CONSTITUENCY POLITICS

CONSTITUENCY POLITICS

A study of
Newcastle-under-Lyme

FRANK BEALEY
J. BLONDEL
W. P. McCANN

THE FREE PRESS : NEW YORK

For information, address:
The Free Press
A Division of The Macmillan Company
60 Fifth Avenue, New York, N.Y. 10011

Collier-Macmillan Canada, Ltd., Toronto, Ontario

Library of Congress Catalog Card Number: 65–27451

© Frank Bealey, J. Blondel
and W. P. McCann 1965

Printed in Great Britain

To
THE PEOPLE AND LOCAL POLITICIANS
OF THE CONSTITUENCY
OF NEWCASTLE-UNDER-LYME

CONTENTS

CONTENTS

ILLUSTRATIONS

FIGURES

11

ILLUSTRATIONS

MAPS

PREFACE

The three authors have worked in association throughout this book, but the primary responsibility for Chapters 5, 8, 9, 10, 11 and 15 rests with J. Blondel; for Chapters 3, 4, 6, 13 and 14 with Phillip McCann; and for the rest with Frank Bealey. The Appendices are the work of whoever was responsible for the chapters with which they are associated.

Such a work, extending into several disciplines, incurs obligations that are diverse and widespread. We are indebted to numerous patrons, above all the Institute of Electoral Research who sponsored and financed this project and its publication. International Computers and Tabulators Ltd. magnificently contributed to our work by doing all our tabulating free of cost. We are also grateful to Ferranti Ltd. of Manchester for aiding us with their computer, and the National and Local Government Officers' Association who financed part of the survey. Last, but by no means least, the University of Keele was exceedingly generous in its financial assistance for both research and publication.

Numerous individuals, both voters and local politicians, gave us information in interviews and documents: we cannot mention them by name as we are pledged to respect their confidences, but their help is acknowledged in the dedication. We should like to thank Mr. C. J. Morton, Town Clerk of Newcastle, Mr. F. W. Ramm, Clerk of Newcastle Rural District Council, and their respective staffs who readily made records available. Dr. J. G. Jenkins, the editor of the Victoria County History of Staffordshire, was good enough to allow us to look at the typescript draft of the volume on North Staffordshire. We must also mention Mr. F. B. Stitt, Librarian of the Stafford County Archives, and his staff; Mr. N. Emery and the staff of the Horace Barks

PREFACE

Reference Library, Hanley; Mr. G. Bradley and the staff of Newcastle Public Library; and Mr. P. J. Bemrose, Curator of the Newcastle Borough Museum. Mr. A. J. Maddock also deserves our gratitude for his assistance in the survey work. Finally we must thank Mr. David Fletcher, Liberal Parliamentary candidate, Mr. John Lovering, Conservative Parliamentary candidate, and Mr. Stephen Swingler, Labour Member of Parliament, for advice and encouragement.

At Keele we have been fortunate to receive the assistance of several departments and individuals. Professor Beaver, Dr. David Herbert and Dr. Brian Turton of the Geography Department helped us with the social and economic background. Professor J. W. Blake and Mr. J. E. Moore advised us on local history. Dr. D. J. Bartholomew and Dr. I. Elce gave us indispensable guidance in statistical matters. Miss Rosemary Cass-Beggs helped in the early stages of the survey; and Miss Patricia Heneage assisted with its organization and did a great deal of work on its statistical tables. Miss Sheila Boyle and Mr. G. Barber of the Geography Department drew our maps while Mr. J. A. Pickavance and the Architects' Department processed them for us. Mr. R. L. Smyth and Mr. R. W. Sturgess helped us with the interpretation of data on local industry and agriculture respectively.

We are also incalculably indebted to about a hundred and fifty Keele undergraduates who responded enthusiastically to our appeal. For no pecuniary reward they interviewed in the streets and countryside in abominable North Staffordshire weather. Without their cheerful co-operation we could have accomplished nothing. Our thanks must also be conveyed to Mr. R. Hambleton for typing the whole of the book.

Furthermore all three authors are grateful to Mr. E. H. Beet, Mr. H. B. Berrington, Professor Peter Campbell, Professor S. E. Finer, Dr. E. P. Hennock, Professor W. J. Mackenzie and Professor W. M. Williams for reading the work in typescript and making various suggestions. The errors that remain, of course, are the responsibility of the authors alone.   F.W.B.

J.B.

Keele   W.P.M.

FOREWORD

Constituency Politics is an important contribution to our knowledge of grass-roots politics in England—if 'grass-roots' is not inappropriate as a description of political life in one of the most intensely industrialized parts of the country. Frank Bealey, J. Blondel and W. P. McCann have examined with great thoroughness the activities of political organizations, party workers, and ordinary electors in the Borough and Rural District which form the Parliamentary constituency of Newcastle-under-Lyme. They have set the area's party conflicts and voting behaviour in their historical and sociological contexts, and have shown the relations between the working of political institutions and the development of private attitudes. The Institute of Electoral Research is glad to have assisted both their research and the publication of their results.

The Institute has had two main tasks since its establishment in 1959 as a non-profitmaking independent trust, whose endowment is too small to enable it to underwrite the whole cost of major projects but which is able to help promote some useful studies. First, it has aided research (such as that on which the present book is based) into the rôle of elections and electoral systems in the political life of the United Kingdom and other countries; second, it has published reference works (such as its annual *Review of Elections*) intended to help the ordinary citizen who wishes to know more about elections and electoral systems. Among the projects that have been or are being aided or undertaken by the Institute are studies of the L.C.C. elections of 1961 (published as *A Metropolis Votes* by L. J. Sharpe, London School of Economics, 1962), of Essex County Council elections, of floating voters, and of the Finnish electoral system. As the Institute

15

FOREWORD

develops it will undertake or aid an increasing number of stndies into the working of the electoral aspects of what James Mill called 'the grand discovery of modern times—the system of representation'.

Institute of Electoral Research Ltd   PETER CAMPBELL
2 Greycoat Place
London S.W.1

CHAPTER ONE

INTRODUCTION

Very old people in Newcastle-under-Lyme can remember the days when sheep were driven down the Ironmarket, the main street; and the faint but unmistakable atmosphere of a market town still pervades the older purlieus of the Borough. Cattle are still sold every Monday about two hundred yards from the Guildhall in the town's centre where the twice-weekly presence of a market with open stalls continues a centuries-old tradition. Other reminders of the nearness of the countryside are the green Crosville buses running from Newcastle, their eastern terminus, into North and Central Wales. By contrast the red buses of the Potteries Motor Traction Company, linking Newcastle with the Five Towns, symbolize the proximity of city life and industrial activity.

Thus the town of Newcastle stands between industrial North Staffordshire and the countryside. During the Middle Ages Newcastle, as the only Borough in the area, was the judicial, commercial and social centre of North Staffordshire, which was then a homogeneous region.[1] The growth of the pottery industry in the eighteenth century and the expansion of coal and iron-ore mining was accompanied by the emergence of a new industrial district, soon known as 'the Potteries'; and the unity of North Staffordshire was shattered by this experience. Newcastle, the 'loyal and ancient Borough', shared little or nothing in this development and the advent of modern communications—a new road, the Trent and Mersey Canal and the railway—all linking Burslem, Hanley and Stoke with London and Manchester,

---

[1] For a discussion of this point see A. H. Morgan, 'Regional Consciousness in North Staffordshire Potteries', *Geography*, XXVII, 1942, p. 95.

by-passed Newcastle with the general approval of the town's population.

In these circumstances an antipathy was born noticed by a late eighteenth-century traveller who remarked that the people of the Potteries seemed 'to deal as little as possible with Newcastle'.[1] In the Chartist disturbances of 1842 the nucleus of the rioting was in Hanley while Newcastle, the centre of law and order, was the place from which the military were summoned.[2] The great novelist of the Potteries summed up the relationship between the Potteries and Newcastle when he wrote of 'the exalted borough which draws its skirts away from the grimy contact of the Five Towns, and employs its leisure in brooding upon an ancient and exciting past. Oldcastle . . . is not industrial; it never will be. It stands for history and carefully conserves its Georgian mansions and that air of distinguished respectability which makes it the secret envy of the Five Towns.'[3]

Yet Arnold Bennett's picture of Edwardian Newcastle must be qualified in two ways. In the first place even in Bennett's day 'grime' and 'industry' were connected with, if not part of, the Borough. In 1885 the Potteries town of Tunstall as well as part of the coalfield was combined with the Borough, in a new Newcastle constituency very different from the former political backwater. Secondly the extension of the Borough's boundaries in 1932, besides more than doubling its area and population, incorporated some of the mining villages within the Borough's limits. Thus the image of Newcastle as a middle-class residential area, which still holds a place in the imaginations of the inhabitants of the Potteries, should have been shattered by the mid-twentieth century. The old animosity, however, has partially survived these changes though it has altered its emphasis and direction. It is the Newcastellians who now fear more. For the possibility always exists that Stoke-on-Trent, the federation of the Five Towns set up in 1910, will make another attempt to swallow up Newcastle. This prospect seems to appal all Newcastle's citizens irrespective of age, sex, political allegiance, or social class.

[1] J. Aikin, *A Description of the Country from Thirty to Forty Miles Around Manchester* (1795), p. 520.
[2] *Staffordshire Advertiser*, 13 August 1842.
[3] Arnold Bennett, *Whom God Hath Joined* (1906), p. 131.

INTRODUCTION

Modern Newcastle, however, has been unable to escape from the influence of the Potteries. Newcastle citizens regularly go to the City of Stoke-on-Trent to work, catch trains and watch football matches. The same gas, water and electricity authorities serve all the inhabitants of North Staffordshire. To the casual traveller who does not see the boundary posts the transition from the Potteries to Newcastle is not one to be remarked. As the draft of the North Staffordshire Development Plan affirmed in 1949 the whole conurbation has a social and cultural life largely centred around the natural capital, the City of Stoke-on-Trent.[1]

Indeed in modern times the salient features of the Potteries have stamped themselves on life at the northern end of the county. These characteristics are largely attributable to the industry on which the existence of the Potteries is based; an industry in which new techniques have only been slowly and reluctantly introduced, in which trade-union activity is, to say the least, lacking in militancy and in which low wages are accepted without great protest. One writer has recently written of the Potteries: 'its people are resistant to outside influences, feel their identity strongly, are vigilant of their reputation and value what they themselves have fashioned'.[2] A low rate of migration and the retention of many attitudes common to an earlier phase of industrialism have thus insulated the Potteries from change and the whole of North Staffordshire seems to have remained out of communication with mid-twentieth-century Britain and its new affluence.

Yet within this larger framework of common social and cultural characteristics Newcastle Borough has retained individual features of its own. And this has not only been a result of the resilience of its traditional independence; but also a consequence of more recent trends. For example, since the 1930's the development of an extensive housing programme has given Newcastle residential estates on a scale that the Potteries has been unable to emulate. With the coming of the motor-car Newcastle, on the main London–Manchester road, was further favoured at the expense of the Potteries. Moreover, the wider confines of Newcastle constituency, outside the Borough, include Newcastle

---

[1] Draft of the North Staffordshire Development Plan (1949), Appendices.
[2] Mervyn Jones, *Potbank* (1961), p. 188.

INTRODUCTION

Rural District, a large area of countryside and mining villages, stretching to the Cheshire and Shropshire borders. Thus the constituency of Newcastle, in spite of the common feature of Labour parliamentary representation, is very different from the three compact urban seats of Stoke-on-Trent.

In fact the outstanding characteristic of our constituency is diversity, a feature complicating the process of investigation, description and explanation, in which several themes recur. Perhaps these should be briefly stated. At all times we make it clear that there is a socio-economic background to politics, an environment which affects political life. Politics is presented as a marginal pastime in which a minority are interested and only a few are really active, a division bridged, to some extent, by the party organizations whose growth and behaviour are here studied in some detail. Within the parties we have emphasized two strata, the rank-and-file and the leaders, and we have tried to relate political leadership to other forms of pre-eminence in the constituency. Especially have we been interested in the social composition of both voters and leaders and we have assayed to connect changes in the social origins of the latter to changes in the way politics has been organized and the methods by which political decisions have been made. Finally we have taken a historical perspective which has enabled us often to assess variations on these themes. After all, the study of change is probably the most important task of the social scientist.

In order to illustrate our points we have been obliged to delve into the minutiae of Newcastle politics; but we hope that our treatment will be not only microscopic but also microcosmic. This is essentially a case study, but we believe that the complexity of this constituency provides a basis for comparison with others where the same features may be found though perhaps combined in different proportions. Thus many of the generalizations we make may be valid for constituencies elsewhere.

CHAPTER TWO

LOCAL POLITICS UNTIL THE
SECOND WORLD WAR

Since the beginning of the nineteenth century two factors have influenced the course of municipal development in the constituency. One has been governmental reform—the great changes of the 1830's and the 1890's and increasing governmental interference in local administration. The other has been social and economic transformation—the Industrial Revolution. Both of these factors have operated to change, often coincidently, the style of local politics, the scope of local control over local decisions and the nature of local political leadership.

We can divide the present constituency into four parts: Newcastle Borough, whose boundaries and form of government were largely unchanged until 1932; the 'farming' area including the parishes of Keele, Madeley and Betley which were marginally affected by industrialization; the parish of Audley; and the three parishes of Chesterton, Knutton (out of which Silverdale was carved in the mid-nineteenth century), and Wolstanton.

To the last three of these districts the Industrial Revolution brought scenic and demographic change. The expansion of the coal industry in Audley, Chesterton and Knutton is a well-known story. Less familiar is the history of the local iron-mining and iron industry which saw its heyday between 1850 and 1870.[1] A local solicitor, Francis Stanier,[2] became an ironmaster owning forges at Knutton, Apedale near Chesterton, and Silverdale, the latter

[1] The best account of these developments is H. A. Moisley, 'The Potteries Coalfield' (Leeds M.Sc. thesis, 1950).

[2] For a short history of the Stanier family see *Staffordshire Sentinel*, 2 December 1882.

township being a creation of nineteenth-century industrialization.[1] The decline of the iron industry brought much unemployment in the later nineteenth and early twentieth century, the last iron-ore mine closing in 1919. Long before that, however, the protrusion of pit banks and slag heaps had rendered these parishes uninhabitable for the landed gentry and the industrialists.

At the same time, as Figure 1 shows, population vastly increased. In 1801 when the first Census was held the population of the farming area was greater than that of either Audley or Newcastle; but between 1821 and 1931 the population of Audley was multiplied more than fourfold, that of Newcastle more than threefold and that of Chesterton, Knutton and Wolstanton nearly ninefold. During the same period the population of the farming area expanded by little more than a quarter. Farming, in fact, decreased in importance from an occupation in which 913 families out of 3,279 were engaged (28 per cent) in 1811 to 1,605 workers out of 22,860 (7 per cent) in 1931.

This upheaval made obsolete governmental institutions in both Borough and County. In Newcastle Borough an elective council was set up by the Act of 1835. In the county the parish vestries and the local Justices of the Peace were deprived of their responsibility for the relief of the poor by the Poor Law Amendment Act of 1834 which grouped parishes with larger adjacent towns. Thus the parishes of Audley, Balterley, Betley, Chorlton, Keele, Madeley, Maer and Whitmore with the Borough of Newcastle made the Newcastle Poor Law Union. Chesterton, Knutton (including Silverdale) and Wolstanton were combined with the pottery towns of Burslem and Tunstall in the Burslem and Wolstanton Poor Law Union; and Ashley, Mucklestone and Tyrley were joined with parishes in Eastern Shropshire and with Market Drayton to form the Market Drayton Poor Law Union. But this was hardly the advent of representative democracy for only the ratepayers were entitled to vote in the elections of the Board of Poor Law Guardians and a system of plural voting gave the largest landowners six votes.

We must now look at the way local politics developed in these four areas.

[1] For an account of early Silverdale see Report of the Commission into the State of the Population in the Mining Districts, 1844, pp. 60 ff.

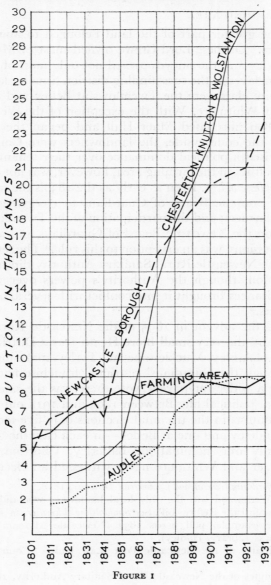

GROWTH OF POPULATION 1801 - 1931

FIGURE I

1. Social and Political Development

(i) THE FARMING AREA

Here the greater part of the land belonged to about twenty landowners.[1] Of these Lord Crewe owned most of Mucklestone and Madeley and the Sneyds owned not only most of Keele but sizeable enclaves in the surrounding district. Smaller landowners of the squire class were the Twemlows at Betley and the Mainwarings at Whitmore. With the exception of the Wedgwoods,[2] who in 1806 purchased Maer Hall and began the exodus of potters to the countryside, the landowners were Conservatives who exercised a political dominance over their tenant farmers.[3]

Local politics in the farming area, however, was not characterized by *noblesse oblige*. Even as early as the 1830's the landowners left service on the Board of Guardians to clergymen and the better-off farmers; and the participation of the Twemlows, father and son, on the Newcastle Board of Guardians and at Stafford Quarter Sessions, was an exception to this rule.[4] The setting up in 1872 of the Newcastle Rural Sanitary Authority did not change this tradition, though the Authority's powers over water and public nuisances brought it into conflict with several of the local landowners.[5]

Nor did the advent in 1895 of the Newcastle Rural District Council, and the very small Blore Heath Rural District Council consisting of Ashley, Mucklestone and Tyrley, make much difference. Though the Guardians' restricted franchise had been replaced by a wider ratepayers' vote there was the same absence of any vital political life. Between 1895 and 1914 out of fifty-six possible contests in the triennial elections only five took place—four at Madeley and one at Betley—in each case the others producing only one nomination. Balterley, Chorlton, Clayton, Keele, Maer and Whitmore never witnessed an electoral fight.

[1] See *Staffordshire General and Commercial Directory*, 1818.

[2] Josiah Wedgwood was the only local landowner who did not sign a manifesto against the Reform Bill. See *Staffordshire Advertiser*, 11 June 1831.

[3] See, for example, poll books 1832 (Newcastle Museum) and 1865 (Horace Barks Library, Hanley).

[4] See Minutes of the Newcastle Poor Law Union (County Archives, Stafford).

[5] See Minutes of the Newcastle Rural Sanitary Authority, 1872–95.

Furthermore the complexion of the representatives changed scarcely at all. When in January 1895 the Newcastle Rural District Council met for the first time the only difference in membership from the 1893 Board of Guardians was the presence of the manager of Madeley colliery, the result of Madeley having been given an extra seat. The other members of this original council were five farmers, a farming innkeeper, the Rectors of Madeley and Whitmore and the Sneyd estate agent. This social composition was to change very little before the First World War. On such a body there was naturally no party politics, and everyone seemed willing to allow the two clergymen to share the chairmanship.

Another innovation of 1894, which it was hoped would bring self-government to the countryside, was the Parish Council. At the first elections, when polls only took place at Ashley, Betley, Keele and Madeley, one finds a majority of farmers among the Parish councillors—52 per cent of the whole compared with 14 per cent for the professional classes and gentry, 14 per cent for manual workers and 12 per cent for shopkeepers and the proprietors of small businesses.[1] But this early excitement soon petered out. By 1897 most Parish councillors were returned unopposed as at Mucklestone where some hoaxer had caused a two-year-old girl to be nominated and returned. Only at Madeley, Betley and Ashley did the councils seem to function with vitality—a situation that has remained to the present day.[2]

In the nineteenth century the landowning class thus ceased to exercise social and cultural leadership in the farming area. Long before the agricultural depression troubled the landlords they had withdrawn from activity in local affairs leaving clerics and farmers to run the countryside. By 1892 of the seventeen principal landowners, cited by *Kelly's Directory*, only seven were J.P.s and two of these latter lived in London. Many of the old halls were let to tenants or fell into disrepair and the communal life of the villages passed away, processes that the First World War was to accelerate.[3]

The war made little difference to rural politics except in one

---

[1] *Staffordshire Advertiser*, 22 December 1894.
[2] Ibid., 27 March 1897 and 19 March 1898.
[3] F. R. Twemlow, 'The Manor of Tyrley', *Staffordshire Historical Collections* (1945–6), pp. 271 ff.

sphere. Asked by the Local Government Board to assess housing needs, the Chairman of the Rural District, in spite of the fact that the 1911 Census had shown that 698 of its 1,900 houses had four or less rooms, said that overcrowding was 'very rare'; but an official of the Board more or less gave orders to build houses and seventy were begun. By 1930 there were 118 and some slum clearance was also under way.[1]

The style of politics, however, changed little. Organization was non-existent even for General Elections—both Blore Heath and Newcastle Rural Districts were in the Stone constituency—and at local elections contests were unusual in most parishes. In 1919 when there were no nominations in three parishes the incumbents were returned against their wills. Newcastle Rural District Council elected in that year contained the usual quota of two vicars and eight farmers, but there was one innovation. The signalman at Madeley station, a Parish councillor since 1913, was supported by his union and came at the head of the poll. Though without the label 'Labour' he represented the organized labour movement and became known as 'the railway-man'. In 1928 he was joined by three other Labour representatives from Madeley who ran him defiantly and unsuccessfully for chairman of the Council; but this was only a distant prologue of events to come and in the 1931 Rural District elections all four of the Labour councillors were defeated.

(ii) AUDLEY

The parish of Audley at the far northwestern tip of Staffordshire had had coal-mines since feudal days, when the Bougheys, Lords of the Manor, were also the largest mine-owning family. When in 1790 the Bougheys moved away their squirearchal function was assumed by the Heathcotes, other mine-owners, who in the late 1830's moved from Longton to live in Apedale Hall between Audley and Chesterton.[2] Thus until the 1870's Audley's social and political order was not dissimilar from the farming area: the Guardians, local farmers, were invariably returned unopposed. Meanwhile the growing and unenfranchised working

[1] Minutes of the Newcastle Rural District Council, 10 January 1919 and 28 April 1931.

[2] J. Ward, *The Borough of Stoke-on-Trent* (1853), p. 124.

class organized its own salvation in friendly societies, co-operative societies and trade unions.[1]

In 1873, faced with the threat of higher rates through Audley becoming a Highway Board, the ratepayers successfully petitioned for their own Board of Health and separation from the Newcastle Rural Sanitary Authority whose inspector of nuisance had just described 939 of Audley's 2,200 houses as 'wretched and defective'. The twelve members of Audley's first autonomous body, chosen by a limited electorate, were T. F. Twemlow, the squire of Betley, three colliery owners, three innkeepers, four farmers and the local schoolmaster.[2]

The Local Government Act of 1894, bringing in the secret ballot and making all ratepayers eligible as candidates, gave some promise of change. At the election of 1894 at Audley nine candidates labelled 'Labour' presented themselves for the twelve seats and eight were elected, of whom five were workers including one colliery checkweighman.[3] There is no evidence to suggest that these candidates were connected in any way with any national organization such as the Independent Labour Party, founded in 1893, and one must conclude that it was an outburst of working-class interest in local politics, an interest which did not last for very long.

None of the local gentry, however, stood in the 1894 election; and the Heathcotes were taking progressively less interest in Audley. In 1882 they had sold Apedale colliery and subsequently Captain Heathcote spent more time in London, seldom attending meetings of the Local Board. Furthermore, though he was M.P. for Northwest Staffordshire from 1886 to 1892, his change from Liberal to Liberal Unionist cannot have endeared him to the Liberal miners. Heathcote's place in the political leadership in Audley was to some extent taken by another coal-owner, R. N. Wood, by the early twentieth century the only J.P. in the Parish. Wood sat on the County Council, until defeated by a farmer in 1904, and on the Audley Urban District Council (as it had become) until he retired in 1910.

[1] The Butt Lane Co-operative Society and the North Stafford Miners' Federation were both founded in 1879.
[2] *Staffordshire Weekly Times*, 1 March, 29 March and 5 April 1873.
[3] *Staffordshire Advertiser*, 6 May 1894.

By the outbreak of the First World War there was a situation that was to last until after the Second World War. Most of the large pits were owned by public companies, and even those that were privately owned were controlled by managers.[1] The Heath-cotes still occupied Apedale Hall and, when they were in residence, still provided some social and cultural leadership. Older inhabitants recall school fêtes and garden parties at the Hall with the Audley brass band in attendance. But the Heathcotes had ceased to exercise any political influence and by 1910 the Council was predominantly composed of local shopkeepers with a sprinkling of colliery officials and one schoolteacher.[2] The 'lower-middle class' had come to power.

In the inter-war years four men held the reins of power in Audley—a farmer, a colliery secretary, a teacher and a secretary of a friendly society. The farmer was an Anglican and a Conservative, the others were Liberals who were prominent in the leadership of the Nonconformist chapels around which social life revolved. In addition to the opportunities for influence which their occupations gave them, they owned numerous houses and acted as the unofficial bankers of the community. The respect which they partially inherited from the colliery owners was thus based partly on social and partly on economic pre-eminence.

Though this lower-middle-class oligarchy had to face electoral contests, both for the Parish and Urban District Councils, they normally ran well ahead of the poll, easily defeating working-class candidates. Their hegemony was based on personal contact with little canvassing or election organization: they tended to nominate one another and other candidates who were amenable. Occasionally there were nominations from other quarters as when in 1919 the North Stafford Miners' Federation put up three candidates one of whom was returned:[3] at the same time the newly-formed Halmerend Labour Party put up two candidates in Halmerend[4] one of whom was successful. But the union backed no more miners in the inter-war years, and the Halmerend

---

[1] *Coal and Iron Diary*, 1897.
[2] *Staffordshire Sentinel*, 5 April 1910.
[3] Minutes of the North Stafford Miners' Federation, 28 March 1919 (Miners' offices, Burslem).
[4] Minutes of the Halmerend Labour Party, 19 February 1919.

Labour Party, an ephemeral body that only seems to have operated at the time of General Elections, did not outlive the 1920's.

Unemployment was even severer in Audley than in the rest of the coalfield throughout the 1920's, and when in 1930 the Midland Coal, Coke and Iron Company, which controlled most of Audley's pits, was sold to a Sheffield scrap merchant disaster stared the parish in the face. Many ratepayers defaulted and between April 1929 and March 1930 there was £5,085 worth of irrecoverable rates.[1] In these circumstances the Audley Urban District Council was no longer viable. Its rulers, however, were not responsible for the predicament, which did not uproot them. It is clear that the depression prevented a challenge coming to them from the one quarter that might have been effective— organized labour.

(iii) KNUTTON, CHESTERTON AND WOLSTANTON

(a) Before Amalgamation

These three parishes, later to become the Wolstanton Urban District, were not a homogeneous area. Knutton (including Silverdale) and Chesterton had, by the 1840's, already acquired the features of industrial villages; but Wolstanton remained fairly rural though first wealthy potters[2] and later less prosperous middle-class people from Burslem and Tunstall came there to live.[3] Consequently Wolstanton had less of a problem of social and political leadership and the resident potters became its Poor Law Guardians. The other two parishes, however, had become too industrialized to be residential and in 1866 had only two J.P.s between them.[4] Chesterton relied on its brick and tile manufacturers to be Guardians but Knutton, which as late as 1882 had only three people qualified for that office,[5] had no natural leadership. Francis Stanier, the Silverdale ironmaster, went to live in Shropshire in 1876 and the Reverend Walter Sneyd who became squire of Keele in 1871, though taking a

[1] Minutes of the Audley Urban District Council, 26 March 1930.
[2] *Staffordshire General and Commercial Directory*, 1818.
[3] P. W. L. Adams, *Wolstanton* (Tunstall, 1908), p. 65.
[4] *Keates's and Ford's Directory*, 1865-6.
[5] *Newcastle Guardian*, 1 April 1882.

charitable interest in Silverdale where the Sneyds owned much of the land, set a precedent of non-involvement in local politics.[1]

As a result, though the parish vestries became inadequate to deal with the problems of industrialization, there were few prominent citizens to persuade the ratepayers to adopt new forms of government. The Wolstanton ratepayers in 1872 rejected a proposal to declare themselves a Local Board under the Public Health Act of 1848[2] and at Silverdale the efforts of Stanier in 1858[3] and of government inspectors in 1872[4] and 1882[5] were vigorously opposed by ratepayers who feared increased rates. In fact until the Local Government Act of 1894 Silverdale remained governed by a plethora of authorities—the Board of Guardians and its Rural Sanitary Authority, a Highway Authority, a Lighting Committee and a Burial Board.

In the absence of guidance from their 'betters' the working class of the two industrial parishes pursued its ends, not through local politics in which it was prevented from participating, but through its own organizations such as friendly societies,[6] the Silverdale Co-operative Society founded in 1861[7] and the North Stafford Miners' Federation of whose branches Silverdale and Chesterton were in 1883 the largest and third largest respectively.[8] Thus by the 1880's collective self-help was a well-established principle of the working class in this area.

As the workers were most interested in forwarding their corporate economic welfare, the 1894 Local Government Act, setting up the Wolstanton Rural District Council elected by ratepayers' suffrage, had no great impact. Chesterton returned a colliery manager and a publican, Silverdale a colliery manager and

---

[1] *Staffordshire Sentinel*, 7 July 1885.

[2] *Staffordshire Weekly Times*, 25 May 1872.

[3] *Newcastle Journal*, 16 October 1858.

[4] *Staffordshire Weekly Times*, 29 June 1872.

[5] *Newcastle Guardian*, 1 April 1882.

[6] On local friendly societies see J. A. Langford, C. S. Mackintosh and J. C. Tildesley, *Staffordshire and Warwickshire, Past and Present* (1884), pp. 581 ff., and P. H. J. H. Gosden, *The Friendly Societies in England, 1815–1875* (Manchester, 1961), p. 59.

[7] Silverdale Co-operative Society Report and Balance Sheet, 11 March 1961.

[8] Minutes of the North Stafford Miners' Federation, 24 December 1883.

a colliery owner and Wolstanton two 'private residents'. There were no manual workers among the candidates. Even in the Silverdale Parish Council elections, in spite of candidates of the miners' union and of a 'Nonconformist council' standing, the chief contest was between lists from Silverdale and Knutton, the two townships having a history of rivalry.[1]

Sectionalism was the keynote of the stormy ten years' history of the Wolstanton Rural District Council which was composed of several parishes around Newcastle and the Potteries. All of the adjacent towns cast greedy eyes on the new authority, while the parishes themselves kept applying for urban district status. The Wolstanton Parish councillors were constantly lobbied in favour of annexation to Burslem, but when in 1901 they were ready to yield to this pressure they were repudiated by the voters. The new Wolstanton Parish Council thought it was expedient to unite with Silverdale and Chesterton in petitioning the County Council for urban powers. Thus in April 1904 the Wolstanton United Urban District Council, combining these three parishes, came into being.[2]

(b) The Wolstanton United Urban District Council 1904-32

Manual workers, as Figure 2 shows, were predominant in the Wolstanton Urban District, though their proportion of the population declined from nine-tenths in 1911 to about four-fifths in 1931. On the Council, however, the proportion of councillors who were manual workers after 1911 remained fairly constant at between a quarter and a third of the whole. But the occupational composition of the manual workers among the councillors changed: in 1911 they were all miners, but by 1931 miners were only half of the manual workers on the Council. The proportion of shopkeepers on the U.D.C. during its short life gradually decreased; but that of clerical workers increased, and it was only with the support of some clerical workers that the Labour Party was able to secure a majority in 1929. Before 1914 manufacturers had been well represented on the Council but after the First World War their role was largely negligible until 1931 when, probably as a foretaste of the 1931 General Election, three

[1] *Staffordshire Advertiser*, 8 May 1896.
[2] Minutes of the Wolstanton Parish Council, 1898–1904.

31

brick and tile manufacturers supplanted three Labour Party candidates.[1]

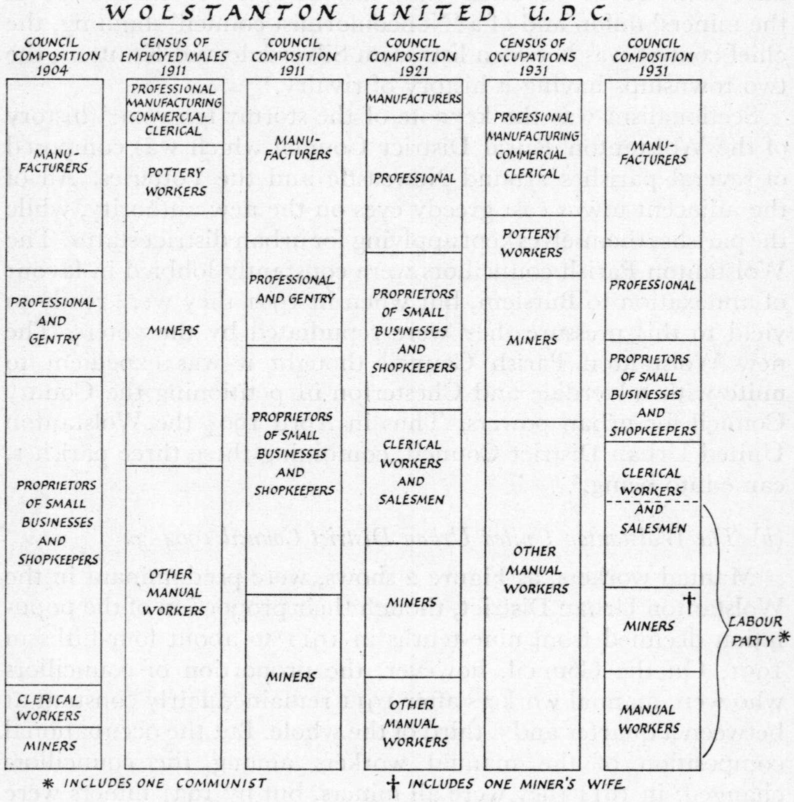

WOLSTANTON UNITED U.D.C.

COUNCIL COMPOSITION 1904	CENSUS OF EMPLOYED MALES 1911	COUNCIL COMPOSITION 1911	COUNCIL COMPOSITION 1921	CENSUS OF OCCUPATIONS 1931	COUNCIL COMPOSITION 1931

FIGURE 2

The First World War was the main landmark in the twenty-eight years' history of the Wolstanton Urban District. Before the war the leadership of the Council was largely in the hands of the pottery manufacturers of Wolstanton who made up half the successful candidatures in that ward. This is the period of the political dominance of the 'five halls', the villas in which the

[1] This account is largely based on Minutes of the Wolstanton United Urban District Council, 1904–32, *Staffordshire Sentinel*, and interviews.

wealthy potters lived. Though most of them were Liberals, the doyens of the Wolstanton potters, the Adamses who lived at Moreton House, were Conservatives. But in local politics all the manufacturers were Independents like the shopkeepers from Silverdale and Chesterton who before 1914 greatly outnumbered the miners elected from these two mining villages.

After the First World War the pattern was much more diversified. Between 1918 and 1932 only a tenth of the councillors in Wolstanton ward were manufacturers, while clerical workers and manual workers were 20 and 30 per cent respectively of the successful candidatures. These last two groups also gained some ground in Silverdale and Chesterton where the shopkeepers proportionately declined. The wealthy potters had now withdrawn from local politics, the Adamses having moved to a country estate in Shropshire during the war. Consequently the U.D.C. was run by much less wealthy suburbanites who, like the pottery manufacturers before them, called themselves Independents. The three most important and long-serving of these were a schoolteacher, who had been a Socialist, a Liberal commercial traveller and a Conservative mining engineer. Between 1918 and 1932 this was the middle-class leadership that had to contend with the growing strength of the Labour Party on the Council.

Before the First World War organized labour had undertaken political action through the branches of the North Stafford Miners' union at Silverdale and Chesterton. From 1904 onwards miners had been candidates in these two wards with an even record of success and failure, though no miners' candidatures were endorsed by the union executive until 1913. In Wolstanton ward the Wolstanton Independent Labour Party, largely working class in membership but with some middle-class members, secured the election of two nominees to the pre-1914 Council. Both the miners' branches and the Wolstanton I.L.P. were at this time connected in the loose type of federation that was the structure of the local Labour Parties before 1918.

After the war Wolstanton and District Labour Party was resurrected and in 1919 ran three candidates in Wolstanton ward, one of whom was successful. The old I.L.P. members in the immediate post-war years were regarded, however, with great suspicion (rather like Communists today, one of them told the authors) and only a few people kept the Socialist cause alive. One of these was a young Co-operative clerk who had lost an arm in the war. In 1923, after his election to the Council, he was asked by Wedgwood to form a General Election organization. The old members were contacted and a new Wolstanton ward Labour Party was formed with a membership of about thirty, of whom about a dozen remained active. With the growth of this body the old I.L.P. seemed to fade away. Meanwhile miners, though not always nominated by their union, were in the 1920's still being returned from Chesterton and Silverdale. After 1927 they were usually supported by the Silverdale Co-operative Society which in 1928 began to contribute a penny per member to its own local Political Council. The Co-operative's effort was not great, but its influence was felt by 1930 through the three members of its Political Council who were then Wolstanton councillors.[1]

In the last years of the Wolstanton U.D.C. the Labour Party was an alliance of a working class organized for collective economic action in the two mining wards and a group of individuals organized as a political movement in Wolstanton ward. As the leadership, usually lower-middle-class, came from Wolstanton there was considerable disagreement in the Labour Group set up in the mid-1920's. At the Group's meetings there was sometimes friction between the leadership and a 'left-wing' faction, predominantly miners or representatives of the two mining wards including one Communist who was allowed to attend. Sometimes the 'left' carried their animus to the Council, and in 1931 one of them was forcibly ejected on the orders of the Labour chairman.

Despite the changes that overtook the Urban District its problems remained distressingly unsolved. The post-war collapse of ironstone mining and the depression in the coal industry brought much misery to Silverdale and Chesterton. In these two wards the difficulty experienced since the inception of the U.D.C.— the collection of rates from poor ratepayers—led to the formation of Excusal Committees (consisting of the wards' councillors), before which ratepayers pleaded to be excused payment of their rates on grounds of hardship. Naturally a very real temptation existed for councillors to excuse their constituents and the Labour

[1] Minutes of the Silverdale Co-operative Society, 23 July 1928.

councillors, who predominated in these two poor wards, were especially vulnerable to accusations of unfair vote-catching. Because of this situation the Labour Party strove for the compounding of rates in order to put the onus of payment on the landlords and not on the tenants, a policy that was effected after Labour gained its majority in 1929. With poverty went squalor. Within the scope of its powers the Wolstanton U.D.C. dealt with this to the best of its ability by the conversion of privies into flush toilets and later by setting a housing programme in motion.[1]

In spite of social and political differences between the wards and between the councillors the Council only divided on clear party lines over such issues as compounding the rates or housing. Caucussing before council meetings was uncommon and the Labour Group that operated in the last few years of the U.D.C.'s history was not, as we have seen, a great success. Debates in Council proceeded usually with little excitement, votes were seldom taken and the chairmanship was rarely contested at the Annual General Meetings, the custom being for the vice-chairman automatically to succeed. When the Labour Party came to power they made a point of announcing that they would not depart from this procedure and an Independent was allowed to become chairman.[2] Anyway, there was always difficulty in persuading people to take office, perhaps owing to the inconvenience of serving on committees whose meetings rotated between the three wards. Especially in Wolstanton ward the councillors showed a propensity to stand down once their terms ended (twenty-one did so—as many as in the other two wards combined); and eventually in order to conciliate the Wolstanton councillors who, after all, represented the area that paid much the heavier rate burden, it was decided in 1917 to acquire Moreton House as a municipal centre.

The annual elections, at which a third of the Council was returned, were rarely characterized by great excitement or display of electoral organization. Among the Independents it was common for the candidates to organize their own machines, often hastily extemporized at public meetings. The Labour Party's

[1] Minutes of the House of Commons Inquiry, 27 May 1930; evidence of Councillor George Hoon, pp. 756 ff.
[2] *Staffordshire Advertiser*, 27 April 1929.

organization was also both sketchy and ephemeral. The personal element as a feature of elections is illustrated by the tendency of the voters to distinguish, sometimes by hundreds of votes, between candidates on both the Labour and Independent slates. In fact the personal nature of electoral support led the leadership of the Labour Party in Wolstanton ward to join local social clubs and emulate the leading Independents as public figures.

Disagreement within the Wolstanton and District Labour Party was already latent, as we have seen, when the party secured its majority in 1929 and it materialized as a result of Stoke's proposal to annex Wolstanton Urban District. Many in the area hoped that Wolstanton would join Newcastle with whom a Medical Officer of Health had been shared since 1920; but the Wolstanton Labour Party at a meeting held to discuss the choice was evenly divided. Half the members, led by a councillor who was a bus conductor, felt that Stoke had more benefits to offer and it was only the casting vote of the chairman that decided in favour of Newcastle. However, 96 per cent of the U.D.C.'s voters expressed a wish in a referendum to amalgamate with Newcastle and at the House of Commons inquiry only the bus conductor supported Stoke. But this dissension split the Wolstanton Labour Party which failed to function effectively for some years.

(iv) NEWCASTLE BOROUGH

Before 1835 Newcastle-under-Lyme was ruled by a self-perpetuating oligarchy. The power of the Corporation lay with its Common Council comprising the Mayor, two bailiffs and twenty-four burgesses known as 'capital burgesses' in order to distinguish them from the other burgesses who had no vote. The body filled vacancies by co-opting burgesses who were favourable to its policy, and its only important political function was to ensure that nominees of the Gower interest were returned to Parliament. Otherwise it enjoyed itself—in 1816 it rented a racecourse—and lined its own pockets. The Royal Commission on Municipal Corporations reporting in 1835 said of the Newcastle Corporation: 'Till late years feasting on an expansive scale prevailed. . . . We have seen that where a magistrate was concerned, public money has been applied to make good the consequences of individual misconduct.'[1] In consequence the Borough was heavily in debt, though Improvement commissioners in the 1820's had introduced gas lighting into the streets.[2]

Though much of the corruption was removed from municipal politics by the Municipal Corporations Act two of Newcastle's fundamental problems remained. Until 1932, except for slight additions, the area of the Borough remained constant though the population trebled. Within this restricted 550 acres development was difficult because of several vested interests. For example the Burgesses' Trust, a body which since the Enclosure Act of 1816 had administered the 99 acres of burgesses' lands and represented the burgesses' interests, had to be conciliated every time land was needed for public purposes, such as for sewerage works in 1855 or a new school in 1874. Another similar body, the Marsh Trustees, owned land, and in 1877 bitterly opposed the transfer of their prerogatives to the Council.[3] Thus until well into the second half of the nineteenth century medieval relics blocked Newcastle's progress.

The shortage of land was connected with the other basic handicap—lack of industry. The pottery industry never took root in Newcastle and the mining of coal and ironstone remained outside the Borough's borders. The hat trade had been important in the eighteenth century and in 1815 it still employed six hundred men, but it was only a 'garret' industry. One cotton and three silk mills were operating in the 1830's in Newcastle, but by the 1840's this nucleus of a potential textile industry had been destroyed by the competition of imported silks from India. Its only relic (extant in the present day) was a cotton-spinning factory employing about a hundred workers.[4] In 1881 Enderley Mills were built for the manufacture of uniforms, but it was only a small firm and its owners, the Hammonds, lived in Manchester. In the last quarter of the nineteenth century the town's largest

[1] We are indebted to Dr. J. G. Jenkins, editor of the Victoria County History of Staffordshire, for information about the early history of Newcastle Borough.

[2] Victoria County History, *A History of the County of Stafford* (1963), p. 29.

[3] *Staffordshire Advertiser*, 20 May 1877.

[4] Appendix to Second Report of the Commission of Inquiry into the state of Large Towns and Populous Districts, 1843, p. 50.

37

enterprise was a small saw-mill and Newcastle's working population in the main fetched and carried for the many shopkeepers, artisans and small traders. Furthermore as time progressed more and more Newcastle workers found employment in the Potteries.

In consequence of its lack of industry Newcastle found itself without the natural leadership that was necessary for it to solve the problems of nineteenth-century urban expansion. Hat manufacturers, the owners of the Borough's traditional industry, served on both the unreformed and reformed corporations, as Figure 3 shows. The 1835 Act was most innovatory, however, in allowing manufacturers in the newer industries to be councillors. In the 1840's W. U. Lester, one of the silk employers, sat on the Council and for a brief spell the Silverdale ironmaster, Francis Stanier, tried to rouse the town. But both as councillor and as Mayor Stanier failed to overcome the vested interests and the complacency. Very few industrialists intervened in the town's affairs and until well into the twentieth century the burden of municipal service was borne by shopkeepers and small businessmen with a sprinkling of the professional classes.

It must be remembered that between the 1835 and 1882 Municipal Corporations Acts there were property qualifications for councillors—they had to be local electors and owners of £500 of real or personal property or a house of £15 in rateable value. Perhaps 250 people fulfilled these conditions in Newcastle in 1835. Yet these stipulations cannot wholly explain the situation because a generation after 1882, when property qualifications were abolished, shopkeepers, hoteliers and small businessmen were still the dominating group on the Council. By the 1920's about a quarter of the Council was composed of workers though more than half of these were clerical workers. Consequently from Municipal Reform in 1835 until amalgamation with the Wolstanton U.D.C. in 1932 Newcastle Borough was governed by the 'shopocracy'.

Table 1 reveals some differences between the two wards from each of which, after the initial election of 1835, three councillors were returned every year. In the earlier period the East ward was the base of the professional men while the manufacturers were preponderant in the West. In the years before 1914, however, the East ward became something of a residential area for the Potteries and some manufacturers served on the Borough Council but after 1918 they disappeared (to more remote residences) and so did the hoteliers and innkeepers. The poorer nature of the West ward in the twentieth century is exemplified by the fact that it returned nearly all the clerical and manual workers on the Council. At no time, however, was the preponderance of small traders threatened in either ward.

TABLE 1. PERCENTAGE SUCCESSFUL CANDIDATES IN NEWCASTLE BOROUGH
1835–1930

	1835–69			1870–99			1900–14			1919–30		
	East	West	Total	East	West	Total	East	West	Total	East	West	Total
	%	%	%	%	%	%	%	%	%	%	%	%
Professions and gentry	28	11	19	32	10	21	11	11	11	14	6	10
Manufacturers	4	14	9	—	3	2	15	4	10	—	—	—
Shopkeepers and proprietors of small businesses	66	70	68	58	56	57	47	52	49	75	52	64
Drink trade	2	5	4	10	30	20	18	18	18	—	—	—
Clerical workers	—	—	—	—	1	1	7	—	3	3	28	15
Manual workers	—	—	—	—	—	—	2	15	9	8	14	11
Total	100	100	100	100	100	100	100	100	100	100	100	100

It is clear from Figure 3 that the Borough Council was never proportionately representative of Newcastle's social structure. The reformed Council of 1835 contained no servants, no labourers and none of the 'manufacturing' classes who made up three-quarters of the Borough's population. The Council of 1911 was almost as unrepresentative: it had no miners, the largest group of workers, though building and pottery workers were present. And the Council of 1931 was even more unrepresentative of manual workers, though clerical workers were well represented and preponderant in the small Labour Party contingent in which small

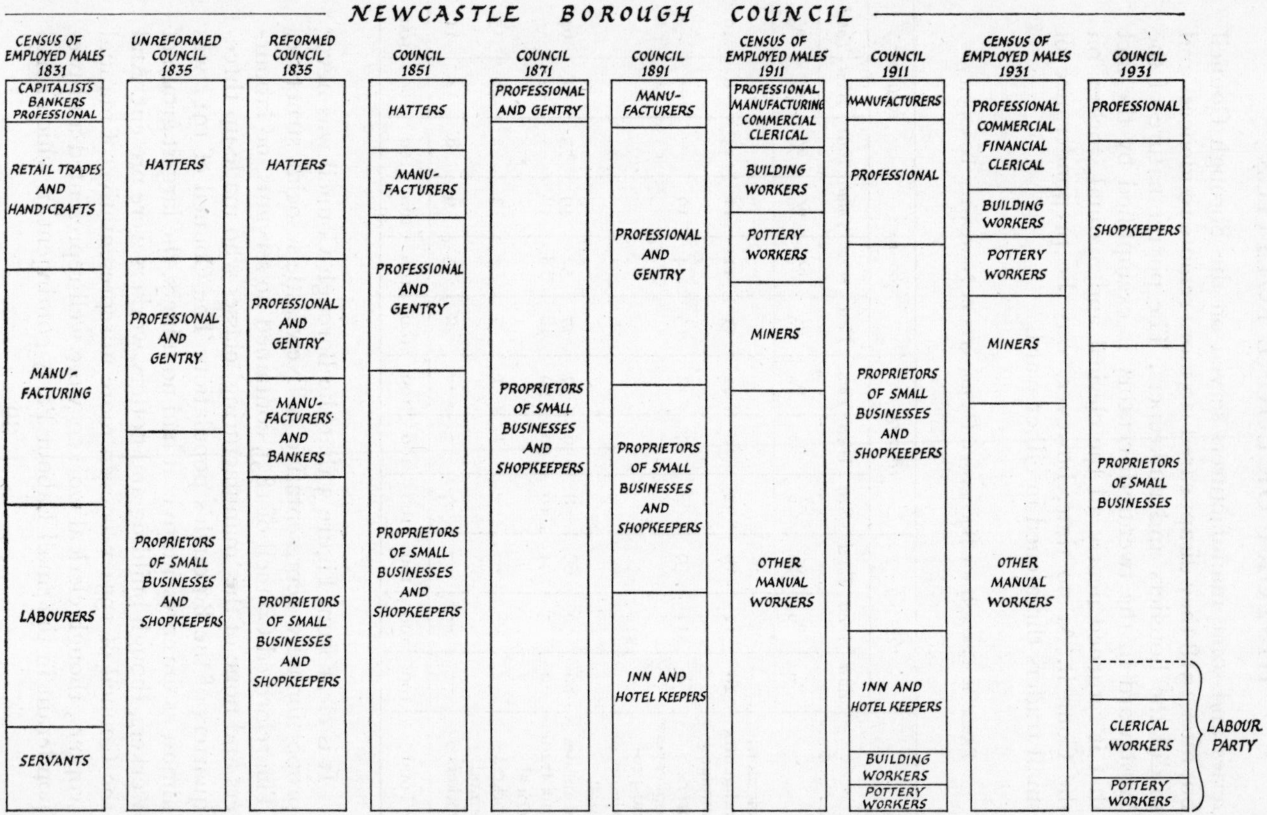

NEWCASTLE BOROUGH COUNCIL

CENSUS OF EMPLOYED MALES 1831	UNREFORMED COUNCIL 1835	REFORMED COUNCIL 1835	COUNCIL 1851	COUNCIL 1871	COUNCIL 1891	CENSUS OF EMPLOYED MALES 1911	COUNCIL 1911	CENSUS OF EMPLOYED MALES 1931	COUNCIL 1931
CAPITALISTS BANKERS PROFESSIONAL	HATTERS	HATTERS	HATTERS	PROFESSIONAL AND GENTRY	MANU-FACTURERS	PROFESSIONAL MANUFACTURING COMMERCIAL CLERICAL	MANUFACTURERS	PROFESSIONAL COMMERCIAL FINANCIAL CLERICAL	PROFESSIONAL
RETAIL TRADES AND HANDICRAFTS	PROFESSIONAL AND GENTRY	PROFESSIONAL AND GENTRY	MANU-FACTURERS		PROFESSIONAL AND GENTRY	BUILDING WORKERS	PROFESSIONAL	BUILDING WORKERS	SHOPKEEPERS
MANU-FACTURING	PROPRIETORS OF SMALL BUSINESSES AND SHOPKEEPERS	MANU-FACTURERS AND BANKERS	PROFESSIONAL AND GENTRY	PROPRIETORS OF SMALL BUSINESSES AND SHOPKEEPERS	PROPRIETORS OF SMALL BUSINESSES AND SHOPKEEPERS	POTTERY WORKERS	PROPRIETORS OF SMALL BUSINESSES AND SHOPKEEPERS	POTTERY WORKERS	PROPRIETORS OF SMALL BUSINESSES
LABOURERS		PROPRIETORS OF SMALL BUSINESSES AND SHOPKEEPERS	PROPRIETORS OF SMALL BUSINESSES AND SHOPKEEPERS			MINERS		MINERS	
SERVANTS					INN AND HOTEL KEEPERS	OTHER MANUAL WORKERS	INN AND HOTEL KEEPERS	OTHER MANUAL WORKERS	CLERICAL WORKERS
							BUILDING WORKERS		POTTERY WORKERS
							POTTERY WORKERS		

LABOUR PARTY

FIGURE 3

businessmen were also a sizeable group. At all periods, however, the working classes remained grossly under-represented.

The under-representation of the poorer classes was partially a reflection of the local government suffrage. By the 1835 Act all male occupiers who resided in the Borough or within seven miles of its boundaries, and who paid their rates, were entitled to vote. Even so in 1837 out of 1,749 ratepayers there were only 533 municipal voters,[1] fewer than the Parliamentary electorate and about a quarter of the adult males. By 1870 about 2,500 voters were on the municipal roll, by 1890 3,054 and by 1919 about 6,000 or two-thirds of the Parliamentary electorate. 'Local democracy' thus came to Newcastle slowly and until the Representation of the People Act of 1944 brought universal suffrage at local elections the franchise was weighted in favour of the middle classes.

But this does not explain the dominance of Newcastle Council by small tradesmen. Like most of the professional classes, many of the shopkeepers and small businessmen obviously had no political ambitions. There were 564 shopkeepers in Newcastle in 1864[2] and only fifteen on the Council. Furthermore though council members were a little better-off, owning on an average nine of Newcastle's 2,800 houses as against the average house-owner's four,[3] they certainly did not comprise all the Borough's leading employers and shopkeepers. The Council was no oligarchy of wealth and political power. Doubtless, as today, self-selection played a large part in the choice of councillors—it was certainly difficult to persuade people to stand—and the attraction of some measure of social prominence was the main spur to political aspiration.

This was an environment in which political contests often ranged around personalities. Before the Ballot Act of 1872 councillors were elected by a form of modified 'hustings'.[4] Under this

[1] B. Keith-Lucas, *The English Local Government Franchise* (Oxford, 1952), p. 60.

[2] Jones's *Mercantile Directory of the Staffordshire Potteries* (1864), p. 98.

[3] Newcastle Poor Law Rate Book, 1867. The authors are indebted to the Borough Treasurer for permission to inspect.

[4] For an account of Newcastle local politics between 1835 and 1872 see Frank Bealey, 'The Municipal Politics of Newcastle-under-Lyme, 1835–1872', *North Staffordshire Journal of Field Studies*, Vol. 3, 1963, pp. 68–77.

system, and with a small electorate, electoral organization was usually confined to a few personal friends, though there was an exceptional situation in 1842 when 'runners' were used and post-chaises were sent at midday to the Potteries to bring back working voters during their lunch hour.[1] By the 1860's meetings of ratepayers were being held to nominate candidates, and they sometimes resulted in the birth of rival factions who would repair to different parts of the hall to construct a party organization on the spot. After the early 1870's some form of electoral machine, always personal and without connection with the national parties, was normally used by candidates at Borough elections.

In view of the social structure of the town and the electorate it is hardly surprising that bribery and corruption were regular and expected features of Newcastle elections. Teetotalism was not the order of the day and accusations of buying and selling votes were bandied about by nearly all the candidates. In this respect the 1872 Ballot Act did not at first seem to make much difference, because the electorate was still small and a section of it had obviously come to regard election day 'treating' as one of the perquisites of enfranchisement. Nor did the various Corrupt Practices Acts quickly bring electoral illegalities to an end. For example in 1882 some of the candidates engaged a private detective from Stafford to check corrupt practices and offered a reward of £5 to anyone supplying information leading to a conviction.[2] But some abuses persisted to the twentieth century. In 1902 one of Newcastle's prominent citizens said he could buy 'hundreds of votes at 1½d. each'[3] (the price of a pint of beer) and some years later one of Newcastle's public houses was still providing free beer on polling day.[4]

Thus to many of the voters the result of the local elections could have been of little importance: it was only occasionally that there was general excitement, and even then among the committed minority. Generally speaking as the electorate increased in size interest decreased. 85 per cent of the voters polled in 1840 but only 59 per cent in 1874. After that, for those years

[1] *Staffordshire Advertiser*, 5 November 1842.
[2] Ibid., 4 November 1882.
[3] *Newcastle Guardian*, 25 October 1902.
[4] *Staffordshire Advertiser*, 16 November 1907.

that we have statistics, the poll was somewhere between 60 and 70 per cent, though in 1887 and 1909 it mounted to 76 per cent. It is significant that in 1919, the first year in which the expanded municipal electorate voted after the Representation of the People Act of 1918, only about half the Newcastle voters exercised their suffrage. Moreover there were many years in which no elections were held because all the candidates were returned unopposed. In the twenty-six elections between 1845 and 1870 there were ten occasions on which the election only lasted for the formality of the first hour, and on nine others only one ward was contested. Thus in only seven of these years did an election in both wards take place. After 1870, however, until the political truce of the First World War there was usually a contest in both wards.

Up to the Second World War the political struggle in Newcastle was largely fought over local issues: only in one year, 1841, were there slates of three candidates in each ward—known as 'Conservatives' and 'Reformers'—from national parties.[1] At all other times the contests were either fought on purely personal grounds, or they revolved around religious feeling, or more frequently they were a clash about the development of the Borough.

The main problem of Newcastle's development was, indeed, adapting the town to its growing population and keeping pace with municipal progress elsewhere. Over this issue two parties arose in no way connected with national parties, for there were Conservatives and Liberals on both sides. A few shopkeepers, small businessmen and professional men, whom we might describe as the 'Improvers', were alive to the Borough's grave social abuses and ambitious for its civic magnificence. Their opponents, best called the 'Economizers', were opposed to any improvement that would increase the rates. They were other shopkeepers and businessmen among whom a 'drink' faction of innkeepers, hoteliers and maltsters, in revolt against the Licensing Act of 1872, were (as Figure 3 shows) quite important. The battle between these two groups shifted ground: in the 1870's and early 1880's it was over the sewerage system whose modernization was vigorously resisted by the 'Economizers'. Later in the 1880's it was over other urban amenities.

[1] *Staffordshire Advertiser*, 6 November 1841.

The support of the ratepayers assured victory to the 'Econo-mizers'. For example, in 1886 a public poll on a Baths and Library scheme showed that 61 per cent of those voting were opposed, the 76 per cent opposition in the West ward emphasiz-ing that the poorer voters were the more hostile to municipal improvement.[1] The result of this defeat was that when the build-ings were erected they were much smaller than originally planned, an illustration of how Newcastle's civic growth was left in a state of half-completion by the 1890's when county and central government began to exert control. Thus the opportunity afforded by municipal independence between 1835 and 1888 was sadly squandered.

For this the 'Improvers' were scarcely to blame. They lacked the business acumen and administrative experience of the Bir-mingham City Fathers whom they probably hoped to emulate. When the leaders of the recurrent ratepayers' revolts accused them of financial mismanagement, there was some truth in the charge, though the vicious circle was not of the 'Improvers'' making, for it was the denial of the proper funds that made them adopt makeshift schemes. When all is said and done they faced an unsurmountable obstacle, the allied opposition of complacent shopkeepers, rascally innkeepers and a hostile working class. It is small wonder that they were unable to avoid completely the electoral corruption practised by others. In 1877 it seems clear that the agent employed by the Municipal Reform Association, the 'Improvers'' organization, used its funds to bribe voters,[2] and one of the 'Improvers', when referring to the election of 1881 as 'the fairest that he ever fought', implied that he had been forced to resort to the tactics of his opponents.[3]

Though the 'Improvers' faded from the scene at the turn of the century the 'Economizers' have remained with us to the present day. Both before and after the First World War the fight against municipal extravagance was led by three puritanical shop-keepers. In November 1906 the 'Economizers' campaigned with the cry of 'Watch the Watch Committee' and promised to fight to reduce the Town Clerk's salary by £150 if they were elected.[4] In 1920 they were still opposing salary increases for the Borough's

[1] *Newcastle Guardian*, 31 July 1886.   [2] Ibid., 22 April 1882.
[3] Ibid., 9 February 1884.   [4] *Staffordshire Advertiser*, 3 November 1906.

employees[1] and in 1925 their stringency was so successful that, with Pembrokeshire, Newcastle had the dubious honour of being one of the only two local authorities that refused to implement the Burnham award to teachers.[2]

But by this time a new group had emerged in Borough politics—organized labour. In the nineteenth century that part of the Newcastle working class that was enfranchised appears either to have been willing to accept bribes or to follow the wishes of their employers. As we have seen it was from the predominantly working-class West ward that most of the manufacturers were returned. Perhaps the nature of the Borough's industry and the presence of the Irish had not encouraged the growth of a Labour movement. The first workingman councillor, a cabinet-maker and a candidate of the 'Improvers', was elected in the East ward in 1890.[3]

The advent of Labour as an organized political force began in 1905 when J. Mayer, a bricklayer, was returned from the West ward.[4] He was chairman of the Newcastle Trade Union Committee, which became the Newcastle Trades and Labour Council in 1913. By that time it was regularly supporting candidates and had four councillors, who made little impact chiefly because, except where education was concerned, they allied themselves with the 'Economizers' and opposed all spending. Nor did they always vote together. Between 1906 and 1913 the Labour councillor from the East ward, a Salvation Army officer, supported the puritanical shopkeepers in a campaign against such abuses as mixed bathing at the Public Baths. The West ward Labour councillors opposed them.

After the First World War the position was virtually unchanged in spite of the foundation of the Newcastle Constituency Labour Party in 1918. A large Independent majority, energized by a few councillors of a Ratepayers' Association in the 1920's, was not seriously challenged by a divided Labour Party with six councillors in 1921 and five a decade later. Both the miners and the Silverdale Co-operative Society, as we have seen, considered

[1] Minutes of the Newcastle Borough Council, 7 January 1920.
[2] *Evening Sentinel*, 8 October 1925.
[3] *Staffordshire Advertiser*, 8 November 1890.
[4] *Staffordshire Sentinel*, 4 November 1905.

that the Wolstanton U.D.C. was a more appropriate field for their activities. In fact the miners' union only endorsed one candidate for Newcastle Borough Council in the post-war decade.[1] The three co-operators who fought the 1920 Borough elections stood as 'Independent Labour' candidates. This rift continued until 1928 when the national agreement between the Labour Party and the co-operative movement brought the Silverdale society back into the fold. However they still made little impact and the main Labour effort in Newcastle Borough still rested with trade-union nominees, invariably members of the Newcastle Trades Council. As many of the latter had been on the Council before a Labour Party had existed locally they were conditioned by the practices of 'non-party politics' and had no inhibitions about consorting with the Independents and accepting chairmanships of committees. In 1925 Ellis Roberts, a railwayman, became the first Labour mayor. Social elevation also accompanied civic distinction. By the late 1920's Roberts had become a coal merchant while Mayer, Labour's first pioneer, was a builder and a Ratepayers' councillor.

But the external threat from Stoke dampened down the political fires in Newcastle in these years. Successfully withstood in 1920 the issue again came to the fore towards the end of 1929. All elements in Newcastle were opposed to the extinction of the ancient Borough's independent existence. Though the plan was conceived by the Labour majority on the Stoke Council, the Newcastle Labour Party would have nothing to do with it: the North Staffordshire Trades Council voted 49 to 1 for annexation,[2] unanimously rejected by the Newcastle Trades Council which joined with the Newcastle Chamber of Trade in an anti-annexation committee.[3] When annexation failed, all parties in Newcastle, in spite of widespread unemployment, were loud in their jubilations.

These were all indications of the failure of the first party nominees to change Newcastle local politics. The electors, who in the nineteenth century had discriminated between candidates of the same faction, were consistent in the 1920's in differentiating between the three candidates that the Labour Party usually put

[1] Minutes of the North Stafford Miners' Federation, 31 October 1921.
[2] *Evening Sentinel*, 9 January 1930.　　　　[3] Ibid., 26 October 1929.

up in both wards. Personal repute was obviously still a political factor and party organization had failed to persuade the voters to 'vote the party ticket'.

These circumstances were reflected in the behaviour of the Council. There was undoubtedly consultation between people with like interests before council meetings, but it is clear that many of the decisions of the Council were actually made in the council chamber; though many of them were foregone conclusions because councillors' reactions were widely known and often predictable. Most decisions anyway were taken unanimously and it was only occasionally that a vote was necessary. Probably the reason for so little disagreement was the powerful guiding influence of the Town Clerks, local solicitors.

2. After 1932

The amalgamations of 1932 created two local authorities where there had formerly been five. Consequently the pattern of local politics in the 1930's was simpler, but otherwise things were not very different. In both the Newcastle Rural District and the Borough the Independents remained in power and, if anything, the Labour challenge receded.

(i) NEWCASTLE RURAL DISTRICT

Thirteen more councillors reinforced the Rural District Council in 1932. Five of them—four farmers and a clergyman—were from the former Blore Heath R.D.C., while from Audley arrived eight unwilling and resentful councillors, the four oligarchs already mentioned, three miners and a greengrocer.[1] These Audley members introduced a new sectional note by immediately challenging for the chairmanship with an Audley candidate; and in spite of inevitable defeat they continued this practice year after year. As a salve for their hurt feelings the Audley Parochial Committee that was set up, unlike Madeley's, was allowed to control its own gas and water undertakings. This did not prevent the Council selling Audley gasworks to the Kidsgrove U.D.C. in 1938—a bitter blow which was not entirely softened by the

---

[1] This account is based on Minutes of the Newcastle Rural District Council, the *Evening Sentinel*, and interviews.

fact that Audley was eventually allowed to have the chairmanship of the Council.

The 1930's were probably even grimmer in Audley than they were in most mining villages. It was a period of soup kitchens and unemployed miners cultivating allotments. Yet amid all this depression, perhaps because of it, the miners did not undertake local political action. Occasionally in this decade local miners' secretaries stood for the Council as individuals, and two of them were elected, but they co-operated with the traditional rulers with whom they had a close connection through the Primitive Methodist chapels. Significantly when the man who after the war was to be Labour County councillor for Audley stood for the Newcastle Rural District Council in 1934, he came bottom of the poll.

In the rest of the Rural District the pre-war decade was a time of similar social and political stagnation. From the countryside the farmers and estate agents still came to represent the agricultural parishes and in the fringe of the coalfield there was little change though in 1937 another railwayman was returned from Madeley. Finally in 1939 the original 'railwayman' was honoured with the chairmanship of the Council. But the choice of the first Labour chairman was not indicative of an appreciation of new social forces: it merely reflected a general feeling among the councillors that everyone should 'have a go'. This episode exemplified a process of government in which personal relationships between the councillors were very important. The Labour councillors, greatly outnumbered, did nothing to upset this style of politics.

(ii) NEWCASTLE BOROUGH

The amalgamation of Newcastle Borough and Wolstanton United U.D.C. proceeded with even less excitement. The eighteen Wolstanton members, unlike the Audley councillors in the Rural District Council, were not performers in a milieu which they disliked. On the contrary co-operation in the defeat of Stoke-on-Trent had created a bond between the two sides and, though Wolstanton's population was about 6,000 larger than that of Newcastle, the Wolstanton councillors, for various reasons, seemed ready to allow Newcastle to lead. The 1930's were undoubtedly years of general agreement in the expanded Borough's politics.[1]

This lack of dissension can be partly attributed to the disastrous economic situation which united all interests. In 1931 over 8,000 or nearly half of the insured workers of Wolstanton and Newcastle were unemployed and though the situation gradually improved, so that by 1938 only 3,000 were out of work, poverty was a familiar feature of life in the Borough during these years. On this issue the Council was at one, expressing unanimous disapproval of the Means Test, protesting against the introduction of the National Assistance economies in 1934 and unanimously asking the County Public Assistance Committee to raise the scales of relief in 1936. Councillors of all political shades of belief supported these remonstrances, a general harmony that was enhanced by the absence of Parliamentary elections.

Moreover there was widespread agreement about the one important undertaking of the Council during these years—a new housing project. In 1921 Newcastle had acquired part of the Parish of Clayton from the Rural District. The Council bought about six hundred acres nearest to the town at a very cheap price, called in the Bournville Trust architect to design a plan of the roads and sold the land in plots to individual buyers. This became the handsome Westlands residential area that people from all over Britain came to look at. The pursuance of this scheme throughout the 1930's was encouraged by all parties, though its chief protagonist was widely acknowledged to be Alderman 'Tony' Moran, a Roman Catholic Post Office worker, chairman of the Housing Committee and Labour's 'strong man' on the Council.

Such disagreement as there was concerned two issues in these years. One was the familiar theme of municipal economy. As the rates remained fairly stable the 'Economizers' devoted their energies to preventing any increase in the Borough officials' salaries and in 1933 and 1934 a battle raged around a proposal to accept a higher scale. Moran, a public employee, was the chief supporter of the increase but the Labour Party was by no means united, some Labour councillors arguing that the officials were

---

[1] This account is largely based on Minutes of the Newcastle Borough Council, the *Evening Sentinel*, and interviews.

likely to become a privileged class. The Independents were divided evenly. The other issue, that of the 'island site', had the similar effect of splitting the Council into two nearly equal factions. In 1936 some dilapidated property in the centre of the town had been demolished. It was proposed that the Council should obtain a loan to rebuild on the site. Nearly twenty councillors, however, were opposed to this step, arguing that the appearance of the town and its traffic problem would be improved by not rebuilding. They took their opposition into the town and a public meeting passed a resolution calling for a plebiscite on the matter. When the Council by 24 votes to 18 refused to accede to this request, the 'island site' became the issue of the 1938 local elections in which the only two candidates who pledged themselves to vote for rebuilding were defeated. The Council, however, refused to accept this verdict as a mandate and the decision to rebuild was finally taken.

Outside the Council Newcastle local politics continued in very much the same style as had characterized the 1920's or, indeed, the nineteenth century. As far as the Independents were concerned they obtained new candidates to the Council by personal recruitment though Independent candidates still occasionally appeared 'out of the blue'. It is clear, however, that there was some attempt to organize against the Labour Party, for between 1933 and 1938 at all the November elections there were only eleven contests out of a possible seventy-two in which there were more Independent candidates than seats. Probably the change in 1932 from three-membered to one-membered wards made this process easier. The Independent ward organizations did not, of course, persist between elections, and they usually consisted of the candidate's friends, especially councillors who did not happen to be standing in that particular year, plus a few helpers who often volunteered their services at the first of the candidate's meetings. Canvassing was often not very thorough and telling and 'knocking up' were seldom practised, though the 1938 local elections were fought so fiercely that they were somewhat different in this respect. The fact that there had been no General Election since 1929 was partly responsible for this lack of organizational efficiency.

The weak Labour Party was no threat to the 'Independent

politics' of the 1930's. In these years the size of the Executive of the Constituency Labour Party was about thirty and of these twenty-five were corporate delegates, largely from trade unions, and only five—two from Wolstanton and three from Newcastle— represented ward parties and individual members. But attendance was slack and by 1937 the Newcastle Borough Labour Party had ceased to function. Anyway it had rarely nominated candidates for the Council: these had usually been trade-union nominees who had felt slight allegiance to the local Labour organization. Thus the pre-1914 tradition had persisted. The involvement of the Labour leaders, and especially Moran, in the policy decisions of a council with an Independent majority made it difficult for solidarity or discipline to be maintained. Though a Labour Group met sporadically only about half of the Labour councillors usually attended.[1]

If the party was weak in the Council in the 1930's it was weaker in the wards. The Wolstanton party never recovered from 1932 and its leadership disappeared. Silverdale and Chesterton (Wards 10, 11 and 12) returned Independents throughout this decade, partly because the North Stafford miners ceased to take an interest in local political action and partly because the Silverdale Co-operative Society was again fighting independently of the Labour Party. Thus a reservoir of potential Labour votes was never tapped and the Labour Party's effort was usually restricted to six wards. This was in marked contrast to Stoke-on-Trent where Labour came back to power in 1934 after three short years in the minority.

In consequence of the failure of the Labour Party to enter local politics in any force the internal arrangements of Newcastle Council were characterized by the traditional absence of stable combinations. Though among the Independent council members there were Liberals and Conservatives it was very uncommon for them to take an active part in the work of their local constituency organizations. Thus there was a fluid situation on the Council. For example, the 'Economizers' on issues of municipal finance were divided on the issue of building on the 'island site'. In these circumstances personal relationships and reputations were important, affecting the choice of committee chairmen

[1] Minutes of the Newcastle Borough Labour Party, 1931–9.

and aldermen. For such positions Labour councillors, never exceeding eight in total strength, were on occasions proposed by Independents; and conversely there were cases of Labour committee chairmen supporting the nomination of Independents for their vice-chairmen.

Decisions were reached in Council by the Independent practice of voting on issues 'according to their merits', a procedure which made it difficult to concert any forward policy. The chairmen of the important committees, however, made it their habit to consult with the Borough officials whose advice was often accepted; and the Town Clerk in the inter-war years, very much one of the 'old school', combining his office with his solicitor's practice, played an important role in the decision-making process of the Council.[1]

In the 1920's two organizations had been founded in Newcastle by the shopkeepers and small businessmen who still largely ran Borough politics. The people who formed the Chamber of Trade in 1925 were almost exactly the same as those who set up the Rotary Club in 1929. The coincidence of membership of the two bodies and of the Council was quite striking. For example, in 1932 seven council officers (including the Town Clerk) and ten council members (including most of the important committee chairmen) were members of the Rotary Club. Thus in the latter body, which had great prestige at this time, was concentrated the group that governed Newcastle. However, by 1939 only four council officers and five council members were Rotarians, and it may well be that the amalgamation with Wolstanton had tended after 1932 to loosen the tight community life of the hitherto small Borough and thus make the centralization of power more difficult.

3. Conclusion

The area which now comprises the Newcastle constituency has had no common social and political history. In the first place the Industrial Revolution made a very differing impact on different parts of the constituency. The farming area remained most stable though its increase of population, and possibly its ablest inhabi-

[1] For a description of this type of Town Clerk see T. E. Headrick, *The Town Clerk in English Local Government* (1962), pp. 22 ff.

tants, were drained away to the towns. Some of the parishes on the fringe of the farming area and Audley, though considerably affected by industrial change, retained some of their rural characteristics. The parishes of Knutton and Chesterton witnessed the greatest social upheaval and industrialization. Meanwhile Newcastle Borough, though its population increased, avoided (almost deliberately) the experience of industrialization and retained many of the features of an older era.

To all these different areas administrative change before the end of the nineteenth century had brought a certain element of representative local government. The Borough experienced this as early as 1835 though, perhaps because the freemen had previously had the Parliamentary franchise, it was not received with any enthusiasm, and in the other areas the greatest change was the Act of 1894, vastly widening the franchise. All these innovations were intended to encourage the development of 'local democracy'. The reorganization of 1932, amalgamating Blore Heath R.D.C. and Audley U.D.C. with Newcastle R.D.C. and Wolstanton United U.D.C. with Newcastle Borough, were to some extent an admission that small authorities, even when like Audley they were communities, were not good models for autonomous local government.

The relative failure of local self-government in the constituency was probably the result of the changes being imposed from above by central direction. Though a vigorous minority of the working class in the nineteenth century agitated for the national suffrage there was no equivalent demand—if Newcastle constituency is typical—for local enfranchisement. The association of the local suffrage with the doubtful privilege of paying rates seems to have discouraged nearly everyone. As we have seen in Newcastle, where some of the working class received the local franchise at a comparatively early date, it was widely regarded as a commodity to be traded for drink. Elsewhere there was strong opposition to local self-government with its concomitant of local financial responsibility.

How much this experience was a result of lack of social and political leadership it is difficult to say, but the local gentry, with the single and honourable exception of the Twemlow family, did not exhibit any pronounced and lasting interest in local affairs.

In the countryside this was the position almost from the beginning of the nineteenth century, while in Audley and the Wolstanton area the manufacturers, after a period of service, left for desirable residences in London or Shropshire at about the time of the First World War. In Newcastle Borough there were scarcely any 'gentlefolk' and leadership was for the most part exerted by shopkeepers and the proprietors of small businesses. Thus taking the constituency as a whole we may say that its leadership was not in the hands of 'top people' but of 'small men' —tenant farmers, clergymen, small businessmen and shopkeepers—in popular parlance 'middle to lower-middle-class people'.

Until the Second World War local politics in the constituency was a reflection of this situation. In all parts of the constituency the personal factor was the most important and 'Independent politics' was the rule in both the Borough and the Rural District. In the Rural District this implied that the most respected people socially were often the political leaders. In the Borough, where the social structure was less simple, the small traders were sometimes divided over policy and struggles for power took place.

In this political climate decisions were *ad hoc* and unrelated to one another. Newcastle Borough never experienced industrial expansion and its consequence, economic buoyancy, so that financial timidity, an obsession with cheeseparing and 'retrenchment', crippled the municipal growth of the town. Audley and Wolstanton, which were industrialized, were by themselves too small and too remote for grand municipal thinking, and the depression in the iron industry shocked their formative years. After the First World War the economic blizzard that swept the coalfield plunged the area into poverty. In these circumstances it is hardly surprising that no tradition of municipal advance, save in the field of housing, ever became rooted in the constituency.

This lack of a general approach to local affairs was no encouragement to the national parties. It is a marked feature of the constituency in the nineteenth century that the people who ran the Liberal and Conservative Parties were rarely prominent in local politics; and in the twentieth century this also became true of the Labour Party. Though the last years of the Wolstanton Urban District were an exception to this rule, on the whole municipal politics were conducted by Labour councillors in an older tradition of trade-union representation that predated the Labour Party; and Wedgwood encouraged the divorce between local and Parliamentary politics which before 1945 proceeded in two virtually separate spheres. We must now turn to Parliamentary politics in the constituency.

CHAPTER THREE

PARLIAMENTARY REPRESENTATION AND PARTY ORGANIZATION IN NEWCASTLE-UNDER-LYME BEFORE 1918

1. Club and Caucus

Modern political life in Newcastle, with its permanent party organization, co-ordinated electoral machines, political headquarters, party officials and mass memberships, had its beginning as far back as the period following the Reform Act of 1867. The progress of political development was uneven, with some elements, such as the caucus system, appearing as early as the 1868 General Election, and others, such as a tiered party structure, not taking final form until the middle 1880's. 1867, nevertheless, represents a break between the old forms of political organization and what we have come to recognize as modern, despite some foreshadowings of later practice in the middle years of the century.

The first Reform Act of 1832 gave the vote to 360 £10 householders and increased the electorate by 55 per cent.[1] The influx of new electors, however, did not destroy the power of the burgesses or hereditary freemen of the Borough, in whose hands the franchise, before the Act, had exclusively rested. In fact they increased in number until in the 1860's they represented nearly three-quarters of the electoral strength of the constituency. Divided more or less equally into Liberals and Conservatives, they contested the elections in consistent rivalry. A retrospective account of Newcastle politics described their role:

[1] *The Parliamentary Pocket Companion* for 1833 (2nd edn., 1833), p. 67.

'Thus successive generations of burgesses ranged on one side had fought throughout a long course of years under the same party colours against successive generations of opposing burgesses wearing opposite colours, both contending with the quenchless zeal of clansmen fighting for hearth and home.'[1]

In the years before the second Reform Act elections were usually fought by middle-class candidates with money and a taste for politics. The campaign would be planned from the residence of the candidate, with a prominent hostelry in the town as local headquarters. For the mass of the population there was little sense of involvement in the process of representation. Workingmen, largely excluded from the franchise, played little part in electoral campaigns. This situation was to be transformed by the Reform Act of 1867.

The Act of 1867 gave the vote to many of the industrial workers, split up some of the largest constituencies in London and the larger towns, and virtually doubled the electorate to a total of two million. In Newcastle the Act added some 1,500 electors to the roll, bringing it up to a total of 2,500.[2] Many of the newly enfranchised were workingmen, and included between four and five hundred Irish Catholics. The constituency retained its right to send two members to Parliament.

The 1868 election, the first to be fought on the new franchise, was contested on behalf of the Liberals by William Shepherd Allen and Henry Salmon, and by Sir Edmund Buckley for the Conservatives. Salmon, the second Liberal, had been nominated by the Radical wing of the party in defiance of the orthodox leadership, which would have been content to have let the two sitting members, Allen and Buckley, have a walk-over. To secure Salmon's return the Radicals set up an organization called the 'Newcastle-under-Lyme Liberal Association', closely modelled on Joseph Chamberlain's Birmingham caucus.

A colleague of Salmon, a Mr. C. B. Becke, was imported from Northants to act as agent and organizer. Under the auspices of the Association, the constituency was divided into districts, wherein local 'captains' were to instruct voters how best to distribute their votes between the two Liberal candidates. During

[1] *Newcastle Guardian*, 26 September 1885.
[2] *Staffordshire Weekly Times*, 5 September 1868.

the course of the campaign, committees in each district carried out a canvass of the electors and organized a series of local meetings. The campaign concluded with a personal canvass by Salmon himself.[1]

The election was a curious mixture of the old and the new, the hustings and the caucus organization being in use at the same time. The Conservatives did not use the word 'caucus' to describe their own organization, though it is clear that they had a central committee which co-ordinated the efforts of local district committees. On polling day, the electors went to various committee rooms to await the orders of the 'captains' before going to record their votes in the booths.[2] Buckley and Allen were returned with 1,443 and 1,081 votes respectively. Salmon, who received 744 votes, failed to get elected.

For the next seventeen years Newcastle returned a Conservative and a Liberal at every election, except for a short period between 1878 and 1880, when a swing towards Liberalism enabled a second Liberal, S. R. Edge, to be returned in a straight fight with a Conservative at a by-election.

It was in this period that the beginnings of stable party structures and well-organized electoral machines made their appearance. The first form of party organization was the political club, which served not only as headquarters but also as a focus of social and political life for party members and sympathizers. The Conservative Club was opened in January 1869 and the Liberal Club four years later.[3] The latter was run by a central committee consisting of delegates from the eleven polling districts of the town, each of which sent three representatives of the Liberal electors to the committee.[4] There is less information about the Conservative electoral organization, but apparently it was run on lines similar to those at the 1868 election.

The political club remained the headquarters of the parties throughout the 1870's. In 1881, however, the Radical wing of the Liberals successfully pressed for a reorganization and the

---

[1] *Staffordshire Weekly Times*, 29 August 1868, 3 October 1868.

[2] Ibid., 21 November 1868.

[3] J. Ingamells, *Historical Records and Directory of Newcastle-under-Lyme* (Newcastle-under-Lyme, 2nd edn., 1881), p. 60.

[4] *Newcastle Guardian*, 4 June 1881.

formation of a Liberal Council on the Birmingham model. The Radicals criticized the conduct of the Liberal leadership in the 1880 election, claiming that the latter had returned to pre-1868 methods of electioneering. The Radicals pointed out that the victory of the second Liberal in the by-election of 1878 was due to the soundness of his organization, which had been based on the Birmingham model. A series of meetings took place in the spring of 1881, resulting in the formation of a Liberal Council, 'for the purposes of organization and the conduct of the affairs of the Liberal Party in the borough', which for the next four years existed side by side with the Club.[1] Before the new organization could be tested in an election, however, the changes brought about by the third Reform Act of 1885 forced the parties to remodel their machinery to meet the challenge of the new electorate and the new political situation.

Under the Reform and Redistribution Acts of 1884 and 1885, the County of Stafford was divided into seven constituencies and Newcastle was made into a one-member constituency. The boundary was extended to include, in addition to the municipal borough, the pottery town of Tunstall plus Wolstanton, Silverdale, Knutton and Chesterton. The population increased threefold to nearly fifty thousand people, and the electorate more than doubled to over eight thousand.[2] Silverdale, Knutton and Chesterton were overwhelmingly mining districts and it was this infusion of miners into the constituency by boundary changes that gave it a characteristic working-class flavour and made the miners henceforward a powerful force.

The 1885 legislation had two immediate and important effects on the political parties in Newcastle: they remodelled their organization in the light of the boundary changes and the increase in the number of voters, and they modified the style and content of their political appeal to suit the increasingly working-class electorate. The Liberal Council was reorganized on the basis of five districts with representatives at the rate of eight per thousand of the population of each district, giving a total of four hundred members, many of them workingmen. The Liberal 'Four Hundred' had a president, five vice-presidents (the chairmen of

---

[1] *Newcastle Guardian*, 30 April 1881, 7 May 1881, 21 May 1881, 28 May 1881. [2] *Dod's Parliamentary Companion* (1886).

the various districts), a treasurer, general secretary and an executive committee.[1] From this date until well into the twentieth century this Council was the political and electoral headquarters of Liberalism in Newcastle, and the Club became purely a social centre. The Council began to play a more active role, and though the contesting of General Elections was still seen as the most important task, the carrying out of continuous work between elections was for the first time given importance. In this it was helped by the county organization, the Staffordshire Liberal Council, which was formed two years later.[2]

The Conservatives on their part formed the Conservative Parliamentary Committee, which, like the Liberal organization, consisted of representatives from each of five districts, on the basis of ten per thousand of the population, resulting in a committee of 500. It was apparent that for all practical purposes the Conservatives' organization was exactly the same as that of the Liberals, though the former hastened to point out that their committee was 'in no sense a Conservative caucus'. Every Conservative, it was claimed, would have a voice in the election of members, and an executive council of 100 would be elected annually by the whole committee.[3] Both the Liberal and Conservative organizations were on a territorial basis, with representatives from each of five communities—Newcastle, Tunstall, Silverdale, Chesterton and Wolstanton. The form of organization was an inverted pyramid, with small local committees and the full council of 400 or 500 members meeting annually as the directing body.

The other main effect of the new franchise of 1885 was to sharpen the political fight between Conservatives and Liberals, and to cause each party to appeal much more directly to the interests of the working class, particularly the miners, a community with great social and political solidarity and Liberal traditions. No longer was it possible, as it had been in the 1870's, for candidates to give a gentlemanly and general exposition of the national programme of their party without reference to the specific needs of their constituents.

[1] *Newcastle Guardian,* 16 May 1885, 23 May 1885, 19 June 1886.
[2] Ibid., 12 November 1887.
[3] Ibid., 27 June 1885.

The change of tone was evident in the 1885 election, the first to be fought after the new legislation. William Shepherd Allen, who once again stood for the Liberals, announced himself as a follower of the working-class policies of Henry Broadhurst, the stonemason who sat as M.P. for Stoke-on-Trent.[1] The Conservative candidate, A. W. Scoble, a London lawyer, became adept at the necessary new double-talk, declaring that he had been a workingman all his life, though he had the grace to admit that 'his work had lain in pleasanter places than the men who worked in the mine, the Pottery shed, the foundry or any other sphere of industry . . .' He was at pains to show that Capital was the best friend of Labour, that the interests of masters and men were identical and that the Conservative Party was not a class party.[2] The local Conservatives produced a well-documented election pamphlet addressed specifically 'To the Working Men'.[3]

The election was won by Allen with 4,031 votes against Scoble's 2,845, and confirmed the Liberal forecast during the campaign that they had the greater proportion of the working-class electors with them. Enoch Edwards, the secretary of the North Stafford Miners' Federation, spoke at one of Allen's meetings in Silverdale. Allen, at the announcement at the poll, declared that it had been a workingman's battle and that the 'swells' were against him.[4]

Within less than a year of his victory, however, Allen had broken with the Liberal Party on the issue of Irish Home Rule. He became a Liberal Unionist, failed to get the support of Newcastle Liberal Council, left politics and retired to his estates in New Zealand. About a third of the Newcastle Liberals went over to the Unionist camp with him.[5] Allen's retirement was not, perhaps, inopportune. A devout Methodist and apostle of Imperial strength and unity, he hardly seemed fitted for the stress of post-1885 politics. First elected in 1865, his conception of the

[1] *Newcastle Guardian*, 6 June 1885.

[2] Ibid., 7 November 1885.

[3] 'A Lesson and a Warning. To the Working Men of the Parliamentary Borough of Newcastle-under-Lyme.' Pamphlet dated November 1885 (Newcastle Museum).

[4] *Newcastle Guardian*, 21 November 1885, 28 November 1885.

[5] Parl. Deb., 3rd Ser., CCCIV (9 April 1886), 1222–6; *Newcastle Guardian*, 19 June 1886, 26 June 1886, 3 July 1886.

duties of an M.P. consisted of a gentlemanly election campaign followed by assiduous attendance but no speeches in the House, an annual report-back meeting to his constituents and a summer fête in the grounds of his seat at Woodhead Hall.[1]

In retrospect, the period between 1867 and 1885 was a transitional one for the Conservative and Liberal Parties in Newcastle, both as regards policy and organization. Their electoral organizations, strongly influenced by the Birmingham model, were ephemeral affairs, brought to life at General Elections and allowed to lapse afterwards. The real centre of party political life was the Club, the headquarters of the party or association and the meeting-place for their social élite. In 1881, however, the Radical wing of the Liberals revolted to form a Liberal Council. After the Reform and Redistribution Acts of 1884 and 1885 electoral organizations of a permanent nature were set up outside the orbits of the Clubs. Both the Conservative Parliamentary Committee and the Liberal Council paid a great deal more attention to propaganda and organizational work between General Elections. The year 1885, therefore, marked the beginning of a new era in political organization, which lasted into the twentieth century.

2. The Rise and Effect of the Working-class Vote

The inclusion of the mining districts in the constituency of Newcastle in 1885 was an event of profound significance for the future of local politics, particularly in relation to the Liberal Party. The latter, having survived the loss of perhaps one-third of their membership to the Liberal Unionists in 1886, were faced within the space of four years with the prospect of a Labour candidate claiming the seat on behalf of the miners. Thus the fissiparous tendencies which were to dog the Liberals in the ensuing period—the danger of losing members to both Conservatives and Labour—were already visible.

As early as 1887 the North Stafford miners had shown a desire

---

[1] For Allen's life and political activities see: G. Rickword and W. Gaskell, *Staffordshire Leaders, Social and Political* (n.d. ?1908), p. 169; W. S. Allen, *Twenty Years of Political Life* (Newcastle-under-Lyme, 1885); *Newcastle Guardian*, 26 September 1885, 3 October 1885, 7 October 1885, 14 November 1885.

for independent labour representation, supporting the National Labour Electoral Association, a body of moderate trade unionists pledged to send workingmen to Parliament in the Labour interest.[1] In 1890 the miners decided to put up their secretary, Enoch Edwards, to contest Newcastle.[2] The Liberals, however, would not agree to Edwards's nomination, nor to the constituency becoming a Labour seat as the miners desired. The latter, for their part, did not at the time feel strong enough to win the seat in a three-cornered fight, and were chary of taking votes from the Liberals and letting in the Unionists. As a result, the nomination of the 1892 General Election went to William Allen, the 22-year-old son of the former M.P., a boy who was still an undergraduate at Cambridge and who appeared to have been chosen on account of whatever magic remained of his father's name and in order to keep out a workingman nominee. After much heart-searching the miners agreed not to put up a candidate in Newcastle and to support Allen. It had been a difficulty, said the *Guardian*, which only 'the loyalty of the miners to their traditional Liberal principles was able to overcome'. In this election the miners decided only to support candidates in North Staffordshire who stood for the Miners' Eight Hours Bill, which, they declared, was the test question of the election.[3]

The miners' decision left Allen in a position of having virtually to transform himself into a Labour candidate in order to win the seat. The support of the miners, the *Guardian* reminded him, 'makes all the difference between victory and defeat'. A Home Ruler and otherwise orthodox Liberal, Allen's election speeches in the 1892 contest could not have been bettered by Edwards himself. The Liberals were friends of the workingman, he claimed, and he personally would fight for all measures of reform which would better the working class, including the Miners' Eight Hours Bill, the Employers' Liability Bill, and the Mines Regulation Bill.[4] The miners' support proved to be decisive. Allen beat Coghill, the Unionist candidate, in a straight fight by 1,268

[1] Minutes of the North Stafford Miners' Federation, 29 February 1888, 4 May 1891.
[2] *Newcastle Guardian*, 25 June 1892.
[3] Ibid., 25 June 1892, 2 July 1892.
[4] Ibid., 25 June 1892.

votes. He declared in his maiden speech in Parliament that he owed his election to his championing of the Miners' Eight Hours Bill.[1]

Allen, to his credit, justified the miners' faith in him, as a glance at *Hansard* for the period shows. Unlike his father, he spoke frequently in the House on questions affecting the welfare and conditions of the working class. But though the voice was the voice of Allen, the hand was unquestionably the hand of Edwards. Had not the young M.P. given a pledge that on all matters he would be guided by the local miners' leaders? English political history is full of ironies, but one of the strangest must surely have been that of a young Cambridge undergraduate of twenty-two acting as the mouthpiece of the hard-bitten North Stafford miners. Allen carried out his duties so well, however, that the miners supported him again in the election of 1895, when Enoch Edwards spoke on his platform, praising him for his work on the Eight Hours Bill and classing him with Sam Woods, Ben Pickard and John Burns as a tribune of the working class.[2] Allen held the seat in 1895 despite the Liberal débâcle of that year, though his Unionist opponent was admittedly not a strong one, being imported from London for the occasion.

Allen's future seemed to be a bright one; he was young, enterprising, eloquent and had a safe seat. But his career was yet to end in tragedy, if not in farce. If his public record at Westminster satisfied his constituents, his private occupations were of such a character as to provide a scandal in Newcastle when they became known. Allen had been unwise enough to become connected with a group of M.P.s who had connections with city financiers and speculators, and had committed the cardinal mistake of taking out shares in a brewery company, despite his pledges on behalf of the temperance cause and his membership (as a temperance representative) of the Liquor Licensing Commission of 1899.[3] The Newcastle Liberals, with their strong Non-

[1] Parl. Deb., 4th Ser., VII (11 August 1892), 369.

[2] *Newcastle Guardian*, 13 July 1895.

[3] Allen signed the Minority Report, the first statement of whose conclusions was: 'A great reduction in the number of licensed houses is of the first importance.' (Final Report of Her Majesty's Commissioners Appointed to Inquire into the Operation and Administration of the Laws relating to the Sale of Intoxicating Liquors, P.P. (1899), XXXV, p. 289.)

conformist and temperance traditions, were shocked beyond measure and accused Allen of betraying his cause and his family. Allen, realizing his political future was bleak, took the romantic way out, volunteered for the fighting in the Boer War, and sought in death the expiation of his misdeeds.[1]

Allen did not die, though he was wounded several times. He even gained the nomination as the Liberal candidate for the General Election of 1900, though by a mere five votes, and that largely on account of his heroic gesture. He could not get leave from the war, however, and his wife and brother fought the campaign in his absence. In an atmosphere of hysterical jingoism and patriotism Allen lost the election by 183 votes, polling 3,568 votes to the Unionist candidate's 3,751. The Liberal vote thus remained solid, for Allen had polled 3,510 votes in 1895. But in such a situation solidity was not enough; an extraordinary effort was needed, and Allen had been in no position to supply it.

3. Josiah Wedgwood: From Liberalism to Labour

The new century began with North Staffordshire politically on the 'right'. Stoke, Hanley, Leek and Northwest Staffordshire all had Conservative or Unionist representation. The Newcastle Liberals were faced with two main problems—to find a new candidate and to reanimate their organization. The situation was complicated by the presence of Labour, more awkward than ever since the formation in 1900 of the Labour Representation Committee, the forerunner of the Labour Party. Newcastle Liberals still refused the claims of Labour to a seat and chose as candidate James Lovatt, a local clothing manufacturer, who had made a fortune manufacturing army uniforms during the Boer War. Lovatt spent some £10,000 building up the organization in the constituency,[2] but the Liberals were still faced with a problem which no money or organization could solve, namely, the extent to which a middle-class candidate could continue to

---

[1] *Newcastle Guardian*, 22 September 1900. The term 'expiation' was used in a *Guardian* editorial in reference to Allen as 'a young man who has erred and suffered, and has risked his life in his country's service by way of expiation' (*Newcastle Guardian*, 6 October 1900).

[2] Unidentified newspaper cutting in *Wedgwood Cuttings Book*, Vol. I (Hanley Public Libraries).

enlist the support of a largely working-class constituency. A solution to the difficulty appeared, however. Lovatt relinquished his candidature on the grounds of ill-health and the demands of business, and Josiah Clement Wedgwood, great-great-grandson of the potter, accepted the nomination in Lovatt's place just before the 1906 election.

He was a remarkable catch. His name was a venerated household word in the area, and he had all the glamour attaching to the scion of the Potteries' most famous industrial family. Wedgwood had a radical and democratic viewpoint, a sympathy for Labour's aspirations and, moreover, some experience of working with his hands.

Wedgwood had been born in Barlaston in 1872.[1] He was educated at Clifton, served an apprenticeship in Armstrong's Elswick Shipyard, studied at the Royal Naval College, Greenwich, and worked as a naval architect at Elswick from 1896 to 1899. From 1902 to 1904 he had been Resident Magistrate at Ermelo in the Transvaal, but had been forced to return to England because of his wife's ill-health. For a Liberal, his political background was unorthodox. In his youth he had been impressed by Edward Bellamy's Utopian Socialist romance *Looking Backward* and he had been associated with the Fabians in London in the 1890's. In 1905 he had become converted to the single-tax doctrine of Henry George and from then on the taxation of land values became, as he said, 'at once my anchorage and my object in politics'.[2]

Immediately after his adoption Wedgwood plunged into the campaign for the 1906 election. The outstanding characteristic of this election and the two following ones of January and December 1910 was the extreme partisanship with which the two political parties fought for victory. It was the era of social distress, Socialist revival and industrial unrest, the age of Lloyd George, Peers *v.* People and Free Trade *v.* Imperial Preference. Politics had a sharp edge and nowhere was this more so than in Newcastle-under-Lyme.

In 1906 Wedgwood opposed A. S. Haslam, the sitting Unionist member, with a policy of 'Free Trade, Free Land, Free Breakfast

[1] J. C. Wedgwood, *Memoirs of a Fighting Life* (1941), pp. 1–59 *passim*.
[2] Wedgwood, *Memoirs*, p. 60.

Table, No Taxes on the Loaf',[1] and he attacked the Unionist protection policies which he claimed would send up the price of bread. When the votes were counted Wedgwood had 5,155 votes to Haslam's 2,948, a majority of 2,207, almost double that of any candidate since 1885. There was an 85 per cent poll, with the heaviest polling in the working-class districts, where Wedgwood was most heavily supported. His supporters carried him shoulder-high through the town amidst scenes which, according to the *Guardian*, had not been seen since the relief of Mafeking.[2] Later in the evening, on a sudden but not untypical impulse, Wedgwood placed the blue ribbon of the Liberal colours round the head of the statue of his great-great-grandfather outside Stoke Station.[3]

Organization had helped in Wedgwood's victory. The Liberal Party had reached, in fact, a pitch of organization unparalleled in its history. The Liberal Council, now augmented to 500 members, was at peak efficiency. It had local committees, an agent in every street (provided with detailed lists of Liberal voters) and squads of knockers-up and tellers.[4] There were also organized sections of women and young people. The latter were particularly active in the election; fifty members of the Newcastle Branch of the League of Young Liberals took part in all the canvassing.[5] Liberals, Free Traders, Radicals and Labour men all rallied round Wedgwood. Perhaps it was significant that the Conservative candidate drove to his election meetings in a carriage and pair, whereas Wedgwood hurried around the constituency in the newest form of transport, the motor-car.[6]

In Parliament Wedgwood rapidly established a reputation for putting questions to Ministers, especially on the issues of land values and foreign affairs. It was his habit, he wrote later, at breakfast every morning to red-pencil every item in *The Times* which annoyed him on Foreign Affairs, Colonies, India, Finance and Land Values, and to draft questions accordingly.[7] Wedgwood's chief work in Parliament, however, was on propaganda for the taxation of land values.

---

[1] Election Card, *Wedgwood Cuttings Book*, Vol. I (Hanley Public Libraries).
[2] *Newcastle Guardian*, 20 January 1906.   [3] Wedgwood, *Memoirs*, p. 61.
[4] Ex. inf. Mrs. Helen Pease.   [5] *Newcastle Guardian*, 6 January 1906.
[6] C. V. Wedgwood, *The Last of the Radicals* (1951), pp. 76–7.
[7] Wedgwood, *Memoirs*, p. 64.

Wedgwood retained his seat at the next two elections of January and December 1910, two bitterly fought contests in which he twice beat the Unionist candidate, E. S. Grogan, an Imperialist and racialist who believed that the mission of the white races was the exploitation of Africa.[1] The General Election of January 1910 has become part of the political folklore of Newcastle-under-Lyme and there is scarcely a person over sixty today in the town who does not remember the Wedgwood-Grogan battles of that famous contest. As Wedgwood said later, it took the place of Agincourt. There were frequent clashes between rival supporters, marches, meetings, songs and heckling. The author has met several people in Newcastle who remember marching through the streets as schoolchildren, their faces painted blue (the Liberal colours) or with blue ribbons in their hair, singing the Land Song and shouting for Wedgwood. Wedgwood and Grogan went to every meeting accompanied by bodyguards. 'From one meeting my football team threw his forty out after a long and bloody fight', Wedgwood recalled. 'Thereafter neither side was allowed to address anything but a sea of fists, and I was bombarded on the Market Cross with shop-soiled produce, using as my shield my most offensive wood-backed posters.'[2] The newspaper reports, however, seemed to indicate that Grogan got somewhat heavier treatment than Wedgwood. A group of Liberal miners would attend every meeting of Grogan's and break into a vociferous rendering of the Land Song as soon as Grogan appeared.[3]

An extreme supporter of Joseph Chamberlain's Tariff Reform League, Grogan concentrated on the effect which Imperial Preference would have on safeguarding the standard of living, whereas Wedgwood attacked the House of Lords, the landowners and the monopolists as enemies of the people who limited the

[1] For Grogan's life and political outlook, see: E. S. Grogan, *From the Cape to Cairo* (1900); N. Wymer, *The Man from the Cape* (1959).

[2] Wedgwood, *Memoirs*, p. 70.

[3] *Staffordshire Sentinel*, 6 January 1910, 10 January 1910. The first verse of the Land Song ran:

> The land, the land, 'twas God who gave the land,
> The land, the land, the ground on which we stand,
> Why should we be beggars with the ballot in our hand?
> God gave the land to the people.

latter's liberty and created unemployment. The main issue of the election, however, was 'the Nairobi incident', an allegation that Grogan had flogged some natives in Kenya a few years previously.[1] There was hardly a meeting at which the accusation of 'flogging the natives' was not flung against Grogan by Liberal supporters. Wedgwood himself, however, refused to make it an issue in his speeches.

Grogan had given Wedgwood the hardest fight of his political life, and though the latter won the election by 5,613 votes to Grogan's 4,245, his majority was down on the 1906 result. Tariff Reform policies apparently had made some appeal to the Newcastle electorate.

It was almost an anticlimax when the Liberal Government once more went to the country at the end of the year, and Wedgwood and Grogan faced each other again in Newcastle within eleven months of their first great struggle. The contest in December was almost an academic one, however, for Grogan, hastily summoned from East Africa, arrived in Newcastle the day before the election, and conducted a campaign which lasted exactly twenty-four hours.[2] The political issues were very much the same as in January, and despite the shortness of his campaign, Grogan succeeded in reducing Wedgwood's majority by 174 votes, polling 4,087 votes to the latter's 5,281.

In the period between 1910 and the outbreak of the First World War, Wedgwood, while consolidating his popularity by nursing his constituency,[3] began to emerge as a critic of the Liberal Government, urging them to carry out their election pledges, attacking their policy on India, and supporting Labour

[1] For the details of this incident see: East Africa Protectorate. Correspondence Relating to the Flogging of Natives by Certain Europeans at Nairobi. P.P. (1907), LVII. Grogan, who was imprisoned for his part in the affair, later appealed against the verdict on the ground that he should have been tried by jury, not by magistrate, and had his appeal upheld (Wymer, op. cit., p. 160 n.).

[2] *Staffordshire Sentinel*, 3 December 1910.

[3] The daughter of a prominent Liberal remembered Wedgwood coming to tea with her father, and how the whole street looked out the windows to see his arrival; Wedgwood was charming, took a great deal of interest in all the members of the family and before he left signed an autograph book: 'Liberté, Egalité, Fraternité, Josiah C. Wedgwood.' (Private information.)

M.P.s at by-elections.[1] In many ways, his niece wrote later, he was more like a Labour M.P. than a Liberal M.P.[2] Newcastle Liberal Council continued to support him, however, but they maintained a less critical attitude than Wedgwood towards the government. They congratulated it on its 'excellent record of progressive legislation', and praised the government's efforts 'to promote peace among the European nations'.[3]

These sentiments were expressed at a meeting on 31 July 1914. Within a week Britain was at war and the Liberal dreams were shattered. Four years later the party was to be split and almost destroyed as a Parliamentary force. Wedgwood himself volunteered for active service, and served with great gallantry in the navy and the army in France, Gallipoli, East Africa and Russia.[4] Before his return the redistribution of 1918 somewhat altered the configuration of his constituency. Tunstall was incorporated into Burslem, and with the break-up of the old Northwest Staffordshire division Audley became part of Newcastle.

Wedgwood came back from the war a hero, a position quite in accord with the popular feeling of the time. It is difficult today to imagine the worship of the returned soldier that took place in 1918, but a glance at the newspapers of the period will satisfy us as to the almost hysterical and uncritical admiration for the man in khaki, and the detestation of the pacifist or of those who had in any way opposed the war. Wedgwood's fellow Liberal M.P., R. L. Outhwaite of Hanley, who had opposed the war from a left-wing point of view, found the local newspaper refusing to print his speeches and virtually advising the electorate not to vote for him in 1918.[5] In Wedgwood's case his Radical opinions were outweighed in the public mind by the glamour of his war record, made all the more meritorious by the fact that he had volunteered despite the fact that he was not only an M.P., but over military age.

[1] Wedgwood, *Memoirs*, p. 38, p. 71, p. 84; *Staffordshire Sentinel*, 1 December 1910.

[2] C. V. Wedgwood, op. cit., p. 90.

[3] Newcastle Liberal Council, Executive Minutes, 31 July 1914.

[4] See J. C. Wedgwood, *Essays and Adventures of a Labour M.P.* (1924), esp. Chapters XV and XIX.

[5] *Staffordshire Sentinel*, 26 November 1918, 12 December 1918, 13 December 1918.

The war years had made Wedgwood more Radical, more independent, and to a great extent disillusioned with the Liberal Party. In 1917, for instance, his name was found among the members of the near-pacifist and revolutionary 1917 Committee.[1] Before the 1918 election he rejected the Coupon or letter of support of the Coalition leaders, the only Liberal, he claimed, who had done so.[2] On the other hand he came to an agreement with the local Unionist Party on the question of Imperial Preference in return for their promise not to oppose him. He agreed, with reservations, to support their policy: the conservation of raw materials and products for the benefit of the Empire and Britain's Allies (provided it was supported by Lloyd George); preferential trading with the Empire and the Allies (provided there was no tax on food), and the prevention of dumping.[3]

These actions were not those of a strict party man; but Wedgwood was laying less and less claim to that distinction. His agreement with the Unionists, he explained, was admittedly a concession, but he claimed that they had met him with such good feelings on so many issues that he was prepared to give way; he wanted their co-operation and was prepared to compromise. As a *quid pro quo* the Unionist candidate, E. P. Hewitt, stood down in Wedgwood's favour.[4]

Wedgwood explained his position in a letter to the editor of the local newspaper, the *Staffordshire Sentinel*. He was not, he pointed out, a supporter of the Coalition. He believed that the nation owed Lloyd George a debt for winning the war, and personally he supported the latter's peace terms, but he did not agree with his domestic policies—in Wedgwood's opinion Lloyd George was reluctant to tackle vested interests and go for fundamentals. Wedgwood preferred, therefore, to call himself an Independent Radical and to hold himself free to join 'those who show serious intentions in the matter of rating and taxing land values'.[5] In whatever other ways his views had changed,

---

[1] *Morning Post*, 12 September 1917.
[2] *Staffordshire Sentinel*, 11 November 1922.
[3] Ibid., 2 December 1918.
[4] Ibid.
[5] Ibid., 18 November 1918.

Wedgwood remained true to the doctrines of Henry George and the single tax.

Despite his self-styled designation as an Independent Radical, Wedgwood was adopted as the official Liberal candidate by the Newcastle Liberals. His nomination forms, however, were signed by a number of prominent members of the Conservative and Unionist Party in addition to his Liberal sponsors. He also received unofficial support from the newly founded Labour Party.[1] The chairman of the Liberal Party, Dr. F. Shufflebotham, spoke of 'the unanimity of all parties in allowing Colonel Wedgwood an unopposed return, on account of his services during the war'.[2]

Wedgwood's election address, despite his arrangement with the Unionists, showed him more in tune with the Radical and Labour sentiments of the period rather than with those of orthodox Liberalism. He wanted to establish a world in which militarism would never again have a place; he supported the League of Nations and President Wilson's Fourteen Points. At home he wanted an end to war-time legislation, the end of D.O.R.A., and of conscription; freedom of the press and an amnesty for all military and political prisoners. The working class, he maintained, wanted justice and the right to work. Inevitably he put forward his views on the land question; the right to the earth and to the land should be restored to the people, with fixity of tenure and right of purchase for allotment holders, the breaking up of big farms and the purchase of land by the Government for distribution to returned soldiers at a rent equivalent to its unimproved value. He also urged a vigorous housing drive (with Government control of building materials), public control of railways and canals, and improvements in education. He concluded by thanking the electors for the free hand they had given him, which few constituencies allowed their members. He was, he claimed, tied to no party and in debt to no man. 'I come before you now the same impenitent Independent Radical that you first elected in 1906.'[3] This was strange talk for an official Liberal candidate and the Liberals might have seen it as a portent of his future behaviour, but at his adoption meeting they

[1] *Staffordshire Sentinel*, 3 December 1918.
[2] Minutes of the Newcastle Liberal Council, 2 December 1918.
[3] *Staffordshire Sentinel*, 22 November 1918.

were uncritically lavish in their praise of his fearlessness, straight dealing, patriotism and courage.[1] They were sincere, and Wedgwood deserved it; but no one queried his professions of independence.

Wedgwood returned to a House of Commons very different from that which he had left over four years before. The great Liberal majority had been reduced to some thirty-odd Free Liberals and virtually a clean sweep had been made of the Liberal ministers. Despite this, Wedgwood believed that if he had been made leader of the 'remnant', had put forward a 'convinced land policy' and led a determined attack on Lloyd George's conduct of foreign affairs, Liberalism might have survived.[2] His Radical views, however, combined with the feeling aroused by his recent divorce action,[3] made it inevitable that he would not be chosen, and the leadership went to Sir Donald Maclean.

During the first months of the new Parliament, Wedgwood's faith in Liberalism, as represented by the Free Liberal remnant, declined even further. By the beginning of April he was writing to his daughter Helen, then a prominent member of Newcastle Labour Party, that he was considering leaving the Liberals in June and joining the I.L.P.[4] The break came earlier, however. On 11 April 1919, he attended a meeting at the Connaught Rooms in London at which Asquith made a policy speech. The Liberal leader began by stating he was going to be deliberately silent on international affairs—a strange decision in view of the recent signs of British intervention in Soviet Russia. Asquith's statement was greeted with a shout of 'Shame!' (was it Wedgwood?). The rest of his speech consisted of a string of generalities about domestic policy; phrases like 'a national minimum of health', 'against extravagance', no preferential treatment of 'particular classes or interests', roused even *The Times* to regret

---

[1] *Staffordshire Sentinel*, 3 December 1918.

[2] Wedgwood, *Memoirs*, p. 143.

[3] In 1918 Wedgwood obtained a divorce from his wife. Though he had acted with integrity in the matter, he received a good deal of public criticism, particularly from the Churches. Cf. C. V. Wedgwood, op. cit., pp. 126–36.

[4] Helen Wedgwood, MS. Diary, 8 April 1919.

that 'so much of Mr. Asquith's ability should exhaust itself in apt but barren phrasing'.[1]

To Wedgwood this lack of a clear-cut lead and vigorous policy was the last straw. Above all, Asquith's repudiation (by omission) of the doctrine of the taxation of land values and his refusal to condemn (again by omission) the beginnings of intervention in Russia, convinced him that nothing was to be expected from the Liberals. The following day he sat down and wrote a letter to the secretary of the Hanley Independent Labour Party, applying for membership. There was, at the time, no branch of the I.L.P. in his own constituency. For those who wanted opposition to intervention and a fight against reaction abroad, he wrote, plus a constructive domestic policy based on taxation and rating of land values and a levy on capital, there was in Mr. Asquith's speech 'no word of hope'. He therefore would be glad if the I.L.P. would enrol him 'as one who will do his best to secure a free co-operative Commonwealth and the brotherhood of man'.[2]

The I.L.P. welcomed him, but neither the Labour Party in the House of Commons nor in his own constituency was immediately enamoured of a new recruit. 'They liked Land Values and all this "brotherhood-of-man" business just as little as did the Liberals', commented Wedgwood somewhat bitterly, and he waited some months before being officially welcomed into the ranks of Labour, poised, as he put it, 'like Mahomet's coffin between heaven and hell'.[3] Why did Wedgwood join the I.L.P. rather than the Labour Party, even though the latter, under the 1918 reorganization, admitted individual members? In the first place, as his daughter noticed, his outlook, despite certain disagreements on economic questions, was much closer to the I.L.P. than to any other party.[4] Secondly, as a commentator in the Newcastle press shrewdly remarked, Wedgwood would have more freedom of action in the I.L.P. than in the Labour Party.[5]

Wedgwood's change of party hit the Newcastle Liberals like a bombshell. The outbreak of the Great War could hardly have

[1] The Times, 12 April 1919.
[2] Staffordshire Sentinel, 16 April 1919; Labour Leader, 17 April 1919.
[3] Wedgwood, Memoirs, p. 144.
[4] Helen Wedgwood, MS. Diary, 8 April 1919.
[5] 'Observer' in Staffordshire Sentinel, 10 May 1919.

been a greater shock to them. As we have seen, they had a somewhat uncritical admiration for Wedgwood and his sudden change of party found them uttering sentiments appropriate to those who feel themselves betrayed without cause. Dr. Shufflebotham, the chairman, called Wedgwood's action 'a betrayal of the trust confided in him at the last election'. Another member of the executive declared that the Liberals felt 'despised' and 'humiliated' by Wedgwood's action, for they had loyally, persistently and energetically supported him, sometimes even against their own better judgment. Wedgwood was described as 'a kaleidoscopic politician, altering the shape and design of his politics with every turn of the hand'. Wounded in their best sentiments, the Liberals unanimously called upon Wedgwood to resign.[1]

A heated correspondence between Wedgwood and the Liberal leadership followed, part of which was published in the local press. The burden of the Liberal case was that Wedgwood had betrayed the trust placed in him at the last election, had acted undemocratically and was guilty of nothing less than duplicity.[2] At times it seemed that it was more the manner of his going than the departure itself which so annoyed the Liberals. Sam Walker, the Liberal secretary, bitterly remarked to Helen Wedgwood, 'We can understand his joining the Labour Party, but why couldn't he do it through the Fabian Society, instead of choosing that bunch of pacifist I.L.P.-ers at Hanley?'[3] In his reply to the Liberal correspondents, Wedgwood reminded them that he had been bound by no pledges at the election and in fact had deliberately proclaimed his future freedom of action; he could not therefore be accused of double-dealing or failure to live up to his undertakings. He thought it was going too far for the Liberals to claim they had supported him—tolerated was a more correct word, and they had done this partly because they liked him personally, partly because his advanced views secured the Labour vote and helped them beat the Tories. His standpoint had been closest to the rank-and-file of the Liberals and now many of

[1] Minutes of Newcastle Liberal Council, 25 April 1919.
[2] Newcastle Liberal Council, Executive Minutes, 6 May 1919, 23 May 1919; *Staffordshire Sentinel*, 29 April 1919, 8 May 1919, 29 May 1919.
[3] Helen Wedgwood, MS. Diary, 1 May 1919.

these were calling him from the ranks of Labour. Many more, he believed, would go that way in the near future.[1]

In an interview he gave to the London *Evening Standard* at the end of April he expanded upon his views:

'I was nominated by all parties . . . and my election address clearly showed that I was independent of any Party. It expressly stated so in my address. I didn't give any pledge, I was unopposed.

'The only pledges I gave were in writing, published in the local paper in connection with tariffs. I didn't have a single public meeting. My election address is clear on the point. I have a clear hand absolutely.

'I was supported by Unionists, Liberals and Labour; that is to say, some of each signed my nomination papers.

'They care so much more about labels than about politics. I don't think my politics have ever varied much. My views have always been more or less in sympathy with them [i.e., the Labour Party]. My election address was very similar to the Labour Party Manifesto.

'What I joined them on was my disappointment at Mr. Asquith's speech—the want of a courageous and clear lead. . . .

'I have left without any ill-feeling. It is not like a sudden change of party, where you suddenly turn upon old friends. I am more or less a licensed person in the House, to do and say what I like.'[2]

Thus Wedgwood left the Liberal Party. Was Liberalism to him the god that failed? Though the manner of his leaving was somewhat abrupt, his disillusionment with Liberalism was no sudden revelation. He had always considered himself, except perhaps in his first few years in the House, to be an individualist to whom the ties of party were secondary to the propagation of what he believed to be right and in Wedgwood's case the right lay in the direction of individualism, freedom and the policies of Henry George. These beliefs he carried into the Labour Party. The effect of his allegiance to the Labour Party in his constituency of Newcastle-under-Lyme and the consequences of his defection from the local Liberals will be traced in the two following chapters.

[1] *Staffordshire Sentinel*, 2 May 1919, 10 May 1919, 12 May 1919.
[2] *Evening Standard*, 30 April 1919.

CHAPTER FOUR

THE LABOUR PARTY SINCE 1918

1. The Wedgwood Era

The early history of Newcastle Constituency Labour Party, founded in 1918, was in many respects similar to that of other Labour parties in working-class constituencies.[1] It took part in political activities in connection with unemployment, strikes and housing conditions, ran some candidates for the local council and campaigned on issues of national and international importance. But to a much greater degree than most constituency parties, Newcastle Labour Party was influenced by the character and activities of Josiah Wedgwood. When he joined the party in 1919, he was an experienced politician, immensely popular in the constituency, and at the height of his considerable powers. The small, newly-founded party gained greatly in numbers and prestige from his accession. On the other hand, the party came to suffer the defects of Wedgwood's virtues. Financially independent, able to defeat any Conservative candidate with ease, Wedgwood seemingly had little need of a strong, well-organized local political machine. His interests lay in the sphere of Parliament and international affairs rather than among the minutiae of constituency issues, although he strongly upheld local traditions and local patriotism. The influence of Wedgwood's

---

[1] The main sources for this chapter are the files of the *Staffordshire Sentinel*, the minute books of Newcastle Constituency Labour Party, and interviews with Labour aldermen and councillors, and members of the Labour and Liberal Parties in Newcastle. We are particularly grateful to Mrs. Helen Pease, daughter of Josiah Wedgwood, who kindly helped us with letters, extracts from her diary kept during 1919, and reminiscences of her father, all of which were invaluable.

political attitudes is evident throughout the first two decades of the party's history.

Newcastle Constituency Labour Party was founded in the summer of 1918,[1] within a few months of the Labour Party Conference which changed the constitution to permit the formation of local parties with individual membership. Its foundation created little notice and went unrecorded in the local press. The original members were a small group of workers—railwaymen, miners, insurance agents and others—who had been active in the unions and in local politics for some years. Though some had been members of the Independent Labour Party or the Social Democratic Federation, they had been forced to travel to neighbouring Stoke-on-Trent to attend meetings, for no branches of these bodies existed in Newcastle itself. There is a record of a Labour Church in Newcastle in 1896,[2] of a branch of the I.L.P. in Wolstanton in 1905[3] and of a short-lived Newcastle Fabian Society in 1910;[4] apart from these, there were no socialist activities on an organized scale in Newcastle in the period before the foundation of the Labour Party in 1918. The latter, therefore, did not inherit a long local tradition of socialist activity as did many such parties founded at this period in the North and Midlands.

Wedgwood's allegiance in the spring of 1919 gave a considerable fillip to the Newcastle Party. In the late summer of that year he spoke at crowded and enthusiastic meetings in various parts of the constituency; at one meeting in September 1919 which he addressed in Silverdale with the purpose of forming an I.L.P. there, almost the whole population of the village, according to the local newspaper, turned out to hear him.[5] Within a few years the party was soundly established. It had the affiliation of an I.L.P. and the Newcastle Trades Council and a flourishing

[1] North Stafford Miners' Federation, Minutes, 27 April 1918, 3 June 1918; Silverdale Co-operative Society, Minutes, 2 July 1918. The exact date of the formation of the Party is not recorded.

[2] Reg. G. Pegler, B.A., *A History of the Old Meeting House, Newcastle-under-Lyme* (n.d. 1920), p. 11.

[3] Wolstanton Urban District Council, Finance and General Purposes Committee, Minutes, 19 October 1905.

[4] *Staffordshire Advertiser*, 19 February and 12 March 1910.

[5] *Staffordshire Sentinel*, 1 September 1919.

Women's Section, whose president in 1919 was Helen Wedgwood, a daughter of Jos's. A little later a Socialist Sunday School was formed by some individual members of the party.[1]

All was not plain sailing, however. During this period of growth in the turbulent economic and political situation of the years after the war, there was a division of opinion in Newcastle Labour Party on I.L.P. and trade-unionist lines, a division which was bound up with a certain amount of trade-unionist opposition to Josiah Wedgwood as M.P. for the Borough. Wedgwood's political and social position presented some problems, particularly to the miners, the most numerous and best-organized of the local unions, whose political influence in the constituency had been increased by the redistribution of 1918.[2] On the one hand he was a member of the best-known family in the Potteries, a political personality of the first order, a war hero who had volunteered for the army though both over age and an M.P. On the other hand, he was a member of the I.L.P., a 'wild Socialist', a type regarded with antipathy by most miners, with their long tradition of Liberal politics and support for Labour representation. Essentially the conflict was a microcosm of the antagonism between the post-war generation of doctrinaire socialists of the I.L.P. and the older type of trade-union official, with a basically Liberal outlook, a conflict which was a feature of the Labour Party nationally at this period.[3]

Opposition to Wedgwood was centred in the person of John Watts, a former miner, who had by his own efforts raised himself to the position of mining engineer. He was a pleasant, middle-aged man of no great personality, with a long tradition of service in the industry and a good record in mining rescue operations. His hobby was running the male voice choir in the mining village of Halmerend. Helen Wedgwood described him as 'quite a nice-looking oldish gentleman', but added 'not much good in the House of Commons, I should think'.[4] The basis of Watts's

[1] *Staffordshire Sentinel*, 30 April 1919 and 10 December 1923.
[2] In 1918 the North Stafford Miners' Federation had 16 branches in Newcastle with a membership of over 5,000 (North Stafford Miners' Federation, District Executive Committee Minutes, 11 October 1918).
[3] Cf. G. D. H. Cole, *A History of the Labour Party from 1914* (London, 1948), pp. 44–54.
[4] Helen Wedgwood, MS. Diary, 5 June 1919.

opposition was founded on the claim that he had been selected as Parliamentary candidate for Newcastle at a Labour Party meeting in the summer of 1919, and that a subsequent reversal of the vote in favour of Wedgwood was invalid.

The controversy raged in a heated correspondence in the local newspaper, mainly in December 1919 and January 1920, and again in September and October 1921. From this correspondence between Watts and Labour Party officials it is possible to piece together the story, which was of more than local significance in the history of the Labour Party at this period.

It appeared that very soon after its foundation Newcastle Labour Party had decided to contest the coming election. A selection conference was called in November 1918, at which three names were put forward. Two withdrew, leaving Watts as the sole candidate. Since Watts had connections with the miners, the question arose of whether the North Stafford Miners' Federation would finance the election. The miners' representative, who was present, declared that this could not be done, so it was decided not to contest the seat.

It was felt, however, that it would be wise to have a Labour candidate ready for future contingencies, so a further selection meeting was called for 12 May 1919. At this meeting H. Drinkwater, the Midlands Organizer of the Labour Party, was present. The names of both Watts and Wedgwood (who had by this time joined the I.L.P.) were before the meeting. Both nominations were apparently open to criticism; Wedgwood's had not been received in writing, and Watts still could not give a financial guarantee. So a further meeting was held on 12 July, at which Watts received 40 votes to Wedgwood's 16, and thus became the official Labour Party Parliamentary candidate. Wedgwood was absent abroad at the time.

After this meeting there was a storm of protest from various members of the Labour Party that the meeting was unconstitutional, that not all delegates were present, that credentials were not checked, and so on; in addition a number of delegates from Newcastle Labour Party had walked out before the vote was taken. The Audley miners dominated the meeting and shouted down opposition to Watts. Members of the Women's Section, who had apparently not received official invitations to the meeting, sent a protest to the national headquarters of the Labour Party. The head office of the party advised the calling of yet another meeting under strict supervision as to procedure. This met in December 1919 and the decision was reversed; Wedgwood was elected as the candidate with only two votes against him.[1]

The basis of Watts's opposition was that the decision of the meeting of 12 July stood, and that the subsequent vote was not binding, since it was made when he was the incumbent of the position. Watts blamed 'dark forces' in the local party, who were intriguing against him, and he was particularly bitter about the actions of Drinkwater, who he felt had entered the controversy uninvited and set in motion the calling of the December meeting. Later he characterized the suggestion of the party head office to hold the December meeting as 'tyranny'.[2] Watts felt that he stood not only for freedom, but also for what he termed 'common-sense trade unionism' against the forces of 'rabid socialism',[3] namely the I.L.P. element of the Labour Party.

Watts's defeat was largely due to the miners' support of Wedgwood. Had he been able to carry the vote of the North Stafford miners, Watts might well have ousted Wedgwood. Support for Wedgwood among the miners was by no means overwhelming. He was nominated as candidate by only two branches, and at a special delegate meeting of the Federation in July 1919, received 38 votes to Watts's 27.[4] But it was enough. The two factors which weighed in his favour, despite his I.L.P. membership, were his political ability, which the miners felt would be important in putting forward their own claims, and the fact that the union would not have to finance him. Wedgwood paid for his own elections and was prepared to spend fairly

[1] Helen Wedgwood, MS. Diary, 10 July 1919, 15 July 1919; Letter of T. Burgess, secretary of Newcastle Labour Party, *Staffordshire Sentinel*, 23 December 1919; letter of H. Drinkwater, Midlands Organizer of the Labour Party, *Staffordshire Sentinel*, 1 January 1920; letter of H. Matthews, treasurer of Newcastle Labour Party, *Staffordshire Sentinel*, 29 September 1921.

[2] Letters of J. Watts in the *Staffordshire Sentinel*, 17 and 27 December 1919, 7 January 1920 and 16 September 1921.

[3] *Staffordshire Sentinel*, 17 December 1919.

[4] North Stafford Miners' Federation, circular to Branch Secretaries dated 2 July 1919; Special Delegate Board Meeting, Minutes, 7 July 1919.

heavily. His election campaign of 1922, it was reported, cost him £800.[1]

Watts did not give in. He continued to call himself the Labour candidate for Newcastle, and maintained enough support to enable him to call a public meeting in support of his candidature in September 1921. J. Matthias, president of the Trades Council, and one or two prominent Labour men were present. Watts confined himself to a moderate programme, stressing his local associations and the 'human factor' in politics as against the professional politicians.[2]

Watts still had some support among the miners,[3] and also in the Labour Party. The latter had been evident in the Newcastle municipal elections of 1920. Matthias and B. H. Dimmock, respectively the president and secretary of the Newcastle Trades Council, were not chosen by the Labour Party to contest the election.[4] The secretary of the Labour Party made it clear that this was due to their well-known support of Watts as Parliamentary candidate.[5] Matthias and Dimmock maintained that they were being discriminated against by the I.L.P. elements.[6] In the event they defied the party ruling and stood as Independent Labour candidates against the official nominees; but they came bottom of the poll in their respective wards.[7]

The lack of unity in the Labour Party remained until the end of 1922, with Watts threatening to stand against Wedgwood as an unofficial Labour candidate in the expected General Election of that year. A fortnight before the election, however, he suddenly withdrew from Newcastle and was adopted as the official Labour Party candidate for the neighbouring constituency of Stoke.[8] His opponent was Colonel John Ward, a former Labour stalwart, now standing independently of the party machine. Despite the shortness of Watts's campaign, he polled the excellent total of 10,000 votes.[9]

[1] *Staffordshire Sentinel*, 6 December 1923.
[2] Ibid., 9 September 1921.   [3] Ibid.
[4] 'Observer' in *Staffordshire Sentinel*, 10 September 1921.
[5] *Staffordshire Sentinel*, 15 October 1920.
[6] Ibid., 23 October 1920.
[7] Ibid., 15 October 1920.
[8] Ibid., 27 October 1922.
[9] Ibid., 16 November 1922.

With Watts's withdrawal, the Newcastle party went into the fight united and confident. As might be expected, the Liberals, still smarting under what they considered to be Wedgwood's 'betrayal' of 1919, refused to support him. The Unionists also, regarding Wedgwood as a sort of apostate Coalitionist, raised the issues of his 1918 pledges during the campaign.[1] Both parties combined to support Alderman Albert Shaw, a National Liberal, as the anti-Wedgwood candidate. Wedgwood replied, in his election address, that he was loyal to principles, not labels, and stood out for a policy of ending unemployment by means of his familiar panacea, the application of labour to land.[2] 'In spite of all, trust me again', he asked, and in spite of his change of party, his divorce,[3] and the long public feud in the Labour Party, the electors did trust him. He gained what a local paper called 'an easy victory' by nearly 5,000 votes.[4]

Thereafter Wedgwood was never seriously troubled about his candidature. He had the support of the miners of the outlying villages and this became the rock on which his unassailable majority was founded. His relationship with the miners was on a personal level. Even today old miners in Halmerend can still recall a picture of Wedgwood striding across the fields on a Sunday morning to have a drink in the workingmen's club. Veteran Labour Party members claim that after the withdrawal of Watts nine out of ten of the electors of these isolated, strongly Nonconformist communities would vote for Wedgwood in a general election. The change of allegiance from Liberal to Labour took place, of course, in other mining areas in the early post-war period, but Wedgwood's change of party no doubt accelerated the process in Newcastle.

Josiah Wedgwood was a Radical, an individualist and a fighter for the underdog. His politics, he declared, were 'hatred of cruelty, injustice and snobbery and an undying love of freedom'.[5] He was never a party man in the narrow sense. He believed that at different times different parties might be the most

[1] *Staffordshire Sentinel*, 3 and 9 November 1922.
[2] Ibid., 9 November 1922.
[3] See Chap. 3, p. 73.   [4] *Staffordshire Sentinel*, 16 November 1922.
[5] From an imaginary interview with his great-great-grandfather, Josiah Wedgwood I, in *Daily Express*, 19 May 1930.

effective instrument for the fulfilment of his political ideals; but he never believed that the whole of political wisdom was embodied for ever in any one party. The taxation of land values remained as the bedrock of his political theories throughout his life, and he never became a socialist in the doctrinaire sense, despite his membership of the I.L.P. and the Labour Party. He did not believe, for instance, in the interference by the state with trade and manufacture, maintaining that employers could look after their own business best.[1] He went against Labour policy in opposing compulsion in education (on grounds of the liberty of the individual)[2] and he publicly contradicted the party's policy for the reduction of unemployment by means of government expenditure on public works.[3]

In his own constituency Wedgwood refused to be guided by the local party, and though the latter might send him resolution after resolution, he would take up only those which interested him. His main interest lay in Parliament and particularly in foreign affairs. He achieved minor office in Ramsay MacDonald's administration of 1924, and became the party's most prominent spokesman on foreign and colonial subjects.[4] In his constituency he saw himself as representing the whole of his constituents rather than the Labour voters, and tried to live up to his local title of 'The Member for the Potteries'. In the 1922 election, for instance, he appealed for support not only from Labour Party supporters but from Liberals, National Liberals and Conservatives,[5] and it was an open secret that some of the latter would vote for him in elections. Fundamentally Wedgwood believed in the personal factor in politics and this was the secret of his popularity. Though he did not have very close ties with the Constituency Labour Party after winning the three General Elections of 1922, 1923 and 1924,[6] he would never fail to take up the case of any constituent, was welcome in every house in the constituency and was liked by all classes of the community. In the inter-war period the

[1] Election Address, *Staffordshire Sentinel*, 22 November 1918.

[2] *Staffordshire Sentinel*, 9 November 1922.

[3] J. C. Wedgwood, *Memoirs of a Fighting Life* (1940), pp. 188–90.

[4] Ibid., pp. 183–6.

[5] Leaflet entitled 'General Election, Nov. 15th, 1922' (by courtesy of Mrs. Helen Pease).

[6] For further information on these elections, see Chap. 5.

strongest opposition candidate at a General Election could hardly hope to get within 4,000 votes of Wedgwood's total, and in 1929 he won by a majority of 11,920 in a total poll of some 30,000, gaining 70 per cent of the votes cast.

Wedgwood's popularity reached its peak in 1931 when he successfully organized the opposition in the House of Lords to Stoke-on-Trent's Bill to annex Newcastle. 'All my individualist instincts, all my hatred of bureaucratic centralism were against the Bill', he wrote.[1] As a result he was welcomed as a hero in Newcastle, made Mayor and Freeman of the Borough, and was given 'carte blanche, apparently, to say and do what I liked for the rest of my political life without having to go to the hustings'.[2]

Few, if any, Labour members have ever achieved such a position. It is not surprising, therefore, to find that the Newcastle Labour Party was affected by his status and by his outlook. It is no exaggeration to say that during the 1920's and 30's Wedgwood's effect upon his constituency party was to restrict its growth and to keep its organization minimal. In effect, Newcastle between 1919 and 1942 was a Wedgwood seat rather than a Labour one. The Newcastle Labour Party functioned chiefly at election times (and between 1924 and 1942 Wedgwood fought only one General Election, that of 1929), and Wedgwood did nothing in between elections to encourage the growth of a local party based on a network of branches, with a strong central Management Committee. This was partly because of his individualist dislike of 'taking orders' from a local political machine, partly because he had little need of a strong party to carry him through elections—he paid his own expenses and always beat his opponent with ease.

To some extent Wedgwood imposed his own pattern on party organization. In the districts where Labour mustered some strength, Wedgwood had his own 'agents'. These were not paid agents in the modern sense, but merely Wedgwood's 'men'. They were often local Labour Party secretaries, but in some cases were devoted Wedgwoodites who might not even be party members. These agents would keep him in touch with local affairs, arrange meetings, and choose suitable chairmen when he visited the constituency, and generally arouse support at election times.

[1] *Memoirs*, p. 209. [2] Ibid., p. 210.

It is interesting to contrast the minimal organization which Wedgwood maintained as a Labour M.P. with the elaborate apparatus of his Liberal days before 1914. The reasons for the difference are not far to seek. The Liberal Party of the 1900's had inherited an excellent electoral organization from the nineteenth century and still had wealthy backers, and Wedgwood, as a budding politician, then had need of this support. By the post-war period Wedgwood had gained vastly in popularity and prestige, making his electoral victories easier. After 1918 he never had to face an election as close as those he fought with Grogan in 1910.

Side by side with the Wedgwood network, the party had its own organization. In the 1920's it consisted of a Borough Labour Party divided into men's and women's sections, and a Constituency Labour Party with delegates from these two sections, the mining villages and the trade-union branches. Even after 1932, with the enlargement of the Borough and its reorganization into twelve wards, the party organization remained unorthodox, reflecting areas of strength rather than municipal divisions. Representatives went to the Management Committee from districts, not from wards. In 1933, for instance, the Committee consisted of delegates from the mining villages of Halmerend, Silverdale, Chesterton, Wood Lane, Talke Pits, Talke, Bignall End, Audley, Cross Heath and Red Street, and one delegate each from Newcastle and Wolstanton, together with seven trade-union representatives and the officers.[1]

During the later 1920's the activities of the party were mainly concerned with economic and industrial issues affecting the working class—the General Strike,[2] the miners' struggle and problems of unemployment and high rents. A certain amount of socialist propaganda was carried out, particularly by the I.L.P., who held open-air meetings at the Market Cross in the centre of the town. No minute books have survived from this period, and

---

[1] Newcastle-under-Lyme Constituency Labour Party, Minutes, 27 May 1933. (Minutes of all meetings of Newcastle Labour Party—Divisional, Executive, Annual, Special, etc.—are hereinafter described as 'Minutes'.)

[2] During the strike Wedgwood addressed several meetings in his constituency. The keynote of his speeches was 'keep cool and observe the law' (*Staffordshire Sentinel*, 15 May 1926).

there was little news about the party in the local press, so a detailed account of its activities is not possible. It is known, however, that the party had to vacate its premises in the centre of the town about 1931, and that this caused a temporary disruption of the organization. For a year or two very few internal meetings took place, and apart from putting forward some candidates at local elections, very little activity was undertaken.

Early in 1933, however, the party was reconstituted by a group of former members, plus one or two new people, including an Independent alderman. Meetings were held regularly and political activities resumed. The 1930's were a period of intense left-wing political activity and though Newcastle party was small— 'We were lucky to get thirty members to a meeting', an old stalwart recalled—the members were active and militant. Undoubtedly the reason for many people joining was a desire to do something about the poverty and unemployment of the time. A member who joined in the early thirties related how he had been shocked by the number of able-bodied men standing workless on street corners, and recalled his amazement when visiting a nearby village to see grass growing in the main street. Local election addresses of Labour candidates of this period reflect the social conditions of the times. A typical policy of 1937 urges 'the feeding of schoolchildren when reported by the Medical Officer to be undernourished', work for the unemployed, and the Government to meet the expense for the Means Test.[1]

It was a period of marches and meetings, of struggles against desperate economic conditions at home and Fascism and the threat of war abroad. The minute books of this period show the party active in many spheres—sending delegates to the North Staffs Peace Council, supporting the League of Nations Union and organizing Aid for Spain. Several members played an active part in the National Unemployed Workers' Movement. On the whole, the policy of the party was to the left of the national line, though it played no part in the United Front movement, rejecting overtures from the Communist Party to this end.[2] As the European situation worsened in the late 1930's Newcastle party expressed its opposition to the Munich agreement and to the

[1] Election address of Sarah E. Matthias, dated 1 November 1938.
[2] Minutes, 23 June and 28 July 1934.

National Government's foreign policy in general; in particular it took a stand against government schemes for Air Raid Precautions and for conscription.[1]

Despite its activities, the party remained small. During the seven years between the reorganization of the party in 1933 and the outbreak of war in 1939, the average number of General Management Committee meetings was 4·5 per year, with an average attendance of 18. Executive meetings averaged only 2 per year, with an average attendance of 13. Throughout the period the average attendance at the annual meeting was 30, a rough and ready indication of the size of the party.[2] A further pointer to the size of the party was the financial position. In 1939 the income was £70 0s. 9d., of which only £33 9s. 1d. was actually spent. Expenditure was mainly on party meetings, printing, and a three-guinea honorarium to the secretary. The party paid a peppercorn rent of £2 12s. 0d. for its premises. The income came mainly from Butt Lane Co-operative Society with £24 7s. 6d. The North Stafford Miners' Federation contributed the next highest total of £7 10s. 0d.[3]

Organizationally, very little changed in the years after 1933. Despite an alteration in the party rules in the following year, which enjoined that local organization should be based on wards, representatives to committees still came from areas, giving particular advantage to the more active and militant groups. In 1938, for instance, a new Executive Committee was created by those present at a constituency party meeting agreeing to constitute themselves an Executive.[4]

The general picture of the party in the 1930's is that of a small, active left-wing body, relying for its finances chiefly on the miners and the co-operators, and basing its organization mainly on the centres of its strength rather than on any organizational blueprint. The relationship between the party and Wedgwood during the thirties was a tenuous one, although as usual he

[1] Minutes, 7 September and 19 October 1935, 12 March and 17 December 1938; 6 May 1939.

[2] Minutes, 1933–9, *passim*.

[3] 'Newcastle-under-Lyme Divisional Labour Party. Balance Sheet for the Year 1939.'

[4] Minutes, 11 April 1938.

maintained excellent personal relationships with his constituents. In this period Wedgwood divided his time between organizing and writing his monumental *History of Parliament* and opposing Fascism and appeasement in the House of Commons. 'I reminded the House', he wrote, 'of the inevitable result of paying Danegeld, of Athens under the Philippics of Demosthenes, of the fate of Carthage. Establish good relations with Russia, rely on the Jews in Palestine, seek not to appease Arabs, Italians, Japanese, Hertzog, Franco and Metaxas. Above all, settle the debt to America, and work in conjunction with Washington on every issue in the Far East, the Near East, Austria, Germany and Spain.'[1]

This sums up the main line of Wedgwood's policy during these years—a line that often conflicted with official Labour Party policy. Many will also remember his work for refugees from Fascism. He saved and succoured hundreds, aided by the local party, his constituents, and indeed all classes and parties in North Staffordshire.[2]

In 1942 Wedgwood was elevated to the peerage, and he retired from the constituency and the Commons amidst the congratulations of the widest circle of both friends and political opponents. He lived for another year only, but he had already become a legend in Newcastle and the Potteries. The miners, his strongest supporters, shall have the last word on his career: 'They have looked up to you as their trusted leader in most things that have affected their lives', wrote the secretary of the North Stafford Federation. 'They have loved you and this love will remain with them as long as they live.'[3]

* * * * *

During Wedgwood's last years as an M.P., a somewhat critical attitude to certain aspects of his stewardship had arisen among some of the party militants. They could not accept his independent attitude to the constituency party, nor his essentially Radical outlook, and it was felt that his successor should not only be a principled socialist, but also form a close relationship with

[1] Wedgwood, *Memoirs*, p. 234.   [2] Ibid., p. 226.
[3] Thomas Dobson, secretary of the North Stafford Miners' Federation, to Wedgwood, 23 December 1941 (Wedgwood Museum, Barlaston).

the local party. The initiative came from a group of party members associated with Silverdale Co-operative Party and the Burslem branch of the National Union of Distributive and Allied Workers.[1]

The successful candidate for the vacant seat was John Mack, an insurance agent by profession and a former Liverpool City Councillor. Mack had impressed the selection conference by his ability as a speaker, his left-wing outlook, but above all (according to local tradition) by flamboyantly throwing his unemployment card on the table to emphasize the fact that he was currently on the dole. Mack, as it proved, differed from Wedgwood in that he had a constituency grant from his union (which would be increased if a full-time agent were employed), and would 'take orders' from the local party and carry out their wishes in the House. In this respect an immediate break with the Wedgwood tradition was made. Mack, who had an unopposed return under the terms of the wartime electoral truce, came to Newcastle at a low point in the fortunes of the local party. The outbreak of war, with its disruption of communications, migration of population and general dislocation of normal life, had dealt a serious blow to the functioning of the Labour Party in Newcastle. Though at the beginning of the war the party had expressed its determination 'to defeat Fascism at home and in Europe',[2] its activities, hampered as they were by the electoral truce and the difficulties besetting organization, were mainly directed to endeavouring to safeguard living standards and maintain morale. In September 1939, for instance, the party suggested to the Town Clerk that rooms should be available for regular meetings at which responsible representatives of the Labour Party could attend to investigate and give advice on complaints from citizens regarding rationing, lighting, air-raid shelters, public assistance and other matters.[3] Apparently an organization of this sort was set up, for in April 1941 a donation to the funds of the Workers' General Advice Bureau is recorded in the minutes. The party also expressed what was a fairly widespread discontent in the Labour movement with the alleged unfair distribution of food

[1] N.U.D.A.W., Burslem Branch, Minutes, 17 February 1942, 10 March 1942. John Mack was the nominee of this branch.
[2] Minutes, 11 September 1939.　　　　　　　　　　　　　　　[3] Ibid.

supplies under the system of controls set up by the Chamberlain Government, especially in relation to the co-operative societies. A little later it protested against 'the unjust purchase tax'.[1]

Few meetings were held during these years. Between September 1939 and the beginning of 1942, only eight meetings of any kind are recorded in the minutes; in 1940, for instance, only the Annual Meeting and a report back of the National Conference were convened. The party at this time was later described as having 'very little organization, a negligible membership and virtually no electoral machinery'.[2] In fact, however, it was on the eve of the greatest expansion in its history.

2. 1942–50—Expansion of the Party

The sudden expansion of Newcastle Labour Party from about the middle of 1942 can hardly be laid to any single cause. As the war progressed, and particularly after the German attack on Russia in 1941, there was a greater unity and sense of dedication to the war effort among the working class. Trade unions in particular were increasingly active in response to war-time conditions of labour and the need for increased production. A Labour councillor recalled that trade unionists in Newcastle were 'brisk' and 'on their toes' at this period. In addition the Labour Party in the Borough was getting increasingly restive at the cramping effect of the political truce; and from 1943 onwards there are several resolutions in the minutes to this effect. The party also applauded the opposition to Conservative policy displayed by the Labour M.P.s' critical attitude to the Beveridge Report in 1942.[3] Allied to this increasing political militancy in the localities was, of course, the national effort made by the Labour Party in 1942 to get the constituency parties back on their feet after the dislocation of the early war years.

The response to the changing political climate was seen in a dramatic way in Newcastle. In October 1942 the secretary reported a 500 per cent increase in individual membership, the formation of three new local parties and meetings being held in

[1] Minutes, 27 November 1939 and 31 May 1941.
[2] Ibid., 19 July 1950.
[3] Ibid., 20 February 1943.

all parts of the constituency.[1] From this time onwards membership continued to increase, and it was not long before the organization of the party was reconstructed to accommodate the new recruits. Ward branches were given representation on the basis of one delegate per 50 members or part thereof and the size of the Executive was increased. No longer a small group of militants, but a party with extending affiliations in all parts of the constituency, it optimistically acquired an office, a car and expensive loudspeaker equipment. Some indication of the improved financial position is given by the party's grant of £80, early in 1945, to the organization fund of the North Staffordshire Federation of Labour Parties, and a gift of £20 to the Labour Party Fighting Fund. In 1944 the honorarium to the secretary had been raised to £10, in contrast to the three guineas commonly given in the late 1930's.[2]

The party's political line at this period was, like that of many other constituency parties, a left-wing one. Resolutions forwarded to the 1944 Labour Party Conference, for instance, ranged from opposition to any attempt to use U.N.R.R.A. for political purposes to support for 'full socialization' as 'the only means' to full employment.[3] It was also very active on behalf of friendship with Russia. Josiah Wedgwood was president of the North Staffs Anglo-Soviet Friendship Committee, and the party had eight members on the local body. At the beginning of 1942 the constituency party sent a letter to the Russian Embassy congratulating the Russian people on their victorious struggle against the Germans.[4]

During the latter years of the war, the party had not only pressed for the ending of the electoral truce, but also, as the possibility of a General Election approached, urged the Labour Party to consult with the other parties of the left with a view to putting up a joint candidate on a minimum programme, a fairly widespread demand in the party at the time. John Mack had, in fact, received practical assistance in his 1945 General Election

[1] Minutes, 15 October 1942.
[2] Ibid., 10 and 24 March, 30 April and 30 May 1945.
[3] Ibid., 14 October 1944.
[4] Ibid., 27 September and 4 December 1941, 3 January and 15 October 1942.

campaign from both the Communist and Commonwealth parties.[1] This election resulted in a striking majority of 17,523 for Mack in a three-cornered contest. Here was undoubtedly the harvest of the general swing to the left, but organization, of a thoroughness unknown in Wedgwood's day, also contributed to the result. A full-time agent was engaged to direct the campaign and a consultative committee of twelve set up to give assistance.[2] Party members who worked in the election all remember the enthusiasm and the hard work put into the campaign, and also the great number of meetings, all well attended. Mack, for instance, often addressed three crowded meetings in one evening. The minute book of Ward 6 Labour Party states that when the election briefing was held 'all present showed great willingness to play their part'.[3] This seemed to be typical of the spirit of the whole party.

In the Borough elections of November 1945, the party improved its position considerably, winning eleven seats and raising its representation to four more than the pre-war total. During the next two years Labour won control of the Council; by 1947 they had 23 councillors as against the Independents' 13, virtually a reversal of the pre-war position.

As a result of these electoral successes and the continued increase in membership, the party decided to employ, for the first time, a full-time secretary-agent. The services of a young Lancashire man, Mr. Leonard A. Dole, were secured and he began his duties on 1 January 1947.[4] From the first the aim of the agent was to build up an organization in all the wards and to increase the membership of the party. In order to accomplish this he saw his first task as that of killing the rampant local particularism. A well-organized constituency party, he believed, could not tolerate 'a party within a party', and he tried to construct a centralized organization based on the model rules. He drew up a constitution, had it printed, and tried to get the party to adhere to it. It was typical of the degree of local autonomy existing in the party at the time that Silverdale Co-operative

[1] Minutes, 9 July 1945.
[2] Ibid., 7 and 30 April and 2 June 1945.
[3] Ward 6 Labour Party Minutes, 14 June 1945.
[4] Minutes, 4 November 1946.

Party immediately raised objections to the working of the new constitution; there followed much argument and correspondence and a series of meetings over a period of some eighteen months before the Co-operative group were satisfied as to their position and agreed to the provisions of the constitution.[1] The agent also introduced standard election addresses for local elections, and all branches were successfully urged to adopt them. By these and other measures Newcastle Labour Party was rapidly given a new look.

There was also a noticeable improvement in the party's work after the arrival of the agent. The minutes show that meetings were held more regularly, work was planned in advance, correspondence conducted in a thorough manner and that peripheral activities—dances, week-end schools, fund-raising activities, public meetings and membership drives—were held at frequent intervals. A duplicated constituency bulletin kept members in touch with news and developments. Old age pensioners were employed to collect contributions from members in return for 25 per cent commission on all they collected. A drive was undertaken to secure greater trade-union affiliation and four new committees, dealing with social events, membership, affiliations and propaganda, were set up.[2]

By these and other means the membership rose in 1948 to over 1,000,[3] nearly 60 per cent higher than the 1947 figures, and within another year or two it was approaching 2,000. At the same time the financial structure of the party became more centralized, and an increasing amount of the party's income was diverted to constituency level in order to meet the costs of the agent's salary and the heavier overheads arising from enhanced size. At the beginning of 1947 the constituency party decided to take half the profits arising from social activities, and three months later the constitution was altered to allow it 75 per cent of the fees of affiliated organizations and 50 per cent of individual subscriptions.[4]

[1] Silverdale Co-operative Party, Minutes, 29 January 1947, 10 February 1947, 18 September 1947, 15 June 1948.
[2] Minutes, 27 February 1947 and 28 February 1948.
[3] Newcastle Labour Party, Membership Register, entries for 1948.
[4] Minutes, 17 February and 30 May 1947.

Undoubtedly, the most striking feature of the period was the growth of the party from a handful of members in 1942 to a figure approaching 2,000 some seven or eight years later. The greatest increases were in the working-class and lower-middle-class districts of Bradwell, Cross Heath, Chesterton, Knutton and Silverdale, on the Northwestern fringes of the Borough. Ward 11, covering Knutton and Chesterton, increased its membership from 22 in 1947 to 234 in 1949. Ward 9 in the Bradwell area improved from 14 to 205 in the same period. In some of the mining districts it was not uncommon to have between 20 and 30 party members in a single street.[1] As a reflection of this increased size, attendance at party meetings also improved. If the seven-year period 1945–51 is taken, and compared with that of 1933–9, the average attendance at Annual General Meetings increased from 30 to 53, and at General Management Committee meetings from 18 to 31. Increased efficiency and greater centralization are noticeable in the increase in the number of Executive meetings—from 2 per year in the first period to 11 per year in the second.

During the five or six years following 1945, Newcastle had for the first time a genuine mass Labour Party. Given the swing to the left which manifested itself in this period, this achievement was undoubtedly the result of organization. The main features of the organizational revolution were three: a strengthening of the powers of the constituency party with a correspondingly augmented financial provision; the supersession of local patriotism and area representation by the creation of a functioning party branch in every ward in the Borough and Rural District; and a greatly increased programme of meetings and social and cultural activities. In fact, during the period of the agency (that is, from 1947 to 1950), the organization of the party was wholly in the letter and the spirit of the model rules—a strong constituency General Management Committee, with affiliations from the rural wards, the trade unions, the co-operatives and the women's organization, and a Borough Party with representation from all twelve borough wards and the affiliated organizations. Figure 4 shows this structure as it was operating in the post-war years.

During this period, the political line of the party continued to

[1] Membership Register, entries for 1947 and 1949.

be left of the official line, particularly on foreign affairs. Although the Newcastle party on the whole supported the early legislation of the Labour Government, it was critical of certain aspects of policy. In 1947, for instance, it pressed for the elimination of the profit motive from the armament industry, and also urged a Labour crusade against 'the pernicious, persistent and poisonous campaign of the capitalist press'.[1] With regard to nationalization, it pressed for more trade unionists on the boards of nationalized industries, and sought to bring down the cost of living by the elimination of the middleman.[2] Newcastle party became increasingly critical of the Labour Government's foreign policy. In March of that year it called on the Government to operate 'a socialist foreign policy in all its spheres',[3] and a year later it criticized the attacks by Labour Party leaders against Communism, and contrasted it with their complacent or even deferential attitude towards Fascism; Communism, the party maintained, had a different approach from that of the Labour Party, but nevertheless the two movements contained a certain common factor, 'i.e., the fight against capitalism'.[4]

The outlook of the Member of Parliament coincided very closely with that of the party at this time. John Mack was a renowned orator and well known as being on the left of the Labour Party. After the war he had become particularly interested in the new states of Eastern Europe then coming under Communist leadership and a much-publicized visit to Bulgaria had earned him the nickname of 'The Uncrowned King of Bulgaria'. Mack gained some notoriety as one of the signatories to both the message of congratulation to German Socialists in February 1948 and to the famous 'Nenni telegram' some three months later; both of these actions were construed by the national party as left-wing infractions of official policy. On each occasion the Executive approved of Mack's actions after hearing a statement from him, in the first case unanimously, in the second case against only two dissentients; a General Management Committee meeting approved his signature on the Nenni telegram against seven votes.[5]

---

[1] Minutes, 8 February 1947.
[2] Ibid., 16 December 1947 and 26 February 1949.
[3] Ibid., 28 March 1947.   [4] Ibid., 11 February 1948.
[5] Ibid., 29 February and 3 May 1948.

Thus Newcastle Labour Party in the four or five years following the General Election of 1945 appeared as united and militant, strong and well organized, eager to push the official Labour Party line even further to the left. These few years were undoubtedly its hey-day and the achievements were very real—an M.P. with an absolute majority of some 12,000 votes, control of the Borough Council, a large and rising membership and a full-time agent. As the strongest and most influential political organization in the Borough the party could, it would seem, face the future with confidence. But the next decade was to confront the party in Newcastle with a number of serious problems.

3. 1950–62. Difficult Years

The employment of a full-time officer had resulted in the building of an excellent electoral machine in Newcastle, with membership in all wards and a party structure fully in accord with the Labour Party constitution. This achievement gave rise to a problem—could the party membership be sustained and increased sufficiently to meet the high and rising cost of the agent's salary?[1] After 1949 it was becoming increasingly obvious that it could not. The income of the party was failing to match the heavy overheads which had been incurred in the spirit of optimism after the war. In 1948, for instance, the main items of expenditure came to over £1,400, which included the agent's salary of £325 per annum, a car account, and rent and office expenses, whereas the basic income from membership and affiliation fees amounted to only £235.[2] Not even a large constituency grant from Mack's union—the National Union of Life Assurance Workers—loans, donations and a bank overdraft could permanently offset this basic imbalance of the party's economy. The only real solution would have been for the party membership to have risen at a rate sufficiently high to have made up the deficit by subscriptions, or for the existing membership greatly to

[1] By agreement with the North Staffordshire Organization Fund, Newcastle party had to pay an increasing share of the agent's salary during each of the first three years of his engagement. In addition his salary increased by increments of £15 per annum. (Minutes 27 November 1945, 17 May and 17 November 1946).

[2] Newcastle Labour Party, Account Book. Entry for 1948.

have increased their activities both in recruitment and fund-raising. From about 1949 to 1950, however, the membership started falling and the existing members were becoming less active. Several reasons can be adduced for this. It is agreed by several prominent Labour Party members that a large number of 'middle-class' members who joined in the hey-day of the 1945 period had left the party by the early 1950's. In addition, the changes in the constituency boundary which took place in 1949 increased the financial and organizational difficulties. The transfer of the strongly Labour Butt Lane area in the north to Leek constituency and the addition of the more Conservative districts of Ashley, Mucklestone and Tyrley in the south meant a net loss in membership, finance and support. More important, perhaps, was that a sense of satisfaction with the party's successes in the constituency, coupled with the improved conditions of life after 1950, made many party members reluctant to go out on the doorstep in membership drives, to collect subscriptions, organize meetings and social functions, and generally undertake the donkey work of keeping the party active and expanding.

As expenditure outran receipts, special Executive and Management Committee meetings were called to discuss the financial situation. Several organizational measures were put in hand to improve the position, including a target of 100 per cent increase in individual membership, and the setting up of a special Financial Committee.[1] By September the agent was talking of 'pressing financial difficulties'. A request for a special grant from headquarters was, however, turned down. During the summer, however, an all-out membership drive was carried out with some degree of success. But the preparations for the General Election of early 1950 came on top of this. Meanwhile the strain was somewhat eased by the sale of the car for £175.[2]

During the summer of 1950, however, the party had received two heavy blows. Both the M.P., John Mack, and the full-time agent gave notice of retirement within one month of each other, the former for reasons of health, the latter on personal grounds. The former's resignation also meant the loss of both an annual

[1] Minutes, 18 June 1949.
[2] Ibid., 27 July, 17 August, 27 September, 6 and 7 October, 30 November 1949.

constituency grant of £250 and an election grant which in 1950 had amounted to £300.[1] After this the party finances gradually returned to a more rational if less spectacular position. By 1953, for instance, the main items of expenditure almost exactly balanced the total of £252 for membership and affiliation subscriptions, although there was still a tendency for payments to outrun receipts to some extent.[2] Not for some years after the departure of the agent was the heavy toll which the constituency party had taken of the incoming finance modified in favour of the lower echelons; in 1956 it was resolved that the borough party take a share of subscriptions equal to that of the constituency party and ward parties retain as much as they sent to the latter.[3]

The candidate chosen to succeed Mack as M.P. was Stephen Swingler, who had been M.P. for the neighbouring constituency of Stafford from 1945 to 1950, and who was well known in the area as a former adult education lecturer. The circumstances of his election are an interesting demonstration of the real sources of power in the party.[4] Swingler was not originally on the short list of delegates chosen by the Executive Committee, but he gained fourth place at a special General Management Committee meeting. The North Staffs miners also decided to throw their votes to Swingler if neither of the trade-union nominees seemed likely to be selected.[5] The short list consisted of Swingler (nominated by the local parties from the mining villages of Halmerend and Audley), J. E. Cooper (nominated by the National Union of General and Municipal Workers), J. M. Inglis, the Railwaymen's nominee, and Ewart Taylor, the 'favourite son' candidate, a young Oxford student and extreme left-winger, whose father was a local butcher. Taylor was supported by the party militants associated with the Silverdale Co-operative movement. In fact he received the backing of Silverdale, Butt Lane and Burslem Co-ops, Newcastle Borough Party, Knutton's Women's Section

[1] Account Book, entries for 1948 and 1950.
[2] Ibid., entry for 1953; Minutes, 23 July 1954.
[3] Minutes, 27 June and 22 September 1956.
[4] The following account is based upon the General Management Committee and Executive Committee Minutes for 25 September, 30 September and 12 October 1950.
[5] Minutes of the North Stafford Miners' Federation, 28 October 1950.

and some local Labour parties, and must have seemed the likely victor.

At the selection conference, however, which was attended by the unprecedented number of 156 delegates, the situation took a different turn. The candidates addressed the meeting, and the subsequent voting showed that although the delegates did not consider the two trade-union candidates to be of Parliamentary calibre, they clearly preferred Swingler to Taylor. In the first ballot Swingler had 65 votes to Taylor's 52, in the second ballot 97 votes to Taylor's 59. An analysis of the delegates gives the key to Swingler's success. The trade unions had 89 delegates, local Labour parties (including Newcastle Borough Party) 32, Co-ops 16 and Women 4. Thus Swingler must have gained the bulk of the trade-union vote. It was an example of where the power in the party really lay. The trade unions, who after all paid the piper, had shown that they could, on occasion, call the tune. They valued Swingler as the more experienced and able man and one likely to favour their interests in Parliament. Swingler, who was elected in October 1951, continued the Newcastle tradition of a left-wing M.P. and later became chairman of the Victory for Socialism group.

* * * * *

During the 1950's Newcastle Labour Party suffered a general decline in numbers, organization and enthusiasm. By the middle of the decade the Regional Organizer was declaring that unless something was done about the membership position the outlook for the party was 'exceedingly bleak'.[1] In fact by 1958 the Divisional membership had become proportionately the lowest in the whole of the Midlands, being 1·8 per cent of the Parliamentary vote.[2] Personal and local rivalries arose once more and overshadowed political activities, leading to a number of expulsions and secessions; this was particularly true of the rural areas.[3] Trade unionists were not exerting their full strength in the organization; the activities of the Women's Section were at a very low ebb and, most serious of all, Silverdale Co-operative Society, a former bastion of Labour, had come under Tory influence and

[1] Minutes, 17 May 1956.   [2] Ibid., 2 May 1958.
[3] See Chap. 16.

for the first time in its history had refused to have Labour Party window bills in its shops at election times.[1] Little wonder that party veterans were lamenting the passing of 'the enthusiasm of the old days'.[2]

This relative decline in the fortunes of Labour was, of course, a national phenomenon, and by no means peculiar to Newcastle. The 1950's were not a fruitful period for left-wing political organizations. The Conservative Party regained much of the initiative lost in 1945 and improved its organization considerably, especially in the localities. This was true to a great extent in Newcastle. Between 1947 and 1957, the Independents and Conservatives increased the number of their seats on the Borough Council by 5 to 18, thus bringing them on a parity with the Labour Party. The latter could not but admit that at the 1957 local elections the Independents had achieved an organization in Ward 9, an old Labour stronghold, with which they had nothing to compare.[3]

During the 1950's, the general decline of the party appeared to have some effect on its political outlook. In the early 1950's, if resolutions forwarded to the Annual Conference and the Head Office can be taken as a guide, the party's line could broadly be described as 'Bevanite', or even left of that. There were a number of resolutions sharply critical of American actions in Korea, and in favour of admitting Red China to the United Nations.[4] There were also resolutions opposing African Federation 'until a majority of the African people are in favour of same', against German rearmament and for the abolition of nuclear weapons.[5] In the latter half of the 1950's, however, the resolutions take on a much more domestic and less militant aspect. In 1955 a resolution asking the National Executive 'to redraft its policy and outlook to meet modern social conditions' was put forward for consideration; what was more unusual was that an amendment urging the Executive to campaign for 'a Socialist Britain now' was lost—which would hardly have happened in the not-so-

---

[1] Minutes, 9 September 1954, 27 June 1955, 2 February 1957.
[2] Ibid., 30 April 1955.   [3] Ibid., 15 May 1957.
[4] Ibid., 11 November 1950, 25 June 1951, 28 June 1952, 5 February 1955.
[5] Ibid., 11 June 1953, 27 March 1954, 12 December 1955.

distant past.[1] In the following years suggestions for the use of atomic power, for the reduction of house-purchase costs, and for the abolition of the office of alderman were put forward.[2]

During the last three or four years, however, there has again been somewhat of a swing to the left, particularly among the younger and more active elements of the party, who have been attracted to the policies of the Campaign for Nuclear Disarmament and of Victory for Socialism. Resolutions by members of these organizations have been put forward and passed— against nuclear weapons, for a national campaign for socialism, and in favour of nuclear disarmament.[3]

Little public activity is currently carried on between elections,[4] which reflects the fact that the constituency party is primarily organized for electoral ends. The main items at internal meetings are constitutional and organizational ones; about 60 per cent of the time at General Management Committee meetings is occupied with these subjects. The emphasis throughout the party is on building the party machine, gaining new members, and organizational tasks of this nature rather than on propaganda and public activity. Members in the stronger areas deliver policy leaflets from time to time between elections to keep up interest, but with rare exceptions there is very little of the continuous struggle against bad social conditions which marked the period between the wars.

In respect of size and organization, however, the party has to some extent returned to its pre-war position. Though the 1947–50 organizational framework has not been jettisoned, the more well-known and active members come from the 'strong' areas and tend to get on to the committees. In addition, the relatively small size (the 1959–60 membership was 426) has necessitated the amalgamation of several branches on an area basis,[5] which is in effect a return to representation by area. The annual number of meetings and average attendance has also returned to something like pre-war level—in the 1953–9 period, for instance, an average of 3·7 General Management Committee meetings were

[1] Minutes, 9 July 1955.
[2] Ibid., 2 July 1956, 28 July 1957, 27 June 1958.
[3] Ibid., 5 September 1958, 7 November 1959, 2 July 1960.
[4] This refers to the period 1960–1. [5] See Figure 4.

held, with an average attendance of 12, and an average of only 27 people went to the Annual Meetings.[1] The financial structure also has resumed many of the pre-war characteristics, with a relatively low income (in 1960 it was £205 plus £235 election grant), and with membership and affiliation fees balancing expenditure. The miners and Silverdale Co-operative Society (£30 and £20 respectively) provided the largest affiliation subscriptions.[2]

LABOUR PARTY STRUCTURE

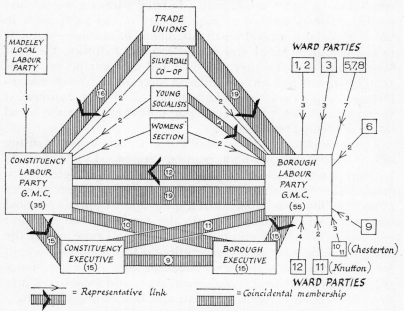

Figures in brackets represent numbers on representative bodies

FIGURE 4

In one respect, however, there has been a lasting break with the pre-war situation. The Member of Parliament, Stephen Swingler, keeps in constant and regular touch with his constituency, visiting the area once per month for consultation and

[1] Minutes, 1953–9, *passim.*

[2] 'The Labour Party. Newcastle-under-Lyme Constituency Party Annual Statement of Accounts for the Year ending June 1960.'

meetings with the party and his constituents, and returning to
support Labour candidates at local elections. In addition he
constantly takes up local issues and local grievances with the
appropriate Ministers and Departments. In this sense he is con-
tinuing the tradition of Mack rather than that of Wedgwood.

*   *   *   *   *

This outline of the history of Newcastle Labour Party points to
several conclusions. In the first place it gives a pointer to the
conditions in which constituency Labour parties grow up and
flourish. The periods of greatest vitality of the party were in
times of social upheaval and realignment of attitudes—namely
in the turbulent social and economic years following the First
World War, and the later war-time and post-war period of the
1940's, when it had an unparalleled increase of growth and influence. People tend to join Labour parties in large numbers, it
would seem, when war or economic upheaval shakes the social
fabric suddenly and violently.

Newcastle also provides a rare but authentic example of the
influence of personality upon politics. Wedgwood's allegiance to
Labour put the Newcastle party on the map and greatly increased Labour sentiment in the Borough. Contrariwise, his very
impregnability as a Labour M.P., quite apart from his personal
sentiments on the matter, made the forging of an electoral
machine in Newcastle an unnecessary luxury. Consequently the
party made do with such organization as was necessary to fight
on local issues. As a result, sectionalism arose. The experience
of Newcastle party in the Wedgwood era would seem to point to
some connection between safe seats and lack of organization.

Good organization, on the other hand, does presuppose a
critical size of party, and it was not until the party had reached
some thousands of members that an organization based on a
model constitution could be built. For some four years during
the period 1947–50 there was a well-organized mass Labour
Party in Newcastle, the only time in the four decades of its history that this has occurred. The decline in membership in recent
years has brought a return in many ways to the pre-war position,
but this has not been complete. Much of the organizational
structure remains, as well as the control of the Council achieved

during the halcyon years. Despite a smaller party, Labour sentiment remains strong and electoral support high; Newcastle is
still a safe Labour seat and the size of the poll at the 1959 election
was 84 per cent, the third highest in the West Midlands area.

In the forty-odd years of its existence, the Labour Party has
undergone many changes. The greatest contrast is between the
pre-war and post-war eras. In the 1920's and 1930's the party
carried out a consistent struggle on behalf of the common man,
against unemployment and for the maintenance and improvement of the standard of living. In the post-war period, though
the thread of social protest has not been lost, there has been
much more emphasis on the electoral aspects of the party's role,
following upon the winning of a majority on the Borough
Council in 1947.

Despite this transformation, which is essentially a reflection of
changed social conditions, the political attitude of the party has,
for the most part, remained fairly consistently to the left of the
national policy of the Labour Party. The Labour M.P.s also
have been far from orthodox. Wedgwood was a law unto himself,
and both Mack and Swingler have been noted left-wingers. In
this respect Newcastle Labour Party has carried forward the
tradition of local dissent which is an important feature of
British political life.

CHAPTER FIVE

THE CONSERVATIVE ASSOCIATION

From the First World War to the early 1960's Newcastle-under-Lyme has been a safe Labour seat: during the whole of the period the Conservatives have never returned a member and they have never come very near victory. However deeply committed and enthusiastic members of an Association can be, such a predicament does affect to some extent the morale of the leaders and of the rank-and-file. Many problems, such as the selection of the candidate, the appointment of a good agent, even the recruitment of new members, are likely to raise greater difficulties when the seat is safe for the other side. Indeed, these problems are not only more difficult to solve: they also arise more frequently. Candidate and agent have an incentive to leave for a better constituency; members, having become disillusioned, fail to renew their subscription. The life of the Newcastle-under-Lyme Association gives some indication of the magnitude and recurrence of such problems.

1. Efforts and Disappointments: 1918–37

In a safe Labour constituency, members of a Conservative Association are constantly faced with the problem of the choice of their parliamentary candidate. In Newcastle-under-Lyme, the difficulty was probably increased in the inter-war period by the fact that the opponent was Josiah Wedgwood. Admittedly the social composition of the constituency—which had become perhaps more working class with the addition of Audley in 1918— put the Conservatives at a great disadvantage, at least up to 1949 when the farming area of the Rural District was in turn included. But all Conservative leaders were not aware of these

106

socio-economic realities. Moreover, national swings were rarely taken into account and electoral fortunes were often attributed to local factors.[1] Leaders were often impressed by the fact that they had to fight Wedgwood; when they decided to leave the seat uncontested in 1918, 1931 and 1935, they never referred to the social composition of the electorate and only once is there in the local newspaper a remark about the national swing which took place in 1931 and about the opportunities which had been missed.[2] On other occasions, reference is made to only one factor, the personality of the opponent whom they had to fight.

Wedgwood obviously had a very strong personal position. It was not only that he was well known; it was also that he occupied a prominent place in the social hierarchy of the Potteries. In fact, many felt that, by turning Labour—albeit remaining a Labour M.P. of a peculiar kind—he had 'betrayed' his class and 'betrayed' his friends. Wedgwood was following the radical traditions of his family, but he was doing so at a time when middle-class radical traditions were often superseded by the fear of the 'excesses' of Socialism.

Wedgwood's 'betrayal' was particularly serious because practically no other personality could appeal to the electorate in the way he did. The business community lacked candidates of standing; there were no prominent families from among whom could be found someone to counteract Wedgwood's attraction: prominent families were few and their members had often contracted out of politics, sometimes by living outside the constituency.

Moreover, and perhaps as a result, deference to Wedgwood was not entirely unknown among Conservative Association leaders, who were usually small businessmen with local interests only and with a much lower status than that of Wedgwood. In the 1930's at least, when some of the bitterness disappeared, deference materialized. The sitting member was instrumental in saving the 'independence' of the Borough from Stoke's attempts at annexation. Wedgwood did cultivate feelings of deference, by

[1] Speech at the adoption of the Conservative candidate in January 1926 by the secretary of the Association, quoted in the *Evening Sentinel*, 30 January 1926. For the results of the General Elections in Newcastle, see Appendix 1.

[2] *Evening Sentinel*, 17 March 1934 (Report of the Annual Meeting of the women's divisional branch).

keeping in touch with Conservative leaders and remaining friendly with many of them.[1]

As Wedgwood had little interest in local matters, difficulties between the M.P. and the local councillors were minimized. Wedgwood never tried to organize the local Labour Party to make it fight on local issues. He became involved in Newcastle matters only once, over the annexation question, when a unanimous population, as was to be shown by a local poll,[2] and a unanimous council were led by their M.P. Local leaders were bound to be grateful and abandon the efforts previously made at fostering opposition against Wedgwood.

These efforts were remarkably slow to start in the 1920's. In 1918, the Member was not opposed, on the assumption that he would become a reliable Coalitionist.[3] Although he did not become reliable, Conservative leaders did not take steps to find a candidate: they followed the Liberals, who were perhaps more embittered than the Conservatives by Wedgwood's new political allegiance. Early in 1922 Liberal leaders met some Conservative Association leaders and a National Liberal candidate, Alderman Shaw, became the common standard-bearer of the two parties. This arrangement was subjected to some stress fairly quickly, however: the candidate tried to paper over the cracks which resulted from the difficulties which the Coalition was encountering nationally by stating that he was both an admirer of Bonar Law and a Lloyd George Liberal and would decide whom to support once elected to the House of Commons.[4] His defeat saved him from having to make an embarrassing choice; he decided not to stand again, largely for health and personal reasons, but also probably because his political position was no longer tenable.

The Association remained without a candidate during the first months of 1923. But Baldwin's decision to go to the country over the issue of Protection forced the hands of the local Conservatives,

[1] Letter to the *Weekly Sentinel*, 18 March 1939.

[2] 98 per cent of the Newcastle voters and over 96 per cent of the Wolstanton United voters were against amalgamation with Stoke. The turnout was 85 per cent in Newcastle and 94 per cent in Wolstanton United U.D.C.

[3] A controversy arose in October–November 1922 about Wedgwood's pledges of 1918; some Conservative leaders claimed that they had believed that the M.P. would support the Coalition.

[4] *Evening Sentinel*, 27 October 1922.

especially since the Liberals were this time divided over the course to follow and preferred not to enter the contest. Yet, several days after the beginning of the General Election campaign, it was still said that Wedgwood might be returned unopposed.[1] In the end, two days before nominations closed, a candidate suggested by Central Office was hurriedly endorsed.[2] This candidate, J. Ravenshaw, had no roots in the constituency and no experience of parliamentary elections; he fought a battle which local people considered to be of pure form, was badly defeated and left the constituency.

The next candidate was not selected until several months later. The 1924 dissolution caught the Conservatives as unprepared as the previous one. However, as more Liberals were inclined to vote against Wedgwood and the Labour Party than a year earlier, the Newcastle Conservative leaders decided, with some difficulty but with rather more enthusiasm than in 1923, to fight the seat on an 'anti-Socialist' basis. The Mayor, A. Hassam, a businessman who had not taken much part in national politics and who was thought to appeal to all classes because of his working-class background, was persuaded to stand.[3] This ill-prepared contest produced a moderately encouraging result (Wedgwood's majority was cut from 6,135 to 3,801); various local causes and in particular the Conservative candidate's personality were mentioned. In fact, the fortunes of the parties in Newcastle closely corresponded to the national pattern: as elsewhere, many Liberals went over to the Conservatives. But for the leaders of the Conservative Association in Newcastle, the result was a success which seemed to forecast the possibility of even greater successes. Up to 1924, Conservative leaders had never really decided to select a candidate; they had only faced the problem at the last moment. The relative success of 1924 seemed to change their attitudes. Their determination to fight Wedgwood became more real; the will to organize for the fight became apparent. The gap had been narrowed: with hard work and much preparation, the

[1] *Evening Sentinel*, 19 November 1923.   [2] Ibid., 10 October 1924.
[3] A. Hassam was supported by the Liberals and indeed called himself 'Conservative and Liberal'. An alliance with the Liberals might have taken the form of a decision to support a Liberal candidate in Burslem under the same label. (*Evening Sentinel*, 15 October 1924. See also Chap. 6, p. 125.)

gap could perhaps be narrowed even more. The optimism with which the 1924 result was received in Conservative circles was probably not justified; expectations were probably too great, as the 1929 election was to show. But this optimism was instrumental in convincing Conservative leaders that a candidate ought to be nominated and that the contest had to be prepared long before the dissolution.

Hassam refused to stand again, partly on health grounds (he was to die in 1926) and partly because he was not inclined to nurse the constituency, and inquiries were made during the course of 1925 in order to find a suitable candidate. They resulted in the adoption of a purely Conservative candidate, Captain P. R. Cooke-Davies, in January 1926.[1] Admittedly, despite what the secretary of the Association said at the adoption meeting, the candidate was in no way ideal: he was unknown (the chairman of the women's branch said that she had met him only a few days before he was selected);[2] he had just retired from the Army and he had no previous experience in politics. However, for the first time since the war, a Conservative candidate was to be seen nursing the constituency, although more by opening bazaars and fêtes than by making political speeches.

The enthusiasm which the candidate showed for the constituency was not to last; after less than two years in Newcastle, he resigned in the course of 1927. But the determination of the Association to fight the seat was not impaired: steps were taken immediately to find another candidate; they resulted in the adoption of C. K. Tatham, a barrister, again without political experience, in June 1928. The new candidate endeavoured to make himself known locally and prepared the Association for the contest of 1929. The General Election of that year, the first since the end of the First World War which the Association had actively prepared, was to be the real test of the new policy.

The preparations of the Association were not confined to the selection of a candidate. While Conservative affairs in Newcastle had been managed by part-time secretaries between 1918 and 1924, a full-time agent was appointed in 1924; under him and his successor, appointed in 1927, organization was deve-

[1] See Figure 6 for a list of Conservative candidates.
[2] *Weekly Sentinel*, 30 January 1926.

loped. In the first few years after 1918, the Association had remained essentially based on two types of bodies, the clubs and the women's branches, an executive council being in charge of the matters affecting the whole of the division. Clubs and women's branches were the only organizations in which the rank-and-file came in contact with the Association: ward branches did not even exist on paper. The Association could count on a nominal roll of between 1,200 and 2,000 members— and indeed the numbers tended to increase from the lower to the higher figure after the appointment of an agent in 1924; but members did not meet and did not even have a place to meet. In this respect, the situation was not very different in the late 1920's from what it had been before 1924.

Efforts at organization concentrated on the development of two main traditional types of bodies, the clubs and the women's branches. Partly because of the dedication of some of their officers, the women's branches increased their activities: in the 1930's they were to become organized on the basis of the old townships, Newcastle, Silverdale, Chesterton, Wolstanton and Audley. They sponsored the creation of branches of the Junior Imperial League, which were to remain under the control of the ladies during the whole inter-war period. Meanwhile, the three clubs—Newcastle, Silverdale and Wolstanton—expanded their membership and increased their turnover. The Newcastle Club, by far the largest, had about 500 members, while the two others, with about 100 members each, constituted subsidiary centres of Conservative activity in the constituency.

Although the Newcastle Conservative Association had not become a modern 'machine' by 1929, some notable developments had taken place in the late twenties. Hopes were therefore fairly high when the candidate was preparing to contest the seat in 1929. But the result did not match up with these hopes: Wedgwood, this time benefiting from the national swing in favour of the Labour Party, obtained 70 per cent of the votes cast compared with only 58 per cent in 1924. Once more interpreting the results on the basis of the local situation rather than as an instance of a national trend, Conservative Association leaders tended to return to the pessimism and despondency which had marked the early 1920's. When the question of annexation arose in 1930, this pessimism turned itself fairly quickly and indeed naturally into a resignation to accept Wedgwood as their M.P. without further contest.

Shortly after the 1929 Election, the forefront of the political scene was indeed occupied by the attempt of Stoke, as we have seen in Chapter 2, to incorporate Newcastle within the city. Newcastle councillors and party leaders turned all their attention to the problem of finding as many allies as possible in London who could help them to defeat Stoke's Private Bill. Wedgwood played a considerable part in the defence of the 'independence' of Newcastle and, when the Bill was defeated in the House of Lords in July 1930, everybody in Newcastle recognized that Wedgwood had been the saviour of the town.[1] The Council decided to offer to their M.P. the freedom of the Borough and the mayoralty for the year 1930–1. Conservatives were no less in favour of that decision than other members of the Council. Meanwhile, a second attack had been started by Stoke, which tried to secure the passage of the Bill at the following session of Parliament, only to receive a bigger rebuff from the House of Lords in March 1931.[2] By then, Wedgwood had been Mayor for five months and his term of office was due to end only in November (he was subsequently re-elected for another year). The formation of the National Government and the dissolution occurred therefore while Newcastle-under-Lyme and its political leaders were only just recovering from what had been a threat to their very existence and a battle in which they had all been united.

The Conservative leaders clearly could not oppose Wedgwood and did not think of doing so. Wedgwood had become popular among them for having defended their interests. They had offered him the mayoralty only a few months before and it would have been politically unthinkable to engineer a contest. The President of the women's divisional branch summed up the situation in her report for 1931 by saying that 'our loyalty to our mayor . . . prevented us from pressing for a national candidate'.[3] Some leaders were later to regret the decision, when it appeared

[1] There was a majority of 18 against the Bill. See above, Chap. 4, p. 85.

[2] The majority against annexation increased from 18 to 42.

[3] *Weekly Sentinel*, 6 February 1932.

that the Association had perhaps missed the chance of a generation to see a Conservative returned for Newcastle.[1]

The activities of the Association were paralysed as a result.
Without a candidate and without an agent, the organization
started to decline. The membership fell by about half from the
late twenties to the middle thirties, possibly partly as a result of
the depression and unemployment as well as through lack of
party activity; the Association survived none the less, thanks to
irregular gifts and bequests rather than donations. Only the
women's branches maintained a lively level of activity.

Meanwhile, many leaders seemed committed to a policy of
withdrawal. Only a few suggested at least a token fight in 1935;
and they were easily silenced by those who pointed out that
Wedgwood's support of the Government over sanctions against
Italy was a sufficient ground for carrying on without a contest.[2]
By 1935, the Association appeared to have gone full circle: the
1924 result had raised hopes and led to action; the 1929 result,
coupled with Wedgwood's stand in favour of the Borough in
1930–1, had led to disillusionment and defeatism. The Association seemed agreed to remain in cold storage as long as Wedgwood was M.P. for Newcastle.

2. Hopes and Deception: 1937–59

The situation was altered in the last few years preceding the
Second World War when a group rebelled against the idea that
Wedgwood would remain unchallenged. A North Staffordshire
Political Union, comprising members of the Conservative,
Liberal and National Labour parties, was created in 1936; its
aims were to promote 'National' candidatures in the Potteries
and neighbouring constituencies and to help such candidates
financially and otherwise. The idea of a Newcastle candidature
gained ground, mainly outside the official leadership. It was
mentioned at the Annual General Meeting of the Newcastle
Conservative Club in 1937: no decision was taken, but the move
had some echo, as the secretary reported that members had come
to be divided on the issue.[3] A few months later, it became known

---

[1] *Weekly Sentinel*, 17 March 1934. [2] *Evening Sentinel*, 16 and 26 October 1935.
[3] Ibid., 27 March 1937.

that a candidate was available and was willing to stand. Head of a pottery firm in Burslem, son of a prominent Liberal who had been Wedgwood's agent before 1914, himself a prominent Liberal up to the middle 1920's and an influential member of the North Stafford-shire Political Union since its creation, Major (later Colonel) Wade had most, if not perhaps all, the qualities which were required of a Conservative candidate if Conservative leaders and rank-and-file were to be rallied and Wedgwood's grip on the town was to be broken. He was adopted as prospective candidate in October 1937, eight years after his predecessor had left the constituency.

Major Wade's adoption ended an era in the life of the Conservative Association. The new candidate was not drawn from the outside and the unknown: he was an influential local business-man. Moreover, Wedgwood's hold, greater on the older genera-tion of leaders, who often knew him as a friend, than on the younger, was diminishing. Thirdly, Major Wade had decided to launch a much more aggressive campaign than any of his pre-decessors. He held meetings in all parts of the constituency, including the mining villages, in the hope of breaking the tradi-tional working-class Wedgwood vote.

Major Wade did not attempt to reorganize the Association drastically, however. An agent was appointed in 1938; financial difficulties were overcome as the candidate was prepared to meet a large part of the expenditure and as businessmen, through the North Staffordshire Political Union, were backing the new ven-ture.[1] But there was no attempt to turn the Association into a mass party. Wedgwood was still setting the pattern: he disliked large machines and preferred to talk to friends or address con-stituents in workingmen's clubs. His opponents of 1938 were equally temperamentally inclined to believe in the virtues of per-sonal contacts. They saw the town as a self-contained and com-pact community and conceived of political action in personal terms. It was only after the Second World War, and then only for a short period, that the idea of creating a mass party came to be adopted by the Newcastle Conservatives.

[1] The Union had a full-time secretary whose function was both to see that the organization of the constituency associations was efficient and that the constituencies which needed financial support received adequate backing. The secretary retired in 1956.

THE CONSERVATIVE ASSOCIATION

The war interrupted the activities of the Association, which was to enter the 1945 campaign totally unprepared. Colonel Wade returned from the Army to fight the seat, but he was badly defeated in the only three-cornered contest which Newcastle has ever known (1962). Wade resigned at the end of 1946, partly to devote more time to his business and partly to leave room for a younger man. The Association quickly selected Major Friend, an ex-regular soldier who had long been interested in politics and was anxious to become a professional politician.

The new candidate could hope to have some personal following in the farming area where he lived and which had been added to Newcastle by the 1949 redistribution. Indeed, the inclusion of this solid Conservative area and of the Westlands— both districts formerly being in the Stone constituency—seemed to alter markedly the balance in favour of the Tory party.

But Major Friend wanted also to turn the Association into a mass party. A membership drive was started: for the first and only time paid canvassers were employed in 1947. An all-time peak of over 5,000 members was reached in 1950. Ward branches were created, both in the Borough (in particular in the marginal Wolstanton area and in the central and southern wards) and in the Rural District. Several branches of the Young Conservatives were started. The activity was fostered, at the centre, by the candidate and his full-time agent.

Major Friend started his political campaign as soon as he was adopted. The rank-and-file was addressed in the ward branches, the electorate in the course of numerous public meetings. The tone was often bitter: personal matters were raised against the sitting Labour M.P. The three weeks of the 1950 General Election campaign were thus only the culmination of three years of intense preparation during which the Association was transformed from a somewhat leisurely committee organization into an efficient, active and even aggressive machine, although it remained perhaps too much the personal machine of the candidate. If organization alone could win seats, Newcastle should have turned Conservative in 1950.

The result was a disappointment. The Labour majority was reduced, but the constituency had gained Conservative areas; 57 per cent of the votes cast still went to Labour, a similar proportion to that obtained by Wedgwood in 1924. When, at the 1951 Election, it appeared that Newcastle did not swing to the Conservatives more than the country as a whole, Major Friend lost hope of ever winning the seat. He resigned early in the spring of 1952, leaving the Conservative Association once more without a candidate.

The decline was not as catastrophic as it had been after 1931, but it was marked and lasted almost a decade. The membership dropped. The agent resigned in 1953 and was not replaced. Ward parties ceased to meet regularly. Even candidates proved difficult to find: although the Association had endeavoured to take steps to find a successor to Major Friend immediately after his resignation, efforts seemed to have been somewhat half-hearted and only in 1954 was Mr. F. H. Taylor adopted as prospective candidate. He was an outsider and had barely come to be known in the constituency when Parliament was dissolved in the spring of 1955. The swing to the Conservatives was to be, as at previous elections, very near the national average.

When the defeated candidate resigned soon after the General Election result was declared, the leaders of the Association became convinced that a local man had to be selected if waverers were to be won over. The search was lengthy and only in March 1958 did the Association select one of its past chairmen, Mr. T. Prendergast, a local builder. The idea was to repeat the developments of the late 1930's, although the new candidate could not be expected to run as active a campaign as Major Wade two decades before. The tone of electioneering was much less aggressive; the candidate did not have the social standing which Major Wade enjoyed. His 'operation' was reminiscent of pre-war contests, however, in that it was based on personal contacts and not on the type of mass-party organization on which Major Friend had relied in the late 1940's. No agent was appointed and the secretary of the North Staffordshire Political Union was called back from retirement only a few weeks before the 1959 Election.

The result did none the less follow the trend of previous results. Conservative gains were patterned on those of the whole country: with or without an agent, with or without an organization, with old friendships or with a relatively unknown candidate, Newcastle Conservatives seemed to incur the same fate.

The 1950's thus ended with a familiar predicament for the Newcastle-under-Lyme Conservative Association. The candidate resigned shortly after the Election; there had been no agent for over half a decade. And the organization, having declined from the level which it had reached in the early 1950's, seemed to return to a pattern similar to that of the middle 1930's. By 1960, there were less than 1,800 members, most of whom had no ward branches where they could easily meet other members and participate in political activities without having to go some distance to a more central organization. The two traditional pillars of the Association, the women's divisional branch and the clubs, did survive, although the links between the Silverdale club and the Association became so tenuous that they were eventually broken and although the two other clubs were losing more and more their political character. Of the other component bodies, very few remained alive. By the late 1950's, only four or five areas could be said to be at all covered by the Association and only in three of these areas could the branches be described as more than an executive committee meeting occasionally. Whole areas of the constituency remained entirely without coverage, let alone membership. As will be seen by the survey of the rank-and-file,[1] it was almost impossible to find members in the solid working-class areas in 1960–1; it was even impossible to find members in the solid Conservative areas of the south of the Rural District. The Association was alive at the centre, but only at the centre. Its Executive Council of 60 members (see Figure 5) and the two sub-committees of the executive—Finance and General Purposes—which met monthly or bi-monthly were the only true organs of policy-making and of deliberation, largely because component bodies were normally inactive outside election times and therefore scarcely capable of putting on the centre any amount of effective pressure.[2]

As in the 1930's, the Association had ceased for a long time to have an agent and it had again to live on a small budget at the end of the 1950's. When Major Friend was the candidate, a combination of three factors had temporarily helped the finances of the Association: the candidate financed much of his campaign, the Political Union provided important funds from the whole of

[1] See Chap. 13.   [2] See Chap. 17.

the Potteries[1] and the increase in membership brought about many subscriptions, even though most of them were at the minimum rate of 2s. 6d. and only a very small number were of more than one or two guineas. After 1952, and even more after 1955, the Association lost on all three counts. Subscriptions came to lapse; no candidate provided regular funds; the Political Union declined and it only contributed about 5 per cent of the Association's income by the end of the 1950's.

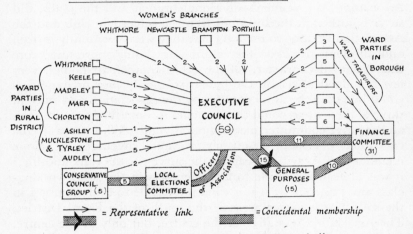

CONSERVATIVE PARTY STRUCTURE

Figures in brackets represent numbers on representative bodies

FIGURE 5

Admittedly, like the Constituency Labour Party, the Association could mobilize the energies of volunteer helpers at the time of General Elections. The enthusiasm of the potential members and of the nominal members seemed to wake up during the few weeks of the election campaign. Even where there were no members and only 'contacts', some canvassing was done, committee rooms were organized and the system of tellers was fairly effective on election day. But, almost immediately after the election, activity was allowed to lapse, in particular since, in

[1] *Evening Sentinel*, 30 May 1956.

many parts of the constituency, local elections were rarely fought on straight Conservative lines and thus did not constitute a training ground for the more enthusiastic members of the Association.

By 1960, the Newcastle Conservative Association seemed to have run full circle for a second time. As between 1924 and 1937, it went through a period of hopes and deceptions between 1937 and 1959. But, during that second cycle, the leaders had been more thorough in trying to break the deadlock. An experiment in intensive organization had been followed by almost a decade of more traditional small-scale electioneering. These efforts seemed to point to one, and only one, conclusion. The Conservative Association could not, by its own actions, modify the course of elections: the swings which took place in Newcastle seemed to depend entirely on the national record of parties. The smoothness of the organization seemed to have no significant impact on the size of the majority.

3. Outlook for the Future

A third cycle started in the early 1960's, but it seemed to differ somewhat from the two previous cycles. For the first time the leaders of the Association decided to appoint an agent before adopting a candidate. By 1961, when an education officer employed by the party Central Office, Mr. J. Lovering, was selected as prospective candidate, the organization had already started to grow. The membership had reached 2,000 and the number of active branches—or active ward committees—had expanded: by 1962, only the mining areas of the northwest of the town were left without a branch. While the women's branches remained active the Young Conservatives became a lively part of the organization and had a membership of about 200.

Moreover, partly under pressure from some younger elements, partly because the Liberal revival had led to a gradual disintegration of the Independent organization,[1] attitudes towards local elections had begun to change. More Conservatives felt that the idea of 'keeping politics out of local government' was unrealistic and came to adopt the view that the Association ought

[1] See Chap. 17.

to fight most of the seats on the local council. The fact that local elections started to be fought on party lines was giving a purpose to branches of the Association. Although the branches were small, their committees did not meet often enough, members of the Young Conservatives remained too few and no effort was being made to organize trade unionists, there was a clear possibility that the Association might develop on a more stable basis than in the past.

The Newcastle Conservative Association, as in the pre-war period, still lacks the widespread organization which British political parties are assumed to have in many constituencies. As a result of historical accidents, perhaps, it has never had a well-established social structure; it has no social hierarchy, even though the Rural District could have constituted a firm ground for such a hierarchical structure. It is an Association of townspeople, mainly professional men and small businessmen, who have in general run the organization on a limited scale by inclination as well as by necessity;[1] they have sometimes seemed to aim at its survival more than at its expansion. Before 1960 and indeed probably still to some extent since 1960, the main cause of difficulties has been the view, conscious or unconscious, that the sole aim of the Association was to return a Member of Parliament. Defeats led to disillusionment, organization suffered and declined; and only time could heal the wounds and restore optimism.

Organization, over more than a generation, has been of little help to produce the desired result. Efforts have perhaps been too rare or too short-lived; but they have never shown rewards. Seen from the angle of the leaders of the Association and of the candidate, the plight of the Conservative Party in Newcastle can appear unbearable; far from being surprised by the ups and downs of the organization, one might perhaps marvel at the recurrent waves of energy and at the sudden outbursts of enthusiasm. Machines and personalities can be more affected by defeats than they can affect the number and size of these defeats. But permanent organization could have one effect. If the Association had had a broader base, if it had had more members, more meetings, more component bodies, its very dynamism and life

[1] See Chap. 18.

CONSERVATIVE CANDIDATES AND AGENTS IN NEWCASTLE
SINCE 1918

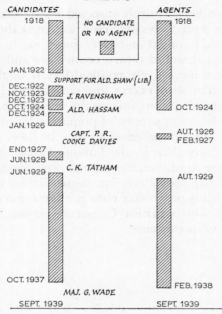

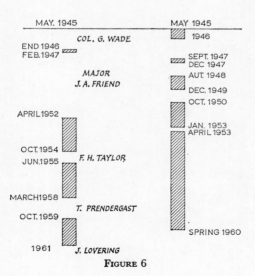

FIGURE 6

might not have been entirely directed to the General Election campaign. If it were to become more active at the periphery, in its local bodies, it might not elect more easily a Member of Parliament; but it would return councillors and it might more generally have a more lively political life. It might thus be less subjected to outbursts of energy and periods of relapse. In a safe constituency, the aim of organizing the minority party cannot be solely the self-defeating process of preparing for another election without much hope of success. This may be more difficult in the Conservative Party than in the Labour Party, as Conservative Associations are traditionally, in the first instance, electoral machines. But the Tory Party has shown that it adapts itself to change: and this is no greater change than some of the 'revolutions' through which British Conservatism has passed in the many decades of its existence.

CHAPTER SIX

THE LIBERAL ASSOCIATION
SINCE 1919

1. The General Elections of the Early 1920's

Although Liberalism as a political force never completely disappeared, the story of the Liberals in Newcastle, following the departure of Wedgwood in 1919, is mainly one of decline. Several attempts at revival proved to be false dawns and it is only in the last five or six years that any real progress has been made, and that has been on quite a different basis from the old Liberalism of previous decades. Although the political weakness of the Newcastle Association has paralleled the national misfortunes of the party, Wedgwood's change of allegiance meant that the descent from the position as one of the two major parties to that of a very poor third came about so sharply as to cause political upheaval in the Liberal ranks.

In the hey-day of Liberalism before the 1918 Election, Wedgwood was undoubtedly the party's chief asset. The magic of his name and the force of his personality attracted the middle classes, and his advanced radical views (as he himself pointed out) had secured the working-class vote. When Wedgwood left, no real political basis for a strong Liberal Party remained. The working class followed Wedgwood into the Labour fold, and many Liberals in the upper social classes either left politics altogether or went over to the Conservatives.

In the stormy years of 1918–24, with their economic hardships, social upheavals and four hard-fought General Elections, the Liberal barque, bereft of its captain, was blown from port to port, finding neither refuge nor sustenance in any. Between 1922 and 1924 the Liberal attachment at General Elections veered from Coalitionist, via support for Labour, to Anti-Socialist; in no case were they able to stand their own candidate.

At first the Liberals had made great attempts to secure a suitable candidate. As the 1922 General Election approached the search became desperate, and they sought out many people, including Arnold Bennett, who refused to stand.[1] With the failure to find a Liberal candidate of any calibre, it was inevitable that verbal opposition to Wedgwood would be the keynote of the Liberal efforts in this election. At the same time they tried to avoid needlessly antagonizing the mass of working-class voters. They attempted to state this position in terms of a formula for ideal candidates: 'level-headed, common-sense men who would realize that the true principles of Liberalism were the wisest and best to forward the interests of all sections of Labour'.[2] Somewhat inconsistently, perhaps, it was decided that a Coalition candidate, representing the will of the people as a whole, would be the best method of fulfilling their hopes. They decided to support Alderman Albert Shaw, a local mineral-water manufacturer, whose political outlook was, to say the least of it, somewhat vacillating.[3] But he apparently satisfied the Liberals of his adherence to their principles.[4] The campaign, despite the fact that it was financed jointly by the Conservative and Liberal Associations, was not, however, very impressive. Only two large public meetings were held.[5] When the votes came to be counted, Wedgwood showed that his appeal was still supreme, winning by some 5,000 votes.

The opportunism and political inconsistency to which the Liberals had been reduced was shown even more clearly at the General Election of the following year. They were saved the trouble of having to search for another candidate, but the price was support for their erstwhile arch-enemy Wedgwood. Baldwin had gone to the country on the issue of Protection, and this united the Asquithian and Lloyd George National Liberals in a last defence of Free Trade. Wedgwood, never one to throw away support where it was obtainable, wrote to his former colleagues

[1] Minutes of the Executive, 11 January 1922.   [2] Ibid.
[3] For Shaw's policy and campaign see Chap. 5, p. 108.
[4] Minutes of the Executive, 14 January 1922.
[5] Ibid., 4 April 1922.

asking for their allegiance, in view of the fact that they were both united on the most important issue in the election, that of maintaining Free Trade.[1] The Liberals could hardly fail to agree and began to recall Wedgwood's fight against Protection since 1906, though they pointed out that they strongly disapproved of many points in the Labour Party programme.[2] Alderman Scott, a prominent Liberal, even spoke at one of Wedgwood's meetings and minimized as far as possible the differences between the Liberal and Labour policies.[3] Several of Wedgwood's nomination papers were signed by Liberals, including those from the mining villages of Silverdale and Chesterton, and prominent Liberal officials added their signatures to others.[4] This support was not decisive, but it helped to increase Wedgwood's majority by 1,200 votes, though the Conservative candidate was admittedly a weak one.[5]

This support for Labour was purely a temporary tactic, a move arising from the conditions under which the election was fought. In the 1924 Election the Liberals once again swung round to support an anti-Socialist candidate in collaboration with the Conservatives. Their decision, no doubt influenced by the Zinoviev letter scare which dominated the election, was based, they stated, on their belief in constitutional government and their view that a Socialist administration would be a disaster.[6] The candidate they supported was a local man and the serving Mayor of Newcastle, Arthur Hassam, a mining engineer and former miner. He stood as an 'Anti-Socialist' and was generally considered to be a strong candidate, much being hoped from his links with the miners. In the event he was more successful than his predecessor and reduced Wedgwood's majority by over 2,000 votes. But Wedgwood's position still seemed to be unassailable.

The Liberal Party, in 1924, must have looked back somewhat ruefully over the previous six years. During that period they had adopted several very different political attitudes, in every case

[1] *Staffordshire Sentinel*, 5 December 1923.
[2] Ibid., 20 November 1923.
[3] Ibid., 5 December 1923.
[4] Ibid., 26 November 1923.
[5] For details of the Conservative candidate see Chap. 5, p. 109.
[6] Minutes of the Executive, 15 October 1924.

from a position of weakness. Although the absence of a candidate and the nature of their various alliances had prevented them from ascertaining the truth about their vote there was no doubt that they had lost all initiative as a political force.

What was the composition of the Liberal Party at this time, and in which part of the constituency were they strongest? Of the seventeen delegates to the North Staffs Liberal Federation in May 1919 there were (excluding the officers) three delegates each from Newcastle and Wolstanton, three from the rural mining area of Audley, three from Silverdale and two from Chesterton.[1] The Liberal Executive of the early 1920's included an accountant, two doctors, a commercial traveller, a building contractor, a pottery manufacturer and several shopkeepers. Nearly all of them were Methodists, and many lived in the residential area of Wolstanton, part of Wolstanton Urban District which, as we have seen, included the mining villages of Chesterton and Silverdale, whose population had always been strongly Liberal.

Newcastle Liberalism, in the period after the First World War, was thus, broadly speaking, an alliance of the urban middle class and lower-middle class of Newcastle and Wolstanton (which mainly provided the leadership) and the miners in the outlying parts of the constituency. After Wedgwood's change of party the majority of the Liberal rank-and-file became Labour voters or actual members of the Labour Party. Exactly how many went over is not clear, but in 1922 Wedgwood stated that between one-half and two-thirds of the former Liberals were now in the Labour Party.[2] The Liberal leadership of the early 1920's, however, showed no sudden change of party. One or two went over to the Labour Party; a few more became Conservatives, including George Wade, a leading pottery manufacturer. But the majority remained true to Liberalism, even though some renounced political activity and others sat as Independent members of Newcastle Borough Council.

In the latter half of the twenties, therefore, very little Liberal activity took place in Newcastle. There were annual meetings, but most of the rank-and-file, in the words of a veteran Liberal,

[1] Minutes of the Executive, 23 May 1919.
[2] *Staffordshire Sentinel*, 3 November 1922.

'went into reserve', that is, gave up all political activity. To a great extent the Labour Party, though still comparatively small, replaced the Liberals on the political stage.

2. Attempts at Revival

In 1929, with the approach of a General Election, there was the first attempt at a Liberal revival. In March of that year a meeting of the Liberal Council was called, a new committee and officials were elected and plans were made for public meetings and a recruiting drive, especially in the mining areas.[1] It was decided, however, not to run a candidate at the forthcoming election, but to give members a free vote and to assist Liberal candidates in neighbouring constituencies.[2] Some successful meetings were held; one at Keele attracted over 100 people. But the revival never really caught alight and few new members were brought into the organization. For two or three years meetings were held regularly and some more council seats were won by Liberals standing as Independents. Finance became a problem; in March 1930 the Association was unable to pay its two-guinea subscription to the national body because of 'the urgent necessity of conserving all money in hand'.[3] Meetings became fewer; only two were held in 1931–2. Furthermore, hope of basing the revival on the old Newcastle Liberal Club faded when the latter applied for a licence to serve drinks and changed its name to the Newcastle Liberal and Social Club. This offended the temperance members who set up a rival (unlicensed) Liberal Club. The Social Club faded out at the beginning of the war but during the thirties the social life of Newcastle Liberals was split on temperance lines.

No meetings are recorded in the minutes between 1932 and 1941. It must be assumed, therefore, that any activities during the thirties were of an *ad hoc* nature. One feature needs to be stressed, however. There were sufficient Liberals willing to stand for the Borough Council—as Independents—to form quite a respectable group. In fact, service on the Council in the guise of Independents was the chief Liberal contribution to local politics

[1] Minutes of the Liberal Council, 20 March 1929.
[2] Ibid., 20 March 1929.
[3] Minutes of the Executive, 7 March 1930.

in this period; during the 1930's the number of Liberal Independent councillors totalled no less than eighteen.

The next attempt at an organizational revival did not come about until 1941. Then, in the darkest days of the war, another meeting was held, attended by thirteen people, only one of whom had been present at the last recorded meeting in 1932.[1] A number of fairly regular meetings followed, mainly of an organizational nature, and 'interesting talks' were held. Thus, in a period when other parties, especially the Labour Party, were finding it difficult to organize, the Liberals managed to hold fairly regular gatherings. In 1942 a Parliamentary candidate, Lt.-Col. N. W. Elliott, was chosen, the first Liberal candidate in Newcastle for twenty-four years.[2] After this, however, there was a lull in activity until the end of the war, when preparations were made for the approaching election. An election campaign committee had to be formed and wards to be allocated to District Committees. Plans were made to form a Liberal '500' with the object of raising money to finance the campaign.[3] A striking feature of the campaign itself was the way in which many of the old Liberals of the 1920's rallied round with funds and support. Significantly, however, very few young people came forward to assist the candidate. The latter came bottom of the poll in a three-cornered contest gaining only 4,838 votes in a total poll of 39,000. The Conservative candidate obtained almost twice as many votes.

The effects of this reverse, and the setting of the political tide in favour of the Labour Party, both locally and nationally, produced its inevitable reaction. Membership fell off, meetings were few and poorly attended and political activity virtually nil. In the five years following the election only fourteen meetings are recorded in the minutes, an average of less than three per year. In April 1946 the old Liberal Club was sold for £1,250 and the money placed in trust.[4] The party had no club rooms for over two years until premises above a shop in a small side street were obtained.[5]

[1] Minutes, 3 June 1941.   [2] Ibid., 2 February 1942.
[3] Minutes of the Annual Meeting, 30 April 1945.
[4] Minutes of the Executive, 8 April 1946.
[5] Minutes of the Annual Meeting, 23 July 1948.

The Liberal Party thus faced the 1950's with grave disadvantages. Though this decade was ultimately to prove a time of revival for the party, it was not until 1957 that there was any real improvement in the situation in Newcastle. Between 1950 and 1957 the party was barely ticking over. In this period it had less than fifty subscribing members, undoubtedly the lowest membership in its history. In 1950, outgoings exceeded income by £97 and cash in hand amounted only to a few pounds.[1] Although the secretary reported in 1952 that £105 had been received from the Club during the year it was becoming increasingly difficult to get helpers to organize whist drives and the Club was in danger of becoming a financial liability. In 1954, however, the situation was somewhat eased by the letting of a room in the Club to the Old Age Pensioners' Association.[2]

The difficult times continued until 1955 when, coincident with the revival of interest in Liberalism on a national scale, a certain amount of activity was carried out. A series of meetings was organized, beginning with a talk on Monopoly, held on 24 February. For the first time for many years the annual meeting envisaged 'more fruitful times ahead'.[3] Contact was also established with Liberal students and staff at the recently founded University College of North Staffordshire.

The Association, however, was still no nearer its goal of obtaining a Parliamentary candidate and at this point in its fortunes a candidate began to be seen less as the Parliamentary expression of Liberal opinion than as the saviour of Liberalism itself in the constituency. To make matters worse there were two schools of thought on the issue. Those who wished to improve the fortunes of the party at one stroke by the adoption of a strong candidate, and those who wished gradually to build up the organization with a series of Liberal candidates in municipal contests. In 1950 the Executive decided that a candidate was necessary 'in order to show wavering members that action is intended', and also in order to maintain and develop an organization.[4] But the 1951

[1] Minutes of the Executive, 21 April 1950.

[2] Minutes of the Annual Meeting, 31 March 1952, and Minutes of the Executive, 1 November 1954.

[3] *Evening Sentinel*, 25 February 1955; Minutes of the Executive, 12 April 1955.   [4] Minutes of the Executive, 6 November 1950.

and 1955 General Elections came and went without the Liberals contesting the seat. From 1955 onwards, however, a degree of independence of the Independents was asserted and one or two Liberal candidates were put up in local elections. This modification of policy, however, brought about a deadlock on the Executive.[1] But eventually it was decided that the best strategy was 'to move by small stages towards securing a sound and effective organization'.[2]

The Liberals of the 1940's and early 1950's inevitably give the impression of being a hangover from the great days of Liberalism of twenty and thirty years earlier. The leadership, though it lacked the mass following of the former period, had the same rather narrow social basis—small shopkeepers and businessmen, and the lower ranks of the professional classes.[3] Their political ideals also had a flavour of the past about them; a document of 1942 put forward the rallying cries of liberty, the fight against monopoly, and the taxation of land values.[4] Furthermore, the 'revivals' of 1929–32, 1942–5, and that of the early 1950's (if indeed the latter warrants the name) all had as their object the renewal of Liberal strength in the old strongholds of the First World War era. There was little recognition that the political and social basis for such a development was no longer in existence, or, if it was realized, the key to future advance seemed elusive or unobtainable. It was clear, however, that if the Liberals were ever to make an impact on the political life of Newcastle, new aims, new methods and new blood were needed.

3. The New Liberals

The renaissance of the Liberal Association in Newcastle dates from the year 1957, and has been part of the nationwide im-

[1] Minutes of the Executive, 3 October 1956. See also below, Chap. 17, p. 345.

[2] Ibid., 13 March 1957.

[3] In 1942 the Executive included a builder, a draper, a timber merchant, two schoolteachers, an insurance agent, a commercial traveller and a civil servant. (Liberal Minute Book, 1942, passim.) In the early 1950's, the eighteen most prominent executive members included no less than seven small shopkeepers or businessmen; the remainder included a commercial traveller, a clerk, an architect and an accountant. (Liberal Minute Book, 1950–2, passim.)

[4] Typescript manifesto, dated 1942 (Liberal Minute Book).

provement in the fortunes of the Liberal Party which occurred from the mid-1950's onwards.[1] In the five years following 1957, the Liberals have forged an entirely new leadership, increased the size of their party more than sixfold, secured the election of a small group of councillors and put a Parliamentary candidate in the field.

This expansion can be dated almost precisely from October 1957, with arrival on the Executive of a former Liberal agent and ex-army officer who had come to live in the district some months before. He was one of a number of younger people, including university students, whose residence in the Potteries was to have a profound effect on the work of the Association. Almost immediately the former agent initiated a certain number of Liberal proposals for a scheduled development area in the heart of the town, and these were sent to the Town Clerk.[2] It was the first time in living memory that any practical proposals for civic welfare had emanated from the Liberal Association. A drafting committee was set up to supply further details of the scheme which the Town Clerk requested.[3]

At the Annual General Meeting in March 1958 the chairman was able to report, for the first time since the war, that the outlook was very promising: 'An influx of young people had given the association new life.' The same meeting passed a resolution critical of the Government's policy on nuclear weapons and called for a positive approach and practical steps to general disarmament and for the strengthening of the United Nations.[4] Another pointer to the revival was the increased numbers attending Executive meetings. At a meeting on 4 June 1958 no less than twenty-one were present, including several young housewives, and it is recorded that: 'The ladies soon proposed various means of developing interest and raising funds.'[5] Jumble sales, bring-and-buy sales, and coffee evenings were planned, and a canvassing session organized. The jumble sale and coffee evening

---

[1] The main sources for this section are the minutes of the Newcastle Liberal Association and interviews with local Liberal officials and councillors.
[2] Minutes of the Executive, 27 November 1957.
[3] Ibid., 8 January 1958.
[4] Ibid., 6 March 1958.
[5] Ibid., 4 June 1958.

both proved very successful and raised no less than £53 for the funds.[1]

The influx of new members and increased activity improved the whole method and spirit of the organization. Canvassing was organized on a regular monthly basis; a *Liberal News* secretary was appointed; and relations with the Independent Civic Association were finally severed. A young and enthusiastic secretary, an economics graduate serving as the local station-master, was elected and a regular programme of interesting social events was drawn up.[2] The rejuvenated Association soon made its mark on the local political situation. In October 1960 a Liberal candidate in Ward 4 easily won a by-election. In May 1961 the secretary was also elected to the Borough Council for Ward 4. A few weeks later a Liberal candidate gained a seat on the County Council at a by-election in the County Council division comprising Wards 5 and 7. A few months later, at an aldermanic by-election, a Liberal candidate beat a Labour opponent in a straight fight (although the seat was narrowly lost to Labour in the following year). In 1962, however, the Liberals won the third seat in Ward 4, thus claiming the whole representation of this ward, and also beat both Conservative and Labour candidates to record their first success in Ward 5 at the Borough elections.

The Liberal campaigns revealed the party as a young, dynamic group who would 'get things done'. Only the Liberals, it was represented, were unhampered by rigid adherence to a party line, by a too-close attachment to national policy, by the lethargy which seemingly afflicted the incumbents of local political office. In fact, an image was projected—that of a go-getting party, in touch with the people, which would put life into local politics without undue emphasis on political programmes or party ideology.

What were the reasons for this sudden improvement in Liberal fortunes? In the first place, the influence of the national Liberal revival must be taken into account. To a great extent it has ended the fear of a wasted vote which had dogged Liberal electoral efforts in previous years. Coincident with this there has been a

[1] Minutes of the Executive, 9 July 1958.
[2] Ibid., 21 March and 11 April 1960.

reaction, particularly among younger people, against the seemingly endless and unfruitful two-party political process. In
addition to these causes, Newcastle Liberalism has had an infusion of strength from some of the younger professional people
who have come to live in the area during the past decade. They
have helped to provide a young and active leadership which has
decisively broken with the old methods of work and political
organization in the party. This leadership has also finally ended
all connection with the Independents and created a more clear-
cut image of Liberalism.

Perhaps the greatest break with the past which the new leadership has made is to devise a much more flexible form of organization, better designed to suit conditions as they exist than the old
stereotyped and rigid pattern. Formally, the Liberal Association
subscribes to rules which were drawn up in 1942. These provided
for a Council, which was an assembly of all members over
eighteen years of age; an Executive consisting of the officers, the
chairman and secretary of each District Committee (based on a
Ward or a group of Wards), delegates from the Young Liberals,
the Women's Association, plus six members elected at the annual
meeting. In addition, an Emergency Committee, in effect a sub-
committee of the Executive, was set up to transact business
between executive meetings. Like most constitutions, this sought
to preserve a balance on the directing committees between, as it
were, the statesmen and the activists. But it also presupposed a
fairly high level of activity in the wards. This, as we have seen,
never occurred between 1942 and the late fifties. In fact, during
most of this period the Executive consisted entirely of people
who were active enough to attend meetings. As late as 1948 a
resolution at the Annual Meeting was urging the implementation of the constitution drawn up six years before.[1] The present
leadership has introduced much greater flexibility into organizational matters with their pragmatic and undoctrinaire approach
to methods of organization.

The present (1962) structure of the Liberal Association is
shown in Figure 7. The effective directing body of the party at
the present time is the Executive Committee which meets
monthly (except in August) and has a maximum membership of

[1] Minutes of the Annual Meeting, 23 July 1948.

thirty-five. As there are only three ward committees in operation at present, active members have sometimes been co-opted on to the Executive. Since 1957, the turnover of members on this committee has been almost complete, and the new and younger members now form the majority. The day-to-day work of the party is, however, carried out by sub-committees of the Executive, and these are the most novel feature of the present set-up. They

THE STRUCTURE OF THE LIBERAL ASSOCIATION

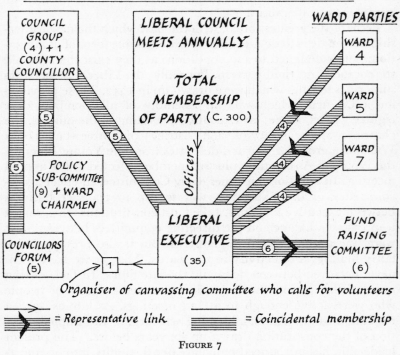

FIGURE 7

are the Canvassing Committee, the Fund Raising Committee, and the Policy Sub-committee. The latter discusses national and local government policies from the Liberal point of view and gives general ideological guidance to the Association; all the important decisions in party policy are taken here. In addition there is the operative staff of the *North Staffs Liberal*, a four-page bi-monthly duplicated news-sheet; this group is in effect also an executive sub-committee. A further committee to deal with trade-union affairs is planned for the future.

With the exception of the Policy Committee, which has nine members, plus three ward chairmen, these committees are fairly small, usually having three or four members who are normally members of the Executive interested in the work which the particular committee undertakes. They give a chance to keen and active members of the Association to concentrate on particular aspects of party work. The Canvassing Committee, for instance, organizes and keeps together all those members who are interested in and see the importance of work on the doorsteps. The *North Staffs Liberal* Committee provides an outlet for those members who are interested in journalism and propaganda. On the other hand there is no danger of these committees becoming autonomous for they are directly responsible to the Executive. It could be argued, however, that the existence of these committees leads to excessive centralization and lack of attention to ward committees. Canvassing, for instance, has often been carried out by the central Canvassing Committee even when a ward committee exists in that particular ward. Increasing membership and the growth of stable ward parties are, however, leading to greater decentralization.[1]

The financial organization of the party again shows a flexible approach in that it is largely a function of canvassing, party activity and social life. There are two main forms of membership —by direct annual subscription, minimum 2s. 6d., but often higher, and by regular subscription to *Liberal News*, which automatically confers membership. Some members pay both subscriptions. There are no regular collectors, however: collection mainly falls upon the Canvassing Committee, either on the monthly canvassing night or when distributing the *North Staffs Liberal*. Because of this regular contact with membership, few (less than 10 per cent) are behind with their subscriptions. This method of collection is facilitated by the fact that the money can be paid at any time and in any amount.

As in the other political parties, subscriptions by no means form the main source of revenue, and this has to be made up by profits from social events—bring-and-buy sales, jumble sales,

[1] See Chap. 17, p. 358.

135

coffee evenings, Christmas draws, treasure hunts, etc. These activities have been very successful of late and in this way a credit balance is maintained despite fairly heavy outgoing expenses on office rates, expenditure on elections, literature and meetings, and contributions to headquarters, and to the national by-election funds. The latter subscriptions run to some £40–£50 per annum.

Mainly because of consistent canvassing and electoral success, the membership of the Liberal Association has improved from less than 50 in early 1957 to over 300 today,[1] and despite the newness of most of the membership, about one-third are considered to be 'active', that is, they undertake the minimum duties of attending meetings and helping in elections. The present strongholds are Wards 4, 5 and 7 where the greatest amount of canvassing has been carried out. On some canvasses as many as seventy new members have been signed up in an evening. Most of the new members come from the intermediate social grades; in some areas recruitment has been good in places which were formerly strongly Labour. Many of these people have obviously joined because of the good local record of the party in fighting for better amenities and the election successes have finally convinced many that to vote Liberal is not to throw one's vote away.

The present picture of the party shows a small but active leadership and a quickly growing but rather inexperienced rank-and-file. To some extent, therefore, an examination of the way in which the party functions is an examination of the centralized leadership. Here again the structure to some extent determines the way in which party policy is fashioned. Not much time, for instance, is spent discussing policy at Executive Committee meetings except in the most general fashion. Detailed discussion of policy is the province of the Policy Committee. At the Executive Committee meetings about 50 per cent of the time is taken up with discussion of party administration; about 30 per cent of the time is spent discussing social activities and how funds may be raised by these; the rest of the time is spent on policy matters. When discussing policy somewhat more time is spent on local issues rather than on national ones, or at least on the local pre-

[1] i.e. December 1962.

sentation of national issues. The initiation of policy tends to come mainly from the officers or the Executive rather than from the lower organizations of the party. This is almost entirely due to the existing small number of ward committees. Important resolutions, especially those dealing with a national or international issue, are sent to headquarters and the local press. It is not the normal practice, however, to send all resolutions to headquarters.

There is no great division of opinion on any of the major issues among the active members. A year or two ago Nonconformity and Nonconformist attitudes were the source of some differences, when the Executive consisted of an uneasy alliance of older people with Nonconformist views and younger people with a less rigid outlook.[1] Now that the direction of the party is in the hands of the latter such differences no longer obtain. The only outstanding point arising from this clash of attitudes is that the money obtained for the old Club cannot be obtained from the trustees because of their views as to its purpose. The Club is now used far more than it was a year ago and serves more as a headquarters for political activity than as a social centre.

A current total of four municipal councillors and one County councillor, and a membership of over 300, give grounds for saying that there has been a genuine Liberal revival in Newcastle during the last five years. What signs are there that this development will continue at the same rate? The initial impetus for the upswing was provided by the influx of younger professional people with Liberal affiliations into the constituency at a time when there was growing disquiet, particularly among younger people, at the seemingly endless stagnation brought about by the Conservative-Labour dominance. Progress has been maintained by the creation of a streamlined organization, dedicated work on the doorstep, and the public presentation of the Liberals as the party who will 'get things done' in Newcastle.

The significant point, however, is that the Liberals initially made the greatest headway not in wards which were Labour or Conservative strongholds but in areas which neither party had cultivated to any great extent, and in which there was little or no formal organization. Liberal candidates were thus able to present

[1] See Chap. 13, p. 263.

themselves as an alternative without running headlong against another party's electoral machine, and were able to turn others' neglect to their own advantage. Whether or not they won the votes of former Labour or Conservative voters depended largely upon the area. In Ward 4 they obviously won over a lot of former Labour voters in the older working-class streets. In other areas with a more middle-class complexion they would tend to take the support of Independent or Conservative voters. In all cases their first-class organization gathered in every possible vote.

To some extent, the initial successes in Ward 4 gave the impetus for later successes against Conservative and Labour candidates, which were much more of a contest between rival party organizations. But the Liberal successes should be seen in perspective. Their strength, in both councillors and functioning ward parties, lies in older and less socially homogeneous areas in the centre of the Borough, i.e., in Wards 4, 5 and 7. A third party wishing seriously to change the balance of political power in Newcastle must ultimately seek to capture at least some of the heartlands of their rivals. There is the possibility that skilled organization, able propaganda and the psychological effect of growing Liberal strength may enable the Association to mop up some of the weaker Conservative, Labour or Independent areas. It is, however, extremely doubtful whether the Liberals can assail the commanding heights of the Labour mining communities or the Conservative residential districts while the social and economic configuration of Newcastle remains in its present form.

CHAPTER SEVEN

NEWCASTLE TODAY: ECONOMIC AND SOCIAL BACKGROUND TO POLITICS

I n the social and political history of preceding chapters we have seen Newcastle, with the advent of the Industrial Revolution, forced to relinquish to the Pottery towns its pre-eminence in North Staffordshire. In our introduction we mentioned how this reversal of fortune affected the nineteenth-century character of Newcastle. After 1932, however, the absorption of the Wolstanton Urban District more than doubled the population of the Borough and greatly diversified its social and industrial structure. Thereafter the comparison with Stoke-on-Trent, as we shall see, is increasingly in Newcastle's favour.

1. Population

The most striking contemporary feature has been the reversal of the nineteenth-century demographic tendency for the Potteries to grow more quickly than Newcastle Borough. During the last thirty years, as Table 1 shows, the increase of population in Newcastle Borough has been well above the national average. At the same time the population of Stoke has been decreasing, in the last decade with accelerating speed. Meanwhile the population increase of Newcastle Rural District, below the national average between 1931 and 1951, has now surpassed it; but the average increase of the Rural District still remains below that of Newcastle Borough.

Population changes are partly caused by changes in the balance between births and deaths and partly by migration. In Stoke the excess of births over deaths between 1951 and 1959, according to the Registrar-General, was 10,000 or 3·6 per cent of the 1951 population. In Newcastle Borough and Rural District the excess was 3,500 and 300 or 5·0 per cent and 1·8 per cent respectively of the 1951 population. The difference between Newcastle Borough and Rural District is thus much greater than between Newcastle and Stoke, in this respect. The natural increase of Stoke, however, was offset in this period by 14,315 of its citizens emigrating, at the same time as 1,364 and 474 people immigrated to Newcastle Borough and Newcastle Rural District respectively. Thus it seems that while the natural increase of population is greater in Newcastle than in Stoke, migration must largely account for the great contrast in their respective population movements.

TABLE I. POPULATION CHANGES FROM 1931, 1951 AND 1961 CENSUSES

	1931	1951	%age increase 1931–51	1961	%age increase 1951–61
England and Wales	39,952,377	43,757,888	9·5	46,071,604	5·3
Stoke-on-Trent	276,639	275,115	−0·6	265,306	−3·5
Newcastle Borough	54,739*	70,036	27·9	75,688	9·1
Newcastle Rural District	16,872	17,930	6·3	18,224	6·3

* Newcastle Borough plus Wolstanton Urban District.

A comparison of the birthplaces of the inhabitants of Newcastle Borough, Stoke and the rest of Staffordshire is set out in Table 2. It shows that the population of Newcastle Borough has a high degree of stability. The proportion of people in Newcastle born outside Staffordshire, though higher than in Stoke, is lower

TABLE 2. BIRTHPLACE OF THE POPULATION OF NEWCASTLE, STOKE AND STAFFORDSHIRE FROM THE 1951 CENSUS

	Staffordshire		Stoke		Newcastle Borough	
	Population	%age total	Population	%age total	Population	%age Total
Staffordshire	1,289,238	79·5	248,564	90·4	60,192	85·9
Midlands (not Staffs)	144,510	8·9	4,821	1·8	1,879	2·7
Wales and Scotland	28,518	1·8	2,812	1·1	1,020	1·4
Eire	8,500	0·5	876	0·3	302	0·4
Outside British Isles	53,100	3·3	7,498	2·8	1,886	2·7

than in the county as a whole. Moreover the foreign-born and overseas element in Newcastle's population is smaller than in the county. On no count can the atmosphere of Newcastle Borough be described as cosmopolitan.

It follows therefore that the exceptional increase of the population of Newcastle Borough over the last thirty years can be accounted for neither by a large increase in the population nor by immigration from outside Staffordshire. The expansion was the result of immigration of people born in Staffordshire, a conclusion borne out by the history of housing development in North Staffordshire. The expansion of housing in the Potteries was restricted by the difficulty of finding suitable building sites, a difficulty not present in Newcastle where, as we have observed, a great housing programme began in the 1930's. Thus whereas in the nineteenth century Newcastle had been one of the middle-class residential districts of Stoke, in the twentieth century it became one of the adjoining city's lower-middle and working-class suburbs.

2. Housing

An analysis of the growth of housing in North Staffordshire since 1931 reveals the remarkable achievement of Newcastle Borough in this field. Table 3 shows that between 1931 and 1951 the increase in the number of households was proportionately more than twice as high in Newcastle Borough as in Stoke.

TABLE 3. HOUSING IN NORTH STAFFORDSHIRE IN THE 1931, 1951 AND 1961 CENSUSES

	Number of households 1951	%age increase 1931–51	Number of households 1961	%age increase 1951–61	Persons per room 1951	Persons per room 1961
England and Wales	13,117,868	28·2	14,702,823	12·1	0·73	0·66
Stoke-on-Trent	79,195	26·2	84,664	10·7	0·84	0·71
Newcastle M.B.	20,637	57·2	24,526	18·8	0·77	0·68
Newcastle R.D.	4,929	16·7	5,636	14·3	0·75	0·66

During the same twenty years the number of people in Newcastle Borough who were living more than two to a room fell from 10·8 per cent of the population in 1931, worse than the Staffordshire average of 9·2 per cent, to 1·6 per cent of the population, better than the county average of 2·7 per cent in 1951.

To sum up, in the last thirty years Newcastle Borough's expansion has been greatly facilitated by its vigorous housing programme. The general effect has been to make the Borough, and more recently and to a much slighter extent the Rural District, something of a dormitory area for the Potteries.

3. Industry and Agriculture

Over the last quarter of a century the general tendency has been for Newcastle's industry to become more diversified. Table 4 shows[1] that while mining has remained the primary industry in the Newcastle employment area the other traditional industry, brick- and tile-making, has diminished in importance. Engineering, greatly stimulated by the Second World War and employing 61 per cent women workers, is now the second most important industry. Services of all kinds and the distributive trades have

TABLE 4. GROWTH OF INDUSTRY IN NEWCASTLE EMPLOYMENT AREA 1939–59 AND COMPARISON WITH STOKE AND GREAT BRITAIN FROM THE MINISTRY OF LABOUR GAZETTE

Industry	1939 Total employed in Newcastle	1946 Total employed in Newcastle	1959 Total employed in Newcastle	Percentage employed U.K. 1959	Percentage employed Newcastle 1959	Percentage employed Stoke 1959
Mining	6,428	5,598	5,159	4·0	19·7	10·7
Brick-, tile- and pottery-making*	3,552	1,874	1,510	1·5	5·8	36·4
Engineering (including electrical engineering) and metal manufacturing	190	1,829	4,476	21·2	17·1	10·3
Other manufacturing industries	1,583	1,131	1,025	19·1	3·9	10·7
Building and contracting	2,312	1,424	2,237	6·4	8·5	5·7
Agriculture	615	604	511	3·0	2·0	0·3
Distribution	2,649	2,534	2,042	11·4	13·6	7·5
All other services	2,507	2,975	7,744	33·4	29·5	18·4

* Wholly brick- and tile-making in Newcastle and almost wholly pottery in Stoke.

[1] We are indebted to Mr. L. Smyth for information about employment in Newcastle-under-Lyme.

also expanded in recent years, the result, no doubt, of Newcastle's growth as a residential area and as a communications centre on the main London–Manchester road.

It should be pointed out, however, that in spite of expansion Newcastle's industries employed only 781 more men in 1959 than they did in 1939. Thus the increase in the labour force over two decades was largely the result of 5,605 more women being employed. In 1939 women were 21·2 per cent of those employed in the Newcastle employment area; but by 1959 the proportion had increased to 37·4 per cent. This is a high degree of female employment compared with other coal-mining districts.

The comparison with Stoke and the United Kingdom reveals that Newcastle in many respects is nearer the national average because though mining predominates in Newcastle, it is not so preponderant as the pottery industry in Stoke-on-Trent. Furthermore the relative superiority of Newcastle in the engineering industry, in services and in building indicates a more modern as well as a more diversified economy.

Table 4, however, underestimates the number of people working in agriculture because the rural parishes at the western end of the constituency are attached to the Market Drayton Labour Exchange; and we must correct for this because, though the numbers are small, the influence of agriculture politically is supposed to be extensive. Actually the Ministry of Agriculture statistics show that 640 people (excluding farmers and their families) worked in agriculture in the Rural District in 1960, a fall from 849 in 1948 and less than the figure for the pre-war period.

The changes in agriculture have indeed been considerable.[1] Obviously the mechanization of farming has been responsible for the decline in the size of the labour force. As the number of holdings has remained around 500 for many decades (in 1960 there were 503) the number of farm workers per holding must have decreased. At the moment we have a position of about 1·3 farm workers (excluding members of the farmer's family) for every farm. Thus on many farms much of the work must be done by the farmer and his family and this factor, coupled with

[1] We are indebted to Mr. R. W. Sturgess for help in assessing agricultural statistics.

the virtual demise of landlordism, implies that the farmers in the constituency have fewer local social and economic ties than ever before. The pattern, therefore, is one of independent farmers farming on an average about sixty acres predominantly devoted to dairying.

Small-scale agriculture in the countryside is paralleled by small-scale industry in the rest of the constituency. Table 5 reveals that the proportion of firms employing between 11 and 24 workers is considerably higher in Newcastle than in the country generally; but that at the level of firms employing more than 1,000 workers there is no great disparity of industrial structure. It is in firms employing between 100 and 500 people that Newcastle is relatively deficient.

TABLE 5. SIZE OF FIRM IN NEWCASTLE PER WORKERS EMPLOYED COMPARED WITH THE UNITED KINGDOM FROM THE CENSUS OF PRODUCTION 1954

Size of firm in terms of workers employed	Number		Percentage of all firms employing over 10 workers	
	Newcastle	U.K.	Newcastle	U.K.
Over 2,000	2	397	0·7	0·7
1,000–1,999	3	731	1·1	1·3
500–999	5	1,532	1·8	2·8
100–499	24	11,446	8·9	20·9
50–99	48	9,388	17·7	17·1
25–49	49	10,346	18·1	18·9
11–24	140	20,903	51·7	38·2
Total employing more than 10 workers	271	54,743	100·0	100·0

The general pattern is for the firms, especially the biggest, to be owned by national or even international concerns. Thus of the five enterprises employing over 1,000 workers two are National Coal Board collieries, and two are light-engineering firms who established themselves before and just after the Second World War. Neither is locally owned or managed. The fifth employer of this size is Newcastle Corporation. The bodies with between 500 and 1,000 employees are the University of Keele, two other N.C.B. pits, the uniform factory whose owners have remained Mancunians, mentioned in Chapter 2, and a bakery, for long owned by a local family, but now 'taken over' by an international combine.

Among the smaller firms local ownership and management are less uncommon. In the 100–499 group there are three old-established tileries, two local builders and one road construction contractor, a large bakery, an old brass foundry, and a firm of heating engineers, all of whom are locally owned and managed. Of the others three are local government authorities, one is an N.C.B. colliery and the remainder are local branches of nation-wide or even, as in the case of Woolworths, international organizations.

The overall pattern, then, is for the largest and newest industry to be financed and managed from outside the constituency. Though there is still some local industry, it is amongst the oldest and smallest. Whatever evidence there is suggests that the tendency will be progressively towards bigger and more remotely controlled industry.

4. Residence and Workplace

In the last section we only dealt with employment *in* the constituency, and it would be neglecting one of Newcastle's chief characteristics if we failed to consider the large number of its residents who work outside its boundaries. Table 6 discloses that rather more than half the workers in the constituency worked outside the limits of their local authority. Nearly as many Newcastle workers went to work in the industrial area to the East as worked in Newcastle Borough. Rather less than half the Borough's worked elsewhere. In the Rural District, on the other hand, Newcastle Borough was the most important workplace except for the Rural District itself. More than half the Rural District's workers also worked outside its boundaries, a considerable proportion crossing into Cheshire or Shropshire to work.

Thus in Newcastle Borough there were 11,000 fewer jobs than employed citizens and in Newcastle Rural District nearly 2,700 fewer. This further emphasizes that the constituency of Newcastle is, to a considerable degree, a residential suburb for the Potteries.

TABLE 6. RESIDENCE AND WORKPLACE FROM THE 1951 CENSUS

Place of residence	Workplace							Total jobs
	Newcastle Borough	Newcastle R.D.	Stoke, Kidsgrove and Biddulph	Stone	Nantwich	Salop	Rest of England and Wales	
Newcastle Borough	16,108	1,781	3,933	108	—	38	390	22,358
Newcastle R.D.	667	3,587	189	—	46	98	85	4,672
Stoke, Kidsgrove and Biddulph	14,200	825						
Stone	871	208						
Stafford	207	28						
Crewe	128	211						
Nantwich	179	185						
Salop	125	228						
Rest of England and Wales	628	285						
Total residents of Newcastle Borough working elsewhere	17,005	3,751	Total residents of Newcastle Rural District working elsewhere					
Total workers	33,113	7,338						

5. Social Structure

Social class is defined by the Census authorities as dependent upon occupation. Thus Class I consists of the 'higher administrative' occupations and includes senior civil servants and larger employers; Class II is composed of farmers, less well-paid professional people such as teachers, shopkeepers and small employers; Class III includes clerks, shop assistants, foremen and skilled manual workers; Class IV consists of the semi-skilled manual workers; and Class V of the unskilled manual workers. Table 7 compares the distribution of these classes in Newcastle, Stoke and England and Wales.

It is clear from the table that in the constituency of Newcastle the 'higher' classes have less and the 'lower' classes more representation than in the national pattern. On the other hand Newcastle is nearer the general pattern than Stoke in respect of

SOCIO-ECONOMIC BACKGROUND

Classes I, II and V, though skilled and semi-skilled manual workers, doubtless owing to the presence of the pottery industry, are a good deal better represented in Stoke than Newcastle. Between Newcastle Borough and Rural District there is also some contrast. In the Rural District there is a low proportion of people in Class III, but a very high proportion of semi-skilled workers in Class IV.

TABLE 7. PERCENTAGE SOCIAL CLASS IN NEWCASTLE, STOKE AND ENGLAND AND WALES FROM THE 1951 CENSUS

	I	II	III	IV	V	Total
England and Wales	3·3	14·5	53·0	16·1	13·1	100·0
Stoke-on-Trent	1·2	8·5	54·7	18·4	17·2	100·0
Newcastle constituency	2·5	14·1	50·1	19·9	13·4	100·0
Newcastle Borough	2·7	13·6	51·9	18·0	13·8	100·0
Newcastle Rural District	1·6	16·2	43·2	27·4	11·6	100·0

For our survey,[1] however, we used different social categories. This was because the Census categories are not very suitable for political study. For example, Class III of the Census groups clerks and skilled manual workers together, people who are often supposed to be in very different political camps. We therefore divided Class III into clerical and skilled manual workers—not a very arbitrary process—and labelled the resulting classes C and D respectively. Census Classes IV and V we combined in class E which thus contained all the semi-skilled and unskilled workers whom we shall henceforth describe as the 'less-skilled' workers. Classes I and II we completely realigned. Anyone whose occupation placed him in these Census Classes was allocated to our classes[2] A and B. Thus our class A consists of business proprietors including all shopkeepers, farmers and publicans. 'Company directors' were placed in this group when they were clearly business proprietors or when we were unable to ascertain

[1] See Appendix 2.

[2] We shall use the term 'class' with some misgivings to describe our categories A, B, C, D, E and X. We realize that this usage is open to serious criticism, but we found such terms as 'occupational grouping' or 'objective social class' too unwieldy for constant reference. We are not, of course, attempting to put forward any new theory of social class.

more about their exact position. In class B we placed all those in managerial, professional and technical occupations. In practice this means that class B consists of all those in Census Classes I and II whom we did not consider to be business proprietors. However there was one further modification. Anyone who ran his or her own business, regardless of where the Census classification might place them, was allocated to our class A.

Everyone in our sample was placed in a class. Housewives were given a class based on their husbands' occupations, as were widows when their dead husbands' occupations could be discovered. When this was not possible, or when there were housewives who were both single and without other occupation, we placed them in X, a class of their own.

Figure 8 demonstrates the method of division diagrammatically, and shows that the Census classification was used to separate our respondents into three groups based on Classes I and II, III, and IV and V. We then modified these on the lines indicated.

The advantage of our categorization of class is that it is more likely to produce statistically significant[1] associations between class and voting. This is especially so because all employers of labour are placed in one class. The main disadvantage—one attached to all personal methods of classification—is the difficulty of comparing it with findings in other places.

Table 8 analyses the class pattern of the constituency. It must be remembered that only 18·7 per cent of the voters live in the Rural District. Consequently the pattern of the Borough naturally dominates the constituency. It will be noted that whereas classes A and B combined are larger than Census Classes I and II combined, class E is smaller than Census Classes IV and V added together. This is doubtless the result of the business proprietors, whatever the nature of their work and its economic reward, being placed in class A.

Whatever the categories used, Newcastle constituency emerges as an area in which the proportion of manual workers is rather high. Skill seems to be slightly less prevalent than in the nation as a whole and in the Rural District there are fewer skilled than less-skilled workers. Probably the proportion of professional and

[1] Henceforward whenever we use the terms 'significant' or 'significance' we mean 'statistically significant' or 'statistical significance'.

MODIFICATION OF CENSUS CLASSES TO PRODUCE SURVEY CLASSES

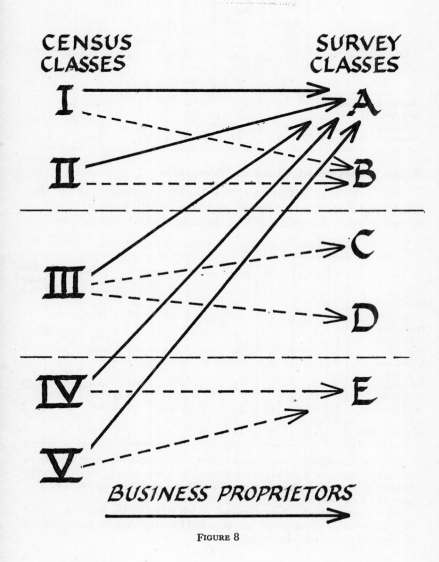

FIGURE 8

SOCIO-ECONOMIC BACKGROUND

clerical workers is relatively rather low. Thus the general
impression is of a fairly old industrial and social structure.

TABLE 8. PERCENTAGE CLASS IN NEWCASTLE[1]

	Business proprietors	Professional and managerial	Clerical	Skilled manual	Less skilled manual	Housewife, no husband
	A	B	C	D	E	X
Newcastle Borough	8	11	9	39	31	2
Newcastle Rural District	16	8	7	29	37	4
Newcastle constituency	9	11	8	37	32	3

6. An Analysis of Class in Newcastle

Besides voting allegiance, class is the category most used in this
study and it is therefore necessary to examine it in some detail in
terms of other factors. Table 9, for example, demonstrates that

TABLE 9. PERCENTAGE AGE AND CLASS: CLASS AND AGE

		21–24	25–29	30–39	40–49	50–59	60 and over	Total	Under 40	Over 40
Business proprietors	A	1	2	14	32	23	28	100	5	11
Professional and managerial	B	2	10	26	16	23	23	100	12	10
Clerical	C	7	9	22	24	15	23	100	10	8
Skilled manual	D	5	8	27	23	19	18	100	47	32
Less-skilled manual	E	2	6	17	23	24	29	100	25	36
Housewife, no husband	X	0	0	12	2	9	77	100	1	3
All respondents		3	7	22	23	21	24	100	100	100

[1] Totals may sometimes add up to 99 or 101 because all percentages from
our survey data are rounded to the nearest whole number. The only exceptions to this rule are when very small numbers—as in the case of 'swing'—
have to be considered.

All the survey tables, henceforward, which relate to the Borough, Rural
District, or whole constituency, are obtained by weighting the wards' figures
in terms of the wards' electorates.

150

it is the professional, clerical and skilled manual workers who are the youngest classes. More than half of all the people in these three groups are under 50, while the other three classes—business proprietors, less-skilled manual workers and housewives without husbands—all have more than half their people over 50. If one turns from the age structure of the classes to the class composition of the age groups it becomes clear that the older part of the constituency's population has less skill and professional qualification, but more business experience.

Another factor usually closely connected with class is house tenancy. It has been estimated that in 1959 (the year of the survey) about 37 per cent of the nation's households were owner-occupied. In Newcastle constituency, despite its rather poor character, 44 per cent of the population owned their own houses. Table 10 shows also that just over a quarter were council house tenants, though this form of tenancy naturally varied

TABLE 10. PERCENTAGE HOUSE TENANCY AND CLASS

	A	B	C	D	E	X	Total
Council tenants	6	13	29	29	39	11	28
Owner-occupiers	74	64	48	42	30	37	44
Other forms of tenancy	20	23	23	29	31	52	28
Total	100	100	100	100	100	100	100

greatly with class, nearly two-fifths of the less-skilled workers living in municipal housing. On the other hand, while the number of those living in other rented houses did not vary overmuch with class, owner-occupation gradually decreased as one moved down our class scale. Even so owner-occupiers were the largest tenancy group at every level except the less-skilled workers, and even 30 per cent of the latter owned their houses. Especially noteworthy was the similarity in the tenancy distribution of the clerical and skilled workers.

There was some variation in this respect between the Borough and the Rural District. Only 15 per cent of the respondents in the Rural District lived in council houses as against 31 per cent in the Borough, where owner-occupation was correspondingly lower—42 per cent compared to 52 per cent in the Rural District.

This difference of 10 per cent was almost wholly accounted for by the greater degree of owner-occupation among the poorer classes in the Rural District where 54 per cent of the clerical workers, 49 per cent of the skilled workers and 42 per cent of the less-skilled workers owned their homes in contrast to 47 per cent, 41 per cent, and 27 per cent of the corresponding groups in the Borough.

Thus a relatively high degree of owner-occupation (30 per cent in Glossop,[1] for instance) coinciding with a comparatively large working class seems to be one of the distinguishing features of the constituency. Newcastle has many manual workers, but they have a good deal more to lose than their chains.

Otherwise the generally rather under-privileged nature of the constituency is reflected in its educational standards. Table 11 shows that late school-leaving is uncommon, only 11 per cent of the respondents having stayed at school until they were 16 as compared with 16 per cent in the nation as a whole. Only in

TABLE 11. PERCENTAGE SCHOOL-LEAVING AGE AND CLASS AND COMPARISON WITH ENGLAND AND WALES

School-leaving age	Class						Total	Percentage England and Wales from 1951 Census*
	A	B	C	D	E	X		
13 and under	25	18	16	22	32	31	25	10
14 and 15	49	33	63	75	66	56	64	74
16 and over	26	50	21	3	2	13	11	16
	100	100	100	100	100	100	100	100

* Occupied people who stated terminal age of education.

the professional group had half—and there only just half—of the voters received a 'higher' education. Only 26 per cent of the proprietorial group, perhaps partly owing to the inclusion of jobbing tradesmen, had had a further education, but probably also owing to the number of 'self-made' men in the constituency. In contemporary parlance this implies a business class that is 'non-U', a factor which may explain, to some extent, the lack of

[1] A. H. Birch, *Small Town Politics* (1959), p. 132.

social and political leadership from which the Conservative Party has particularly suffered.

This latter point is further emphasized by the association between class and self-assigned class designated in Table 12. Respondents were asked to place themselves in one of the social classes indicated. In spite of this, 6 per cent asserted that they were not in any class. The 'lower-middle' class, as always, was unpopular though the professional class was most ready to admit to it as it was also the class most conscious of being 'middle class' and least ready to claim 'working-class' allegiance.

TABLE 12. PERCENTAGE CLASS AND SELF-ASSIGNED SOCIAL CLASS

Self-assigned class	A	B	C	D	E	X	Total
'Upper middle' and 'middle'	50	52	34	15	12	28	23
'Lower middle'	12	23	18	11	6	11	11
'Working'	32	22	42	68	75	51	59
'No class'	6	3	5	7	7	10	6
	100	100	100	100	100	100	100

59 per cent of respondents said they were 'working class' (as against 58 per cent in Bristol N.E.[1] and 70 per cent at Glossop[2]). In this self-assigned category there was little difference between the skilled and less-skilled workers. Quite a high proportion of the clerical workers placed themselves in the 'working class', and nearly a third of the business proprietors. Here again, perhaps, we see the factor of 'non-U-ness' amongst the constituency's businessmen.

There were some important variations between Borough and Rural District. The Rural District considered itself more 'working class' than the Borough—67 per cent as against 58 per cent. Moreover this difference of around 10 per cent applied to all occupational levels, perhaps representing the more 'old-fashioned' nature of the Rural District, with its older people, older housing, older industries and older pattern of consumption. In such an area it is possible that older attitudes to class persist, and that manual workers and people whose parents were manual

[1] R. S. Milne and H. C. Mackenzie, *Marginal Seat* (1958), p. 56.
[2] A. H. Birch, op. cit., p. 108.

workers are less likely to label themselves as 'middle class' than similar people might in newer, younger, expanding industrial towns.

The general picture is of an area to which many of the modern occupational trends are only slowly penetrating, though in this respect Newcastle may be ahead of the neighbouring Potteries. The small size of the clerical and professional classes and the high proportion of manual workers connote a proletarian atmosphere, an impression strengthened by the relative lack of further education even among the 'higher' social groups. Yet though the manual workers may be fairly class-conscious and strong in numbers their lack of militancy may be partly explained by their involvement in house ownership.

7. The Wards

There are twelve wards in the Borough numbered impersonally one to twelve. In the Rural District there are eleven parishes, all of which are wards except for Audley, which is so large that it is divided into three wards—Audley, Halmerend and Bignall End. Some of the other ten parishes have such a small electorate that, for the purposes of our survey, we combined them. We put Balterley with Betley, Chorlton with Maer, Keele with Whitmore and Mucklestone with Tyrley. Thus in the Rural District we had nine survey areas or, as we shall call them, 'wards'.

(i) POPULATION OF THE WARDS

At the time of the 1931 Census the boundaries of the Borough wards were being changed as part of reconstruction of the Borough in 1932. At that date there was, as Table 13 shows, something near to parity of population between the wards. The great decrease of population in the central wards, largely owing to slum clearance, and the remarkable increase of population in the more peripheral wards, the result of new estates being built, have led to a marked disparity between ward and ward. For example, Wards 3 and 9, with 32·6 per cent of the Borough's population, are represented by only a sixth of the Councillors.

In the Rural District the situation is very different. It is the

SOCIO-ECONOMIC BACKGROUND

TABLE 13. POPULATION CHANGES IN THE BOROUGH WARDS FROM THE
1931, 1951 AND 1961 CENSUSES

Ward	1931	1951	Percentage increase or decrease 1931–51	1961	Percentage increase or decrease 1951–61
1	6,441	5,870	–8·9	4,819	–17·9
2	5,037	4,270	–15·2	3,679	–13·8
3	3,014	7,312	46·2	13,423	83·6
4	4,636	3,014	35·0	2,095	30·5
5	4,152	5,033	21·2	4,172	17·1
6	5,783	9,176	58·7	8,430	8·1
7	4,123	4,642	12·6	3,706	20·2
8	4,273	5,666	32·6	4,945	12·7
9	4,386	9,782	123·0	11,264	15·2
10	4,239	5,462	28·9	7,669	40·4
11	4,257	6,304	48·1	6,640	5·3
12	4,398	3,505	–20·3	4,846	38·3

wards nearest Newcastle and the Potteries that have increased
most in population: Keele with its University has contributed to
this. On the other hand, the places on the edge of the constituency, on the borders of Shropshire and Cheshire, have lost
some population during the last decade. In general the population movements in the Rural District have been less spectacular
than in the Borough. In some wards there has been a gradual
ageing and decline of the population and in others an influx of
'commuters' and some elderly retired people.

TABLE 14. POPULATION CHANGES IN THE RURAL DISTRICT WARDS
FROM THE 1931, 1951 AND 1961 CENSUSES

Ward	1931	1951	Percentage increase or decrease 1931–51	1961	Percentage increase or decrease 1951–61
Ashley	1,027	1,149	11·9	1,237	7·7
Audley	8,533	8,273	–3·1	8,018	–3·1
Balterley and Betley	916	833	–9·1	819	–1·7
Chorlton and Maer	886	1,140	28·7	1,032	–9·5
Keele and Whitmore	974	1,172	20·3	2,174	85·5
Madeley	2,823	2,844	0·7	3,444	21·1
Mucklestone and Tyrley	1,611	1,715	6·5	1,500	–12·5

SOCIO-ECONOMIC BACKGROUND

(ii) THE GEOGRAPHY OF VOTING

Maps 1–4 based on our survey after the 1959 General Election are self-explanatory; but one point of interest should be noted especially in relation to the later chapters on local politics.

It is clear that there is a great difference between the absolute and relative voting strengths of the parties at the ward level. For example, Ward 9 is a strong Labour ward, safely returning three local councillors and piling up the largest Labour vote in the constituency at the General Election. However, this does not prevent it from also presenting the Conservatives with the second largest bundle of votes from any ward. In contrast Ward 5, which in our later account emerges as the ward with the strongest Conservative Association, ranks fifth among the wards in terms of Conservative turn-out. Similarly on the Labour side Ward 6, in no sense a safe Labour municipal seat, has the second highest turn-out for Labour while Halmerend with the highest proportion of Labour voters is surpassed in numbers of Labour voters by twelve wards. Success in local politics is thus likely to be an indication of the relative strength of the parties; but not necessarily a guide for organizers at Parliamentary elections to where the largest blocks of party supporters reside.

(iii) PROFILE OF THE WARDS

Whether a ward has 'character' or not will depend, to a great extent, on its geographical and social cohesion. Wards will tend to lack cohesion when they are composed of more than one community or parts of several, or more than one estate housing very different types of people. In Newcastle constituency the Rural District wards are both more geographically distinct and more socially homogeneous; and they have clearly more autonomous personalities than the Borough wards.

Neither Ward 3 nor 5 is homogeneous though both are characterized by affluence, Conservatism and the most highly rated residential areas in Newcastle—the Westlands and the Brampton respectively. Ward 3 has 38 per cent of its inhabitants living in the Clayton council estate,[1] while Ward 5 in contrast

---

[1] See Appendix 3 for distribution of various factors by wards.

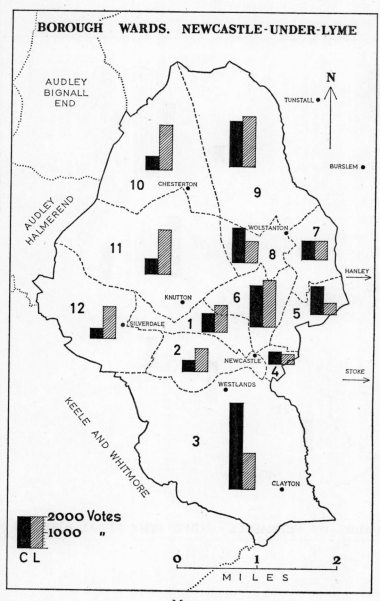

BOROUGH WARDS. NEWCASTLE-UNDER-LYME

AUDLEY
BIGNALL
END

TUNSTALL •

BURSLEM •

N

AUDLEY
HALMEREND

10   CHESTERTON •

9

WOLSTANTON •

11   KNUTTON •

8   7

HANLEY →

12   6   5

1

• SILVERDALE

2   NEWCASTLE •   STOKE →

4

• WESTLANDS

KEELE AND WHITMORE

3   CLAYTON •

2000 Votes
1000 "

C L

0   1   2
M I L E S

MAP 1

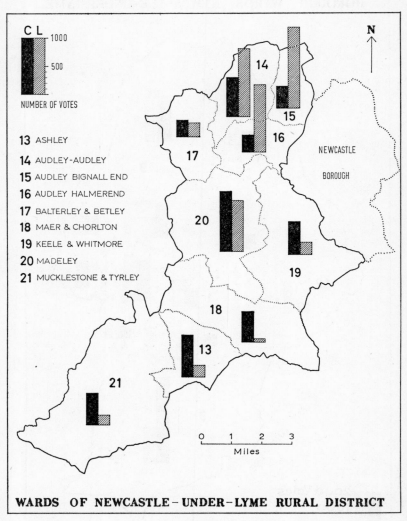

WARDS OF NEWCASTLE-UNDER-LYME RURAL DISTRICT

Map 2

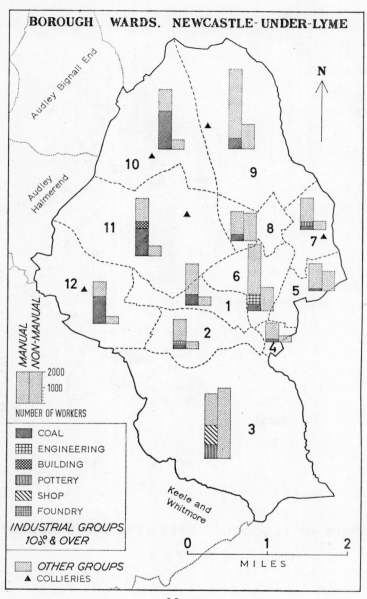

BOROUGH WARDS. NEWCASTLE-UNDER-LYME

Audley Bignall End

Audley Halmerend

N

MANUAL
NON-MANUAL

2000
1000

NUMBER OF WORKERS

COAL
ENGINEERING
BUILDING
POTTERY
SHOP
FOUNDRY

INDUSTRIAL GROUPS
10% & OVER

OTHER GROUPS
▲ COLLIERIES

Keele and
Whitmore

0   1   2

MILES

Map 3

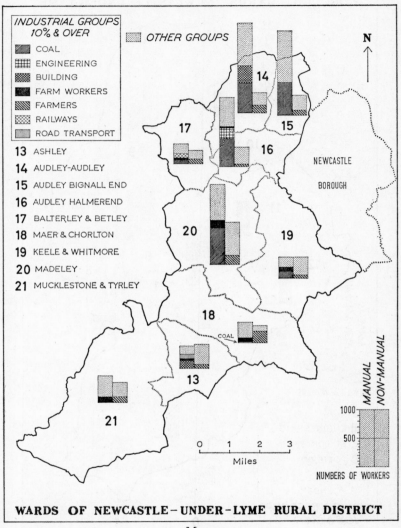

INDUSTRIAL GROUPS
10% & OVER

OTHER GROUPS

COAL
ENGINEERING
BUILDING
FARM WORKERS
FARMERS
RAILWAYS
ROAD TRANSPORT

13 ASHLEY
14 AUDLEY-AUDLEY
15 AUDLEY BIGNALL END
16 AUDLEY HALMEREND
17 BALTERLEY & BETLEY
18 MAER & CHORLTON
19 KEELE & WHITMORE
20 MADELEY
21 MUCKLESTONE & TYRLEY

N

NEWCASTLE

BOROUGH

COAL

MANUAL

NON-MANUAL

1000

500

NUMBERS OF WORKERS

0   1   2   3
Miles

WARDS OF NEWCASTLE−UNDER−LYME RURAL DISTRICT

MAP 4

has several streets of old working-class housing. Thus there was a difference between these two middle-class wards. Ward 3 had newer houses, younger people and a high ownership which extended to its manual workers of consumer durables. This was not the case in Ward 5 where the manual workers seemed older and poorer. The largest group among them was steel workers, a traditional local occupation; but in Ward 3 the shop assistants were the largest group. Thus Ward 5 gives an impression of social conservatism while Ward 3 seems to symbolize expanding prosperity.

Wards 1, 2, 4 and 6, all part of the pre-1932 Borough, one might describe as the 'central wards'. Their atmosphere of dilapidation, so characteristic of the districts behind the main streets of towns, has recently been palliated by some signs of 'urban renewal'.[1] Even so many of their houses are old and even the extensive council estates in Wards 1 and 2 date from the inter-war era. In these wards more than three-quarters of the people were manual workers and more than half were over fifty. In spite of these similarities, however, there was a strange variation in their politics. Ward 4, for long totally Independent, is now represented on the Council by three Liberals. Ward 6 has wavered between Labour and the Independents. Ward 1, which once elected a Communist, and which in 1961 returned a Liberal at a by-election, is now a Labour stronghold. Ward 2, also a safe Labour seat, has a reputation of being a Roman Catholic preserve, and in the late 1930's it was certainly represented by a Roman Catholic priest,[2] but only 12 per cent of its respondents were Catholics when our survey was conducted in 1959.

Wards 7, 8 and 9, the eastern part of the old Wolstanton Urban District, have little in common except geographical contiguity and the fact that, facing towards the Potteries rather than Newcastle, a large number of their inhabitants work outside the Borough. For example, in Ward 7 the largest occupational group was the pottery workers. In fact skilled workers were a high proportion of the manual workers in Ward 7 and many of them

---

[1] See W. M. Williams and D. T. Herbert, 'The Social Geography of Newcastle-under-Lyme', *North Staffordshire Journal of Field Studies*, Vol. 2, 1962, p. 108.

[2] *Evening Sentinel*, 19 March 1937.

owned their own houses. These factors, as we shall see in the next chapter, would lean its workers towards Conservatism and they may explain the classic marginality of the ward. Ward 9 differed from Ward 7 in every way, save for the high proportion of skilled workers. A much larger number of Ward 9's population lived in council houses and they were younger and possessed many more consumer durables. The largest occupational group, one-tenth of all respondents, was miners. Ward 9 regularly returns Labour councillors, but as Map 1 shows, it is not overwhelmingly Labour in its voting habits. Ward 8 is a good deal wealthier and more middle class. Only half its respondents are manual workers and not surprisingly the ward is strongly Conservative and elects three Independent councillors.

As in Wards 10, 11 and 12 over 40 per cent of the population are miners we shall refer to them as the 'mining wards'. Ward 12 is homogeneous, comprising most of the township of Silverdale; but Chesterton is divided between Wards 10 and 11 and part of Knutton is included in the latter. Though the pits and pit banks give these wards the familiarly grim look of mining communities, 40 per cent of their people live in post-war council houses. Ward 10 differs somewhat from the other two. Only 5 per cent of its respondents are over forty compared with 67 per cent and 57 per cent respectively in Wards 11 and 12; and this age difference is probably reflected in Ward 10's far higher ownership of consumer durables. But in these 'mining wards' this factor obviously has no bearing on political allegiance and in the post-war years all three have returned Labour men without fail.

In contrast the three wards of Audley Parish—Audley ward, Bignall End and Halmerend—are mining communities of a past age. Save for a few 'footrails' no coal is mined today in Audley, but the legacy of industrialization remains in the landscape and at Halmerend in the still-gaseous ruins of the Minnie Pit where in 1918 so many of the village's men lost their lives. Mining, however, is still the most common occupation employing 31 per cent at Halmerend, 28 per cent in Bignall End and 25 per cent in Audley ward, all lower proportions than in the 'mining wards'. The character of these wards is predominantly working class though Audley ward differs from the other two in having fewer manual workers, more ownership of consumer durables and younger people. The contrast is also apparent in relation to the two outstanding characteristics of Audley Parish—Nonconformity in religion and a high degree of house ownership. Audley ward is less Nonconformist than either Bignall End or Halmerend, the latter being the only ward in the constituency where Nonconformists are both more numerous than Anglicans and more significantly disposed to favour the Labour Party with their votes. In spite of its relative affluence and Conservatism, Audley ward also had considerably fewer owner-occupiers, 43 per cent as against 69 per cent in Bignall End and 73 per cent in Halmerend. This strange combination of working-class proprietorship and Nonconformity in rather remote small communities may well have occasioned the sort of politics we later describe in Chapter 16.

On the fringe of the coalfield the wards are less Labour than Audley, but more Labour than the 'rural parishes'. The villages are part industrial, part agricultural and part residential. At Balterley and Betley, nearer to Crewe than Newcastle, farming, working on the railway and mining were, in that order, the three most common occupations; but 41 per cent of the respondents were non-manual workers. At Madeley the industrial influence may be declining for both the pit and the railway are now closed. Here 29 per cent were employed in mining compared with 13 per cent on farms and 6 per cent on the railway. At Keele, nearer Silverdale, nearly a third of respondents were miners. Perhaps the complicated social structure of these parishes is reflected in the variety of the local politics. While Balterley and Keele usually return unopposed Independents, Betley, with a reputation for contested elections with high polls, was represented for many years until his death in 1962 by a Labour councillor who depended on a large personal following. Finally Madeley throughout the 1950's consistently elected three Labour men and one Independent.

The six 'rural parishes'—Ashley, Whitmore, Chorlton, Maer, Mucklestone and Tyrley—are predominantly Conservative and usually return Independents unopposed to the Newcastle Rural District Council. They are all, to a greater or lesser extent, characterized by a division between the older, indigenous manual workers and the more recently arrived non-manual workers who 'commute' every day to the Potteries. Ashley is the one large village and it is distinguished by a vigorous community life. It is different also in that only 12 per cent of its inhabitants are engaged in farming: the largest occupational group is the 17 per cent employed in the building trade and 10 per cent are lorry drivers. Whitmore, Chorlton and Maer are so rich in wealthy 'commuters' that they might be considered together as a sort of 'stockbroker' belt for North Staffordshire. Farming, however, is their largest occupational group. Thus these three parishes combine the traditional Conservatism of the countryside with the business Conservatism of the town. This distinguishes them from Mucklestone and Tyrley where farming was even more predominant and where the 'commuters' were not so numerous. These two latter parishes had the lowest ranking in the constituency in their proportion of owner-occupiers and skilled workers. In spite of this they were more Conservative than Wards 3 and 5 in the Borough, an example of rural Conservatism, resting on strong working-class support, with little of the commercial Conservative element.

The main factor in determining the relative support for the political parties would appear to be the location of the coalfield. As one moves away from it there is a tendency for all groups to be less Labour and more Conservative; and where there is no contact with the coal industry, in the West of the Rural District, the nature of the wards seems to depend on the importance of farming and the amount of penetration of the countryside by urban people using it as a dormitory. In the South and East of the Borough, away from the coalfield and nearer the Potteries, there is again a tendency, among all groups, for Conservatism to increase.

8. Conclusion

The general impression of the constituency is thus one of industrial and economic backwardness alleviated in recent years by some change. While Stoke has retained its pattern of traditional industry, Newcastle, owing to the war and Government policy, has become less dependent on coal-mining and has developed a more diversified economic structure based partly on light engineering. And although a large proportion of Newcastle's labour force is employed in Stoke the other side of the coin is that many former Stoke people are resident in Newcastle. Aided by a vigorous housing programme in the last thirty years Newcastle has expanded at the expense of the Potteries.

The overall economic pattern in both industry and agriculture is still one of small-scale concerns; but change has overtaken both. The tenant farmer has almost disappeared and mechanization has largely displaced the farm labourer. In industry the locally owned and managed firms are scarcer than they were and those still operating are the smaller establishments. The largest firms have come under the control of international, national and nationalized bodies. Thus in agriculture and industry many local economic relationships have ended and there is a trend, though perhaps less marked than in other places, towards larger, more impersonal organizations.

The social reflection of this situation is that of a population relatively unskilled among whom further education, even among the better-off groups, is not very widespread. Professional and technical qualifications are less common than in general. However, the higher incidence of these factors among the younger age groups shows that change is taking place. Furthermore, though the population by these indications is necessarily poor it is also thrifty as the very high proportion of owner-occupiers testifies. On the newer estates, moreover, there is some evidence of a higher standard of consumption among the manual workers, especially the younger ones.

The expansion of Newcastle's population has been very uneven and consequently the disparity between the size of the electorate in different wards is very great. Thus a high proportion of votes for a party in a ward is not necessarily an indication of a large absolute vote for that party. Relatively speaking, however, the Labour vote is greater in the Northern and Northwestern wards of the constituency, while the Conservative vote is higher in the residential wards and rural parishes.

CHAPTER EIGHT

THE SOCIOLOGY OF THE VOTERS

S tudies of voting behaviour have helped to circumscribe the limits of the influence of 'class' on political allegiance in Britain. Conservative supporters may be preponderant in the upper strata and Labour supporters in the lower strata; a large minority exists in both groups, and it is particularly large in the working class, where the Conservative Party has always had a notable following. It seems therefore necessary to consider the influence of many other components of the social structure and voting studies have indeed shown that some of these components, such as sex, age, school-leaving age, religion, tended to diminish the influence of straight 'class' divisions in British politics. Admittedly, these factors are partly subjected in turn to the influence of prevailing class divisions; but it would seem equally difficult to sustain that these factors have no independent influence on voting behaviour.

We shall examine the possible influence of these factors in the case of Newcastle-under-Lyme. But it appeared interesting to try to consider also the influence of 'class' in somewhat greater detail and to try to ascertain in particular whether supporters of each party, within each class and especially within the working class, were distributed at random in relation to two factors which play an important part in the day-to-day life of individuals, their occupation and the community in which they live. Miners may be more prone to vote Labour than engineers, out of tradition, trade-union organization or any other cause; residents of working-class estates may be more prone to vote Labour, irrespective of their occupation, because of the psychological pressures exercised by the community. Clearly, the conclusions which we tentatively draw here are limited by the smallness of the groups

THE SOCIOLOGY OF THE VOTERS

which were reached in our sample. But it was felt that the investigation of voting behaviour in the constituency, based on twenty-one samples, could at least give some indication of the magnitude and direction of variations due to occupational or environmental influences.

1. The Sample Findings and the Swing

At the 1959 General Election, Labour won Newcastle with 55·6 per cent of the votes cast in a straight fight against the Conservatives. The swing was 1·2 per cent to the right on a turn-out of 84 per cent (an increase of 4 per cent compared to 1955). In the sample, there were some discrepancies from these percentages; they are analysed in an Appendix.[1] By far the largest discrepancy concerned the turn-out—93 per cent of the respondents said that they had voted, but 'real' abstention had been 16 per cent: this was to be expected, however, as the register was old while the sample includes only persons who were interviewed.

TABLE 1. PERCENTAGE 1959 VOTE AND 1955 VOTE

| | 1959 vote | | |
1955 vote	Conservative	Labour	Did not vote
Conservative	81	1·5	27
Labour	8	87·5	30
Did not vote	11	11	43
(among whom:			
too young)	(3·8)	(2·1)	(9)
	100	100	100
Percentage of sample	43·5	49·5	7

The swing—which was a little larger in the sample than at the Election (2·8 per cent instead of 1·2 per cent)—was found to be fairly uniformly spread from ward to ward: it varied from + 4 per cent to − 1 per cent in favour of the Conservatives, except in one ward, where the number of Labour supporters was very small. It was a genuine swing and not, as in Bristol North-east in 1955, an overall advantage obtained by the Conservatives as a result of a large number of cross-currents: 1·5 per cent of the

[1] See Appendix 4.

167

Labour voters of 1959 were Conservative voters of 1955, admittedly, but 8 per cent of the Conservative voters of 1959 were Labour voters of 1955. The groups of electors who fluctuated in that way were too small to be analysed from the point of view of their social characteristics, but there is no evidence suggesting that these floating voters were overwhelmingly to be found among certain sections.

2. Class and Voting

As in other surveys class was found to have a notable influence on voting behaviour in the Newcastle survey. As described in Chapter 7, broad groupings of occupations, based on modified versions of the five Census Classes, were adopted for this study. The respondents were thus divided into business proprietors, professional and managerial people, clerical workers, skilled manual workers and less-skilled manual workers. In 13 wards out of 16 where the association could be tested,[1] there was a significant association between classes (defined in this way) and voting at the 1959 General Election. For the whole of the sample, the party allegiance of each of these classes was distributed in the following way:

TABLE 2. PERCENTAGE CLASS AND 1959 GENERAL ELECTION VOTE

Party	Percentage business proprietors	Percentage professional and managerial	Percentage clerical workers	Percentage skilled manual	Percentage less-skilled manual	Total
	A	B	C	D	E	
Conservative	87	85	72	43	22	47
Labour	13	15	28	57	78	53
Percentage of sample in each group	9·0	10·5	8·4	37·3	32·1	97·3*

* The table excludes unemployed women without husbands (X), who were 2·7 per cent of the sample.

[1] In the other wards, the number of supporters of one of the parties was too small.

Business proprietors—who include farmers as well as shop-keepers and businessmen—were found to be overwhelmingly Conservative; so were people engaged in professional and managerial occupations; in both cases the ratio was over 5 to 1. Labour had more support among clerical workers, but the Conservatives still had a majority of over 2 to 1 in this group. Taken together, the three non-manual sections of the population voted Conservative at the rate of just over 4 to 1.

The voting patterns of manual workers were very different: they divided in the ratio of 2 to 1 in favour of the Labour Party, a slightly higher proportion than was found in some other areas. Indeed, the discrepancy with some parts of the country is even greater when skilled workers are distinguished from less-skilled workers. In Newcastle, 57 per cent of the first group voted Labour and 43 per cent Conservative, while 78 per cent of the second group voted Labour and 22 per cent Conservative. Judging from the 1959 Abrams survey, the 'upper manual working class' does not vote very differently from the 'solid working class' over the whole country (60 per cent voted Labour in the first category and 65 per cent in the second). In Newcastle, on the contrary, differences were larger. Some characteristics of the Newcastle electorate may account, as we shall see, for these variations.

3. Other Influences on Voting

It was to be expected that some general components of the social structure, such as sex, age, education, religion or home ownership, would have, in Newcastle as elsewhere, some influence on patterns of voting. But the analysis of this influence remains impaired because it is not generally possible to isolate each of these factors from the others and from the socio-economic background of the electors. Class has an indirect influence through other factors. This is for instance the case with school-leaving age: it is preposterous to try to find out whether school-leaving age has a direct influence on voting unless the sample is large and the class factor can be controlled. But the sample needs to be very large, as only a small proportion of the electorate leaves school after 16 or 17. The same difficulty arises, although in a somewhat more diffuse fashion, when the influence of sex, age or religion on voting is examined. Women are not engaged in hard manual jobs to the same extent as men. In Newcastle-under-Lyme at least, some working-class communities include a much larger proportion of Nonconformists than middle-class and lower-middle-class communities. Finally, as was pointed out in the Bristol surveys, members of the non-manual groups have—and even more so had—on average a longer life expectancy than members of the manual groups; and people do, in the course of their life, move up the social ladder to some, if often only to a limited, extent. In practice, it was found in the Newcastle survey that age and class were often associated: in six wards, there was a significant association between these two factors. The influence of age deserves to be analysed as the influence of the various components which have been mentioned, but it is difficult to test unless the survey is very large; yet, unless each factor is isolated, its real influence remains unknown.

Moreover, although class may thus increase indirectly the apparent influence of these components of the social structure on voting, this apparent influence itself remains much smaller than the influence of class. As we noted, there was a significant association between class and voting in 11 wards out of 16 where this question could be tested. But there were only four wards where the association between school-leaving age and voting was significant, and one where both the association between voting and religion and between voting and age was significant; the number of significant associations was only large—nine—in the case of the type of occupation of houses, rented or owned. These factors have all some influence on voting behaviour, but they seem to modify some of the details of the picture rather than alter the main lines of the design.

(i) SEX AND VOTING

As in other areas, women appeared to be slightly more Conservative than men in Newcastle-under-Lyme. Overall, nearly 47 per cent of the sample voted Conservative and just over 53 per cent Labour; but, among men, the Conservative vote dropped to 44 per cent, while it increased to 50 per cent among women. It seems thus that, if only women were voting, the constituency of Newcastle would become very marginal, although, as was mentioned earlier, the sample did overestimate the Conservative strength by about 2 per cent.

TABLE 3. PERCENTAGE SEX AND GENERAL ELECTION VOTE

	Party distribution within each sex		
	Percentage male	Percentage female	Percentage both
Conservative	44	50	47
Labour	56	50	53
	100	100	100

(ii) AGE AND VOTING

An overall table of the voting behaviour of respondents in different age groups shows some appreciable differences between very young and very old people, who appear more Conservative, on the one hand, and people between 25 and 50, who seem more Labour-inclined, on the other. Yet the detailed analysis of ward results does not show consistent trends: one ward table was found to be significant—and this only at the 10 per cent level. As the

TABLE 4. PERCENTAGE AGE AND 1959 GENERAL ELECTION VOTE

Party	21–24	25–29	30–39	40–49	50–59	60 and over	All ages
Conservative	57	44	44	43	49	53	47
Labour	43	56	56	57	51	47	53
Percentage of sample in each group	3	7	22	23	21	24	100

association between age and class was significant in six wards, the apparent tendency for older age groups to be more Conservative is probably the reflection of the class structure of the various age groups. At the other extreme of the scale, Conservatives were also rather more numerous among respondents under 25; the same tendency was observed over the whole country at the time of the General Election of 1959; but the numbers interviewed in Newcastle were too small for this association definitely to be ascertained. In fact, the influence of age on voting, as that of sex, appears to be much more limited than the influence of class.

(iii) SCHOOL-LEAVING AGE AND VOTING

There is an apparent overall association between school-leaving age and voting, but it is probably more difficult to analyse than the associations between voting and sex and voting and age. Among the best educated, the Conservatives have a clear lead: tables were not usually significant at ward level, but this was because numbers were usually too small to allow for a test to be conducted. Obviously, however, the strength of the Conservatives among these groups is connected with the strength of the Conservatives among the non-manual groups. The Conservatives were also found to be stronger than average at the opposite extreme of the scale, among respondents who left school at 12 or 13; this is probably in part the reflection of the connection which has already been mentioned between Conservatism and age, as only older people are likely to have left school at 13 and very old people are likely to have left school before 13.

TABLE 5. PERCENTAGE SCHOOL-LEAVING AGE AND 1959 GENERAL ELECTION VOTE

Party	Percentage left school at							All groups
	12 or under	13	14	15	16	17	18 or more	
Conservative	53	47	38	57	79	93	98	47
Labour	47	53	62	43	21	7	2	53
Percentage of sample in each group	3	22	57	7	6	3	2	100

However, as we also saw, this connection between age and voting is probably in turn influenced by the connection between voting and class, as the proportion of non-manual workers is above average in the older age groups. Admittedly, in a more general fashion, education is clearly part of the complex which helps to build the 'class structure' of the country; the connection between school-leaving age and class simply shows that the prospects of a managerial or professional career are very much greater among children who went through the grammar school and university system. Class has therefore to include education. But the measurement of the separate effect of education, within each class or alongside class, would require the use of much more refined instruments than those which straightforward comparisons between voting and school-leaving age can provide.

(iv) RELIGION AND VOTING

The influence of religion on voting also seems to be rather limited in Newcastle. Only Nonconformists (and more so the small number of electors who profess to be of no religion) diverge sizeably from the average and are more Labour-inclined; Roman Catholics, on the contrary, seem to be distributed between the parties in the same way as Anglicans.

TABLE 6. PERCENTAGE RELIGION AND 1959 GENERAL ELECTION VOTE

Party	Percentage Church of England	Percentage Roman Catholic	Percentage Nonconformists	No religion	All
Conservative	51	51	41	25	47
Labour	49	49	59	75	53
Percentage of sample in each group	65	8	26	1	100

As with school-leaving age, however, the precise impact of religion on voting behaviour cannot be adequately determined. The findings about Roman Catholics are tentative, as these constituted only 8 per cent of the sample; however, they appear to distribute their vote much more evenly between the parties than is often assumed locally, an assumption which probably comes from the belief that Roman Catholics have played a large part in the leadership of the Constituency Labour Party. But it is not possible to state firmly that Roman Catholicism plays, in Newcastle at least, a large part in the determination of voting patterns. In the case of Nonconformists, however, there is some evidence—backed by a significant association in two of the wards where they form a sizeable percentage of the population—that class and religion are somewhat intertwined. Overall, followers of the Church of England are probably somewhat more Conservative-inclined than Nonconformists, but they are also rather more middle class. If the impact of religion on voting exists in Newcastle-under-Lyme, it is far from being as large as it was shown to be in other areas where surveys have taken place; it is not decisive and could indeed be very small.

(v) OWNER-OCCUPATION AND VOTING

It is often said that owner-occupiers are more likely to vote Conservative than occupants of privately-rented houses or of council houses. Indeed, an examination of the Newcastle results seems at first to confirm this view. There was a significant association between voting and house ownership in nine of the wards: the number of significant tables was thus much larger than in the case of the four factors which have previously been analysed; only the association between class and vote was found to be more significant.

TABLE 7. PERCENTAGE TYPES OF HOUSE TENANCY AND 1959 GENERAL ELECTION VOTE

	Owner-occupiers	Tenants in private houses	Council house tenants	Overall
Conservative	65	43	27	47
Labour	36	57	73	53
Percentage of sample in each group	44	28	28	100

Yet it is not certain whether this association is, any more than the previous ones, a direct association between house ownership and voting. The link between class and house ownership is clear; a significant association appears in nine wards. The relationship between house ownership and voting may therefore be similar to the one which had been observed in the case of education, class and voting. House ownership is part of a syndrome: middle-class voters are more likely to own a house, in the same way as they are likely to have remained at school longer than manual working-class voters. Meanwhile, the detailed situation is complicated because, as has been mentioned in Chapter 7, some wards have practically no owner-occupied houses, while others have no council houses. The proportion of manual workers who live in owner-occupied houses varies considerably—as does of course the type of property which is owner-occupied. In the middle-class Ward 3, less than a quarter of the manual workers interviewed owned their house; in two of the three wards of Audley, over half the manual workers owned their house. Trends are therefore somewhat erratic. The measurement of the precise impact of house ownership would require more than the bare knowledge of the legal position of the tenant. The association between house ownership and voting behaviour is thus clearly not a simple one. The impact of ownership is at best that of one component among many other variables and it may often just be the sign of belonging to a class.

4. The Influence of Class and its Variations

(i) SELF-ASSIGNED CLASS

Education and house ownership are to a fairly large extent the reflection, or a component, of the class structure of the community. The same may even apply to the influence of other factors, such as the distribution of the votes between the sexes, among age groups or according to the religious denominations. There are, however, some variations within the class pattern itself. We have defined class according to the division of the population into five large occupational groupings. But subdivisions of these groupings may lead to variations; the assessment which individuals give of the broad grouping to which they feel associated can also introduce further differences.

Self-assigned class has often been analysed. In this survey, persons who were interviewed were asked to state whether they considered themselves to belong to the 'upper-middle' and 'middle class', to the 'lower-middle class', to the 'working class' or to 'no class'. Overall tables showed a marked association between this subjective assessment and voting and this association was indeed found significant in eight wards (Table 8).

The similarity between the spread of Conservative and Labour support in the subjective groupings and in the objective groupings shown in Table 1 is striking. In fact, the association between class groupings and subjective assessment is very marked at ward level: the tables were found to be significant in 12 cases out of 13 where the association could be tested.

TABLE 8. PERCENTAGE SELF-ASSIGNED CLASS AND 1959 GENERAL ELECTION VOTE

Party	'Upper-middle and middle'	'Lower-middle'	'Working'	'No class'	Overall
Conservative	79	61	33	51	47
Labour	21	39	67	49	53
Percentage of sample in each group	24	11	59	6	100

But self-assigned class is not an exact replica of the objective groupings. Overall, only 59 per cent of the respondents considered themselves as being members of the 'working class', while, by an objective assessment, 70 per cent of the sample belonged to the two groups of manual workers. Although subdivisions could not be tested at ward level, an overall table clearly indicates that the tendency to 'upgrade' themselves into the 'lower-middle class' or 'middle class' is greater among Conservative manual workers than among Labour manual workers.

TABLE 9. PERCENTAGE CLASS, SELF-ASSIGNED CLASS and 1959 GENERAL ELECTION VOTE

Party	Non-manual (A, B and C)		Manual (D and E)	
	Self-assessment: 'working class'	Other	Self-assessment: 'working class'	Other
Conservative	28	72	54	46
Labour	81	19	76	24

Figures in the non-manual categories, particularly among Labour voters, are purely indicative, as the proportion of respondents in this group is small (5 per cent). Moreover, Conservative voters in these groups include more members of the proprietorial and managerial classes, while Labour voters include more members of the clerical workers. But the differences occurring in the manual categories are based on a much larger proportion of the sample and clearly reflect a real distinction. Moreover, in three wards where the question could be tested, skilled manual workers did not show a significant tendency to upgrade themselves more into the 'lower-middle' or 'middle class' than less-skilled workers. As was shown in other studies, and indeed in other countries, 'right-wing' voters did seem to have in Newcastle a greater tendency to upgrade themselves than 'left-wing' voters.

However, this association between voting and self-assigned class is not a sufficiently sharp one to constitute more than a guide to differential voting behaviour within the class pattern. As will be shown later in this chapter, there are differences in the self-assigned class of Conservatives from one part of the constituency to the other and these differences are not entirely distributed at random. Moreover, over half the Conservative manual workers describe themselves as 'working class' and these respondents cannot therefore be distinguished from Labour voters by their self-assigned class: the subjective assessment thus constitutes only a limited complement to the general differences which emerge from the class groupings. Finally, the self-assigned class does not explain, it only indicates, that some respondents consider themselves as members of a certain class. Many workers vote Conservative; these workers have a tendency to consider themselves as members of the 'middle' or 'lower-middle class'. The two phenomena may be associated; one may even influence the other. But neither phenomenon can be considered as being an 'explanation' in itself; they both call for an 'explanation' on a different and 'objective' plane.

(ii) INDIVIDUAL OCCUPATIONS AND VOTE

Voting is broadly associated with certain class groupings. But these classes are composed of very different occupations and, indeed, the whole of these categories are to a considerable extent arbitrary. If the voting behaviour of persons engaged in each occupation could be analysed, the real characteristics of the influence of class on political support could be assessed much more precisely.

The main difficulty in such an analysis comes from the small size of many of the groups. A very large survey would be required if the voting behaviour of persons engaged in non-manual occupations were to be examined. The difficulty is not as great with all manual occupations, although, in Newcastle as in most urban areas, the range of working-class occupations is very wide. In this study, only miners constituted a sufficiently large group (18 per cent of the sample) to allow for firm conclusions;[1] most other manual occupations employed between 2 per cent and 4 per cent of the respondents, and no occupation employed more than 6 per cent. Skilled workers had therefore to be considered together with less-skilled workers in the general table and conclusions become thus in most cases purely indicative.

The occupations listed in Table 10 cover about 45 per cent of the whole sample, or about two-thirds of the manual workers who were interviewed; other manual occupations were represented by such small numbers that even an indicative table was clearly not justified. If the figures corresponding to the occupations listed in the table do have some representative value, they do seem to indicate that the spread of the Conservative vote throughout manual workers is far from being entirely even. The average of 34 per cent for the whole of the group seems to be the result of a fairly wide support, in most occupations, of about 40 to 45 per cent combined with a very small support, of perhaps even less than 20 per cent, among a few occupations.

Coal-mining is the main source of Labour's strength. The Labour share of the poll among miners is not only much higher than among manual workers in general (85 per cent instead of 66 per cent): it is higher even than among all less-skilled workers (78 per cent). While conclusions concerning builders or railwaymen remain very tentative, since these workers constitute a small part of the sample, the overwhelming strength of Labour among

---

[1] Even in the case of miners, tables were not significant at ward level.

miners seems to be derived more than partly from the fact—noted earlier—that Labour's share of the manual working class is greater in Newcastle than it is in the country as a whole.

TABLE 10. PERCENTAGE VOTING BEHAVIOUR BY INDUSTRIAL OCCUPATIONS

Party	Miners	Builders	Railway-men	Electricians	Rubber workers
Conservative	15	20	31	34	39
Labour	85	80	69	66	61
Percentage sample in each group	18	4	3	3	3

Party	Engineers	Pottery workers	Road transport	Steel and foundry workers	Average all manual workers
Conservative	40	43	43	46	34
Labour	60	57	57	54	66
Percentage sample in each group	6	3	4	3	69

Many of the occupational groups show, on the contrary, a tendency to divide more evenly between the two parties. Differences in the voting behaviour of manual workers in older and newer trades do not emerge from the examination of the occupations represented in Newcastle. Potters were not found to be more Labour-inclined than engineers and steel and foundry workers. This result may have occurred by chance. It may also be that the pottery trade is not a good example of an 'old' industry and that the 'newer' industries are not well represented. Yet, with the very notable exception of coal-mining and, perhaps, of building, the occupational groups which were found among Newcastle workers did not seem to lead to marked variations in voting behaviour.

(iii) VOTING PATTERNS AND ENVIRONMENT

Supporters of the Conservative and Labour parties are thus fairly well spread among most manual occupations. But another line of inquiry has yet to be pursued. Are manual workers—and indeed non-manual workers as well—influenced by the prevailing patterns of voting in the area in which they live? Can it be said that manual workers divide between the two parties in exactly the same proportions whether they live in middle-class, lower-middle-class or working-class districts? Or, if there are variations, are these variations distributed entirely at random?

Ward results did show considerable variations in the range of Conservative support within three broad groups of roughly equal size, the non-manual workers, the skilled workers and the less-skilled workers, as can be seen by Table 11.

TABLE 11. PERCENTAGE CONSERVATIVE MAXIMUM AND MINIMUM SUPPORT AT WARD LEVEL IN THREE BROAD CLASSES*

	A, B and C Non-manual	D Skilled	E Less-skilled
Maxima	97–94	80–66	57–44
Minima	60–55	21–10	8–0
Average	82	43	23

* Ward 18 is excluded, as the Labour vote in that ward was very small.

These variations were not random ones, however, and two fairly clear patterns did emerge, at least in the two manual workers' groups (the Conservative support was overwhelming among non-manual workers in some wards and definite conclusions seem precluded). Firstly, except in one ward (Madeley) the Conservative received a greater share of the skilled workers' vote than of the less-skilled workers' vote, both in the wards and on average for the constituency. Secondly, in two-thirds of the wards, the share of the Conservative vote in *both* groups was simultaneously either above or below the average for the group in the constituency. Only in seven wards (Chorlton and Maer with very few Labour voters was excluded) did the Conservative Party receive more support than average in one group of manual workers while receiving less support than average in the other group of manual workers.

The case of these seven wards deserves closer examination. Wards can be divided into three groups: some are middle class (residential and farming), others are solidly working class and the rest are mixed, either because they include a balanced sample of various occupational categories or because they are made of two well-defined sections which are geographically contiguous but have little in common socially: Ward 1 has small businesses in its eastern part and slum properties and a mining community in its western part; Betley and Madeley have farmers as well as miners and railwaymen.

The homogeneous or mixed character of a ward seems to have a definite influence on the way the Conservative strength among industrial workers is distributed on each side of the average. In almost all the wards where a social group is dominant, the percentage of the Conservative vote in both categories of industrial workers fluctuates on the same side of the average; conversely, in almost all the wards which are socially mixed, the percentage of the Conservative vote in the two categories is on two different sides of the average or very near the average in one category and far from it in the other.

TABLE 12. FLUCTUATIONS OF THE CONSERVATIVE SHARE OF THE POLL
IN THE TWO CATEGORIES OF INDUSTRIAL WORKERS

A. Wards where both groups fluctuated on the same side of the average in both groups:

Conservative share in both groups:

	Under average	Average	Above average
1. Clearly defined social units	10, 11, 12 Three Audley wards		3, 5 Ashley, Chorlton and Maer, Mucklestone and Tyrley
2. Socially mixed units	4	6	

B. Wards where both groups do not fluctuate on the same side of the average in both groups:

	Above average in one group Under average in the other	Above or under average in a group. Average in the other
1. Clearly defined social units	—	2 Keele and Whitmore
2. Socially mixed units	1, 7 Balterley and Betley, Madeley	8, 9

One can pursue the investigation further and consider the wards which constitute clearly defined social units more in detail. Table 12 lists the wards where the Conservatives are under average (and Labour is above average) and the wards where the Conservatives are above average (and Labour is under average). In the first group, one finds the three 'mining wards' of the Borough and the three wards of Audley; there is also the small central Ward 4 in the Borough. In the second group, one finds the two middle-class wards of the Borough (3 and 5) and three parishes of the Rural District which are mainly inhabited by farmers and commuters from the Potteries. A distinct pattern emerges: in a working-class area, such as the mining areas of the northwest of the Borough or in Audley, the *proportion* of industrial workers who vote Labour is above the average for the whole constituency; conversely, in residential and farming areas, the *proportion* of the industrial workers who vote Conservative is above the average for the whole constituency. In mixed wards, where one group tends to be above the average and the other under the average, voting patterns seem to fall between those of solid middle-class areas and those of solid working-class areas: indeed, in one case (Ward 6) both groups of industrial workers divide between the two parties exactly as the whole constituency does. Although such a tendency would have to be sustained by similar findings in other constituencies, it does seem that the type of district influences to some extent the voting patterns of industrial workers in Britain.

It might perhaps appear that the importance of mining in the Newcastle constituency accounts for the Labour strength in some of the most solid working-class areas. We noted earlier that miners vote overwhelmingly Labour; it should not be surprising that districts which include many miners should show a greater proportion of Labour voters among industrial workers than other districts. This would not necessarily invalidate the fact that the environment plays a part in the determination of voting patterns: the strength of the Labour Party among miners might come to some extent from the fact that mining tends to be an occupation where workers are heavily concentrated in a few housing estates. This concentration might account for their loyalty to the Labour Party.

But the differential voting behaviour of manual workers and

even of respondents in other social categories living in solid working-class areas also appears in other ways. Firstly, as was pointed out in Chapter 7, there are many more miners in the Northwestern part of the Borough than in Audley: yet Labour does not share a higher proportion of the vote of manual workers in the mining wards of the Borough, except for one of the two industrial groups in Ward 10. Secondly, manual workers who are not miners seem to divide more favourably in favour of the Labour Party in the working-class wards than they do in other wards. Thirdly, a similar tendency can be found among non-manual workers. It is in Wards 10, 11 and 12 of the Borough and in the three Audley wards that the proportion of Conservatives among non-manual workers is at its lowest. Even if the respondents who belong to the professional and managerial class and to the business proprietors' groups are drawn from the lower strata of these social categories and earn less money than the members of these social categories who live, for instance, in the middle-class Wards 3 and 5, differences in voting patterns are still sufficiently marked to constitute an indication. It is only in these working-class wards that the proportion of Labour voters among non-manual workers is less than a trickle.

Environment does therefore seem to play a part in voting behaviour—although it has to be considered within the general framework of class. Environment also seems to affect the subjective assessment which voters give of their class. We noted earlier that Conservative manual workers had a greater propensity to assign themselves to the 'middle' or 'lower-middle' class than Labour manual workers. But at ward level, Conservative manual workers are more likely to assign themselves to the 'working class' in solid working-class wards and to the 'lower-middle class' and 'middle class' in middle-class areas. As there are some important exceptions, however, and as numbers are in general rather small, this trend would require further confirmation elsewhere.[1] Yet it seems reinforced by the more general tendency

[1] Above the average of 54 per cent of self-assessed 'working-class' Conservative manual workers: Wards 1, 2, 3, 4, 7, 10, 11, Ashley, Audley ward, Bignall End, Balterley and Betley, Chorlton and Maer, Madeley, Mucklestone and Tyrley. Under the average: Wards 5, 6, 8, 9, 12, Halmerend. Average: Keele and Whitmore.

among all Conservative voters in working-class wards to assign themselves to the 'working class': all the wards which have more Conservative self-assessed members of the 'working class' (in absolute numbers) than Conservative manual workers are working-class wards, while the wards which have less Conservative self-assessed members of the 'working class' than Conservative manual workers are predominantly middle-class wards.

TABLE 13. SELF-ASSIGNED CLASS AND MANUAL WORKERS AMONG
CONSERVATIVE RESPONDENTS

Wards where the numbers of self-assessed 'working-class' Conservatives:

• exceeds the number of Conservative manual workers	is equal to the number of Conservative manual workers	is lower than the number of Conservative manual workers
1, 4, Audley ward, Bignall End, Halmerend	2, 7, 10, 11, Ashley, Balterley and Betley, Chorlton and Maer, Keele and Whitmore, Madeley	3, 5, 6, 8, 9, 12, Mucklestone and Tyrley

Only one clearly defined working-class ward (12) was found to have fewer self-assessed 'working-class' Conservatives than there were Conservative manual workers. The farming districts, on the whole, occupy an intermediate position, which seems to come from the fact that, with only one exception (Keele and Whitmore) the respondents in the non-manual categories (many of whom were farmers) were not as prone to consider themselves as members of the 'middle class' as members of the same broad categories in many solid middle-class areas.

Although environment thus seems to influence voting behaviour, it is difficult to define more precisely this general influence. Various factors which might have been expected to play a part in shaping social attitudes in each district do not appear to be connected with voting behaviour. There are not more members of clubs in well-defined social units than in more mixed areas; in this respect the difference between middle-class and working-class areas is as great as is the difference between mixed areas and homogeneous districts. The length of residence in a particular area does not seem to contribute to create the 'climate' of that area: the wards which have a high proportion of long-term residents do not include all the working-class areas, as large sections of the mining community live in fairly recent Corporation estates, particularly in the Borough. Admittedly, the feeling of community could have been transplanted from the older working-class estates to the new Corporation estates; there is no way of proving such a hypothesis, however, and, in general, tables which aimed at examining the influence of length of residence on voting behaviour were found to be not significant. The political allegiance of friends does not seem to play any material part in voting behaviour either; there is perhaps some difference between the political allegiance of friends of Conservative and Labour voters over the whole constituency, but the political allegiance of friends of respondents of either party in their strongholds or in the more marginal areas does not seem to show any pattern.

Such an inquiry suggests therefore that there is something deeper and also more subtle than just an objective criterion such as the length of residence or the political allegiance of friends in the determination of the influence of the environment on voting behaviour. It may appear to be to some extent side-tracking the issue to say that tradition is probably responsible for the permanent strength of a political party in a particular area. Traditions have to be explained, especially if one remembers that the traditions to which one refers in electoral sociology date back to one or two generations only. But a relatively long period of time needs to be investigated; and yet the instrument with which one analyses voting patterns, the survey, is by nature incapable of giving to the political scientist more than the means of investigating a few years of the political history of respondents and of the community.

The analysis of the influence of the environment on voting behaviour perhaps also throws some light on the structure of the political parties. We know that, except for brief intervals, political parties have not been organized on a 'modern' pattern in Newcastle-under-Lyme; this situation can be explained to some extent by historical accidents; but it is also accounted for by the characteristics of the social structure and of the geographical structure. Homogeneous communities seem to put pressures on

THE SOCIOLOGY OF THE VOTERS

voters, irrespective of the action of political agents and Parliamentary candidates. If it is true that, as it seems in Newcastle, areas which are socially diverse are under less pressure to conform politically and if the voters are more likely to divide around the average for their groups or to some extent at random, one understands why other constituency parties may feel a need for organization which Newcastle political parties did not generally feel in the past.

CHAPTER NINE

HOW INTERESTED ARE THE VOTERS IN POLITICS?

Before we examine some of the opinions of the Newcastle respondents at the time of the 1959 General Election, it is perhaps useful to attempt to assess the degree of interest which they displayed in political matters. Moreover, in an election such as that of 1959, interest in politics was apparently affected by the widespread use of the mass-media and in particular by television. If interest can be assessed, one may be able to measure the 'temperature' of the electorate and to describe the influences which raise or lower this temperature.

But such a measurement can be obtained only through using 'subjective' criteria. Objective tests are precluded because they lead only to separating relatively small groups of electors at both extremes of the scale. At one end, a small percentage of electors are party members—the percentage was indeed smaller in Newcastle than elsewhere, as we saw; about 9 per cent of the Newcastle respondents stated that they had attended political meetings: this proportion, though small, is in no way untypical. At the other end of the scale, 7 per cent of the respondents claimed to have abstained at the General Election and 16 per cent of the registered electors did abstain. An analysis of local elections may help to distinguish between broad categories of voters: the question will be discussed in Chapter 12; but General Election abstention is a relatively rare phenomenon. Three-quarters of the electors both vote and do not seem to participate otherwise in political activities. If political interest is to be measured, the scale will have to allow for distinctions within this large group, and such a scale has to be based on subjective and somewhat imprecise criteria.

Three questions were thus used in this study to assess the political interest of the bulk of the electors. Firstly, respondents had been asked to state whether they had discussed politics outside the family at any time during the month preceding the election: one could assume that those who answered 'Yes' were somewhat more interested than those who answered 'No'. Secondly, respondents had been asked to state what were the politics of three of their friends: it could be considered that those who did not know were rather less politically interested than those who knew. Finally, interviewees were asked to state which issue had been, in their opinion, the most important at the General Election: those who did not know of any such issue could be described as less politically interested than those who could mention an issue.

Admittedly, respondents were likely to make factual mistakes which could not be discovered. They could be wrong about the politics of their friends; they might believe that they had discussed politics outside the family while in fact they had discussed only with relatives. It seemed none the less possible to accept the answers as they were given, since the aim was not to test knowledge of the accuracy of impressions, but the impressions themselves. If respondents did think that they had discussed politics or that they knew the politics of their friends, they thereby showed some political interest. Indeed, even if respondents answered with a straight lie—probably if they felt that they 'ought' to have discussed politics or to know the politics of their friends—the kind of guilt which they were showing was also indicating a degree of (admittedly very passive) interest.

The possible impact of the mass-media introduced further and more serious difficulties. There was in the first place a theoretical problem: should newspaper-reading and television-viewing be considered as a purely passive activity? Should such an exposure be taken on the contrary as being a form of political interest, albeit very passive? Electors who do not read newspapers may not read them because they are not interested at all in the life of the community. Persons who had a television set and switched it off when the election programme came on the air could, in theory, be regarded as having very little interest in politics. However, the introduction of such a distinction would have created further difficulties, theoretical as well as practical. More-over, previous surveys had clearly indicated that viewing of television programmes was passive, as common experience also shows. An 'active' dislike for political matters is rarer than a very passive neutral attitude.

Even if the exposure to mass-media is taken to be purely passive, the measurement of the influence of television or news-papers is only possible if one can adequately compare the atti-tudes and knowledge of respondents who are not subjected to this exposure to the attitudes and knowledge of respondents who are subjected to it. It was hoped that by using three different criteria and by trying to assess the influence of the mass-media on each of them, one could distinguish to some extent the 'natural' in-clination of the interviewee for politics from the interest which was created as a result of the influence of the press or television. The use of three different criteria had also another aim: if respondents could be scaled in relation to these three criteria, it might be possible to subdivide the bulk of the electors into broad categories corresponding to different degrees of interest.

1. Scale of Political Interest

Table 1 shows how respondents divided on the questions designed to test their political interest and also gives the propor-tion of respondents who read a national daily newspaper and saw at least one television election programme.

TABLE 1. PERCENTAGE POLITICAL INTEREST AND EXPOSURE TO THE MASS-MEDIA

	Percentage 'Yes'	Percentage 'No'
Attended meetings	9	91
Discussed politics outside the family	39	61
Stated an issue	72	28
Knew the politics of their friends:		
1. Among those who had friends	81	19
2. Among all voters	70	30
Saw at least one television election programme	62	38
Read a national daily newspaper	81	19

These findings show a great similarity with comparable find-ings elsewhere. In Leeds, Dr. Trenaman found that 57 per cent of his sample had seen a television election programme:[1] they were 62 per cent in Newcastle. In Bristol in 1955, three-quarters of the respondents read a daily newspaper regularly:[2] in Newcastle, 81 per cent stated that they had read a newspaper *'yesterday'*. Moreover, also in Bristol in 1955, 42 per cent of the Conservative respondents and 41 per cent of the Labour respondents declared that they had discussed politics:[3] they were 39 per cent in Newcastle. Finally, the proportion of people who went to meetings seems to have consistently been, from one election to another, in the course of the 1950's, of about 6 to 10 per cent: it was found to be 9 per cent in Newcastle in 1959.

These figures vary only moderately from ward to ward and for two criteria of interest (discussions and knowledge of issues) variations seem erratic. More respondents appear to know the politics of their friends in urban than in rural areas, but the discrepancy is not large and the trend exists only in a majority of wards in each case. Differences between urban and rural areas are greater from the point of view of exposure to mass-media and attendance at meetings, but they are still not very marked: as might be expected, greater use is made of the traditional means of propaganda (meetings and newspapers) in the rural areas and of television in the urban areas. In the Rural District, more people went to meetings than in the Borough: the proportion exceeds 10 per cent everywhere in the Rural District except in the two areas of the extreme South of the constituency (Ashley and Mucklestone and Tyrley) where the number of meetings was in any case small and from which it was more difficult to go and attend meetings in the town. In the Borough, variations from ward to ward are erratic, although people living in the outlying areas attended less meetings than people living in the central wards. The proportion of newspaper readers is also larger in most of the rural wards (but not in two of the three Audley wards): in rural wards, readers always exceeded 85 per cent of the electors and in four wards they even constituted 92 per cent of the sample, while the average for the constituency was 81 per cent. The elec-

[1] J. Trenaman and D. M. McQuail, *Television and the Political Image* (1961), p. 81.
[2] R. S. Milne and H. C. Mackenzie, op. cit., p. 98.
[3] Ibid., from answers collated in Table 1, Chap. 10, p. 143.

torate is thus slightly, but only slightly, less 'modern' in the rural than in the urban wards.

Table 1 shows that there are more electors who know the politics of their friends and who know the issues at the Election than there are electors who discuss politics outside the family. It seems reasonable to assume that electors who knew the politics of their friends, mentioned a General Election issue and claimed to have discussed politics outside the family are more interested than those who gave negative answers to all three questions. But it is interesting to examine the intermediate cases. More specifically, if definite associations do exist between any two of these three criteria, it would appear that a kind of scale can be devised, with those who discussed politics at the top and those who only knew the politics of their friends at the bottom.

Such associations were found to exist, particularly between the question on discussions and the two other questions: the association was found to be significant in four wards, while in many other wards figures were too small to be tested. There was also a tendency for respondents who were able to mention the politics of their friends to be able to mention a General Election issue, but figures were too small to be tested in 17 out of the 21 wards and the trend was not sufficiently marked to be significant in the other four. The link between these criteria does exist, and a scale of political interest, however imperfect, does emerge from the answers to these three subjective questions (Table 2).

The electorate is thus not an altogether amorphous mass of equally unpolitical people. There are gradations and they can be measured to some extent. About a third of the respondents in the Newcastle survey were sufficiently 'active' to discuss politics occasionally. Only a small minority of these electors appeared unable to mention an issue at the General Election or to state the politics of a few of their friends.[1] Another and larger section, comprising perhaps two-fifths to half the electorate, does not discuss politics, but politics appears to be in their panorama. They are often sufficiently aware of political matters to mention a General Election issue or to know the politics of their friends and in many cases they can do both. But these electors are 'passive':

[1] Only a very small number of these respondents were unable *either* to state a General Election issue *or* to mention the politics of their friends.

they do not show enough interest to discuss and they only receive and register. Finally, at the bottom, just before those who refused to answer out of complete lack of interest in politics, about a tenth of the respondents did not show any apparent concern. They did not know the issues, they did not know the politics of their friends. They were the truly unpolitical.

TABLE 2. 'SCALE' OF POLITICAL INTEREST

1. Discussions outside the family and knowledge of issues:*

	Percentage all respondents	Percentage among those who discussed politics	Percentage among those who did not
Stated an issue	72	82	68
Did not state an issue	28	18	32

2. Discussions outside the family and knowledge of friends' politics:†

Knew the politics of their friends	81	88	75
Did not	19	12	25

3. Knowledge of friends' politics and ability to state an issue:‡

	Percentage among those who stated an issue	Percentage among those who did not
Knew the politics of their friends	81	83	68
Did not	19	17	32

* Ward 7 is excluded: the question was not asked in that ward.
† Wards 6 and 7 are excluded. The answers are taken among those who had friends only.
‡ Ward 3 is excluded. The answers are taken among those who had friends only.

2. Exposure to Mass-media

Political interest can be excited, and indeed perhaps created, by the mass-media. The question was analysed here in respect of two of these—newspapers and television. Tables were drawn in order to find whether newspaper readers and viewers of the

election programmes on television were more likely to have discussed politics, to mention an election issue or to know the politics
of their friends. These six sets of tables did not produce any significant associations, but, although in many wards tables could not
be tested because figures were too small, there seemed often to be
a tendency for television viewers to be more likely to mention an
issue, whether they had, incidentally, seen only one or seen several
programmes. On the contrary, newspaper reading did not seem
to have an influence on the interest shown for, or the knowledge
in, political matters. Those who read the *political* news may have
been better informed, but the wording of the question did not
allow for subdistinctions between types of newspaper readers.

The impact of television is therefore more apparent than that
of the newspapers. Yet even television seems to have had a somewhat limited impact: it affected knowledge, but it did not seem
to stimulate interest in other ways. Those who discussed politics
were found to be as numerous among the viewers of the television programmes as among the non-viewers. This broadly confirms the findings of the Leeds survey of 1959.[1] Television seems
to affect the receptivity to politics, but it does not seem to create
—or to create yet—as much interest as is sometimes thought.

3. Scale of Interest and Voting Behaviour

Political interest appears spread fairly evenly among supporters
of both political parties. Labour has a slight disadvantage, but,
as can be seen from Table 3, the discrepancy between the two
parties is not very large.

TABLE 3. PERCENTAGE POLITICAL INTEREST AND VOTE

	Conservative	Labour	Both parties
Attended meetings	5	12	9
Discussed politics outside the family	41	37	39
Mentioned a General Election issue	75	69	72
Knew the politics of their friends	83	80	81
Saw at least one television election programme	65	59	62
Read a newspaper	85	77	81

[1] J. Trenaman and D. M. McQuail, op. cit., p. 233.

Labour electors seem a little less interested and, except for attendance at meetings, slightly less exposed to politics than Conservative electors; indeed more Labour electors may have attended meetings in Newcastle simply because the constituency is predominantly, and in parts even overwhelmingly, Labour. Yet, overall, even though the Conservative electors seem to display a slightly greater interest than Labour electors—a fact which is underlined by significant associations in some wards[1]—the tendency is not very marked. The gradation from unpolitical electors to active party members follows roughly the same steps in both political parties.

4. Class and Political Interest

Class, as defined in this study by means of occupational categories, was found to affect the political interest of respondents. The extent of this association was not as large and as marked, admittedly, as for instance the association between class and voting: tables were found to produce significant associations only in three wards for each of the criteria of political interest, although the same trend appeared in the other wards. But, as it is, this association is at least as marked as the association between voting and some of the social factors which were examined in the previous chapter, such as age or religion. Moreover, this association between class and political interest deserves further examination since, as we said, the association between voting and these criteria is rather limited and does not seem to exist at all when voting behaviour is examined in relation to discussions outside the family. Two factors, party allegiance and discussions, are apparently related to a third, class, although they do not seem to be related to each other.

When tables associating class and the proportion of respondents who discuss politics are analysed at ward level, three of the five occupational categories of respondents seem to divide very erratically from ward to ward. The proportion of interviewees who discussed politics outside the family varies considerably on both sides of the constituency average among skilled workers,

[1] Two tables associating the knowledge of friends' politics and the General Election vote and three tables associating the knowledge of issues and the General Election vote were found to be significant.

less-skilled workers and business proprietors. But the two other groups, those of professional and managerial people and of clerical workers, seem more consistent and appear to discuss politics rather more than average, although, even among these groups, there are some exceptions at ward level. This is why the significant tables are found only in the wards where the proportion of respondents belonging to the professional, managerial and clerical classes is large and constitutes the bulk of the non-manual categories. As a result, significant associations are not found either in the strong working-class wards, where the non-manual groups are often too small or are mainly composed of business proprietors (usually shopkeepers) or in the rural wards, where the non-manual groups are partly composed of farmers. It is in the middle-class and some of the lower-middle-class wards of the Borough that the professional and clerical classes are large enough to outnumber the business proprietors' group among non-manual workers: it is precisely in these wards that significant associations between the class of respondents and the level of discussions are to be found, although the middle-class Ward 3 constitutes a major, but the only major, exception. In that ward, respondents belonging to the professional group seemed not to discuss politics more than business proprietors and skilled workers, while clerical workers discussed even less. But in all the other middle-class and lower-middle-class wards, professional people and clerical workers seem to differ from other social groups from the point of view of discussions, even where the discrepancy is not large enough to be significant.

Yet, despite the fact that class has an influence on discussions, there is no association between discussions and political allegiance. As class greatly influences political allegiance, the lack of apparent association between political allegiance and discussions requires further examination. Admittedly, the lack of association between political allegiance and the level of discussions could simply be due to the fact that the Conservatives take almost half the voters in the skilled workers' group, which is a far larger group than those of non-manual workers, and indeed also take almost a fourth of the voters in the less-skilled workers' group. Moreover, we saw that the influence of class on discussions was marked in the middle-class and lower-middle-class wards: it could be that 'environment' also plays its part in limiting the association between discussions and political allegiance. We noticed in the previous chapter that, the less working class a ward is, the greater the proportion of working-class voters who vote Conservative, while in mixed wards the proportions tend generally to come nearer the average for the whole constituency. The influence of class may therefore become more or less marked according to the direction in which environmental factors seem to operate.

It is therefore difficult to decide, on the basis of this study alone, whether the lack of a significant association between political allegiance and discussions outside the family, combined with significant association between class and discussions and class and political allegiance, firmly shows any specific characteristics of the Conservative and Labour voters. But differences are so large in three wards (5, 6 and 8), and more particularly in Ward 8, that they seem to point to a possible contrast between the political involvement or interest of Conservative manual workers. In these three wards, it is difficult to understand how the overall proportion of Conservative and Labour voters who discuss politics can be the same while the proportion of non-manual and manual workers who discuss politics is widely different, unless one admits that Conservative voters among manual workers discuss rather less than average and in particular less than Labour voters among manual workers.[1] This would seem to confirm the fairly common assertion that 'politicized' workers are more likely to be found among Labour voters than among Conservative voters. One should not exaggerate the difference between the level of political interest among manual workers on both sides: we noted earlier that the trends were not general in Newcastle. But there is an indication that Conserva-

[1] Figures are not so marked in Wards 5 and 6 as in Ward 8. In the latter ward the respondents who discuss and those who do not discuss are found almost evenly distributed among the two parties (18 to 21 for the Conservatives, 13 to 11 for Labour); yet among non-manual groups, those who discuss are in a two to one majority (22 to 9) and the Conservatives have an overwhelming majority (25 to 4). In the other two wards, Labour respondents tend to discuss a little more than manual workers, while the Conservatives take the overwhelming majority of the vote of the respondents in non-manual occupations, who also discuss much more than manual workers.

tive industrial workers are perhaps drawn from the 'less politically interested' section of the manual working class.

The other two criteria which were used here to test the political interest of the respondents do not allow similar conclusions to be drawn. As has already been said, there is some association, however small, between these criteria and political allegiance as well as an association between these criteria and class. But it is perhaps interesting to note the indirect effect which television seems to have on the knowledge of issues among voters and more specifically among Labour voters. Although Labour industrial workers may tend to discuss more, as we said, Labour voters are also at a slight disadvantage in respect to their exposure to the mass-media: they read less newspapers and saw less television election programmes. As there are associations both between class and the knowledge of issues and between political allegiance and the knowledge of issues and as we saw that television had the effect of spreading such a knowledge among the population, it seems reasonable to conclude that television has probably tended to reduce somewhat the gap between the classes and between the parties in this respect. Labour might thus have benefited more from the television election programmes than the Conservatives, at least in the restricted sense that more of its supporters became aware of the issues at stake than they would otherwise have done.

5. Other Social Factors

(i) SPREAD OF POLITICAL INTEREST AMONG THE SEXES

Most other social factors do not seem to have any marked influence on the level of political interest of the electors. Variations according to age and even education (given the very limited amount of information available in respect to the better-educated social groups) are small and certainly rather erratic. No difference emerges between the members of the various denominations or between regular churchgoers and more lukewarm church or chapel supporters. Results vary so much from ward to ward in respect of religion that a significant association appears in both directions: in one predominantly Church of England ward, the more devout are found more prone to discuss politics, while in one predominantly Nonconformist ward, the less devout are more prone to discuss. General conclusions are therefore out of the question.

The one factor which does seem to be significantly associated with political interest is sex. Women discuss politics rather less than men (in almost all the wards the tables are significant) and they are less aware than men of the issues of the General Election; they even seem to attend meetings rather less than men, although figures are too small to be more than indicative. Only on one criterion, the knowledge of friends' politics, is there no difference between the two sexes.

The fact that women differ from men on most accounts and not on the knowledge of the politics of their friends may not be entirely fortuitous. Admittedly, it may be that women have, on the whole, less opportunities to discuss politics outside the family, simply because they do not in fact see people outside their family as often as men do. But it must be remembered that this question covered the whole period of the election campaign: the proportion of women who did not have an opportunity to discuss politics outside their family must have been very small. It seems also difficult to sustain the view that women did not have the possibility to come to know the issues which were mentioned during the Election. Television helped to propagate that knowledge as we saw; tables do show that the proportion of men and women who watched the election programmes was broadly similar; there are variations from ward to ward, but they are erratic. It is in fact very likely that most television programmes were followed by husbands and wives together, although some women may have had to interrupt their viewing from time to time in order to do some of the housewives' chores.

It seems therefore more logical to conclude that the discrepancy between men and women on some of the criteria does indicate a difference in the degree of political interest of the two sexes, an assertion which is commonly made on the basis of casual impressions. If this is so, one must try to explain, however, why as many women as men knew the politics of their friends. As for class and political discussions, we encounter here three factors, two of which are associated with the third without being related to each other. Although it may be that the lack of association is accidental, and although the 'scale' of political interest which is being examined in this chapter is far from perfect, there is perhaps here an indication of the fact that the knowledge of the politics of friends constitutes the 'lowest' degree of political interest which can be displayed by respondents. It is indeed the knowledge which is the most widespread, since only 19 per cent of the respondents who had friends were unable to state their politics. The knowledge of politics of friends would thus be the most 'passive' of the three criteria; it would be part of the knowledge of friends, rather than part of politics. If this were so, it would not be inconsistent to find women both as aware as men of the politics of their friends and yet less aware than men of the issues at stake and less prepared to discuss politics outside the family. Women would have attitudes of spectators more than that of actors. They would appear to observe the political panorama in their neighbourhood, but would not seem as likely to participate in discussions or even to absorb the knowledge of issues which comes through newspapers, television or indeed discussions. This difference between the sexes may perhaps also to some extent account for the fact that the contrast between the supporters of both parties on questions of political interest was smaller than the association between class and political interest: Conservatives have more women supporters than Labour and, indeed, Labour might have more 'politicized' electors among manual workers partly because it has more men among its electors.

(ii) THE INFLUENCE OF CLUB MEMBERSHIP ON POLITICAL INTEREST

The membership of clubs also suggests that the knowledge of the politics of friends is of a somewhat different character from the knowledge of issues or the propensity to discuss politics. This is the only 'environmental' factor which appears to have a bearing on political interest: whether respondents have lived for a long time in the same area or whether they live in a council estate does not seem to affect the intensity of their political interest. There are no 'areas' of political interest as there appear to be areas of Labour or Conservative predominance. The interest displayed for politics seems to be a personal one, which might be influenced by class or sex, but not by the environment.

The membership of clubs and other associations seems associated with political interest, however. Overall, those who belong to associations, whatever the character of these associations, appear to be more politically interested than those who do not. Tables associating club membership with discussions outside the family were found to be significant in three wards. Although tables associating club membership with the knowledge of issues were found not to be significant; there was a trend, not large enough to be significant, appearing in many wards.

The interpretation of these findings bears some similarities to the interpretation of the findings concerning the political interest of the two sexes. Admittedly, as for men, it may be said that opportunities to discuss are greater among members of clubs than among voters who do not belong to clubs. But it is also true that people often become members of clubs because they choose to join them. Politics is one of the social activities and it is perhaps logical that socially active persons (relatively speaking) should be more politically aware, although it is of course impossible to say whether people become more interested in political matters because they have joined clubs or whether the sheer fact that they join clubs is in itself a sign of social interest which extends to political as well as to other social activities.

Moreover, as when political interest is being examined among the two sexes, the knowledge of politics of friends appears to be the same among club members as among non-club members. The impression is therefore reinforced that the knowledge of politics of friends is a criterion which denotes only a very passive level of political interest, while the other two criteria, discussions and the knowledge of issues, however affected they may be by the development of television, indicate a somewhat more active and personal degree of political interest. The randomness of the spread of the knowledge of friends' politics, whatever the group or the situation, contrasts with the greater apparent influence of certain social factors on the amount of discussions or the amount of knowledge of General Election issues.

Perhaps these differences between various categories of interested voters are exaggerated: the criteria which have been analysed here do not indicate—with the exception of that of attendance at political meetings—a very large degree of interest in absolute terms. One does not show a considerable amount of political participation if one discusses politics occasionally outside the family during the time of an election campaign. Yet there is none the less a scale. This scale makes it possible to divide the mass of the electors into a group which seems almost unconcerned and passive and a group which appears to belong somewhat to the 'political society'. At both extremes, there are very small groups which are very active—members of parties, electors who attend meetings—and small groups which are completely passive—respondents who do not even know the politics of their friends, in many cases electors who refuse to answer. The divisions which can be found within the broad mass of the electors correspond to some, although admittedly not to all, the divisions of the social structure. What is perhaps most striking is that this association does not have any marked effect on political allegiance. Political interest is distributed, broadly speaking, evenly between the two parties—despite the fact that the social differences which can be found among the electors of the two parties can be very large. This may at first seem normal; it can be argued that the parties would not have developed and become two large and fairly equal political and electoral machines if something like the same degree of political interest was not equally shared by both sides. Yet, with the marked difference in the class basis of the two parties, a sizeable discrepancy in the degree of political interest of their electors could equally have been expected. Whether this relatively even spread of political interest accounts, in the last resort, for the fairly even support of the two parties or whether, on the contrary, the fairly even strength of the two parties accounts for a fairly similar degree of interest among Conservative and Labour supporters is a problem which is unlikely to be answered without much further study.

CHAPTER TEN

THE OPINIONS OF THE VOTERS

1. Issues, Images and Comparative Political Attitudes

Election studies which have been undertaken in Britain have more and more emphasized the importance of the party image: often unconsciously, electors associate a political party with a number of general phrases, some of a stereotyped nature, such as 'the Labour Party stands for the working class' or 'the Labour Party is the party of nationalization'. On the other hand, election studies have also shown that individual election issues are a much poorer indication of party inclinations. Their importance as a record of the sort of problems which were discussed during the election campaign may remain, but they are no longer likely to be given much prominence as a guide towards understanding political behaviour. Whatever issues are at stake, only a small fraction of the electors switch their political allegiance because of these issues; many may disagree with the stand taken by the party which they support on a particular issue, but this fact seems to have little bearing on their actual voting behaviour. Analyses of the floating vote do not indicate that change can be directly linked to disagreements on issues. 'Floaters' have even been sometimes described as being less well-informed and less interested politically than other electors;[1] even if this is not the case, changes in party allegiance seem more motivated by alterations in personal living standards and in the environmental conditions of the floaters than by General Election issues: in Newcastle in 1959, the issues mentioned by floaters as being most important at the time of the General Election were scattered throughout the same range of problems as those which non-floaters chose to mention.

[1] See for instance in R. S. Milne and H. C. Mackenzie, op. cit., pp. 191–2.

The description of issues mentioned at the General Election does not therefore provide an 'explanation' of voting behaviour: it is not valueless, however. Election campaigns remain important, although their role is not as decisive as it is sometimes assumed to be. Party leaders and candidates spend much energy in developing certain themes: the examination of the issues which electors deemed most important is thus a means of testing the capability of the political parties to communicate with the people at large and it is a means of testing indirectly the influence of the mass-media.

Meanwhile, in order to examine the more permanent attitudes of the electors towards the parties, one has to turn to images, which are vague and yet more revealing. Paradoxically, images give a more adequate idea of the way in which the electors define the parties, although this 'definition' may perhaps vary in time and, indeed, in space as well. But even if these images vary, even if, as the authors of *Marginal Seat* suggest, new images gradually 'come through the gateway',[1] they have a prolonged life and a meaningful and almost permanent reality for the electors.

Party images also reveal other aspects of political attitudes, moreover. Firstly, they indicate how much consensus there is in a society. An elector who applies the same image to both parties reveals a low degree of partisanship at least on one point. If the same image is applied to both parties by many electors, the degree of consensus, at least on that question, appears rather large.[2] Secondly, electors can respond differently when presented with different types of images about the parties. Some images are concerned with 'policy' or long-term aims. Others are concerned with organization or leadership. Attitudes may differ about the same party when one passes from one type of image to the other.

If comparisons are to be made and if the degree of consensus is to be assessed, the same kind of questions have to be asked about both parties to all the respondents. In the Newcastle survey, interviewees were therefore presented with descriptions which they could apply, if they wished, to one, both, or neither of the

[1] R. S. Milne and H. C. Mackenzie, op. cit., p. 188.
[2] This approach has tended to be more commonly used in recent studies. See in particular J. Trenaman and D. M. McQuail, op. cit., Chap. 8, and M. Abrams and R. Rose, *Must Labour Lose?* (1960), Chap. 1.

political parties. One hoped to find whether some electors disliked both parties and seemed to display a kind of negative or 'Poujadist' attitude to politics. One hoped to find how partisan the electors were by analysing the proportion of electors who were prepared to see virtues in one party and the proportion of those who attributed qualities to both. Finally, one hoped to be able to see how discontented respondents were about their own party, not only because of its general aims, but also because it was inefficient or not very practical. The analysis of issues was aimed at finding the awareness of the respondents and the impact which the election campaign had on the public; the examination of images was aimed at considering the degree of identification between electors and the parties and the degree of consensus which existed on party matters among members of the general public.

2. The Electors and the Issues at the General Election

The question on issues was open-ended: interviewees were asked to state the issue which they thought had been the most important during the 1959 General Election campaign. Few respondents mentioned two issues and, as was already said in the previous chapter, over a quarter of the respondents did not mention any issue at all. The order in which these issues came to be placed in Newcastle widely differed from the order in which issues were mentioned in previous surveys and it differed to some extent from the order in which they were mentioned in Leeds in 1959;[1] but the results of both the 1959 surveys in Leeds and Newcastle are much more similar to each other than to those of any previous survey (Table 1).

By far the most important issue was old age pensions, which was mentioned by 30 per cent of the respondents. Nationalization came second with 18 per cent and the cost of living and prosperity third with 11 per cent. Foreign affairs and problems connected to external questions come much lower down the scale: only if all the issues concerned with peace, nuclear disarmament, etc., are taken together do they form a slightly larger group than the cost of living and prosperity issues.

[1] J. Trenaman and D. M. McQuail, op. cit., p. 174.

THE OPINIONS OF THE VOTERS

There are differences between the issues mentioned by the supporters of the Conservative and Labour parties. Indeed, old age pensions stand well above the other issues only because they were mentioned on the Labour side by over two-fifths of the respondents. Among Conservatives, their place was much more modest: they came after nationalization and were only slightly more popular than the cost of living and questions of prosperity. On the other hand, the relatively large importance attributed to nationalization by Conservatives is not surprising. As less than one Conservative respondent in four mentioned this issue, the anti-nationalization campaign launched by the party and some other organizations did not seem to have as much impact locally as might perhaps have been expected.

TABLE I. PERCENTAGE MOST IMPORTANT ISSUE AT THE GENERAL ELECTION

	Percentage Conservative voters	Percentage Labour voters	Percentage both
Old age pensions	16	43	30
Nationalization	23	13	18
Employment, unemployment	3	5	4
Cost of living, standard of living, prosperity, better pay	13	8	11
Tax and economic issues	6	3	5
Housing	1	2	1
Education	3	1	2
Colonies	—	1	1
Foreign policy	8	6	6
Peace	3	3	3
H Bomb, nuclear disarmament	5	5	5
Miscellaneous	19	10	14
	100	100	100

Dr. Trenaman concluded from the findings at Leeds that, despite the campaign launched by the Labour Party, the pensions issue did not reach the mass of the electorate either. The Newcastle findings seem to show on the contrary that this campaign had a greater effect than at Leeds. It is not directly known whether it was the Labour television campaign which brought the issue home to two-fifths of the Labour voters in Newcastle (as well as to 16 per cent of the Conservative voters); but, both in Newcastle and in Leeds, pensions were mentioned more often in 1959 than at previous elections. On the other hand, two other issues which Labour voters used to place very high, unemployment and peace, seemed to have lost their popularity, at least in Newcastle, despite the fact that the Labour candidate mentioned them frequently during his campaign. The peace issue appeared to have receded very markedly: only a tiny proportion of supporters of both parties mentioned it in Newcastle in 1959.

Issues are thus transient and influenced by the campaign. Moreover, the television campaign on an issue seems to have a greater impact on the categories of electors who are least interested in politics. Women, older people and manual workers were more prone to mention pensions. Older people were directly affected by the issue, admittedly; manual workers were also affected indirectly. But these groups are also those which have least interest in politics: if pensions were often mentioned because the issue was of immediate relevance to many respondents, it was probably selected also because it was in the news and had been often referred to in the television programmes and in the campaign in general.

3. The Electors and the Party Images

When images which electors have of their parties are being analysed, one aim is to try to discover whether these electors are strong supporters of their own party or how far they are choosing the lesser of two evils. This is another way of looking at the temperature of the electorate: in the previous chapter, the test was the interest in political matters; in this case, it is the degree of attachment to one of the parties.

Although, in order to discover this temperature, the comparative approach seems the most fruitful because it gives an idea of the partisanship of the electors, the method raises some difficulties, in particular because the same 'definition' cannot always easily fit both political parties. We noted earlier that some 'images' concern the efficiency of political parties and others their policy or their long-term aims. In the case of the latter, the descriptions which have to be used must not be so loaded with emotional content that they automatically refer to one political party rather than the other. This is why respondents were not

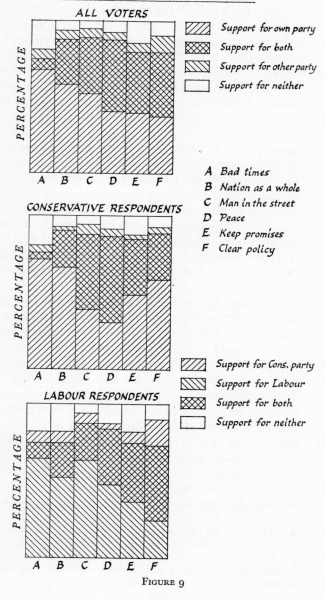

OPINIONS ABOUT THE PARTIES

ALL VOTERS

PERCENTAGE

A B C D E F

Support for own party
Support for both
Support for other party
Support for neither

A Bad times
B Nation as a whole
C Man in the street
D Peace
E Keep promises
F Clear policy

CONSERVATIVE RESPONDENTS

PERCENTAGE

A B C D E F

Support for Cons. party
Support for Labour
Support for both
Support for neither

LABOUR RESPONDENTS

PERCENTAGE

A B C D E F

FIGURE 9

asked in this survey whether one or both political parties appeared to them to 'stand for the working class'. Other descriptions seemed more appropriate, even if they were more likely to be applied to one party than to the other. Interviewees were asked to state whether they felt that either, both, or neither of the political parties 'stood for the nation as a whole' and 'stood to raise the standard of living of the man in the street'. In order to measure to some extent their partisanship in international affairs, they were also asked whether they felt that the parties stood 'for peace'.

These three questions concerned 'general aims'; two others were designed to assess how respondents viewed the relative efficiency and honesty of the parties. They were both presented in a negative way: interviewees were asked to state whether the parties 'did not keep their promises' and 'did not have a clear policy'. At a time when Labour was going through an internal crisis, it appeared interesting to examine whether the party was being censured because of a lack of 'clear policy' and whether it was censured to the same extent by the supporters of both parties.

Finally, a sixth and last question, in which interviewees were asked to state whether each party was the 'party to vote for when times are bad', aimed at measuring the extent of the support on which each party could count in the last resort and, conversely, the size of the potential floating vote. It was also designed to test whether there was a sizeable negative anti-party feeling among the respondents, as those who felt that neither party was the 'one to vote for when times are bad' would appear to have only a limited faith in the present structure and aims of the party system.[1] Finally, this question could also be used to check the overall meaningfulness of all the party image questions, as it seemed barely logical to answer that both parties were 'the party to vote for when times are bad'. If a large proportion of respondents had answered in that way, some doubt would have been cast

---

[1] Only this question could circumscribe the group of electors who were 'anti-party'. An answer 'neither' on the other questions might have meant that the respondents felt that on this particular question the parties did not satisfy them, although they might satisfy them on other questions and, indeed, in general.

on the comparative approach. In fact, the percentage of respondents who answered in that way was small (6 per cent), by far the smallest percentage in the category 'both' on all six questions.

(i) THE ATTACHMENT TO THE PARTY IN THE LAST RESORT

This question was primarily aimed at measuring the proportion of respondents who were attached to their party in the last resort; however 70 per cent of the voters selected the party for which they voted in 1959. But they were somewhat unevenly divided: Conservatives were rather more attached to their party than Labour voters. Only two-thirds of the latter against just under three-quarters of the former stated that they would vote for their party if times were bad. The proportion of respondents who, as already noted, rather strangely answered 'both' (6 per cent) was also divided unequally between the supporters of the two main parties: only 3 per cent of the Conservative respondents, but 8 per cent of the Labour respondents, answered in this way. In many cases this type of answer was probably a kind of polite refusal or a sign of lack of political interest. As this answer was more often given by Labour respondents, it is perhaps not surprising to note that it was also given more often by manual workers. More generally, voters less interested in politics had perhaps a greater propensity to answer that both parties were equally good out of general apathy and relative ignorance.

The last quarter of the respondents can be divided into two groups of very unequal size. Four-fifths of them (19 per cent of the sample) appeared to be anti-party. They did not find it possible to support either party in 'bad times', although they did vote at the 1959 General Election. Admittedly, for a proportion of these respondents, this answer may not have meant a profound disgruntlement about the parties in general, and may have indicated only a rather superficial outburst of 'Poujadist' feeling. Yet the impression that the answer 'neither' is a sign of anti-party feeling is reinforced by the fact that the proportion of those who rejected both parties is larger among abstainers than it is among voters. Interestingly enough, among voters, respondents who answered in this way divided almost equally between the two parties, Conservative voters being only very slightly more anti-party than Labour voters (20 and 18 per cent respectively). These respondents were also scattered at random among all social groups.

The rest of the respondents (6 per cent) singled out as 'the party to vote for when times are bad', not the party for which they voted in 1959, but the party for which they did not vote. These electors, a majority of whom were Labour (4 against 2 per cent), seemed to consider themselves as potential floating voters.

(ii) POLICY IMAGES AND THE TWO PARTIES

How did the electors consider their own party, or the other party, in relation to certain policy images? As was to be expected from previous surveys, Conservative and Labour voters alike did credit the Conservative Party for 'being for the nation as a whole' more than they credited it for 'raising the standard of living of the man in the street'. The situation is reversed for the Labour Party. However, the extent of this credit is not the same in the two parties. As Figure 9 shows, the credit given to the Conservative Party is almost the same on both questions, while the credit given to the Labour Party rises very steeply from the first to the second question. This characteristic obtains both among Conservative and Labour voters: in both cases, about 90 per cent of the Conservatives and slightly under a third of the Labour voters give credit to the Conservative Party; on the other hand, the credit given to Labour varies from just under three-quarters to almost 90 per cent among Labour voters and from a quarter to half among Conservative voters.

On balance, all Newcastle respondents thus agree about the fact that the Conservative Party is more 'for the nation as a whole' and that the Labour Party is more 'for the man in the street'. But this is true only in a relative fashion. In absolute terms, the Conservative Party is equally credited for being 'for the man in the street' and for being 'for the nation as a whole'. The Labour Party is not. It receives a lower credit on both sides when respondents are asked whether it is 'for the nation as a whole'. These answers seem to indicate a fairly high degree of consensus: the general objectives of the two parties are not seen in the light of 'dramatic' differences; they are seen in terms of pluses and minuses.[1]

The answers to the question on peace indicate yet another trend. Voters of both parties seem equally prepared to show their generosity about the other party, while they are not particularly anxious to be generous about their own party. The Conservatives credit the Labour Party with the highest mark of the three policy questions (60 per cent) and Labour voters credit the Conservative Party with the highest mark as well (38 per cent). At the same time, the credit which voters give to their own party is not the highest, but the second of the three marks. The gap may not be large and could well be accidental;[2] but it is interesting to note that far from there being unanimity among voters of one party in stating that *their* party is 'for peace', there are fewer respondents who say that their party is 'for peace' than either 'for the nation as a whole' or 'for the man in the street'. Perhaps this discrepancy occurred, however, because some respondents considered achievements as well as policy when they answered the question.

If all three questions are taken together, two main trends emerge: Conservative respondents are more likely to credit the Conservative Party than Labour voters are likely to credit the Labour Party; moreover, more Conservative voters tend to credit the Labour Party than Labour voters the Conservative Party. While the first two questions concerned aims of policy about which a cleavage of opinion was expected, the third question was

[1] One of the difficulties in interpreting these questions, as will be stated later, comes from the fact that Conservative voters seem less ready to refuse to give credit to their party than Labour voters are. Since, however, the credit given to the Conservative Party on both questions is stable among both Labour and Conservative voters, there seems to be a genuine consensus of opinion among respondents to say that Conservatives are 'for the man in the street'; a different answer might have been given if the emotionally-loaded expression 'for the working class' had been used instead of that of 'man in the street'. It is still interesting to note that a small proportion of Conservative voters have singled out the *Labour* Party as being 'for the man in the street'.

[2] On the Conservative side, 88 per cent, while the maximum is 92 per cent for the question of being 'for the nation as a whole'; on the Labour side, 85 per cent, while the maximum is 89 per cent for the question of being 'for the man in the street'.

expected to give a higher proportion of bi-partisan answers: this is indeed what happened, but not to an extent which would indicate a difference of kind between attitudes of respondents on that question and attitudes on the other two questions. On the contrary, the same characteristic attitudes of the voters of the two parties can be found from the answers to all three questions. Labour respondents are more partisan: on the question of peace, only a third of the Labour voters credit the Conservative Party; the proportion is even lower on the two other policy questions. Three-fifths of the Conservatives, on the other hand, are prepared to credit the Labour Party on the 'peace' question and half on the 'man in the street' question. This discrepancy comes perhaps from the attacks launched by the Labour Party against the Conservative Party since the war on the issue of peace; it might even have come from certain aspects of the Conservative policy itself.[1] But, as Labour voters appear more reluctant to concede virtues to the Conservative Party on questions concerned with party aims than Conservative voters to concede virtues to the Labour Party, the discrepancy seems more fundamental and indicates that more Labour electors than Conservative electors view the party conflict in terms of a conflict over general aims.

(iii) HOW COMPETENT ARE THE PARTIES?

The picture of Conservative voters almost generously inclined in favour of the Labour Party aims and of Labour voters reluctant to recognize the value of Conservative policy is reversed when one examines how respondents judge the efficiency and the competence of the parties. The difference is slight on one question: 39 per cent of the Conservatives give credit to Labour and 44 per cent of the Labour voters give credit to the Conservative Party for being able to 'keep their promises'. But it is very pronounced on the other question: nearly two-thirds of the Labour voters seem to think that the Conservative Party has a 'clear policy',

[1] It must be remembered that these Conservative voters who credit Labour on the issue of peace tend to credit also the Conservative Party. Those who support Labour but not their own party constitute a very small proportion of the sample (3 per cent).

while only one-third of the Conservative voters are prepared to say the same about the Labour Party.

The discontent which Labour voters show *vis-à-vis* their party is not large on either question but it exists: in both cases nearly three-quarters of Labour voters appear to be satisfied with their party, but a quarter of them seem to be somewhat disgruntled, while almost the same majorities of Conservative voters give credit to their party (86 and 89 per cent respectively) for the manner in which it conducts its affairs efficiently as on its general aims. The confidence which Labour voters have in their party does therefore tend to fall, if only to a limited extent, when one passes from the 'policy' matters to the practical presentation of the party's views.

This relative lack of confidence in the Labour Party expresses itself differently when one considers the answers to the two questions. Labour voters who do not think that their party 'keeps its promises' tend also to think that the Conservative Party does not keep them either: only 7 per cent of the Labour respondents single out their own party and not their opponents' party while 18 per cent are disappointed by both parties. There is much more specific discontent of the Labour Party when Labour voters are asked whether the parties have a 'clear policy': 16 per cent of them accuse the Labour Party alone and only 11 per cent accuse both parties. Indeed, on this question, Labour voters do not seem to credit their own party much more than they credit the Conservative Party: almost half the Labour voters are happy about both parties; one-ninth blame both. In the middle about two-fifths of the Labour respondents single out one party and blame the other: but over a third of these electors (16 per cent) find the Conservative policy clearer than that of their own party. The support enjoyed by the Conservative Party among Labour electors is thus almost equal to that which the Labour Party enjoys; this is the only question in which both parties stand almost equal in the eyes of Labour electors. Asked about which party keeps its promises, Labour voters who single out one of the parties single out their own party in the proportion of five to one; on the 'general aims' questions, they favour their party even more. But, when asked about which party has a 'clear policy', Labour voters are much less ready to praise their party and much more prone to credit the Conservatives.

THE OPINIONS OF THE VOTERS

(iv) PARTISAN AND NON-PARTISAN ATTITUDES

If one excepts the question which was aimed at testing the basic attachment of respondents to their own party ('which is the party to vote for when times are bad?'), the attitudes of the voters of both parties contrast rather sharply. 90 per cent of the Conservative voters are prepared, on all issues, whether of 'general aims' or of 'efficiency', to give credit to their party. Differences from one question to the other, on the Conservative side, are almost entirely about whether the Labour Party is given credit *as well* as the Conservative Party: Conservative voters rarely blame the Conservative Party, whether or not they associate the Labour Party with the blame.

Conservative voters vary much more in the judgments which they pass on the Labour Party. On the 'general aims' of that party, they mostly think that it is not 'for the nation as a whole', but half of them or more recognize that it is 'for the man in the street' and 'for peace'. The blame placed on the Labour Party is therefore the classic one, namely that it is not a 'national' party in the true sense of the word, that it contributes to the division of the nation. Moreover, Conservative voters are, on questions of party 'efficiency', inclined to be partisan: only about one-third of them are prepared to give credit to Labour on these questions. By stretching the point somewhat, one could almost say that, while Conservatives are perhaps prepared to credit the Labour Party as for some of its general aims, they base mainly their partisanship on patriotism and on a 'practical' appreciation of the way policies should be presented and implemented. The views expressed by the Conservative rank-and-file thus echo attitudes commonly held by Conservative leaders and Conservative thinkers, for whom the Conservative Party is the 'national' party and the party of realizations. Newcastle supporters appear to choose, or to claim that they choose, on that basis between the two parties.

Labour voters seem to have almost exactly the converse attitudes. They find it difficult to credit the Conservative Party for its 'general aims'. On all three questions about 'aims', more than twice as many Labour voters give credit to their party than give credit to the Conservative Party. Only on one question concerned with 'aims' ('which party is for the nation as a whole?') were Conservative voters found so highly partisan. This happens despite the fact that, on all three questions concerned with 'general aims', there are always as many Labour voters who single out the Conservative Party—as distinct from giving credit to both parties—as there are Conservative voters who single out the Labour Party, and, indeed, while on one of these questions ('which party for the nation as a whole?') there is a substantial number of Labour voters in this category.

The fact that there are more Labour voters who prefer their party on 'general aims' contrasts with the relatively smaller credit which Labour voters give to their party on competence and efficiency. The difference is discernible in two ways: in the first place, the extent to which Labour voters credit their own party tends to fall slightly although it remains relatively high; in the second place, the 'partisanship' of Labour voters, which was noted on the questions dealing with 'general aims', tends to fall even more sharply, particularly when respondents were asked if the parties had a 'clear policy'. Labour voters prefer the Labour Party for reasons which are on a different plane from the plane at which Conservative voters pass judgment on the parties. The latter express their partisanship with reference to the 'national' character of parties and with reference to their competence; Labour voters express their partisanship in terms of general aims. Conservative voters seem to judge parties on what they do; Labour voters, on the contrary, concede virtues to their opponents on the practical implementation of policy, not on aims. Here again, one finds a similarity between the attitudes of Labour respondents and the general pronouncements of Labour leaders and Labour thinkers. Whatever the party may do in fact, whatever its troubles and the difficulty it may have in presenting and even preparing its case, the main virtue of the Labour Party, in the eyes of both voters and leaders alike, lies in the 'general aims' of the party.

(v) ATTITUDES ABOUT PARTIES AND EXTERNAL INFLUENCES

These differences seem to be independent from the external influences, social or economic, which affect voting behaviour. Variations are erratic and random. Moreover, the mass-media do not seem to play much part in the building-up of the images which the respondents have of the two parties: there is no direct association between the viewing of the television programmes and the images which the respondents have of the parties. Those who saw the programmes of one party only—who are not very numerous—do not give answers which differ from those given by respondents who saw programmes of both parties, and those who did not see any of the programmes divide in the same way as those who saw some of them. Even the newspapers, to which respondents were exposed over a longer period, do not seem to affect party images in a discernible fashion. Labour respondents who read Conservative newspapers were not more prone to give credit to the Conservative Party on aims and were not more prone to blame the Labour Party on competence than Labour respondents who read Labour newspapers. Although there are wards where as many as two-thirds of the Labour respondents took a Conservative (or Conservative-inclined) newspaper, these wards, most of which are rural wards, do not appear to be inhabited by electors who have a different image of the political parties. Perhaps the changes arising out of newspaper-reading permeate gradually through the whole of the electorate and do not remain the preserve of those who read newspapers which, directly or indirectly, tend to put forward certain specific party images. But the influence of newspapers, in this respect as in others, is either very concealed or not very profound.

The same negative conclusion arises out of the consideration of the influences of friends supporting the other party. No definite association can be traced. The proportion of respondents who have friends with different political views varies from ward to ward; it seems to be linked to the character of the ward. In solid Conservative areas, Labour voters tend to have more friends in the Conservative Party, while in Labour areas, Conservative voters tend to have more friends in the Labour Party; on the whole, Conservative voters tend to have friends with a more mixed political view than Labour voters, but this may only be because the whole of the area is predominantly Labour (particularly if the Potteries are considered together with Newcastle).

The political attitudes of friends are ordered by geography, but they do not seem to affect the image which people have of their party and of their opponents' party. Attitudes *vis-à-vis* the parties probably change over a period of time, but, as Trenaman and McQuail pointed out, the personal element and the individual history of the electors seem more important than the mass-media, or even perhaps than the influence of friends.[1] Whatever influence is exercised in this way is so slow and so vague that it is difficult to analyse it with very simple and 'measurable' questions. Perhaps the very passivity of the electors towards politics even helps to prevent the spread of the influence of the mass-media and of friends. The slowness with which images move seems in any case to indicate that opinions on parties belong genuinely to individuals and constitute divisions within and across the parties which socio-economic factors either do not account for or only account for in an indirect and complex fashion.

4. Conclusion

The influences which help to form opinions are much less easy to circumscribe than the influences which are exercised on voting behaviour. Opinions are difficult to measure; they are slow to change; they show perhaps personal views and personal prejudices and they do not, as voting does, imply a social commitment. But, over an area such as the Newcastle constituency, they clearly indicate both the reality and the limits of the consensus which exists in British society. There is a community of thinking between the two main groups of electors. These groups are not clustered, entirely devoted to the defence of their own party and never ready to recognize any value in the party for which they do not vote. Yet supporters of each party seem to have, at the same time, a fairly well-defined political 'philosophy'. The left is more ideological and less prone to base its political allegiance on purely practical realizations: this is true of the electors, and not only of leaders, 'activists' or party members. The right may be, fundamentally, as ideologically committed; but it is less conscious of its ideology and it is more prepared to think in practical terms and in terms of the 'whole nation'. The two main parties are thus well-rooted in the community; their support is

[1] J. Trenaman and D. M. McQuail, op. cit., pp. 203 ff.

THE OPINIONS OF THE VOTERS

not only one of votes, but it is one of feeling and approach as
well. Whether this support is diminishing, elsewhere or in Newcastle, is clearly beyond the scope of this study. But it is still
sufficiently strong for the party system to be alive and real,
whereas the consensus is sufficiently large for the electors, as well
as the parties, to be prepared to coexist.

CHAPTER ELEVEN

LOCAL ELECTIONS IN NEWCASTLE

Interest in national politics is widespread and most electors are prepared to express opinions on the political parties and on General Election issues. In local politics, on the contrary, interest and knowledge are much less common; the turn-out is often only half what it is at General Elections and it is sometimes much lower. Even in fairly large authorities, uncontested returns are not rare and, in rural areas, they are still sometimes the norm. Patterns of participation at local elections and attitudes about local matters are therefore likely to show interesting contrasts with attitudes and participation at the level of national politics.

Before this participation and these attitudes are examined, however, the results of the local elections themselves need to be considered in some detail. They have not attracted much attention on the part of British political scientists; yet the characteristics of contest and turn-out in the various types of local elections are somewhat dissimilar. Although comparisons are often hampered by the number of uncontested returns, the examination of the results, carried over a relatively long period, does point to some consistent trends in the behaviour of the British public at local elections.

1. Contested and Uncontested Seats in Newcastle

Seats are often uncontested, even in the Borough. Indeed, the discrepancy between the Rural District and the Borough is not as large as the nature and the size of the authorities would perhaps have suggested. Just over half the seats have been contested in the Rural District and County Council elections since 1932; in the Municipal Borough, slightly over three-quarters of the seats have been contested.[1] As has been already said in previous chapters, the Rural District is only partly 'rural' and the more industrial parishes have provided a large number of contests; the Municipal Borough is composed of a large number of working-class areas where, in the post-war period, the support enjoyed by the Labour Party has been overwhelming.

In the Borough, parties seem to contest seats only in the wards where they appear to think that they have a reasonable chance of victory. Contests have normally been straight fights between the Labour Party and 'Independent' organizations which, under various names, have succeeded in avoiding a division of the 'anti-Socialist' camp.[2] In thirty years, there were only 19 three- or four-cornered contests in the 12 wards of the Borough, although there were a further 15 contests in which Labour did not oppose an 'Independent', but one of these last two was opposed to a third party or a candidate neither belonging to any party nor officially supported by the Independent organization.[3] However, even if these are taken into account, 83 per cent of the contests which took place in Newcastle opposed Labour to Independents, and candidates who were left unopposed always belonged to one of the major parties, with the exception of one Communist in the inter-war period.

The pattern of contested and uncontested seats reflects the marked increase in Labour's strength in the early post-war period. In the 1930's the Independents controlled three-quarters of the seats, but by the late 1950's Labour held five safe seats and one fairly safe seat while the Independents could count only on three safe seats and two fairly safe seats. Only one ward was very mar-

[1] Borough: 264 seats between 1933 and 1961: 203 contests, 61 uncontested returns.

Rural District: 174 seats between 1934 and 1961: 90 contests, 89 uncontested returns.

County: 63 seats between 1934 and 1961: 35 contests, 28 uncontested returns.

[2] See Chaps. 15 and 17.

[3] Communists contested nine seats over the whole period; their only successful candidate was elected before the war. Liberals started to contest seats in the late 1950's: see Chaps. 6 and 17. Conservative candidatures became more numerous in the late 1950's and early 1960's: see Chaps. 5 and 17.

ginal, but, even if the Independents won it, they were just at parity with Labour.[1]

TABLE I. UNCONTESTED SEATS AND SEATS WHERE A MAJOR PARTY WAS ABSENT FROM THE CONTEST

	1932–8	1945–9	1950–61	Total
Labour unopposed by Independent	7	0	33	40
Independent unopposed by Labour	24	0	12	36
	31	0	45	76

Although Labour and the Independents had almost the same aggregate number of uncontested seats, Labour won most of its uncontested victories since the Second World War and, indeed, since 1950. Before 1939, Labour often left unopposed some of the very solid working-class areas of the West and Northwest: Labour contested only 10 of the 18 seats in these wards between 1933 and 1938. After the war, Labour contested these wards and won them from the Independents. The Independents tried to recover them, and up to 1950 all the wards were contested by both parties; indeed, 8 of the 19 three-cornered and four-cornered fights took place during the period 1945–50. By 1950–1, however, the Independents seemed to abandon the hope of winning back the working-class wards of the Northwest, and ceased to contest them. Although, in 1961, the Conservatives fought local elections with more determination, two of the safe Labour and working-class wards (11 and 12) remained un-opposed.

In the Rural District, a similar evolution took place. Labour, always in a minority before 1939, gained control of the Council after the Second World War. The Independents remained un-challenged and victorious in the rural parts of the Rural District,[2] but in Audley, Betley, Keele and Madeley, once Labour secured

[1] Between 1933 and 1935 the parties' strength among councillors only was: Independents 27, Labour 8, and C.P. 1. Between 1958 and 1960 Labour had 21 seats and the Independents (with the Conservatives) 15.

[2] Ashley, Balterley, Chorlton, Maer, Mucklestone, Tyrley and Whitmore. Whitmore was contested twice, in 1928 and 1961, but in both cases by Independents.

a majority, the number of contests tended to diminish. In 1958, the only two contests which took place were at Ashley and at Betley. Moreover, the contests which took place in Audley during the 1950's were due mostly to 'Independent Labour' candidates, very often breakaway members of the Labour Party. In 1961, however, the Conservatives seemed more determined to oppose Labour[1] and contests may become more common in the 1960's than they were in the 1950's.

County Council contests also diminished in the 1950's. Before the war, although it contested 26 of the 35 elections which took place after 1932, Labour never came very near to winning a majority of the seven seats which the Newcastle area has on the council (five for the Borough, one for Audley and one for the rest of the Rural District). As at other elections, Labour made a considerable advance in 1946 and, after 1949, the Independents left two seats unopposed, while Labour also ceased to contest two of the Borough wards. In 1961, there was no contest in the Borough. Contests took place sporadically in the Rural District; in Audley, the County Council elections were often the battleground for the various factions of the Labour Party in the parish.

The year 1962 may be a turning-point: local elections may become more keenly contested and contested by more efficient machines.[2] But the 1950's were a period of stabilization during which both parties, and the Independents even more than Labour, seemed to have ceased to hope for any dramatic electoral changes. The fighting spirit of the parties and the interest of the electors can therefore be adequately tested only in a few marginal wards where elections took place more consistently.

2. The Turn-out. Does a Higher Turn-out Help the Left?

It is sometimes alleged by political leaders that a higher turn-out at local elections is more likely to help the left, as if right-wing electors comprised a larger group of permanently conscientious voters. While too few seats were contested in the Rural District for this hypothesis to be examined in that part of the constituency, it can be analysed in the Borough. As a rule, the turn-out has been around 40 per cent since 1932, except at by-elections where it often fell below 30 per cent, but it has fluctuated

[1] See Chap. 16.   [2] See Chap. 16.

from year to year and from ward to ward around that figure. Some movements are erratic, but a general picture of the evolution of the turn-out since 1945 does none the less emerge. There were two years of low turn-out just after the war (1945 and 1946) which were followed by a sharp increase in 1947 and 1949 (55 per cent for the whole of Newcastle).[1] Abstention rose steeply in 1950 (40 per cent voted) and, after a last increase in turn-out in 1952 to 46 per cent, the percentage of voters fell often under 40 per cent and never went above 41 per cent in the 1950's and early 1960's (it was 37 per cent in 1961).

The sharp increase in turn-out in the late 1940's appears linked with the sudden change in the party fortunes in Newcastle, which had, as we saw, the other consequence of increasing the number of contested seats. However, the increase in turn-out which took place in 1947 and was to continue in 1949 was not mainly owing to Labour electors; as in other parts of the country, it seems to have been the result essentially of the reawakening of the right and of the reorganization of the Conservative Party. Labour thus had fared much better in Newcastle—and nationally as well—on the two low turn-outs of 1945 and 1946 than it did on the high turn-outs of 1947 and 1949.

TABLE 2. PARTY VOTES AT NEWCASTLE BOROUGH ELECTIONS BETWEEN 1945 AND 1949

	1945	*1946*	*1947*	*1949*
Independents and allies	8,996	8,305	13,781	13,087*
Labour	12,004	9,852	13,225	12,991

* Plus 610 Independent Labour votes.

After 1947, Labour ceased to win a majority of the votes cast, the Independent vote having increased much more than the Labour vote. These results may conceal a genuine 'swing' to the Independents, but this swing was probably small. The Labour vote remained stable in many parts of the Borough, and in particular in the safe Labour wards as well as in the middle-class Ward 3 in the South, while the Independents had dramatic

[1] There were no municipal elections in 1948, as a result of the change of the date of local elections from November to May.

increases in many wards, particularly in their safest areas (Wards 3 and 5) and in some of the marginal areas, most of which are located in Wolstanton (Wards 6, 7, 8 and 9). The bulk of the increase in the right-wing vote seems therefore to have come from abstainers at previous elections: as these increases took place mainly in the safe Independent wards and in the marginal areas, they seem to have been connected with efforts made by the right to try to organize their vote and to reconquer some of the seats which they had lost.

An analysis of the results of the 1950's does not suggest either that a high turn-out tends to favour the left. Once the fighting spirit of the late 1940's receded, the Independent vote diminished proportionately as much as the Labour vote. Admittedly, Labour's victory in 1952 coincided in Newcastle—as in other parts of the country—with a fairly high poll. But, since 1953, results did not suggest that a high turn-out either favoured the left or, as in 1947 and 1949, favoured the right. There seems to be a kind of general 'consensus' among electors. In exceptional cases, supporters of one party abstain in greater numbers, apparently as a result of opposition to the government of the day (1952 and, possibly, 1946). In most cases, however, feelings of national protest do not seem to enter the preoccupations of electors when they vote at local elections, and the percentage of abstainers of each party seems to remain very similar.[1]

3. Is Abstention Larger in Safe Seats?

The answer to this question can only be tentative in Newcastle, as many safe seats were not contested over long periods. However, the analysis of the post-war period shows that, with only one exception, seats which changed hands do not have higher turn-outs than safe seats. Variations in turn-out from ward to ward are often very marked, but they are also often erratic. In the four wards which changed hands at least once since 1945 (see Figure 10), the turn-out has normally been between 2·5 per cent higher and 3 per cent lower than in the Borough as a whole; in one case, in 1956, it was 11·5 per cent higher; in two cases, in

---

[1] See Chap. 12, p. 229, for an analysis of the characteristics of local election abstainers.

1950 and 1959, it was 6 per cent lower. In the period 1949–60 the turn-out was six times above the average and five times below.

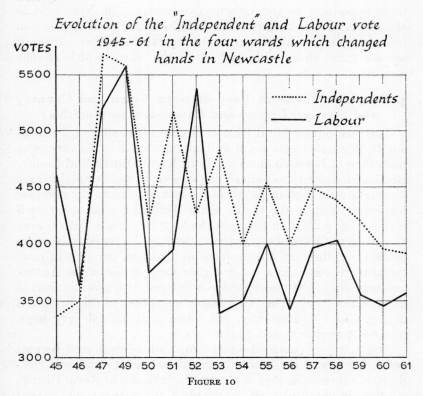

Evolution of the "Independent" and Labour vote 1945–61 in the four wards which changed hands in Newcastle

FIGURE 10

The one exception is constituted by the very marginal Ward 7 since 1957. Labour retained this ward by a majority of 22 in 1960 and lost it to the Conservatives by a majority of 12 in the following year. Up to 1956, the turn-out in the ward had been similar to the average turn-out in the Borough and had remained in the neighbourhood of 40 per cent. Since 1957, on the contrary, it has always been above 50 per cent. Both parties have taken great interest in the fate of the ward; the Independent and later the Conservative organization became efficient. The result was a 50 per cent poll. But even this percentage is lower than the overall percentage for the whole Borough in 1947 and 1949, when the Conservative organization was at its peak and when many electors were probably using their local election vote to manifest their opposition to the Labour Government, in Newcastle as elsewhere. Given a better organization, marginal wards can probably have a higher turn-out, but these higher turn-outs are far from always achieved in all the wards which change hands.

4. Does the Turn-out Vary between Town and Country and between Upper- and Lower-tier Authorities?

The turn-out in Rural District elections is similar to the turn-out in Borough elections; it is distinctly lower at County elections than at Borough elections. Both Rural District and County elections followed the pattern of elections in the Borough: there were relatively high turn-outs in the late 1940's and the decrease was often sharp in the 1950's. Rural District elections attracted even higher polls than Borough elections in the late 1940's: over 60 per cent of the electors voted in three of the parishes in 1949. Since 1952, the turn-out dropped to about 35 per cent in most cases; there was even a much higher drop in one of the Audley wards in 1955, but the contest was between two rival factions of the Labour Party. The one notable exception to this decline is Betley, where, consistently, the turn-out remained very high, between 70 per cent and 75 per cent.

At County elections, the turn-out, both in peak and bottom years, is lower in the Borough area than it is at municipal elections, but it remains very similar to the turn-out at Rural District elections in the rural areas. In the town, the peak was 38 per cent in one ward in 1949; it remained between 20 per cent and 34 per cent at the following elections. In the Rural District, the peak was 66 per cent in 1949 and the percentage poll never fell under 38 per cent. Some County Council contests in the Rural District area have been very heated, much more heated than County Council contests in the Borough areas: this accounts perhaps for the fact that the percentage poll never fell as much in the Rural District area as in the town. But Rural District electors are perhaps also more aware of the role of the County Council than electors in the Borough, as Borough electors are more likely to be screened from the County by the larger part played by the Borough in local government.

As for municipal elections, differences in turn-out between County and municipal elections do not appear to have a permanent effect on the fate of the parties. Results at County elections and at municipal elections are difficult to compare as uncontested returns are common. However, in the twelve cases where comparisons can be made over the period 1932–61, Labour and Independents shared equally the benefit of the lower turn-out at the County elections. There is perhaps a very slight tendency for Independents to fare better at County elections when the turn-out is very low, as in three occasions before 1949 and in one case in 1952. But such an advantage did not occur after 1952 and it may have been accidental. On the whole, the differential abstention between municipal and County elections seems to be shared equally between the two parties as is the differential abstention between General and municipal elections.

The analysis of local elections at County, Borough and Rural District levels thus seems to show that abstainers are fairly evenly spread between the electors of the two parties. There are variations in some cases; as in the late forties, one party sometimes benefits from an increased turn-out: in such cases, the advantage enjoyed by one party seems to be the consequence of a sudden increase in the level of the *national* interest in politics. When this occurs, all the local authorities concerned are affected and the advantage which one party temporarily enjoys from a higher turn-out is projected in equal proportions throughout the whole range of local elections. Such periods are none the less exceptional. During the whole of the 1950's, local elections in Newcastle have tended to reflect rather faithfully the results of General Elections. The same conclusions thus emerge from the examination of the turn-out at local elections as from the examination of the degree of political interest. The proportions of more 'active' electors among the supporters of both parties is fairly even. Labour electors do not appear to be less interested in local elections than Conservative or Independent electors.

CHAPTER TWELVE

THE ELECTORATE AND
LOCAL POLITICS

Earlier chapters revealed that more than four-fifths of Newcastle electors cast their votes at the 1959 General Election. In local elections, as we have seen, only about two-fifths of the electorate usually participate, demonstrating a much lower degree of involvement in municipal affairs. In this chapter we shall examine the outlook of the local government voter and non-voter, and attempt to explain the relative lack of interest in local politics.[1]

1. Voting and Non-voting

All respondents were asked: 'Did you vote in the last Borough (Rural District) Council elections?' This was a straightforward question in the Borough where elections take place annually; but in the Rural District, where elections are triennial, the 'last election' had been eighteen months before the survey, not nine months as in Newcastle Borough. Moreover in the Rural District elections of May 1958 only two parishes had polled, the others having returned councillors without contest. The 'last election' in Whitmore had been in 1928, while in both Chorlton and Maer there had been no contested election since the setting up of the Rural District in 1894. Consequently in the Rural District the answers to the question were likely to be much less reliable and the data on Rural District voting need to be treated with some scepticism.

[1] For earlier studies see L. J. Sharpe, *A Metropolis Votes* (1962), and F. Bealey and D. J. Bartholomew, 'The Local Elections in Newcastle-under-Lyme, May 1958', *British Journal of Sociology*, September and December 1962.

Table 1 makes it clear that far more people claimed to have voted than was actually the case. In Newcastle Borough, where calculation is possible, 38 per cent of the electorate had voted at 'the last Borough election', though nearly twice as many said they had done so, a discrepancy between actual and alleged voting that could be explained in various ways. It may be that people felt rather guilty about not exercising their civic duty and were ashamed to admit their remissness; or it may be that they confused the 'last Borough election' with the last Parliamentary or County Council election, or with other Borough elections

TABLE 1. PERCENTAGE VOTING AND NON-VOTING AT LOCAL ELECTIONS IN BOROUGH, RURAL DISTRICT AND WHOLE CONSTITUENCY

	Borough		Rural District		Whole constituency	
	Voted in last Borough election	Didn't vote	Voted in last Rural District election	Didn't vote	Voted in last local election	Didn't vote
1959 General Election vote:						
Conservative	73	27	49	51	69	31
Labour	71	29	71	29	71	29
Class:						
A Business Proprietors	75	25	58	42	70	30
B Professional	82	18	47	53	77	23
C Clerical	68	32	47	53	65	35
D Skilled manual	65	35	61	39	64	36
E Less skilled	70	30	63	37	68	32
X HW/f no husband	46	54	56	44	48	52
Self-assigned social class:						
'Middle'	72	28	50	50	69	31
'Lower-middle'	71	29	44	56	67	33
'Working'	67	33	71	29	68	32
'No class'	65	35	21	79	57	43
Age:						
21–24	47	53	20	80	41	59
25–29	71	29	39	61	67	33
30–39	70	30	28	72	65	35
40–49	67	33	66	34	67	33
50–59	72	28	67	33	71	29
60 and over	65	35	59	41	64	36
Sex:						
Men	72	28	55	45	69	31
Women	63	37	53	47	61	39

	Borough		Rural District		Whole constituency	
	Voted in last Borough election	*Didn't vote*	*Voted in last Rural District election*	*Didn't vote*	*Voted in last local election*	*Didn't vote*
Form of house tenancy:						
Council house tenants	70	30	57	43	69	31
Other tenants	63	37	48	52	60	40
Owner-occupiers	70	30	66	34	69	31
School-leaving age:						
15 or less	68	32	61	39	67	33
16 or more	79	21	41	59	72	28
Religion:						
Church of England	71	29	56	44	68	32
Roman Catholic	69	31	18	82	66	34
Nonconformist	63	37	69	31	64	36
Workplace:						
Locally	67	33	58	42	66	34
Not locally	71	29	60	40	69	31
Length of residence in home:						
Less than 11 years	72	28	53	47	69	31
11 years or more	65	35	63	37	65	35
Club membership:						
Club member	68	32	57	43	66	34
Not club member	65	35	53	47	63	37
Ability to name councillor:						
Correctly	82	18	74	26	79	21
Incorrectly	65	35	57	43	64	36
All electors	69	31	59	41	67	33

before the 'last'. Most probably both guilt and confusion were responsible for the discrepancy.

Table 1 also shows that non-voting at local elections is, with a few notable exceptions, distributed fairly evenly among the voters. Political allegiance, sex, education, religion, place of work, length of residence in present home and being a club member or not, seemed to make little difference to local voting throughout the constituency.

With regard to class, however, there were some differences. Single or widowed women without employment were very much less prone to vote than any other grouping. The professional and managerial class had the best voting record and skilled workers the worst. This pattern is reflected in the incidence of voting among the 'classes' to which people assigned themselves. The 'middle class' has the greatest proneness to vote and the 'working class' is least prone, though the variation is very slight, especially in the Borough. It is very interesting to note that the respondents who claimed they were without 'class' had the lowest voting record of all.

Among age groups, people in their 50's emerged as most likely to vote while the youngest voters were outstanding as abstainers. This must be qualified, however, by noting that many among the 21–24 grouping may not have been legally entitled to vote at the time of the 'last' election. Even so it is probable that inclination to vote in local elections is a habit that develops with a growing interest in politics and that this is encouraged by the opportunity to use the franchise. Interest is clearly greater among those people upon whom the local council makes most impact. Both council-house tenants and owner-occupiers have a better voting record than those voters who live in other people's houses. Finally, those most knowledgeable about politics, by virtue of being able to name one of their councillors, had a considerably greater propensity to vote than those who were less knowledgeable in this way.

So far we have been dealing with the whole constituency. Variations between the Borough and the Rural District must be treated with care for reasons already given. As far as it is safe to draw conclusions from Table 1 it shows that the Labour voters, the manual workers, the 'working class', and the less well educated are all more prone to vote in the Rural District, a reversal of the situation in the constituency as a whole. Among religious groups Nonconformists, in the constituency as a whole, have the lowest propensity to vote in local elections, but they are the most likely to vote in the Rural District. Conversely, the Roman Catholics in the Rural District, where they are very few in numbers, have a very low voting record; but in the whole constituency their proneness to vote is rather higher than the Nonconformists.

The higher voting among Labour voters and manual workers in the Rural District may be caused by many more electoral contests taking place in those parishes such as Audley and Madeley where Labour voters and manual workers are a larger section of the electorate. Even so the differences between the Borough and the Rural District are so great as to suggest that in the latter, among the less-privileged section of the population, there is a greater propensity to vote than among the more privileged. This may be because the less-privileged people are a higher proportion of the population in the Rural District; and it may well be that groups in a minority are less prone to vote in local elections.

Support for this last view can be gained from a study of abstention at local elections within the wards. Though the abstention rate of Conservative and Labour voters was almost the same for the constituency as a whole, the local voting record of these two groups varied between Labour and non-Labour wards. In five out of the seven Borough wards where Labour held all the seats in 1959 there was a higher proportion of Conservative than Labour abstentions. Conversely in the five non-Labour wards there was a greater degree of abstention by Labour voters. Where in the Rural District one can make a comparison—as at Madeley which has returned three Labour councillors out of four since 1946 and where there is more Conservative than Labour abstention—the same holds good.

These facts suggest that, besides all the factors affecting voting and non-voting, the past electoral history of a ward is important. Wards acquire a reputation of impregnability and the supporters of the party not in possession become disheartened and are much less ready to go to the poll. On the other hand a ward like Ward 7, the most marginal ward in the constituency, where either side may win, had the lowest abstention rate in the Borough at the 'last' local elections.

2. Reasons for Abstention

It was in Ward 7 that, in order to investigate the problem of non-voting in local elections in more detail, we carried out a survey on the eve of the Borough election in May 1960. 89 per cent of respondents said they were going to vote. Immediately after the election all respondents were again visited and their promises checked against their performance. Only two-thirds of those who had said they would vote—59 per cent of all respondents—had voted, though a small group amounting to 4 per cent of all respondents had polled in spite of saying they would not do so. Thus 63 per cent of all respondents in the post-election survey claimed to have voted. In the actual election 50 per cent of the electorate voted. Thus even allowing for sampling error, and the fact that among the 'Refusals' there was likely to be a higher proportion of non-voters, there is still an appreciable proportion of the electorate who do not like admitting their failure to register their franchise.

The voters who confessed to not voting gave various reasons for their lapse. Such phrases as 'sick' or 'too busy' were often used. One woman said she was out house-hunting with her husband, while another complained, 'My feet hurt.' Altogether 17 per cent said they were ill, 21 per cent said they were 'too busy' or 'away from home' and 29 per cent said they were 'indifferent', 'not interested', or words to that effect. These last included some who said they didn't 'get anything for voting' and one man who admitted that he had forgotten.

The important question, Why was abstention 62 per cent at the 'last' Newcastle Borough elections when it was only 16 per cent at the last General Election?, was thus hardly answered by the investigation in Ward 7. Obviously it would be unrealistic to assume that there was a wave of illness, an epidemic of sore feet and a sudden rush of social and business commitments in May 1960 that kept people from the polls who had not been thus prevented from voting in October 1959. Clearly a more detailed study of the voters' assessment of the relative importance of local and national government is needed before the important question can be answered.

It is possible, however, from the data about Ward 7 to compare three groups of voters—those who in the pre-poll survey said they would vote and later confirmed that they had voted, those who intended to vote and later admitted to abstaining and those who said they wouldn't vote (or were doubtful about voting) and didn't. These three groups are shown in Table 2. It must be remembered initially that this analysis is only of one ward and that the groups involved are quite small.

TABLE 2. PERCENTAGE VOTING AND ABSTENTION IN WARD 7

	Intended to vote and did	Intended and didn't	Didn't intend or D.K., and didn't
Men	58	34	5*
Women	65	14	21
Age: 21–29	60	20	20
30–49	55	24	14
50 and over	60	24	13
Business proprietors	100	—	—
Managerial and professional	75	—	13
Clerical	50	25	25
Skilled	69	19	9
Less skilled	46	42	13
All non-manua	71	7	14
All manual	59	29	11
'Middle' class	56	33	11
'Lower-middle' class	71	14	5
'Working' class	51	28	19
Owner-occupiers	76	15	7
Council tenants	33	33	27
Other tenants	27	36	32
Left school at 12 or 13	63	17	21
Left school at 14 or 15	60	27	11
Left school at 16 or later	45	27	18
At local elections would vote for 'man' rather than 'party'	73	10	13
At local elections would vote for 'party' rather than 'man'	51	34	13

* Some rows do not add up to 100 per cent because the small category (4 per cent of the whole) of people who didn't intend to vote and did has not been included.

There are two groups among abstainers—those who intended to vote and those who didn't intend. We will call them the 'unintentional' and the 'intentional' abstainers—26 per cent and 11 per cent of all respondents respectively. It is interesting to note how the proportion of these two types of abstainers varies between different groups. Thus women were much more prone to be 'intentional' abstainers, but when it came to the actual poll they had a rather better voting record because 'unintentional' abstention amongst the female sex was a good deal lower. 'Unintentional' abstention with men was much greater than 'intentional', perhaps reflecting the difficulty many men find in getting themselves to the poll after a hard day's work. Men are more conscious of their civic duties, and find it more difficult to admit of the possibility of their not voting. Women, less anxious on the whole to exercise the suffrage, nevertheless have more opportunity: for example, they can vote in the middle of a shopping expedition.

Among owner-occupiers—61 per cent of respondents in this ward—there was a very low degree of both 'intentional' and 'unintentional' abstention which contrasted with the very high degree of both types of abstention among council-house and other tenants. The non-manual workers had a very low rate of 'unintentional' and 'intentional' abstention, while among manual workers there was a sharp contrast between the skilled and less-skilled, the 'unintentional' abstention rate of the less-skilled being the highest of any group. The relatively low abstention rate of the skilled workers, the largest class in the ward, was also partly responsible for the good voting record of the self-styled 'lower-middle' class and of the owner-occupiers, the proportion of skilled workers in Ward 7 among both the 'lower-middle' class and the owner-occupiers being very high compared with the Borough as a whole. Here then in the largest class many of the factors making for a high rate of voting are combined.

3. Knowledge of Local Politics

All respondents were asked one question about the Staffordshire County Council and all, except in Ward 7, were asked one about their own ward. These questions, which it was hoped would be criteria for assessing knowledge of local politics, were 'Which party has a majority on the Staffordshire County Council?' and 'Can you tell me the name of your local Borough (Rural District) councillor?'

Only eleven respondents gave the correct answer—'Conservative and Independent coalition'—to the first question. On the other hand 52 per cent of the constituency held that the Labour Party was in the majority at Stafford, a situation that had terminated in 1955. Furthermore if either the answer 'Independent' or the answer 'Conservative' was 'partially correct', then there were only two wards in the Borough where more than ten respondents were correct or 'partially correct'. But in the Rural

District at Madeley 23 per cent of respondents gave a 'partially correct' reply and at Audley 15 per cent.

Besides this regional difference the only marked variation was between the sexes. Only one woman gave the correct answer, women being a good deal less likely to render a 'partially correct' reply and much more ready to admit their ignorance. Men were much less inclined to say 'Don't know', illustrating the male tendency to feel that at least a show of knowledge about politics was seemly.

A much higher proportion of respondents—25 per cent of the whole—were able to name one of their councillors. When a respondent gave one correct answer we neglected any other incorrect answers he might give. There were many incorrect answers, the most prevalent being the name of the Member of Parliament proffered perhaps more in desperation than hopefulness; while a much smaller number of respondents put forward the name of the last Conservative Parliamentary candidate. As each ward in the Borough had three councillors while in the Rural District the average is a little more than two; and as the Borough poll is annual but triennial elections are the rule in the Rural District, the Borough's respondents had a great advantage. Even so 39 per cent in the Rural District gave a correct name compared with 22 per cent in the Borough.

There were no significant associations in any ward between political knowledgeability and either class, school-leaving age, or the propensity to discuss politics with people outside the family. On the other hand the form of house tenancy, age and 1959 General Election vote were sometimes significantly associated with political knowledgeability, and in Ward 2, where Labour voters, council-house tenants and older people were the groups with greatest success in naming one of their councillors, all three factors were significantly interrelated. In general, however, the form of house tenancy and the 1959 General Election vote did not seem to affect political knowledge which, as Table 3 shows, was distributed fairly evenly. Surprisingly there was little difference between those who thought it was right to vote for the 'party' and those who voted for the 'man' at local elections; and the main variations were between age groups and, not unnaturally, between voters and abstainers. The strange political ignorance of the 25–29 age group ought to be noted and the fact, which may be an indication that political knowledge is decreasing, that those over 60 were best informed. More probably, however, this is a local characteristic associated with generation rather than age group: for in the Rural District the 50–59 group were the best informed. The superior political knowledge of the voters as compared with the non-voters is to be expected, though it is important to note that the non-voters in the Rural District were better informed than the voters in the Borough.

TABLE 3. PERCENTAGE KNOWLEDGE OF LOCAL POLITICS

	Borough		Rural District		Whole constituency	
	Correct	Incorrect	Correct	Incorrect	Correct	Incorrect
1959 Conservatives	18	82	48	52	24	76
1959 Labour voters	21	79	29	71	23	77
Council house tenants	19	81	49	51	22	78
Owner-occupiers	16	84	40	60	22	78
Other tenants	22	78	32	68	25	75
Men	20	80	44	56	24	76
Women	18	82	34	66	21	79
Age: 21–24	22	78	18	82	21	79
25–29	7	93	25	75	9	91
30–39	18	82	36	64	20	80
40–49	24	76	39	61	28	62
50–59	17	83	43	57	22	78
Over 60	28	72	40	60	30	70
Would vote for 'man' in local elections	19	81	42	58	24	76
Would vote for 'party' in local elections	23	77	37	63	25	75
Voted in last local elections	23	77	46	54	27	73
Didn't vote in last local elections	11	89	29	71	15	85
All respondents	22	78	39	61	25	75

Table 4 analyses the response by wards and shows considerable variations that cannot easily be ascribed to factors such as class, political allegiance and industry. For example, Wards 1 and 2 are very similar in such respects, but vary greatly in political knowledgeability. Consequently it is likely that the personality of the councillor plays a large part here. In the Rural District the six parishes that usually return councillors without contest had a very much lower political knowledgeability than the other parishes, demonstrating that electoral activity in itself helps to keep the electors informed. Rural District respondents, however, sometimes confused Rural District councillors with Parish councillors. In the Borough many respondents named aldermen who had once represented their ward, showing that the process by which familiar councillors are removed from the electors' notice by election to the aldermanic bench weakens the link between the voters and their representatives.

TABLE 4. PERCENTAGE POLITICAL KNOWLEDGE BY WARDS

Borough		Rural District	
1	8	Ashley	52
2	55	Audley ward	38
3	14	Bignall End	37
4	18	Halmerend	45
5	14	Balterley and Betley	66
6	21		
7	—	Chorlton and Maer	23
8	10		
9	17		
10	16	Keele and Whitmore	27
11	28	Madeley	46
12	31	Mucklestone and Tyrley	14

In Ward 7 the name of a councillor was not requested because the survey in this ward took place on the eve of the election, but respondents were asked what they thought was the most important election issue. By the time this question was put most voters had received literature from the candidates and the poll was less than a week away. In spite of this 28 per cent of respondents—the largest group of all—said 'Don't know' or 'None'. Of the 72 per cent who offered some reply 15 per cent maintained that 'Old Age Pensions', an echo of the General Election of seven months earlier, was the issue on which the campaign was being fought, showing the inability of some voters to dissociate local from national politics. 12 per cent of respondents, the third largest group, did mention a local issue, 'lower rates', as the most important. Altogether, however, only 26 per cent of respondents mentioned an issue which could be construed as relevant to the activities of the

Borough Council, as against 34 per cent who gave replies indicating that to them something that was the prerogative either of the County Council or of the national government was the most important issue of the campaign.

For this reason the ability to name an election issue in Ward 7 was not a very reliable criterion of political interest or knowledge. There was no significant relationship between the ability to name an issue and the disposition to vote or abstain, though, as we have seen in Table 3, there was a considerable difference between the political knowledge of voters and non-voters. Furthermore when in Ward 7 we associated ability to name an issue with age we obtained significant results: only 53 per cent of those under 50 named an issue as against 78 per cent of those over 50. Club membership was also significant, 40 per cent of those who were not club members naming an issue compared with 70 per cent who belonged to clubs. The ability to name an issue, however, was not the same as the ability to name a relevant issue so these findings must be treated with caution.

The overall picture is complementary to the figures of the incidence of voting in Newcastle local elections. The electorate are poorly informed about local political personalities and policies, though the Rural District voters are conspicuously better informed than those in the Borough. The general impression is that this political ignorance is widespread and not confined to any particular social group.

4. Party in Local Politics

Only about half as many people voted at the local elections as at the General Election and many cannot name one of their councillors. It is not therefore surprising that the voters often cannot remember the exact label of the candidate for whom they voted.

Table 5 clearly demonstrates this fact. The most marked feature of the respondents' memories of their vote at the 'last' Borough election was their obsession with our two largest national parties. For example in Ward 2, where voting was about average, only 1 per cent claimed to have voted for the Liberal candidate who had actually received 18 per cent of the votes against 26 per cent for Labour. 23 per cent of Ward 2 respondents, on the other hand, alleged they had voted 'Conservative' in spite of there being no Conservative candidate at that election.

TABLE 5. ACTUAL AND ALLEGED VOTING IN THE BOROUGH WARDS
PERCENTAGE TOTAL ELECTORATE AND TOTAL SAMPLES

Party supported at last local election:

Vote	Conservative		Labour		Liberal		Independent		All voters	
	Act.	Alleg.	Act.	Alleg.	Act.	Alleg.	Act.	Alleg.	Act.	Alleg.
Ward										
1	—	25	17	31	—	—	6	1	23	57
2	—	23	26	51	18	1	—	1	44	77
3	—	40	13	22	—	2	29	16	42	80
4	—	37	12	36	—	—	31	1	43	74
5	31	39	13	15	—	—	—	6	44	60
6	—	6	13	33	—	—	22	34	35	73
7	—	36	30	45	—	—	25	6	55	87
8	—	25	13	22	—	—	27	22	40	69
9	—	14	21	48	—	—	15	11	36	72
10	—	5	24*	54	—	2	4*	4	28	64
11	—	9	29	56	—	—	16	6	45	71
12	—	5	18†	44	—	—	0·15 (C.P.)	5 (Ind.)	32	54

* Here there was a casual vacancy and therefore two seats to be filled. Average vote taken of two Labour and two Independent candidates.

† Here there was one Labour, one Independent Labour and one Communist candidate. The Labour and Independent Labour were added together.

Similarly Independent candidates, with a few exceptions, made little impact on the mind of the electorate. In Ward 4 where an Independent candidate polled 31 per cent of the votes only 1 per cent of respondents claimed to have voted for her while 37 per cent of respondents claimed to have voted 'Conservative'. A very similar situation appertained in Ward 7. In fact in spite of there being only one Conservative candidate at the 'last' Borough election the party was credited with votes in all wards and in nine of the eleven seats it did not contest more respondents claimed to have voted for a 'Conservative' than for Labour's actual opponent in those wards.

In two Borough wards, however, the idea of Independent candidates had established itself in the minds of the voters. In Ward 8, where there was a long tradition of Independent councillors,

22 per cent of the respondents said they had voted Independent, only 5 per cent less than had actually done so; and in Ward 6, where 22 per cent of the voters had supported the victorious Independent candidate in May 1959, 34 per cent of respondents actually claimed to have voted Independent. This was the only ward in which the Independents—unlike the Conservative and Labour Parties who were in this position in all twelve Borough wards—had an alleged voting support that outran their actual figures. As we shall see later in Chapter 17 there were special reasons why the 'Independent' character of Ward 6 should have impressed itself on the Ward 6 voters' minds.

In the Rural District the same phenomenon seems to have been present. At Madeley, where a popular Independent had been one of the councillors since 1949, only 6 per cent of the respondents claimed to have voted Independent at the 'last Rural District election'. At Ashley 10 per cent said they had voted Labour and 34 per cent Conservative in May 1958, when the two Ashley seats on the Rural District Council had been fought for by three Independent candidates, and 100 per cent of those who voted must have voted Independent. But only 14 per cent of respondents admitted to so doing.

The degree to which the electorate conceives of the local political rift in the national Conservative/Labour terms is borne out by the very high correspondence between General and local election voting. Those who said they had voted Labour at the 'last' local election in nearly every case said they had voted Labour at the 1959 General Election and those who said they had voted either Conservative or Independent at the last local election in nearly every case said they had voted Conservative at the 1959 General Election. Only in two Rural District parishes was this pattern disturbed. In both Audley ward and Balterley and Betley an appreciable number of respondents who had voted Conservative at the General Election admitted to having voted for a Labour candidate at the local election. Here personal factors were working to favour party, not non-party, candidates.

On the whole, as we have seen, the average Newcastle voter finds it difficult to conceive of politics of any sort without the two large national parties. This is the case in the Borough where an 'Independent tradition' has lingered on into the 1960's and it is the case in the Rural District where personal factors are so important. Yet there are data to show that the voters do have some residual feeling that party labels are not entirely desirable in local politics. Many of the voters, like the 19 per cent who said one should vote for the 'man' rather than the 'party' at General Elections, were probably motivated by a vague idea that this was the correct thing to say; and this may also apply to the two-fifths who thought one should vote for the 'man' at local elections. Even so the strength of support for the concept of voting for the individual merit of the candidate at least must show that the national parties have not completely succeeded in monopolizing the mind of the electorate.

As the reader might expect, the answer 'man' to the question, 'At local elections do you think one should vote for the man or the party?' was not spread uniformly throughout the constituency. Table 6 shows there was 10 per cent more support for voting for

TABLE 6. PERCENTAGE VOTING FOR 'MAN' OR 'PARTY' AT LOCAL ELECTIONS ACCORDING TO LOCAL ELECTION VOTE

	Conservative	Labour	Liberal	Independent	Non-voters	All
Borough wards						
'Man'	36	34	43	52	45	39
'Party'	64	66	57	48	55	61
Rural wards						
'Man'	48	46	51	61	50	49
'Party'	52	54	49	39	50	51
Whole constituency						
'Man'	38	37	45	53	46	41
'Party'	62	63	55	47	54	59

the 'man' in the Rural District. Among party supporters at the local elections it is the Labour voters who are most party-oriented though the Conservatives are only a little less so. The Liberals, very few in number, true to their party's principles, are rather less party-oriented than the two major parties while the non-voters are almost the same as the Liberals. The Independents, not unnaturally, are the least party-oriented group though even 47 per cent of them thought one should vote for the 'party' at local elections.

It was possible to pursue this analysis further and to examine those respondents—24 per cent of the whole—who, while thinking that one should vote for the 'party' at General Elections, thought one should vote for the 'man' at local elections. In Table 7 we have related this factor to the General Election vote, and shown that the Conservative voters were more prone

TABLE 7. 1959 GENERAL ELECTION VOTE, CLASS, AND PERCENTAGE MOVEMENT FROM VOTING FOR THE 'PARTY' AT GENERAL ELECTIONS TO VOTING FOR THE 'MAN' AT LOCAL ELECTIONS

	Borough						Rural District						Whole constituency					
	A	B	C	D	E	Total	A	B	C	D	E	Total	A	B	C	D	E	Total
1959 Conservatives:	32	43	26	26	22	30	38	54	36	45	40	42	34	45	28	28	26	32
1959 Labour voters:	20	39	38	24	4	15	18	46	24	23	26	25	20	41	35	24	8	17
All voters:	31	43	29	25	10	22	36	53	33	31	29	33	32	44	30	26	12	24

to move from a 'party'-oriented position at General Elections to a 'man'-oriented position at local elections. Furthermore the voters in the Rural District were a good deal more inclined than the voters in the Borough to move in this way.

But class was the factor that provided most evidence of significance, and the professional and managerial class was clearly the one most likely to move from support for the 'party' at General Elections to support for the 'man' at local elections: in fact it was nearly three times as prone as the less-skilled workers who were at the opposite end of the scale in this respect. The business proprietors, clerical and skilled workers differed a good deal less from one another and were somewhere in the middle of this scale.

Most noteworthy is the fact that in this respect the Labour and Conservative voters who were in the professional, clerical and skilled manual classes did not greatly differ. However, the business proprietors and the less-skilled workers among the Labour voters were a good deal less inclined than their counterparts among Conservative voters to move from 'party' to 'man' between General and local elections. Thus it seems that there is some socio-economic factor, not connected with voting allegiance, that affects attitudes to party candidatures as between General and local elections. It seems to correspond neither to propensity to vote nor to political knowledge, but to be associated with both type of district and occupation independently of party connections.

These generalizations must be qualified by Table 8 which shows the variation between wards of the change from voting

TABLE 8. PERCENTAGE MOVEMENT FROM VOTING FOR 'PARTY' AT GENERAL ELECTIONS TO VOTING FOR 'MAN' AT LOCAL ELECTIONS BY WARDS

Borough Movement of voters		Rural District Movement of voters	
1	0	Ashley	34
2	19	Audley ward	35
3	9	Bignall End	17
4	23	Halmerend	3
5	47	Balterley and Betley	49
6	28	Chorlton and Maer	38
7	26	Keele and Whitmore	32
8	30	Madeley	31
9	29	Mucklestone and Tyrley	48
10	18		
11	12		
12	22		

for the 'party' at General Elections to voting for the 'man' at local elections. Within the Borough Wards 3 and 5 with very similar occupational structures (21 per cent and 22 per cent of the professional class respectively) have a very different outlook to 'party' in local politics. But puzzlingly it was Ward 5, with its three Conservative councillors, that had the highest rate of movement in the Borough while Ward 3 with three Independent councillors had a low rate of movement. In two Borough wards with strong Independent traditions, 6 and 8, the voters were less disposed than the voters in Ward 5 to move to the 'man' at local elections. In the Rural District Bignall End and Halmerend, with very similar characteristics, stand out as party-oriented wards while Balterley and Betley and Mucklestone and Tyrley are at the other extreme.

These data are difficult to interpret and one can only conclude that among the voters there is a general feeling that the merits of a candidate should be considered at local elections a good deal more than at General Elections. The feeling is somewhat more prevalent among Conservative than Labour voters, and more common in the Rural District than in the Borough. These variations might be expected as both Conservatives and Rural District voters are more likely to be voting 'Independent' at local elections. Yet a further phenomenon, the variation among classes, seemed largely unconnected with either 1959 General Election vote or local government area. Thus attitudes to party in local politics may be related to other social attitudes as yet unexplored.

5. Satisfaction with the Local Council

Respondents' impressions of the functions of their local council were as vague as their ideas about local politics, and we must treat with some reservation the answers to the question 'Are you satisfied with the services provided by your local council?' In many cases it is probable that the reply was an assessment of *all* services for, as we have seen in Ward 7, respondents had adjudged Old Age Pensions to be a function of local government; and even where confusion did not exist the answers may have been little more than a general verdict on local government.

Yet a study of the data does establish various patterns. 24 per cent of all respondents were dissatisfied with their council's services, 22 per cent in the Borough and 32 per cent in the Rural District. 1959 Conservative voters were dissatisfied with both local authorities to the same extent—28 per cent; but Labour voters were more dissatisfied in the Rural District than in the Borough—23 per cent as against 17 per cent. Among classes there were no significant differences, but Conservative manual workers were a good deal more dissatisfied than manual workers who were Labour voters. In Ward 11, for example, 47 per cent of Conservative manual workers were dissatisfied with council services as against 19 per cent of Labour manual workers.

The same situation, less strikingly illustrated than in Ward 11, was present in nearly all the other wards, and perhaps reflects the fact that Conservative manual workers feel themselves to be the least privileged group in a constituency where (in 1959) both local authorities had a Labour majority. As we have observed, a higher proportion of Labour manual workers live in council houses than Conservative manual workers. It may be that those Conservative voters who are manual workers feel more resentment about such a position, and are thus more dissatisfied with their Labour-dominated council than Conservative non-manual workers.

6. Conclusion

Only about two-fifths of the electorate, it seems, participate in local elections—about half the proportion who vote at General Elections. There are many similarities between local election voters and non-voters; but an important difference is that of age. Clearly older people are much more likely to vote. Otherwise such factors as class appeared to be unimportant in the constituency as a whole, though it is noteworthy that, at the ward level, voting tended to be more common among the dominant social and political groupings. For example, the turn-out of Labour voters was higher in Labour-held wards. There was also a good deal more inclination to vote in the Rural District in spite of its less frequent elections and its usually higher proportion of uncontested seats.

Knowledge of local politics was not great and people were especially ignorant about the Staffordshire County Council; but generally speaking ignorance of local affairs was spread fairly evenly among different social groupings and between the political parties. Where there was knowledge it was often connected with political activity. For example, knowledgeability was higher among voters than abstainers, and older people were not only more inclined to vote, they were also more knowledgeable about local politics. In the Rural District there was both a higher turn-out and also more knowledge amongst the voters than in Newcastle Borough.

The lack of interest in local politics is probably the result of a feeling that they are no longer important. Likely as this explanation is, it did not emerge from respondents' answers to the question 'Why didn't you vote?' No respondent replied that local elections were unimportant and many of them insisted that they had intended to vote but for various reasons had not done so. The relative weakness of party organization and the almost total absence of the impact of a campaign, as compared with General Elections, may be another important factor in explaining the much greater abstention rate at local elections.

It is clear that there is ignorance of the functions of the respective councils though this has not prevented some dissatisfaction developing especially in the Rural District and among Conservative voters. The electorate is not totally unaware of the councils but it would be difficult for an active and informed public opinion to grow, particularly in the scattered and heterogeneous Rural District, without a considerable improvement in the quantity and quality of information provided about the councils' activities.

This absence of a public opinion about local politics has provided a vacuum which the national parties have filled so successfully that the electors visualize local elections as contests, fought largely on issues of national policy, between the candidates of the Conservative and Labour Parties. Thus a century of Independent candidatures seems to have left little impression on the minds of the voters. But perhaps at a lower level of consciousness there does exist a feeling, especially strong in the Rural District and among the professional class and varying from ward to ward, that in voting for local government candidates one should consider individual merit rather than party affiliation.

Such generalizations as one can make from the example of one constituency do not encourage great optimism about the future of local representative government. If the relative political inactivity and ignorance of the young is an indication (and it is not necessarily so, as we have said) increasingly smaller interest is likely to be taken in local politics. The fact that in the much less densely populated and much less urbanized Rural District political activity and knowledge were greater than in Newcastle Borough, while the politics of the Staffordshire County Council occasioned most ignorance, is hardly auspicious in an era of increasing urbanization, centralization and amalgamation of local authorities into larger units. If so few know who rules at Stafford how many would be likely to know who would rule at some future Midland regional seat of government? Presumably in such a situation the domination of the national parties over the minds of the voters would be even more complete.

It is to the three national parties and their membership that we must now turn.

CHAPTER THIRTEEN

THE MEMBERSHIPS OF THE POLITICAL PARTIES

P revious chapters have dealt with the electorate as a whole and the extent to which its political behaviour has been affected by social, economic and other influences. In this and the following chapter we turn to a more politically active section of the population, the members of the three main political parties. For the great majority of the electors, political activity is limited to voting in General and local elections, with perhaps an occasional attendance at a political meeting. The party member, however, is expected not only to mobilize support at election times and help organize meetings, but also to do whatever day-to-day political work the party decides upon. Party members, therefore, form a distinct group of the population, involved in active politics to a much greater extent than the average elector.

This chapter examines the three main political parties in New-castle in order to discover the social classes from which they draw their members, the kind of political activity in which the latter are involved and the attitude of the rank-and-file to their own party and to local council affairs. For this purpose a survey was carried out among the Conservative, Labour and Liberal Parties. A hundred names were chosen, by means of the random sampling method, from the latest available membership rolls of each party, and each person was interviewed in his home by student interviewers. The returns are as set out in Table 1.

These samples represent 6 per cent of a Conservative membership of 1,500, 20 per cent of a Labour membership of 426, and 67 per cent of a Liberal membership of 130. On this evidence, political activity in Newcastle is clearly a minority concern. The total membership for the three parties, at the time when the surveys were taken,[1] amounts to 2,056 out of an electorate of 63,504, or 3·2 per cent of the whole.

TABLE 1. TOTAL SAMPLE OF THREE PARTY MEMBERSHIPS

	Answered	Refused	Ill	Dead	Out	Moved	Total
Conservative	83	6	4	2	—	5	100
Labour	85	4	2	2	—	7	100
Liberal	87	6	—	1	4	2	100

The questionnaires were divided into three sections. The first dealt with objective questions such as age, sex, class, working condition, education and so on; the second part covered local political activity, and the concluding section was concerned with the different political issues facing each party at the time of the survey. This chapter deals with the answers to the first two sections of the questionnaire.

1. Occupation, Work and Residence

The criteria for class were the same as in our constituency survey,[2] with which in the following table the total for each party is compared.

TABLE 2. PERCENTAGE CLASS STRUCTURE OF THE PARTY MEMBERSHIPS

	Conservative	Labour	Liberal	Constituency Survey
A. Business proprietors	31	2	16	9
B. Professional and managerial	33	8	26	11
C. Clerical	18	13	21	8
D. Skilled manual	14	42	33	37
E. Less skilled	4	35	4	32
	100*	100*	100*	97*

* The category X, housewife without both employment and husband, was not used in the surveys of party membership.

[1] The survey of the membership of the Labour Party took place on 8–9 December 1960, and that of the other two parties on 19–20 June 1961.
[2] See Chap. 7, pp. 147 ff., for an explanation of this.

POLITICAL PARTY MEMBERSHIPS

64 per cent of the Conservative members are in the first two
social groups, and only 14 per cent of the membership are skilled
workers. The Labour Party is almost a mirror-image of the
Conservative with nine out of every ten members in the three
lower categories.

The Liberal Party, on the other hand, has the greatest proportion of its membership in the three intermediate groupings,
with a slightly higher proportion of clerical workers than the
other two parties. Like the Conservative Party, however, it
attracts a mere 4 per cent of less-skilled workers. The Labour
Party is distinctly working class in its composition and reflects
fairly closely the occupational structure of the constituency as a
whole, with a slight over-representation of skilled manual and
clerical workers and a considerable under-representation of
business proprietors.

An inquiry was also made as to the working condition of each
respondent. Where the respondent was a non-working housewife,
she was recorded as such and her husband's occupation also
noted.[1] The following table is an analysis of the results:

TABLE 3. PERCENTAGE WORKING CONDITION OF PARTY MEMBERSHIPS

	Conservative	Labour	Liberal
At work	52	67	69
Retired	12	6	11
Disabled, ill	—	—	—
Unemployed	—	—	—
Housewife	36	27	20
	100	100	100

The main difference between the parties lies in the fact that the
Conservatives contain a greater number of retired people and
housewives than the other two parties—nearly one in two of the
membership, compared with about one in three of the membership of Labour and the Liberals.

If we turn to the specific occupations in which members of
each party are employed we find that 16 per cent of the Labour

[1] In the case of the Labour Party, the husband's occupation was not
recorded.

members in employment work in the coal industry, and 10 per cent in engineering; slightly fewer—8 per cent—are employed in pottery. Thus over a third of the working membership is employed in the three main industries of the district. The highest single group in both the other parties are clerical workers, with 11 per cent each. 8 per cent of Liberals and Conservatives are employed in shop work. 5 per cent of the Liberals are teachers, and the only industries represented to any extent are pottery and engineering, employing 8 per cent each. Conservatives are also employed in the building and engineering industries (6 per cent each), presumably mainly as contractors and in managerial positions. 7 per cent are also employed in the newer electrical industry, and 6 per cent are farmers.

The proportion of trade unionists among the working members of each party reinforces the picture that has so far emerged. One would, of course, expect the Labour Party to have the greatest number, as the rules enjoin members to become trade unionists wherever this is possible. But in view of the efforts of the Conservatives and Liberals to recruit trade unionists, the small proportion of trade unionists in their ranks could be a disappointment to both of these parties.

TABLE 4. PERCENTAGE TRADE UNIONISM AND PARTY MEMBERSHIPS

	Conservative	Labour	Liberal
Members of trade unions	5	69	28
Non-members	95	31	72
	100	100	100

Grouping unions to which members belong into three broad categories—'industrial-manual', 'general' and 'clerical'[1]—we find that of the trade unionists in the Labour Party, just over

[1] These categories are purely arbitrary and have been set up for purposes of comparison only. The 'industrial-manual' group includes the National Union of Mineworkers, the Amalgamated Engineering Union, the National Society of Pottery Workers and several others. The 'general' group includes the Transport and General Workers, the General and Municipal Workers, the Shop, Distributive and Allied Workers and others. The 'clerical' group includes unions catering for clerks, teachers, civil servants, etc.

half are in the industrial-manual category. In the Liberal Party, exactly half of the 28 per cent of union members fall in the clerical group. The total of trade-union members in the Conservative Party was too small for any useful comparisons to be made. But 20 per cent of the Conservatives were members of professional associations, and a similar proportion of the Liberals.[1] This preliminary examination shows that the Labour Party, as compared with the other two parties, has the majority of its membership among the skilled and less-skilled workers, with over a third of its working membership in the basic traditional industries of the district.

There are also interesting differences in the geographical distribution of the members of the three parties. The twenty-one wards of the constituency can be grouped into three socioeconomic areas—the urban residential wards (Wards 1–9), those containing the mining villages on the Northwestern edge of the Borough (Wards 10, 11 and 12), and those comprising the Rural District. The latter, it must be remembered, is not entirely homogeneous as it contains both mining villages and purely agricultural districts.

TABLE 5. PERCENTAGE GEOGRAPHICAL DISTRIBUTION OF PARTY MEMBERSHIP

	Conservative	Labour	Liberal
Area 1: Urban residential	80	49	91
Area 2: 'Mining wards'	—	26	6
Area 3: Rural District	20	25	3
	100	100	100

Both the Conservative and Liberal Parties have their greatest strength in the Borough residential area, whereas the Labour Party has less than half its membership there, and a quarter of it in the mining villages of Silverdale, Knutton and Chesterton. Two-thirds of Labour's rural membership is in the Audley mining villages. On the other hand, a breakdown of the above

[1] Professional Associations include the Library Association, the Institute of Quantity Surveyors, the Builders' Federation, National Farmers' Union, and many others.

table reveals that nearly a third of the Conservatives reside in the middle-class Ward 3, and that much of their rural strength is in Chorlton, Maer, Keele and Whitmore, residential areas favoured by middle- and upper-middle-class commuters from the Potteries.

The distribution of Liberal support should be treated with reservations. Many of the Liberal Party members are of recent date, and the fact that a breakdown shows that 54 per cent of their members reside in Wards 4 and 7 represents the direction of their canvassing efforts as much as anything. But it is noticeable that in these two wards neither the Labour nor the Conservative Party has made much, if any, headway, mainly because they have neglected to develop them. On the whole, the strongholds of the Conservatives are in the middle-class residential areas, and those of the Labour in the working-class mining areas; the Liberals have made headway in wards where neither of these two parties is strong.

The preceding analysis has dealt with objective criteria and established an initial profile which associates the Labour Party with the working class and the Conservative Party with the middle class. The profile of the Liberal Party is less well-defined. Now let us examine the members' own assessment of their class position. Respondents were asked to assign themselves to one of five given categories, with the following result:

TABLE 6. PERCENTAGE SELF-ASSIGNED CLASS AND PARTY MEMBERSHIPS

	Conservative	Labour	Liberal
'Upper-middle class'	3	1	3
'Middle class'	51	12	27
'Lower-middle class'	24	5	20
'Working class'	11	73	37
'No class'	11	9	13
	100	100	100

A majority of the Labour Party considers itself 'working class', whereas in the Conservative Party the majority sees itself as 'middle class'. If we compare these figures with those of Table 2, however, we find that Labour Party members have a slight tendency to overrate their social position. Although, according to Table 2, 77 per cent are in the manual workers' categories D and E, only 73 per cent of the party are willing to call themselves 'working class'. The Conservatives find the 'middle-' and 'lower-middle-class' categories the most popular, with 75 per cent of the membership placing themselves there, avoiding the extremes of 'upper-middle' and 'working class'; though 18 per cent are manual workers according to Table 2, only 11 per cent call themselves 'working class', and though 64 per cent are in the upper-class groups A and B, only 54 per cent so assign themselves. The Liberals place themselves much more evenly in the class scale, with a tendency to underrate their social position; only 30 per cent call themselves 'upper-middle' or 'middle class', though 42 per cent fall within groups A and B.

2. Other Social Factors

The profiles of each party can be further filled out if we consider an analysis of their membership according to sex, age, educational standard, religion and newspaper-reading habits. The sex distribution in the parties is as follows:

TABLE 7. PERCENTAGE SEX AND PARTY MEMBERSHIP

	Conservative	Labour	Liberal
Male	45	54	68
Female	55	46	32
	100	100	100

As might be expected from the known tendency of women to be somewhat more Conservative in politics than men, the Conservative Party has a preponderance of women—55 per cent. The Labour Party has about the same proportion of men, but the Liberals have two males to every female in their ranks. It is not easy to explain this discrepancy except on the grounds that the greater number of young unmarried people in the Liberal ranks tends to reduce the number of wives who might otherwise have joined with their husbands.

POLITICAL PARTY MEMBERSHIPS

The age distribution in the parties does not differ very greatly:

TABLE 8. PERCENTAGE AGE AND PARTY MEMBERSHIPS

Age group	Conservative	Labour	Liberal	Constituency
21–25	4	4	4	3
25–29	5	1	8	7
30–39	8	18	17	22
40–49	26	27	29	23
50–59	34	28	18	21
60 and over	23	22	24	24
	100	100	100	100

All three parties are under-represented in the under-forty age range and over-represented in the over-forty group, the Conservative Party to the greatest extent and the Liberals the least so. The latter are, in fact, the only party over-represented in the 21–29 age range. The Labour Party shows a striking failure to win younger people: only one in every hundred of their members is aged between 25 and 29.

As might be expected from the characteristics of each party already defined, the educational standards of members of the three parties vary:

TABLE 9. PERCENTAGE EDUCATION AND PARTY MEMBERSHIPS

School-leaving Age	Conservative	Labour	Liberal	Constituency
12 or less	—	2	6	3
13	16	33	14	22
14	21	47	36	56
15	22	7	8	8
16	16	5	19	6
17	16	2	9	3
18 or more	9	4	8	2
	100	100	100	100

More than 8 out of 10 Labour members left school before the age of 15, i.e., they can be assumed to have had an elementary or secondary modern type of education. Only 37 per cent of the

Conservatives fall into this category, and 56 per cent of the Liberals. One-quarter of the Conservatives, in fact, carried on their schooling to the age of 17 or beyond. Again the Labour Party has the lowest proportion in this category and the Liberals have an intermediate 17 per cent. In educational standards, as in other characteristics, the Liberals are closer to the Conservatives than to the Labour Party.

The Conservatives and Liberals attract a much greater proportion of people with a grammar school or higher educational background than is found in the constituency as a whole. Only 11 per cent of the population continued their schooling to 16 years or beyond, compared with 41 per cent of the Conservatives and 36 per cent of the Liberals. The Labour Party on the other hand has exactly the same proportion in this group as in the constituency. These figures reflect, of course, the class basis of the parties and the customary association of middle-class position and higher educational qualifications.

The religious affiliations of the party members also reflect a traditional state of affairs. The Conservatives are overwhelmingly Church of England; just under half the Labour Party members are Anglicans, with a strong (29 per cent) infusion of

TABLE 10. PERCENTAGE RELIGION AND PARTY MEMBERSHIPS

	Conservative	Labour	Liberal	Constituency
Church of England	82	49	43	65
Roman Catholic	4	11	2	8
Nonconformists	14	29	46	26
No religion	—	11	9	1
	100	100	100	100

Nonconformists; the Liberals have a slight majority of Nonconformists over Anglicans—46 per cent as against 43 per cent. In comparison with the constituency proportions, there is obviously a strong over-representation of Nonconformists in the Liberal Party, whereas Anglicans are over-represented in the Conservative Party. Thus the religious affiliations of the two parties established in the later nineteenth century still hold good. The Labour Party has the highest proportion of Roman Catholics, and to a small extent an over-representation of Catholics in comparison with their strength in the constituency. The Labour Party also contains the largest proportion of people who subscribe to no religion.

It is always difficult to decide how far religious affiliations influence an individual towards joining a particular political party or whether the policy of a party appeals strongly to people of certain religious views. A similar difficulty presents itself when considering newspaper-reading habits. To what extent does a newspaper have of representing a party viewpoint and convert new readers to its cause? Or are people won over to join a party for other reasons, such as economic hardship, and then begin to read a paper which corresponds to their newly-formed outlook? It is necessary to bear in mind such reservations when considering the reading habits of the members of the three parties under review.

The newspaper-reading habits of the respective party members conform to what one would expect. The majority of the Labour Party membership (56 per cent) is faithful to one newspaper—the *Daily Herald*. Admittedly this has been—and to some extent still is—very much more of a 'party paper' than most national dailies, but recent changes in its sponsorship and outlook do not seem to have affected its standing among Labour members. Significance tables reveal that by far the largest readership of the *Herald* comes from the working-class social groups D and E. If we include the *Daily Mirror* and the *Guardian* with the *Herald* as ostensibly 'non-Conservative' papers, we find that no less than 80 per cent of Labour members read one of these three papers.

On the other hand, if we group the *Daily Express*, the *Daily Mail* and the *Daily Telegraph* together as ostensibly 'non-Labour' papers, we find that the Conservative Party is as true to them as Labour to the non-Conservative papers; 86 per cent of Conservatives read one of these three papers, with the *Daily Mail* (44 per cent) the most popular. The Liberal Party is much more eclectic in its newspaper reading. Only 23 per cent read the traditionally Liberal *Guardian*, as compared with 24 per cent of *Mail* readers. Some of the latter are, undoubtedly, former readers of the defunct *News Chronicle*, as is evident from the ques-

POLITICAL PARTY MEMBERSHIPS

tionnaires, which sometimes had '*News Chronicle*' in answer to the question on reading habits. *Express*, *Herald* and *Mirror* readers are also found in the Liberal Party. The general bias is in favour of the 'non-Labour' group of papers, however. 51 per cent of the Liberals read these in contrast with 37 per cent of readers of the 'non-Conservative' papers.

Finally we come to consider the extent to which the party members have roots in the area. To what degree are the members of the parties linked to the constituency by birth and residence? In order to discover this, two categories—place of birth and length of residence in the constituency—were combined in order to produce the following table:

TABLE 11. PERCENTAGE NATIVES AND IMMIGRANTS AMONG PARTY MEMBERSHIPS

	Conservative	Labour	Liberal
Born in constituency and lived there more than 20 years	26	67	41
Born outside constituency and lived in it less than 20 years	29	12	25
Others not in above categories	45	21	34

If we consider these categories—natives with a long and continuous length of residence and immigrants with a residence of under twenty years—we see that the Labour Party has by far the greatest proportion of the first category—nearly seven out of ten of the members were born in the constituency and have resided there for two decades or more. Conversely, only one in four of the Conservatives come into this category. The latter also have the highest proportion of immigrants—29 per cent. The Liberals show a high proportion of both natives and immigrants, with one in four of their members in category two. Once again this is characteristic of a party with a long tradition in the constituency which has recently started recruiting younger people. The high number of immigrants in the Conservative Party is related to the large proportion of highly educated members of the 'upper' social groups for whom it is customary to migrate in search of salaried posts. The opportunities in this sphere open to workers who left school at a relatively early age are correspondingly fewer.

Generally speaking, a fairly clear picture of the differences between the three parties emerges from the above analyses. The picture can be seen most clearly if certain outstanding characteristics of the membership are gathered together in order to build up a composite picture of the typical member of each party.

Conservative

    belongs to the 'upper' occupational groups;
    assigns himself to the 'middle' or 'lower-middle class';
    Anglican in religion;
    an immigrant of less than twenty years' residence;
    educated to the age of 15 or later;
    reads the *Daily Mail* or *Daily Express*;
    does not belong to a trade union.

Labour

    belongs to the 'lower' occupational groups;
    assigns himself to the 'working class';
    Anglican or Nonconformist in religion;
    a native of Newcastle with more than twenty years' residence;
    left school before reaching the age of 15 years;
    reads the *Daily Herald*;
    is a member of a trade union.

Apart from religious affiliations, the typical members of each party are at opposite poles on all points. It is not possible to characterize the typical Liberal in quite the same way, as the party is essentially a party in transition, moving away from a Nonconformist middle-class orbit towards a lower-middle-class and working-class membership. Bearing this in mind, the following description can be given.

Liberal

    belongs to the intermediate occupational groups;
    assigns himself to the 'middle', 'lower-middle' or 'working class';
    slightly more likely to be Nonconformist than Anglican in religion;

a native rather than an immigrant;
reads the *Daily Mail* or *Guardian*;
likely to have left school before 15 years of age;
not likely to be a member of a trade union.

On the whole, the typical Liberal shows a tendency to incline more towards Conservative than Labour.

The profile of the three main political parties in Newcastle has shown that each party has clearly recognizable characteristics even if examined solely from the point of view of social composition. This, however, gives a merely descriptive picture of each party, and it is now necessary to discover the extent to which the members are active in party affairs and their attitude to the local political process in which the parties participate.

3. Activities and Attitudes of the Party Members

The activities of political parties depend upon the quality and enthusiasm of the membership, the degree to which the members are willing to work in order to carry out the programme and to fulfil the aims of the party. Any examination of the rank-and-file of a political party must seek the answers to certain questions: Into which age group do the most active members fall? Does the party continually recruit an adequate number of new members? Can it rely on a sufficient turn-out of members at crucial election periods? In addition, there is an area of more subjective inquiry, concerning the attitude of members to their own party and to the local democratic process.

In examining the dates at which members joined the parties, two things must be borne in mind: firstly, lack of knowledge of the rate at which members have left the party, and secondly the different size of each party. In absolute numbers the Conservative membership, for instance, is nearly four times the Labour Party's. From the following three tables, therefore, only some general comparisons between the parties can be drawn. A further point is that the categories in each table are slightly different—partly because of the different dates at which the survey was taken, partly because, in the case of the Liberals, a narrower breakdown was made in order to throw more light on their recent heavy recruitment.

261

POLITICAL PARTY MEMBERSHIPS

The Conservative and Labour tables reveal a not dissimilar pattern of recruitment. About a fifth of each membership dates from pre-war. The Labour Party, however, had retained about twice as many members from the war-time period as the Conservatives. It has also shown a slower pattern of recruitment, or a greater wastage of members, during the period from 1955. The Liberals show a striking difference from that of the other parties, and this is almost entirely due to the fact that they doubled their membership in the eighteen-month period between the beginning of 1960 and the date of the survey in June 1961.

TABLE 12. PERCENTAGE RECRUITMENT OF PARTY MEMBERSHIPS

Joined	Conservative Party	Joined	Labour Party	Joined	Liberal Party
Before 1930	10	Before 1930	14	Before 1930	7
1930–39	10	1930–39	9	1930–39	6
1940–45	10	1940–45	21	1940–45	6
1946–54	36	1946–54	35	1946–54	8
1955–61	34	1955–60	21	1955–59	23
				1960–61	50
	100		100		100

The survey revealed some interesting information concerning the new Liberal recruits.[1] An analysis of religion, educational standard and other factors suggests that a different type of person is now joining the Liberals. This is partly the result of the fact that canvassing has mainly taken place in the lower-middle-class and working-class areas of Wards 4 and 7. A significantly greater number of those who joined in 1960–1, for instance, left school at fifteen years or under. A higher proportion of these new recruits also belongs to manual and general unions than to clerical unions. Conversely, significantly fewer are members of a professional association, as compared with pre-1960 members. Also a smaller number of Nonconformists are found among the more recent members than among the older members. As there is a

[1] The high percentages in the last two categories of the Liberal table made it possible to produce a number of significant associations with religious, educational and other factors. The Labour and Conservative tables, with a more even spread of percentages, did not produce any significant associations.

significantly larger number of Nonconformists in social categories A and B, the above analysis suggests that as far as the social composition of the party is concerned, a break has been made with the traditions of Liberalism in Newcastle, and that the revival of 1960–1 has broken new ground. The well-educated Nonconformist middle class are being outnumbered by members from the middle class and working class, a proportion of whom are members of trade unions, catering for manual and general workers.

The pattern of recruitment gives a rough and ready guide to the appeal of a party at different times, but tells us nothing about the amount of party work carried out by members, whether old stalwarts or new recruits. In order to discover the proportion of active members within each party, questions were asked concerning attendance at party meetings, service on a party committee, and help given at local and General Elections. Finally, an analysis was made of the proportion of members taking part in all four activities. The latter table will provide an accurate indication of the size of the solid core of activists upon which each party can draw.

Firstly let us examine the primary form of party political activity, attendance at party meetings. A great difference is found between the parties. Figures for the Conservative and Labour Parties are as follows:

TABLE 13. PERCENTAGE PARTY ACTIVITY AND PARTY MEMBERSHIP

Attended a ward party meeting	Conservative	Labour
Less than 2 months ago	8	39
2–6 months ago	9	13
7–12 months ago	5	10
More than 12 months ago	16	33
Never	48	—
Don't know	14	5
	100	100

The Labour Party has five times more people who had attended a meeting in the eight weeks preceding the survey than the Conservatives. This period was, however, an extremely

crucial one for the Labour Party and the debate on foreign
and home policy and questions of leadership probably stimulated
attendance. Conservatives who last attended a meeting between
two and six months before the survey are not greatly fewer than
the same category of Labour members. Nearly half the Conservative members, however, never attended a meeting of any
kind. This is mainly due to the low level of organization in
the wards, in some of which there is no organized group in existence.

Because of the lack of any ward organization at all in the
Liberal Party during the preceding few years, figures for the
Liberal Party could not be included in the previous table. But it
was possible to compare those members in each of the three
parties who had served on a committee during the last ten years.

TABLE 14. PERCENTAGE COMMITTEE MEMBERSHIP OF PARTY
MEMBERS DURING LAST TEN YEARS

	Conservative	Labour	Liberal
Committee member	20	40	29
Not a committee member	80	60	71
	100	100	100

In relation to the previous table, it is clear that since attendance
at meetings is confined to just about half the membership of the
Conservative Party, the proportion of those active on a committee during the last decade is virtually the same as that of the
Labour Party. In absolute terms, the number of members
actually involved on Conservative committees is, of course,
greater, even allowing for the great proportion of stable members
in the Conservative Party in that period. As far as the Labour
Party is concerned, this means that there is either a greater
rotation of office, or, more likely, a greater number of offices to
be filled in relation to the size of the membership than in the case
of the Conservatives. Of the 29 per cent of the Liberal committee members, there is a significant tendency for those members
who joined the party before 1955 to have served on committees rather than later recruits. Even so, a third of those who

have been or are at present committee members joined the party during the 1960–1 period, a pointer, perhaps, to the number of posts to be filled in a rapidly expanding party.

One of the most important pointers to a party's vitality is the number of members on whom it can call for help at election times. In the General Election of 1959 in Newcastle, there was a straight fight between Conservative and Labour candidates: 75 per cent of the Labour Party turned out to help, but only 39 per cent of the Conservatives. Of the Labour helpers, 44 per cent undertook canvassing, whereas 8 per cent was the highest proportion of those undertaking any other task, which ranged from addressing envelopes to helping at polling stations. Of the Conservative helpers, 37 per cent preferred to canvass, though a high proportion of others helped with cars. Significantly fewer Conservative women than men gave help, despite their higher absolute numbers in the party. There were, more expectedly, significantly fewer helpers in the higher age ranges.

In order to compare the degree of magnitude of help given to each party in the election, we can express the percentage of helpers as a proportion of the total party membership. If one takes the proportion of 39 per cent for the Conservatives and 75 per cent for Labour, then the numbers of helpers would have been 585 and 319 respectively. There is thus some indication that the Conservatives, though able to call on a smaller fraction of its membership, could put a larger force into the field.

Local elections show a similar pattern, though the turn-out is somewhat smaller. Labour had an election force representing 56 per cent of its membership at the last local elections, the Conservatives only 16 per cent, of whom nearly one-third provided cars. A number of Independent candidates stood in these elections, to which some Conservatives would have given help. More than half the Labour helpers went canvassing and no more than 7 per cent undertook any other activity. In terms of the forces engaged, however, the proportions were almost exactly equal; the percentage of active members expressed as a number gives figures of 240 for the Conservatives and 239 for Labour.

The Liberals had 38 per cent of their members active at the local elections; half of these went canvassing and one-third addressed envelopes and undertook other clerical tasks, a reflection of the importance which Liberals have attached to door-to-door work plus a wide distribution of literature. A significantly fewer number of the 1960–1 recruitment helped at local elections than those who joined earlier. Many of the members recruited in this period were made, however, while canvassing for the elections of October 1960 and May 1961. This is emphasized by the fact that significantly more committee members helped at local elections than non-committee members; much of the canvassing of course was, as we have seen, carried out by the canvassing committee.

The above figures emphasize the importance which elections, especially General Elections, play in the life of the parties. It is the one single activity which can arouse a large number or even a majority of the rank-and-file. Even so, compared with the total electorate, the numbers involved are small. If we assume that the notional figure of 904 party members (585 Conservative and 319 Labour) gave help to the two candidates at the 1959 General Election, this represents but 1·4 per cent of an electorate of 63,504. The same calculation for the local elections gives a figure of 531 helpers (240 Conservative, 239 Labour and 52 Liberal, i.e., 38 per cent of a total membership of 130), or 0·8 per cent of the electorate.[1] The democratic process would seem to operate on a very narrow basis.

Returning to the individual party members, we can obtain a reasonable guide to their range of activity if attendance at meetings, committee membership, and help at General Elections are combined in one table and members are graded according to participation in these activities. Thus '100 per cent active' members are those who helped at both elections, had served on a committee in the last decade and had attended a party meeting during the six months previous to the survey. '75 per cent active' members are those who took part in any three of these activities, and so on.

For Conservative and Labour members the table is as shown on the following page.

[1] In the calculations of the local elections it is assumed that the turn-out of Labour members in 1961 was the same as that in 1960. The local elections referred to in the Labour survey were those of May 1960, those referred to in the other two surveys those of May 1961.

TABLE 15. PERCENTAGE SCALE OF ACTIVITY OF CONSERVATIVE
AND LABOUR MEMBERS

	Conservative	Labour
100% active	3	22
75% active	10	21
50% active	16	31
25% active	34	12
100% inactive	37	14
	100	100

This shows that 43 per cent of the Labour Party are thus in the first two categories of activity compared with 13 per cent of the Conservatives. If we include the third category as well, about one in three of the Conservatives is involved, as compared with about three out of four Labour members. In the case of the Liberals it was possible to include only three of the above categories, because a Liberal candidate did not stand in the 1959 General Election. This gives the following table:

TABLE 16. PERCENTAGE SCALE OF ACTIVITY OF LIBERAL MEMBERS

100% active	16
66% active	8
33% active	20
100% inactive	56
	100

The Liberals have by far the largest group of inactive members, but this is certainly due to the fact that there has not been time to draw the newest members into activity. There is, in fact, a significantly larger group of members in the two least active categories among those who joined in the period 1960–1 than among those who joined before this. Many of the most recent members were enrolled during the local election campaign which took place in the month preceding the survey.

Tables 15 and 16 reveal an interesting comparison between the parties on the question of activity. The Labour Party has a solid core of 22 per cent of their members (i.e., the 100 per cent active group) who keep the wheels of the party turning both at election times and in between. The Liberals come next with 16 per cent and the Conservatives last with 3 per cent. To some extent this reflects the fact that the Labour Party is the 'ruling' party in the constituency, but it is, perhaps, more indicative of the conception which the parties traditionally hold of the role of the individual member. Are there any pointers to the type of member involved in these spheres of party work? Significance tables show that in both the Conservative and Labour Parties the younger members appear to be less active politically; there is a tendency for the most active members of the Conservative Party to be drawn from those who joined before 1955, i.e., the somewhat more experienced members. The same trend is even more pronounced in the Labour Party, whose active members of the first two categories are found in a significantly higher proportion among the older and more experienced members who joined the party before 1939. In the Liberal Party, on the other hand, political activity is in the hands of the younger age groups—there is a significantly larger number of less active members in the over-forty age group. There were, as might have been expected, a greater number of *Liberal News* readers among the members in the first two categories of activity than those in the others.

Thus, in the case of the Labour and Conservative Parties there is a tendency for the most active members to be among the older and more experienced members. The large influx of new members into the Liberal Party has yet to be organized for activity and much of the work of the party is carried on by those younger members who joined before the great intake of 1960–1. The association of relative youth, high political interest and activity and membership dating from before 1960 suggests that the current leadership of the Liberals is in the hands of a group intermediate between the old Nonconformist middle class and the newer influx of more plebeian elements.

Finally the opinions of party members were discovered on certain questions relating to their own organization and to local political affairs. Members were asked how, in their opinion, the work of their party could be improved. The answers were grouped as shown in Table 17.

POLITICAL PARTY MEMBERSHIPS

TABLE 17. PERCENTAGE CRITICISM OF THEIR PARTIES
BY PARTY MEMBERS

	Conservative	Labour	Liberal
Suggestions for improvement	40	67	55
Don't know	54	28	39
Satisfied	6	5	6
	100	100	100

Firstly, the fact that the question was a leading one probably accounts for the very small proportions of those who declared themselves satisfied. Secondly, not a little difficulty lies in the interpretations of the proportions of those members offering suggestions for improvement. Does a high percentage indicate dissatisfaction with current methods of work or is it indicative of the extent of greater democratic discussion and interest? What may be described by others as an internal dispute may be seen by its own members as vigorous concern for the welfare of the party. The actual improvements suggested can throw some light on this. 16 per cent in the Labour Party wanted the recruitment of more younger members, and an equal number suggested better organization was needed. The highest proportions among the other suggestions were 14 per cent for more public activity of all kinds, and—very significantly—the same proportion wanted more co-operation and less 'bickering' within the party. The latter desire of course stems not only from the disputes on policy but also from the personal feuds which seem endemic in Newcastle Labour Party. Over a quarter (27 per cent) of the Conservatives believed that more enthusiasm was needed in their party, and 15 per cent wanted more members. Understandably, the latter suggestion received the most votes from the Liberals—21 per cent. The second largest group (13 per cent) thought more canvassing was necessary.

The picture which can be drawn from these suggestions and figures indicates that the Labour members see themselves as an ageing party in which internal bickering is frequent, and are concerned about inadequate public activity. The Conservatives regard themselves as a party without much rank-and-file enthusiasm, whereas the Liberals are very conscious of their relatively small size.

The party members were also questioned on two aspects of local politics designed to show their political awareness and their attitude to council affairs. Firstly, respondents were asked to give the names of their local councillor; in each case they had a choice of three but only one was required by the question.

TABLE 18. PERCENTAGE POLITICAL KNOWLEDGE AND PARTY MEMBERSHIPS

	Conservative	Labour	Liberal
One or more correct	61	47	60
Wrong name(s)	12	34	14
Don't know—no answer given	27	19	26
	100	100	100

The Liberals and Conservatives seem equally knowledgeable here, but the Liberals have an unfair advantage in that a large proportion of their membership is in Ward 4, which has recently returned two Liberal councillors. Probably the concentration of Conservatives in Ward 3, in which the councillors are well known and of long standing, has also improved the Conservative figures. A significantly greater number of active members could name their councillor than inactive ones. The fact that about one-third of the Labour respondents gave them wrong names suggests that names of Labour councillors of other wards were given in many cases. Perhaps this is understandable in a constituency which has had a Labour majority for fourteen years and has provided many of the aldermen and all the mayors during that period.

The attitude of the Labour Party to the work of the Council is very different from that of the other two parties. Members were asked their opinion on whether the work of the local council should be conducted on party lines or on a non-party basis (see Table 19).

What is surprising is not the fact that three-quarters of both the Liberals and Conservatives are against the Council being run on party lines, but that nearly one-third of the Labour respondents also think the same. Conservatives have a long tradition of co-operation with the Independents against the 'party politics' of the Labour Party; Liberal candidates have made opposition to council work being run on party lines a feature of their election addresses. But the official Labour Party policy has always been to run candidates as Labour candidates and operate as a

TABLE 19. PERCENTAGE PARTY MEMBERS' OPINION OF PARTY POLITICS IN LOCAL GOVERNMENT

	Conservative	Labour	Liberal
On party lines	10	51	18
On non-party basis	76	32	78
Don't know	14	17	4
	100	100	100

party at all levels of council work when in a majority. Significantly more pre-1939 Labour members favoured the 'party lines' view, and so did the more active members. The latter is not surprising in view of the fact that the more active members tend to be those who have had a longer membership. These are the people, of course, who fought for, and were eventually successful in obtaining, a Labour majority on the Council. Perhaps they are much more likely to favour the Council being run on party lines than those to whom a Labour majority is merely an accepted fact rather than the product of long years of struggle.

4. Conclusion

The preceding analysis enables us to distinguish some of the salient features of each of the three main political parties in Newcastle. The Labour Party is indubitably a working-class party which finds the greater part of its members among skilled and less-skilled manual workers, particularly in the three main industries of the region—coal, engineering and pottery. The majority of the members are in their appropriate trade union. Most of the party are natives of the district with long residence there, and nearly a quarter live in the Rural District's mining villages. The Labour Party has every claim to be considered as the party of the Newcastle working class.

271

The Conservative Party, on the other hand, attracts mainly the business and professional section of the community, many of whom have come to Newcastle from other parts of the country to take up their posts. A third of the party lives in the Westlands estate in Ward 3, the residential area of the respectable middle class; about half the Conservatives call themselves 'middle class', and a further quarter 'lower-middle class'. A good education, membership of the Church of England, and a liking for popular Conservative newspapers are further features of the Conservative membership. The Newcastle Conservative Party is not the party of the upper class or even upper-middle class, nor do its members consider themselves so; it is the political expression of the smaller businessmen and company directors and the managerial and professional people of Newcastle.

The most important factor differentiating the Labour and Conservative Parties is social class. Many of the other characteristics of the membership, such as education, place of birth and length of residence, the type of newspaper that is taken, can be traced to this factor. The thesis that political parties are basically the expression of different class interests finds some support in this context.

The Liberal Party, however, stands outside such a clear-cut analysis. It has all the attributes of a small party enlivened by recent heavy recruitment in different areas of the borough, attracting professional people, clerical workers and skilled industrial workers in somewhat similar proportions. Consequently it does not bear the characteristics of one particular social class; its members have varied educational, religious and residential backgrounds.

The size of the active membership of each of the parties varies as much as their social characteristics. No less than a fifth of the Labour Party are consistently active in attendance at meetings, service on committee and in help at elections. The Conservatives on the other hand, though much larger in numbers than the Labour Party, have a comparatively small corps of activists, and half the membership never attend ward meetings. The Liberals present a similar picture, but for different reasons. The large number of inactive members are mostly new recruits enrolled a few weeks before the survey was undertaken.

POLITICAL PARTY MEMBERSHIPS

It is indicative of the extent to which parties are organized for electoral purposes that the one issue which activates the greatest number of members is a General Election. Members who normally are unwilling to attend meetings or accept office will turn out with cars or serve as tellers on polling day, or will canvass the constituency beforehand, as the experience of both the Conservatives and Labour in 1959 reveals.

General Elections apart, however, local political party activity is a minority occupation even among party members in Newcastle, reflecting the low level of interest in local political affairs noticed in other chapters. Only about 3 out of every 100 of the electorate are members of political parties, and of the total number on the party rolls, only a minority are consistently active. Putting an X on a ballot paper at stated intervals still remains the one political activity which involves an overwhelming majority of the English electorate.

CHAPTER FOURTEEN

POLITICAL OPINIONS OF
PARTY MEMBERS

This chapter examines the opinions of members of the Conservative, Labour and Liberal Parties on current political issues. Some of the questions in this part of the survey were concerned with internal party policy, others with topics which were agitating the country as a whole. The Labour Party survey was held about eight weeks after the party conference which voted for unilateral nuclear disarmament and the retention of Clause 4 of the Constitution, and these, together with the question of Mr. Gaitskell's leadership, were the burning issues at the time. The Conservative and Liberal surveys took place some seven months later, when such issues as the possible restriction of immigration, the relationship between corporal punishment and crime and, in particular, the debate on whether or not Britain should join the Common Market, were in the public mind.

The questions for each party were related to its outlook and policy. There was no attempt to make a full comparative survey of political attitudes. For this reason, although there were one or two identical questions in the Conservative and Liberal questionnaires, it will be most convenient to treat each party separately.

1. The Conservative Party

The questions put to the Conservative members dealt with party leadership, the connection of crime and corporal punishment, West Indian immigration and the Common Market. The first question asked of the members was whether or not they

OPINIONS OF PARTY MEMBERS

knew which body chose the leader of the party. As this was the only question to appear on all three questionnaires, the replies of Liberal and Labour members are also given for comparison:

TABLE 1. PERCENTAGE MEMBERSHIP AND KNOWLEDGE OF METHOD OF ELECTING PARTY LEADER

	Conservative	Labour	Liberal
Correct	8	33	13
Incorrect	21	31	34
Don't know	71	36	53
	100	100	100

The relatively high correct score for Labour can be explained by the greater clarity regarding the workings of the party which the then-current discussion on leadership gave. The lower Conservative figure is not surprising; the election of a Conservative leader is a complex process which is seldom carried out. A similar criterion must be applied to the Liberals.

Conservative members were then asked: 'Whom would you like to see becoming the leader of the Conservative Party when Mr. Macmillan retires?' The replies were:

TABLE 2. PERCENTAGE CONSERVATIVE MEMBERS' PREFERENCE FOR ALTERNATIVE LEADER

Butler	24
Lloyd	7
Macleod	2
Eden	2
Others	10
Don't know	55
	100

The fact that a majority of the party were unable to name a successor suggests that this was not an issue to which the members had given great thought. On the other hand, of the 45 per cent of the party who named a successor, Butler took 24 per cent, or more than half of the votes. The only significant association was that the less active members were more predisposed to Butler

275

than to the other choices. The preferences of the Newcastle Conservatives are in close agreement with Conservative opinion
nationally. A Gallup Poll survey of July 1961 showed that 24
per cent of Conservative voters chose Butler as Macmillan's
successor, with Lloyd and Macleod in second and third places
respectively.[1]

The remaining questions all covered subjects of national political concern in which Conservatives might be assumed to have
special interest.

The first of these questions was: 'Some people think that new
laws in favour of corporal punishment would diminish crime. Do
you agree?' The replies were:[2]

TABLE 3. PERCENTAGE CONSERVATIVE MEMBERS
AND CORPORAL PUNISHMENT

Yes entirely	52
To some extent	28
Not at all	20
	100

Compared with Conservative opinion in the country as a
whole, the figure of 52 per cent for those who believed in corporal
punishment as a deterrent is very low. Conversely the figure of
20 per cent for those who believed it would have no effect is high.

According to Gallup Poll surveys, a much higher percentage
are in favour of corporal punishment as a deterrent. A poll conducted in March 1960 revealed that 79 per cent of Conservative
voters believed that flogging or birching would reduce the number of crimes of violence or sexual assault;[3] only 9 per cent
thought it would have no effect. Some eighteen months later
80 per cent of Conservative voters wanted the return of corporal
punishment.[4] Though these findings are not strictly comparable,
they are close enough to suggest that on this issue Newcastle

[1] Gallup Political Index. Report No. 19, July 1961, p. 14.
[2] 'Don't knows' and 'Refusals' are eliminated from this table, and from
Tables 4 and 5, in order to facilitate the composition of Table 7.
[3] *Capital Punishment and Corporal Punishment.* A Gallup Poll conducted for
the *News Chronicle*, March 1960, p. 21.
[4] Gallup Political Index. Report No. 23, November 1961, p. 40.

Conservative members are relative moderates, the more so because the voters in both parties are usually regarded as less extreme than the party members. Men were significantly more certain than women that legal measures would definitely diminish crime, a position which to some extent contradicts the traditional image of the 'Tory dame' calling for increased floggings as a deterrent to crime. There were no other significant associations here. Members in the 'higher' social groups, for instance, did not differ significantly in their replies from those in the 'lower', nor did religion, age, educational standard or any other factor have a significant effect in the attitude to this question.

'Do you think that compulsory national service should be reintroduced?' was the next question, which revealed very little support for conscription:

TABLE 4. PERCENTAGE CONSERVATIVE MEMBERS
AND NATIONAL SERVICE

Yes	22
No	78
	100

A question of greater moment concerned immigration: 'Some people think that West Indian immigration to Britain should be restricted. Do you agree?' Only about four out of ten were in entire agreement, and one in five was completely against restriction. Answers were not affected by differences of social

TABLE 5. PERCENTAGE CONSERVATIVE MEMBERS
AND RESTRICTION OF WEST INDIAN IMMIGRATION

Yes entirely	38
To some extent	41
Not at all	21
	100

class, religion, age or education. As in the case of corporal punishment, the figure of 38 per cent in agreement with restriction is a very low one, just over half the figure of 73 per cent for

Conservative voters in the country as a whole.[1] In this, as in other questions, the Conservatives show a definite 'liberal' bias.

A further analysis was made of the reasons which respondents gave for restriction. Of the 80 per cent in the first two categories, 90 per cent gave a reason for complete or partial restriction. These are expressed in the following table:

TABLE 6. PERCENTAGE CONSERVATIVE MEMBERS' REASONS
FOR RESTRICTION ON WEST INDIAN IMMIGRATION

Take British workers' jobs; compete with British workers	20
Not enough jobs for them here	18
Insufficient housing in Britain	28
Bad behaviour, lower standards, insufficiently trained and educated	17
Others	17
	100

It is interesting to note that the reasons most often given for restricting immigration concerned alleged difficulties of employment and housing. A total of 38 per cent wanted restriction on the grounds that West Indians would oust British workers, or be unable to find jobs themselves. A further 28 per cent thought there was insufficient housing to accommodate them in England. Only 17 per cent would restrict immigration on the grounds of alleged low standards of behaviour or education. These reasons for opposition to West Indian entry reflect, of course, the current rationalizations on the subject, for they certainly do not arise from conditions in Newcastle which has few, if any, West Indian immigrants.

Answers to the above three questions have varied, though all have shown a tendency to moderation. In order to discover whether or not there was any tendency to give positive or negative answers to all three questions, a joint table combining the answers was constructed. It was assumed that positive answers to the three questions constituted a 'right-wing' outlook; three other categories were then placed in descending order of agreement. Those who entirely or partly agreed that legislation in favour of corporal punishment diminished crime, those who wanted the

[1] Gallup Political Index. Report No. 24, December 1961, p. 10.

reintroduction of National Service and those who were wholly or partly in favour of the restriction of immigration were placed in the first category. The following categories show two agreements with the above out of the possible three, two disagreements out of the possible three and three disagreements. This latter category, in contradistinction to the first, could thus be considered a 'left-wing' outlook.

TABLE 7. PERCENTAGE CONSERVATIVE MEMBERS' ANSWERS
TO THREE QUESTIONS

Three agreements	13
Two agreements	56
Two disagreements	27
Three disagreements	4
	100

On the evidence of this table, there is only a very small group —about one-eighth of the membership—who could be said to form a 'right-wing' bloc. (And the figure of 13 per cent, it should be noted, includes those who were only in partial agreement with two of the questions.[1]) This confirms the impression already gained that the Newcastle Conservatives, in relation to Conservative opinion in the country at large, are political moderates on these issues on which a strong line might be expected. Factors such as social class, religion or education had no influence on the answers to the above table, but one interesting association was noted—members over fifty years of age tended to be more in favour of the first two categories, i.e., to lean more to the right than those under fifty. The age level in this case, however, is rather too high to speak of a 'younger generation', for many of those under fifty could have been active in the 1930's.

While the survey was taking place the debate on the Common Market was beginning to rise to its height in the press and on television, though the Prime Minister had not then announced the decision to negotiate. In view of the public interest in the topic, a three-part question on the Market was included in the Conservative and Liberal surveys. The first question was a simple

[1] It could not, of course, be higher than the lowest total for a positive answer in any of the three tables, i.e. the 22 per cent of Table 4.

factual one: 'Have you heard of the Common Market?' and 96
per cent of the Conservative membership had done so. The
second question was: 'Can you tell me which countries are
members?' The answers fell into the following categories:

TABLE 8. PERCENTAGE CONSERVATIVE MEMBERS
AND KNOWLEDGE OF COMMON MARKET

5 or 6 names correct	14
Less than 5 correct	49
Incorrect answer	9
Don't know	28
	100

This table does not show much greater political knowledge than
has previously been shown by the Conservatives. The names of
the Market members, however, had not at that stage gained the
familiarity which frequent press and television comment later
gave them. There were some significant associations here—there
was a tendency for social classes A and B to give more correct
than incorrect answers; possibly this reflected higher educational
standards. Men rather than women were also more correct in
their answers; active members were also more correct than less
active ones. A connection between male members and activity
has already been noticed. No doubt party activity which includes
discussion of policy and current political issues is a stimulus to a
knowledge of foreign affairs.

The third question was an attitude question: 'Do you agree
with Britain joining it?' (i.e., the Common Market):

TABLE 9. PERCENTAGE CONSERVATIVE MEMBERS'
ATTITUDE TO COMMON MARKET

Yes	38
No	21
Don't know	41
	100

These answers do not differ greatly from those obtained at the
time by Gallup Polls from Conservative voters. In a survey made
in the same month as the present one, 48 per cent approved of
Britain joining the Market, 23 per cent disapproved, and 29 per

cent gave the answer 'Don't know'.[1] Newcastle Conservatives have fewer in favour and a greater proportion of 'Don't knows'. The association with newspaper readership—the obvious source of opinion after the Government itself—shows some interesting and not unexpected results. Readers of the *Daily Mail* were much more in favour of joining than readers of other papers, who were split almost evenly on the issue. On the other hand, readers of the *Daily Express*, the only mass-circulation newspaper which was in unequivocal opposition to Britain's entry, were against joining the Market as compared with readers of the rest of the press. This would suggest that on this issue some members of the Conservative Party were influenced by the newspaper which they read. The Beaverbrook campaign against the Common Market found an echo in at least some Conservative hearts in Newcastle.

2. The Labour Party

The questions asked of the Labour Party ranged around the very controversial issues of unilateral nuclear disarmament, Clause 4 of the Labour Party Constitution, world peace and problems of leadership. Answers to these questions, it was felt, would give some pointers as to the extent of the left-wing influence in the party, the degree to which the views of the M.P., Stephen Swingler, are followed, and the attitude of the party towards the leadership of Gaitskell.

The first question was concerned with the decision of the recent Labour Party Conference to support unilateral nuclear disarmament for Britain. Respondents were asked if they had heard of this decision; 92 per cent of the party had heard of it. These respondents were then asked if they agreed with the decision; they divided in the following categories:

TABLE 10. PERCENTAGE LABOUR MEMBERS
AND UNILATERAL DISARMAMENT

Agree entirely	37
Agree to some extent	18
Not at all	38
Don't know	7
	100

[1] Gallup Political Index. Report No. 18, June 1961, p. 13.

OPINIONS OF PARTY MEMBERS

Labour Party members were thus polarized into two almost equal groups on this issue, with an intermediate group of about half the size inclining towards unilateralism. The percentage of the total membership calling themselves unilateralists is 34 per cent. There were two significant associations—a greater proportion of women, rather than men, were wholly or partly in agreement with unilateralism, and members in non-manual occupations more strongly in favour than those in manual jobs. The latter would indicate a somewhat more militant and left-wing line among the white-collar section of the party. A question directly bearing on international affairs followed. This was in two parts; the first part read: 'Do you think that there is any *one* country whose policy is an obstacle to world peace at the present time?' The members were divided on the issue:

TABLE 11. PERCENTAGE LABOUR MEMBERS AND BELIEF IN ANY
SINGLE COUNTRY BEING AN OBSTACLE TO PEACE

Yes	52
No	36
Don't know	12
	100

How far this bare majority giving a positive answer represented an open-minded attitude to world affairs and how far a lack of real knowledge of the world situation it is difficult to say. Those who answered 'Yes' to the above question were then asked: 'Which country would you say?' The respondents who supplied a name divided as follows:

TABLE 12. PERCENTAGE LABOUR MEMBERS
AND SINGLE COUNTRY

America	59
Russia	34
Others	7
	100

The answer to this question may be influenced by the fact that America is traditionally regarded with suspicion by many sections of the Labour movement, a tradition, as we have seen, which has been alive in Newcastle party since the war. To believe that America is an obstacle to world peace is not necessarily evidence of a left-wing outlook, though in the context there is a strong assumption in favour of it.

The question on Clause 4 of the Constitution does not divide the party on quite the same political lines as the above questions. Though 'left-wingers' are of course in favour of it, the national conference showed that some who would be classed as 'right-wingers' on the above criterion did not want Clause 4 struck out of the Constitution. The first part of the question sought a knowledge of the issue itself: 'Have you heard of Clause 4 of the Labour Party Constitution?' The answers were:

TABLE 13. PERCENTAGE LABOUR MEMBERS
AWARE OF CLAUSE 4

Heard of Clause 4	46
Not heard of Clause 4	54
	100

This was a somewhat surprising and disappointing result, considering the publicity that the clause had received in the months preceding the survey. One can only assume that specific and more technical issues, which are before the public eye for a relatively short time, make less impact on the public, and also on members of the party concerned, than international and other issues which one 'lives with' for years and decades.

The 46 per cent who were aware of the clause were then asked: 'Do you think it should be kept as it is, altered in any way, or dropped from the Constitution?'

TABLE 14. PERCENTAGE LABOUR MEMBERS
AND RETENTION OF CLAUSE 4

Kept as it is	57
Altered	20
Dropped	8
Don't know	15
	100

Here the majority was much more clear-cut. Of those who had heard of the clause, fewer than one in ten wanted it dropped from the Constitution, and were outnumbered more than seven to one by those who wished to retain it intact. The figures should, however, be brought into perspective. Expressed as a proportion of the whole of the party membership, the proponents of Clause 4 numbered only 26 per cent.

From the above data it is possible to construct a table which amalgamates the answers to the political knowledge questions. It will be remembered that the level of political knowledge varied greatly, from the 92 per cent who had heard of the conference decision to support unilateralism to the 46 per cent who had heard of Clause 4 and the 33 per cent who knew of the way in which the leader was elected. If the answers are combined the following table is the result:

TABLE 15. PERCENTAGE LABOUR MEMBERS'
POLITICAL KNOWLEDGE

Yes to all three questions	26
Yes to any two questions	31
Yes to any one question	41
No to all three questions	2
	100

Just over a quarter of the party can be considered to have a sound political knowledge on this evidence. Men were more knowledgeable than women (i.e., were in the first two categories of the table); clerical and general workers more than industrial workers; members who joined in 1945 and before more than those who joined later; the three 'higher' social groups more than the 'lower' ones. 'Higher' social class and education thus seem to be the decisive factors making for political knowledge among Labour Party members.

If, in the case of the political opinion questions, we assume that the following answers constitute a 'left-wing' line—those who wholly supported unilateral nuclear disarmament (34 per cent of the whole party); those who considered America the greatest obstacle to peace (31 per cent of the party) and those who agreed to retain Clause 4 unaltered (26 per cent of the party)—then from these data somewhat less than one-third of the party comes into this category. These figures can be compared with the proportion who took a 'right-wing' line on the same issues: 35 per cent of the party were wholly opposed to unilateralism, 18 per cent considered Russia a threat to peace and a mere 4 per cent wanted to drop Clause 4 from the Constitution. Support for 'right-wing' policies was thus on the whole low, except in the case of unilateralism. These figures are, of course, merely indications; there are many other issues by which a left- or right-wing tendency might be measured; nor, taken together, do they constitute a syndrome. But they give a rough and ready guide to the polarization of opinion within the party. Intermediate groups must also be borne in mind—the 17 per cent of the party who agreed with unilateralism 'to some extent' and the 9 per cent who wanted Clause 4 'altered' but not dropped. These, of course, must be accounted as coming nearer the 'left-wing' than the 'right-wing' line.

Because of the complexity of the questions on these issues it was not possible to amalgamate the answers to form a single table. An analysis of the completed questionnaires, however, shows that only 5 per cent of the membership answered 'Yes' to all three questions. The 'left-wing' bloc is thus very small, and suggests that support for each of the above policies is made on an *ad hoc* basis by most of the members.

The above analysis allows us to make a tentative answer to an important question—to what extent does the policy of Stephen Swingler, the M.P., who is on record as a supporter of unilateralism and the retention of Clause 4 and in general can be counted among those who consider America rather than Russia as an obstacle to world peace, command support among the members of his constituency party? On any one of these issues the answer is about one-third of the members; on all three issues, one-twentieth. The M.P.'s position would thus appear to be reasonably strong, especially if we remember that there is a sizeable intermediate gathering of partial supporters on unilateralism and Clause 4.

We have analysed the support given to the M.P. on various political issues. The last question on the survey was designed to find the extent of support for the leadership of the late Hugh Gaitskell. The question concerning the leader of the party was somewhat different from that asked of the Conservatives and

Liberals. The form of the question: 'If you were in a position to do so, who would you vote for as leader of the Labour Party?' was, in effect, a test of the membership as to whether or not they agreed with the leadership of Gaitskell; they were not asked to suggest a successor, but to say whether or not the current leader commanded their sympathies.

TABLE 16. PERCENTAGE LABOUR MEMBERS'
SUPPORT FOR PARTY LEADER

Gaitskell	58
Wilson	9
Others (right wing)	6
Others (left wing)	9
Don't know	18
	100

In the circumstances the support given to Gaitskell was sound, if not overwhelming. No other candidate came within striking distance, and the much-fancied Wilson, the 'official' opposition to Gaitskell, received a mere handful of votes. The remaining candidates, none of whom received more than two or three apiece, were loosely classified into 'right-wing' and 'left-wing' groups; the totals are probably too small to have much significance, but for what it is worth the left-wing proportion was slightly higher. The high percentage of the 'Don't knows' reveals a degree of uncertainty about the whole issue.

In order to discover what reasons, if any, guided the choice of leader, respondents were then asked: 'Why would you choose this person?' Not every respondent gave a reason, and the reasons were so varied that it was necessary, in the case of Gaitskell, to classify them into two main groups—those who chose him because they agreed with his political outlook, and those who chose him on the grounds of his personal qualities. The proportions falling into these two categories showed that in Newcastle Labour Party Gaitskell commanded support mainly on the latter ground (see Table 17).

An analysis of significant associations shows that though, among Gaitskell's supporters, there is a significantly larger number plumping for his personal qualities as against agreement with

286

his political outlook, amongst supporters of the other choices for Labour leader the reverse is the case. How far does this fact strengthen the view that a great part of Gaitskell's support came about because no alternative candidate of sufficient stature was available, and that he received the votes of those who disagreed with his political views? Did he, in fact, receive the votes of many of the left wing in Newcastle, or were his supporters concentrated

TABLE 17. PERCENTAGE LABOUR MEMBERS SUPPORTING GAITSKELL FOR POLITICAL VIEWS OR PERSONAL QUALITIES

Agreed with Gaitskell's political views	31
Admired his personal qualities	69
	100

among the right-wing elements of the party? An analysis of significant associations shows that though the unilateralists are split fairly evenly for and against Gaitskell, the anti-unilateralists are very significantly in his favour. Similarly, those who saw America as an obstacle to world peace divided almost evenly for and against Gaitskell, whereas those who thought Russia an obstacle to peace were significantly pro-Gaitskell. As far as newspaper readership is concerned, readers of the *Herald* and *Mirror* were strongly on Gaitskell's side. Apart from the fact that these papers conducted a pro-Gaitskell campaign before the conference, they are read, as we have seen, mainly by the manual workers, who are significantly pro-Gaitskell as compared with the clerical workers. Those who rated least knowledgeable on the political knowledge questions were also significantly in favour of Gaitskell, and this category, as we have also noted, were strongly made up of industrial workers from the 'lower' social classes.

Thus the main body of the Gaitskell supporters were, broadly speaking, found amongst the more right-wing elements of the industrial workers. But it is obvious that he received some support from the political left wing as well.

3. The Liberal Party

The Liberals, as we have seen, present a rather different case from that of the other two parties, in that half of their membership is of very recent date. This raises the possibility that some

287

will have been in the party so short a time as not to have assimilated the Liberal policy on all issues.

Perhaps this is evident in the answers to the question of a successor to Grimond, which did not produce a positive result. To the question: 'Who would you like to see becoming leader of the Liberal Party when Mr. Grimond retires?' the following rather inconclusive table resulted:

TABLE 18. PERCENTAGE LIBERAL MEMBERS' CHOICE
OF ALTERNATIVE LEADER

Jeremy Thorpe	6
Ludovic Kennedy	3
Frank Byers	3
Others	5
Don't know	83
	100

Thus more than eight out of ten could not suggest an alternative to Grimond. A significantly larger number of *Liberal News* readers and members who joined before 1959 were able to supply a name than other non-readers or those who joined after 1959; this is in keeping with the greater political knowledgeability of the more experienced members noticed before.

Another question peculiar to the Liberals concerned future voting behaviour in the unlikelihood of a Liberal candidate standing at the next General Election. In view of the scarcity of Liberal candidates in recent years and the fact that, at the time of the survey, no Liberal candidate had been chosen for a future election, members were asked: 'If there is no Liberal candidate standing in Newcastle at the next General Election, which party, if any, will you vote for?'

TABLE 19. PERCENTAGE LIBERAL MEMBERS' GENERAL ELECTION
VOTE IF NO LIBERAL CANDIDATE

Conservative	39
Labour	17
Others	5
Won't vote	25
Don't know	14
	100

OPINIONS OF PARTY MEMBERS

Thus only one-quarter of the party would abstain from voting, whereas 61 per cent would vote for one party or another. The two-to-one majority in favour of Conservatism on this issue is in line with the anti-Labour and pro-Conservative trend already seen in the party. A further pointer to this is shown in the answers to a question in the earlier part of the survey which is relevant here: 'Have you ever been a member of any other political party? If yes, which one?': 83 per cent had never been members of any other party, but 10 per cent had been members of the Labour Party, 5 per cent members of the Conservative Party, and 2 per cent members of other parties. The figures are not large, but they suggest a slightly greater dissatisfaction with Labour than with the Conservatives.

One or two associations between possible future voting behaviour and type of member are worth noting in connection with the answers to Table 19. Not surprisingly, readers of the non-Labour papers—the *Mail*, *Express* and *Telegraph*—were more likely to vote Conservative than readers of other newspapers. The recruits of 1960–1, on the other hand, were less likely to vote Conservative than those who joined the party before them. In the previous chapter it was shown that these new recruits tended to come from the lower-middle and working class, and to be members of manual and general unions. Evidently, though dissatisfied with Labour, they are sufficiently within the working-class and trade-union ambit to reject Conservatism.

The last question on what might be called internal party attitudes concerned electoral reform. For many years the Liberals have campaigned for a reform of the electoral system on the lines of proportional representation. The first part of this question was: 'Are you satisfied with the present electoral system?' The replies were tabulated thus:

TABLE 20. PERCENTAGE LIBERAL MEMBERS' ATTITUDE TO ELECTORAL SYSTEM

Yes	55
No	39
Don't know	6
	100

OPINIONS OF PARTY MEMBERS

It is possible that even the recent modest electoral successes of the Liberals may have blunted the edge of their enthusiasm for such a reform. If successes can be won under the present electoral system, reform may seem less pressing. On the other hand, many of the new recruits may be simply unaware of this traditional item of Liberal policy. That the latter may be the truer state of affairs is suggested by the fact that committee members were significantly more in favour of reform than non-committee members, and *Liberal News* readers rather than non-readers. This position is confirmed by the fact that those who joined before 1959 are significantly more in favour of reform than those who joined in the period 1960–1. Of the 39 per cent who were dissatisfied with the electoral system, 85 per cent were in favour of some form of proportional representation; 6 per cent wanted voting to be made compulsory, and the remaining 9 per cent were made up of those in favour of various other schemes. The proportion of the whole party who want proportional representation amounts, however, to only 33 per cent.

The general picture which arises from the answers to these questions does not contradict the previous impression of a party with a dynamic and well-informed leadership and a large number of members who have not yet assimilated traditional Liberal attitudes or even elementary political knowledge.

The question on West Indian immigration was exactly the same as that set for the Conservatives. For the purpose of comparison the answers are set against those of the latter. The

TABLE 21. PERCENTAGE LIBERAL AND CONSERVATIVE MEMBERS' ATTITUDES TO RESTRICTION OF WEST INDIAN IMMIGRATION

	Liberal	Conservative
Yes entirely	22	38
To some extent	36	41
Not at all	42	21
.	100	100

Liberals are more 'liberal' on this issue than the Conservatives, with four out of ten against any restriction at all. The main factors influencing this decision seem to be the standard of

290

education and Liberal principles. Those who left school at 16 or more were significantly more in favour of unrestricted immigration than those who left at 15 or under. Committee members were more in favour of no restriction than non-committee members. Readers of the *Mail* and *Express* were more in favour of restriction than readers of the *Guardian*.

Reasons were given by 81 per cent of those who favoured complete or partial restriction, and are analysed into categories in the same way as was done for the Conservatives, with whose figures they are compared:

TABLE 22. PERCENTAGE LIBERAL AND CONSERVATIVE MEMBERS' AND WEST INDIAN IMMIGRATION

	Liberal	Conservative
Take British workers' jobs; compete with British workers	43	20
Not enough jobs for them here	3	18
Insufficient housing in Britain	15	28
Bad behaviour, lower standards, insufficiently trained and educated	26	17
Others	13	17
	100	100

The Liberal restrictionists feared West Indian competition with British workers for jobs to a much greater extent than the Conservatives, more than twice as many giving this as a reason. We can only speculate why Conservative restrictionists should see the major evil of immigration in the field of housing whereas Liberals most fear economic competition. It is a reflection, perhaps, of their different social composition and outlook. Do the Conservatives fear intrusion into the 'residential' areas? Do the working-class and lower-middle-class members of the Liberal Party feel that their jobs might be threatened?

On the question of unilateral nuclear disarmament, the Liberal replies can be compared with those of the Labour Party. Liberals were asked: 'Do you approve of the policy of unilateral nuclear disarmament for Britain?' The answers were divided for and against as shown in Table 23.

OPINIONS OF PARTY MEMBERS

TABLE 23. PERCENTAGE LIBERAL AND LABOUR PARTIES
AND UNILATERAL DISARMAMENT

	Liberal	Labour
Yes	31	37
No	61	38
Don't know	8	7
	100	82

The figures for the Labour Party exclude the 18 per cent who supported unilateralism 'to some extent'. The Liberal supporters of unilateralism are thus not very greatly fewer than those in the Labour Party, which was officially committed to unilateralism as a policy at the time of the survey.

The three-part question on the Common Market had the same wording for the Liberal survey as that given to the Conservatives. To the question: 'Have you heard of the Common Market?' the following replies were given, with the Conservative answers for comparison:

TABLE 24. PERCENTAGE LIBERAL AND CONSERVATIVE MEMBERS
HAVING HEARD OF THE COMMON MARKET

	Liberal	Conservative
Yes	72	96
No	28	4
	100	100

The large percentage of those who had not heard of the Common Market again reflected the fairly large reservoir of political unawareness among the Liberals.

The 72 per cent who answered 'Yes' to the question were split in the proportions shown in Table 25 when asked to name the member countries.

The Liberals who had heard of the Market were able to supply more correct names than the Conservatives. In both parties, however, the percentage giving one or more correct names was about the same—66 per cent for the Liberals, 63 per cent for the

292

Conservatives. As a percentage of the total party membership, the Liberal figure was, however, 48 per cent as against the Conservatives' 60 per cent. In the case of the Liberals, education again was a factor in their ability to name members of the Market; those whose schooling finished at 16 were able to give more correct answers than those who left school before this age. In addition, men were significantly more knowledgeable than women and those under 40 more so than those over 40.

TABLE 25. PERCENTAGE LIBERAL AND CONSERVATIVE MEMBERS' KNOWLEDGE OF THE COMMON MARKET

	Liberal	Conservative
5 or 6 correct	27	14
Less than 5 correct	39	49
Incorrect answer	6	9
Don't know	28	28
	100	100

Those who had heard of the Common Market were then asked the third part of the question: 'Do you agree with Britain joining it?' Over half the Liberals did agree:

TABLE 26. PERCENTAGE LIBERAL AND CONSERVATIVE MEMBERS' SUPPORT FOR BRITISH MEMBERSHIP OF COMMON MARKET

	Liberal	Conservative
Yes	56	38
No	17	21
Don't know	27	41
	100	100

Perhaps the most interesting deduction from this table is that even before negotiations for Britain's entry had officially begun, and while there was a good deal of debate, and also a certain amount of confusion on the issue, there was only a small minority in each party (two in ten or less) who were definitely opposed to Britain's entry. Taking the party membership as a whole, the proportion of Liberals who were in favour of Britain joining the Market was only slightly larger—40 per cent—than that of the Conservatives—36 per cent. Significant associations reveal that those most in favour of Market membership were *Liberal News* readers, those who had entered the area within the last twenty years and those who had served on committees during the last ten years. These groups, as we have already seen, are the ones from which the leadership is drawn; there is no doubt that on this issue, as on others, the dynamic of policy has been theirs.

4. Conclusion

Questionnaires are necessarily selective, and it is not maintained that a comprehensive picture of the political attitudes of the rank-and-file of the three parties can be drawn from an analysis of the answers to the above questions. Nevertheless, comment can be made on some of the more interesting and significant trends revealed by the survey.

In the case of the Conservative Party, two points are worthy of note—the relatively low level of political knowledge, and a sense of moderation on certain important issues on which Conservatives traditionally take a strong line. The fact that only 8 per cent of the party know the way in which the leader is elected, and only 14 per cent can name five or six members of the Common Market, is consistent with the picture of party activity drawn in the previous chapter. The answers to the policy questions, however, raise some interesting problems. On some issues, members of the Newcastle Conservative Party differ little in their attitude from Conservative supporters nationally—on whether Britain should enter the Common Market, or on the question of a successor to Macmillan. But on the issues of conscription, corporal punishment and immigration, the Newcastle members show a surprising moderation, nor does the number of 'diehards' on these questions exceed one in eight of the party.

This rather striking 'liberal' trend has no simple explanation beyond that which can be found in the environmental and historical situation. It has already been noticed that Newcastle is an area of relative political moderation, and certainly during the last fifty years or so it has lacked any long-drawn-out or large-scale political or industrial unrest. Above all, time has yet to eradicate the influence of Josiah Wedgwood. It will be remembered that he always maintained good personal relationships with Conservatives, some of whom, it was said, would secretly vote for him. In 1931, in an excess of local patriotic zeal, they even agreed not to oppose him at future elections. These attitudes laid the basis for a tradition of political moderation.

In contrast to the Conservatives, the Labour Party has an aspect of greater political awareness, activity and militancy. The key to the relatively high state of political knowledge would seem to lie in the involvement of a large proportion of the membership in party work of various kinds. Politically, however, Newcastle Labour Party cannot claim wholly to belong to the left. About a third of the party take a 'left-wing' stand on certain issues, but only a small fraction—a mere 5 per cent—were found to be consistently 'left' on the three important issues of unilateralism, world peace and Clause 4. This suggests that on any single issue a fair measure of left-wing opinion can be aroused (and the partial supporters of left policies should not be forgotten). But the hard-core support for the policies of the Member of Parliament, an office-holder of the Victory for Socialism group, is small indeed, and suggests that a left-wing M.P. does not necessarily imply an overwhelmingly left-wing constituency party.

To some extent the near-60 per cent support for the leadership of the late Hugh Gaitskell supports the above picture. Admittedly only a third of those who supported him agreed with his policies, but there was, on the other hand, no great demonstration in favour of an ostensibly left-wing rival. The fact that the greatest opposition to Gaitskell tended to come from the clerical workers, who were also among the most politically knowledgeable of the membership, suggests that the centre of gravity of activity and militancy could be moving towards this class in Newcastle Labour Party.

The Liberals, lastly, have no clear-cut political tendencies. They reveal a mixture of radicalism on some issues with a tendency to conservatism on others, which is entirely a reflection of their mixed social and political composition at the time of the survey. As far as votes at a future General Election are concerned, they lean heavily to the Conservatives, and a greater proportion of them want Britain to join the Common Market

OPINIONS OF PARTY MEMBERS

than the latter. On the other hand, nearly a third of the Liberals are unilateralists, and they have a much more radical attitude on immigration than the Conservatives, moderates though the latter might be on this issue. Not surprisingly, the highest level of political knowledge and grasp of party policy comes from the better-educated professional elements who form the greater part of the leadership. If recruitment in the Liberal Association is continued, however, on the scale of 1960–1, the above trends of opinion may alter.

CHAPTER FIFTEEN

COUNCILLORS AND CANDIDATES

P arty members constitute the middle part of the chain which
links the people with their political leaders: they are relatively numerous but many of them, as we have seen, are
almost totally inactive and many of the more active do not
participate very much in politics. Councillors and candidates are
fewer and more politically involved. Though Newcastle has
about two thousand of its citizens on the rolls of the political
parties, only seventy-five people in the Borough and Rural
District belong to one of the two local councils at any given
moment. There are perhaps another hundred who were members of these councils in the past and have retired and a further
hundred who are eager to stand at future elections despite previous defeats or little hope of a safe seat. The study of councillors
and candidates does therefore have a logical place after the study
of the membership: both councillors and candidates participate
fairly actively in politics and councillors occupy positions where
they can wield some administrative power, while, at the same
time, the number of persons involved has become fairly small.

Distinctions have to be made within the whole group, however. Some councillors and candidates show a greater zeal for
local politics and contest seats repeatedly at local elections. Some
are always unsuccessful while others are elected. Some are elected
for a short period and others remain several terms on the councils and are elected aldermen. These long-term councillors tend
to become chairmen of committees and thereby to have more
influence. The boundary between influential and less-influential
councillors is difficult to draw, but the bulk of the councillors
clearly falls within one or the other group. There are thus three
levels of councillors and candidates which a study should help to

distinguish. At the bottom, unsuccessful candidates, and among them those who contest only one election, play a very limited part in local government life. In the middle, councillors elected for one term or two do have some power, but do not exercise it for long. At the top, the rest of the councillors and aldermen may sometimes—although not always—have much power.

Such distinctions can be made only by an analysis of the personnel who stand for local elections over a relatively long period. Otherwise, the group is too small to constitute an adequate sample and the period is too short to allow for an examination of the length of tenure of office of councillors and of the number of contests of candidates. In this chapter, all the candidates who stood for the Newcastle Borough Council and the Newcastle Rural District Council between 1932 (the date of the local government reconstruction) and 1962 are considered. The war and the starting and terminal dates all raise some unavoidable problems; but the duration of a generation is surely a long enough period to give an idea of the characteristics of the personnel involved in Newcastle local elections.

1. Candidates

(i) SELECTION

Methods of selection of candidates are analysed more in detail in other chapters.[1] But it must be remembered that the party structure in local government is somewhat different on the right from what it is on the left. The Labour Party, both in the Borough and in the Rural District, tends to apply the same formal procedures for the selection of its candidates as in other parts of the country, although, as the party organization is weak in many areas, the adoption procedure often consists only of the informal decision taken by a few keen party members who agree to approach another member. On the right, the selection of candidates was informal for a very long time almost everywhere in the constituency and still is to some extent in many parts of the town and the Rural District. An Independent organization based on small committees in each ward helped to put up candidates and supported their campaign. Since the late 1950's,

---

[1] See Chaps. 16 and 17.

however, the revival of the Liberal organization and the gradual development of the Conservative organization tended to spread to the right and centre procedures more akin to those of the Labour Party. As for most of the period, however, Independents tended to contest most seats and to receive the bulk of the non-Labour vote, the analysis conducted in this chapter is based on the examination of Labour and Independent candidates. Conservative candidates, who appeared only in the late 1950's, have been added to the latter.

(ii) CANDIDATES AND CONTESTS

In the Borough at least, the average political career of candidates is short. Between 1932 and 1962, 305 candidates stood for the Council and these candidates entered an aggregate number of 676 fights and uncontested elections, including by-elections: on average, each candidate thus contested only slightly more than two elections (2·23). If one excludes twelve candidates who stood for the reconstructed 1932 Council only once (and were immediately elected aldermen because they had been prominent on one of the previous councils), the average number of contests per candidate rises slightly to 2·28. Local elections thus had a rapid turnover, particularly if it is remembered that they take place every year and that there is a fairly large number of by-elections.

TABLE 1. NUMBER OF CONTESTS PER CANDIDATE IN NEWCASTLE BOROUGH

	Number of candidates	Percentage	Number of contests	Percentage
Contested once	130	44·5	130	19·5
Contested twice	57	19·5	114	17
Contested three times	51	17·5	153	23
Contested four times or more	55	18·5	267	40·5
	293 (+ 12 aldermen)	100	664	100

If these 293 candidates are divided into four categories according to the number of contests they fought, over two-fifths of them appear to have contested an election only once; but these two-fifths contributed to less than a fifth of the total number of elections: a large group of candidates takes a very small part in local elections. Some leave the district unexpectedly, are too ill to stand again, or die; but others are not sufficiently interested to participate further in local affairs and to want to be inconvenienced more than once by the relatively light burden of a local election campaign.

At the other end of the scale, 55 persons, or less than a fifth of the candidates, stood four times or more and contributed to two-fifths of the contests over the period 1932–62, while a further 51 contested three elections. One hundred and six persons thus can be said to have constituted the hard core of the personnel engaged in local election campaigns over a whole generation in Newcastle-under-Lyme: they were the only really persistent candidates and they contributed in fact to two-thirds of the contests.

(iii) DISCREPANCY BETWEEN RIGHT AND LEFT

Candidates who only stood once thus constitute a large proportion of the total. They can be found among all parties, although Labour seems to attract slightly more of the keen candidates than the other political organizations. Small parties or 'non-party' candidates tend naturally to form a larger proportion of the candidates who only contested one election: two-thirds of the seventeen candidates who did not belong to the Labour Party or to the Independent or Conservative organizations fell in that category.[1]

The difference between Labour and Independents is not as marked, but it exists. There were more Independent candidates, but the number of Labour candidates who stood four times or more is larger. This is partly owing to the fact that, in the pre-war period, Labour did not succeed in securing a seat on the aldermanic bench for many of its councillors, although, in the post-war period, Independents suffered to some extent from the same disadvantage. But it is also probably true that, overall, more Labour candidates were anxious to stand for the Labour Council, while Independent candidates seemed more ready to

[1] These candidates include 6 Liberals, 5 Communists, 3 'Progressives' and 3 'Non-party'.

abandon the fight once they had been unsuccessful. There seems to be a hard core of Labour members for whom local politics have an importance which is rarely attained—or attained for so long—on the Independent side.

TABLE 2. CANDIDATES AND CONTESTS IN EACH PARTY IN NEWCASTLE BOROUGH

	Independents		Labour		Other		Total	
	No.	*Per-centage*	*No.*	*Per-centage*	*No.*	*Per-centage*	*No.*	*Per-centage*
Contested once	72	46·5	46	40	12	70·5	130	44·5
Contested twice	29	19	22	19	4	23·5	57*	19·5
Contested three times	29	19	19	16·5	1	6	51†	17·5
Contested four times (or more)	24	15·5	28	24·5	—	—	55‡	18·5
	154	100	115	100	17	100	293	100

* Including two candidates who left the Labour Party to become 'Progressives'.
† Including two candidates who left the Labour Party to become Independents.
‡ Including three candidates who left the Labour Party to become Independents.

The situation in the Rural District cannot easily be compared with that in the Borough: many Rural District seats remained uncontested and elections occur only every three years. But Rural District candidates seem to have been somewhat more persistent than Borough candidates. Two hundred and ninety-three candidates in the Borough competed for an aggregate of 276 seats (not counting by-elections), while 112 candidates in the Rural District competed for an aggregate of 195 seats. There was thus, on average, about one candidate per seat in the Borough, and one candidate per 1·7 seats in the Rural District.

(iv) SOCIAL CLASS OF CANDIDATES

The analysis of the occupations of candidates has to be limited to the two major party groupings: other candidates were few and belonged to a wide range of very different organizations, from Communist to 'non-party'. But, if one uses the same class categories as for the survey, several contrasts appear. The class of Independent candidates contrasts with that of Labour candidates; the class of candidates in general contrasts with that of the electors; finally, the class of the candidates of each party grouping contrasts with the class composition of the electors of that party.

TABLE 3. SOCIAL CLASS OF CANDIDATES IN THE BOROUGH

	Independents		Labour		Both	
	No.	*Per-centage*	*No.*	*Per-centage*	*No.*	*Per-centage*
Business proprietors among whom:	60	39	3	2·5	63	23·5
shopkeepers	31	20	3	2·5	34	12·5
Professional and managerial	28	18	7	6	35	13
Clerical	24	15·5	23	20	47	17·5
Manual workers among whom:	9	6	61	53	70	26
miners	4	2·5	17	15	21	8
railwaymen	2	1·5	9	8	11	4
Others: housewives	8	5·5	9	8	17	6·5
unknown, not stated	25	16	12	10·5	37	13·5
	154	100	115	100	269	100

Manual workers are under-represented: they form 26 per cent of the candidates and 70 per cent of the electors in the Borough. Business proprietors and clerical workers are over-represented, with 23·5 per cent and 17·5 per cent of the candidates against 8 per cent and 9 per cent of the electors. Among business proprietors, shopkeepers form the majority and builders constitute an important fraction of the others (7 out of 29). Managerial and professional people have a fair representation, but on the Labour side this group is mainly composed of teachers.

Manual workers are at a disadvantage in both parties, although the discrepancy is much larger on the Independent side. Indeed, the bulk of the nine Independent manual workers were candidates before the war. Like Conservative M.P.'s, Independent candidates are far from constituting a microcosm of the electors; they are mainly drawn from the 'middle classes'. But, on the Labour side as well, manual workers are under-represented: only slightly over half the Labour candidates were manual workers and over a fourth were 'middle class', while 87 per cent of the Labour electors of 1959 were found to be industrial workers and 13 per cent only were drawn from the non-manual groups. As in Parliament, not only do the candidates who come from the working class tend overwhelmingly to be Labour (or, to put it differently, were it not for the Labour Party, manual workers would remain almost totally unrepresented); but also the non-manual groups tend to be over-represented among both Labour and non-Labour candidates. On the other hand, while non-Labour candidates tend mainly to come from among the business proprietors and managerial and professional people, Labour candidates who are not drawn from the manual working class are essentially clerical workers.

An analysis of occupations on a party basis has little meaning in the Rural District, as Labour entered few contests in the rural parishes. But a geographical analysis, based on the division between the rural parishes, the 'fringe of the coalfield' and Audley, shows on the contrary very marked contrasts. In the rural parishes, farmers are by far the largest group and are in a majority, although, in some parishes situated near Newcastle, professional and managerial people have come forward to contest seats. In the parishes on the fringe of the coalfield, the candidates are more mixed: farmers are less numerous, while manual workers, most of whom contested Madeley, are a sizeable proportion of the candidates. In Audley, the representation of the occupational categories tends to follow the same pattern as in the Borough, although professional and managerial people are fewer and manual workers are more numerous. Indeed, the social origins of the candidates in that parish have changed drastically since the pre-war period: the old 'middle-class' type of representation has tended to be replaced almost entirely by a purely 'working-class' representation (see Table 4).

Fluctuations in the occupations of candidates follow therefore to a considerable extent the fluctuations of occupations in the area, but the manual workers are at a disadvantage everywhere in the constituency. This discrepancy comes perhaps to some extent from the fact that political interest is less widespread among manual workers, but manual workers are also more reluctant to contest seats than non-manual workers whose background and occupations prepare them more often for committee work and administrative decisions. Social 'superiority' as such has probably little influence, although it might have played some part in the constituency before the war and may still have played a part in some rural areas since 1945. The 'technical' qualifications of members of non-manual groups, even of the clerical workers, are much more likely to be a decisive factor.

TABLE 4. OCCUPATIONS OF CANDIDATES IN THE RURAL DISTRICT

	Rural parishes (Ashley, Chorlton, Maer, Mucklestone, Tyrley, Whitmore)		The fringe of the coalfield (Balterley, Betley, Keele, Madeley)		Audley	
	No.	Percentage	No.	Percentage	No.	Percentage
Business proprietors	19	70·5	12	35·5	11	21·5
among whom:						
farmers	15	55·5	5	15	1	2
shopkeepers	3	11	6	18	8	15·5
Managerial and professional	4	15	7	20·5	2	4
Clerical	1	3·5	1	3	9	17·5
Manual workers	—	—	8	23·5	20	39·5
Others: housewives	—	—	2	6	3	6
unknown or not stated	3	11	4	11·5	6	11·5
	27	100	34	100	51	100

2. Councillors

(i) SOCIAL CLASS OF COUNCILLORS

The class background of Rural District councillors does not differ markedly from that of unsuccessful candidates, but, in the Borough, councillors appear to be even more 'unrepresentative' than unsuccessful candidates. Manual workers and shopkeepers are less likely than the other groups to be selected for a safe seat on the Council.

TABLE 5. SUCCESSFUL AND UNSUCCESSFUL CANDIDATES IN THE BOROUGH

	Independents				Labour			
	Unsuccessful		Successful		Unsuccessful		Successful	
	No.	Percentage	No.	Percentage	No.	Percentage	No.	Percentage
Business proprietors among whom:	28	41	32	37	1	2	2	3
shopkeepers	17	25	14	16	1	2	2	3
others	11	16	18	21	—	—	—	—
Professional and managerial	7	10	21	24·5	—	—	7	10·5
Clerical	8	12	16	18·5	8	16·5	15	23
Manual workers among whom:	6	9	3	3·5	30	61	31	54
miners	2	3	2	2·5	7	14	10	15
railwaymen	1	1·5	1	1	4	8	5	7·5
Others: housewives unknown, not	4	6	4	4·5	5	10	4	6
stated	15	22	10	12·5	5	10	7	10·5
	68	100	86	100	49	100	66	100

Manual workers are at a disadvantage in both parties: in the Labour Party miners and perhaps railwaymen are less likely to be given difficult seats to contest than other manual workers, but their chances of being given a safe seat are less good than those of a non-manual worker. Overall, however, in contrast with what happens at Westminster, safe seats are not more likely to be 'trade-union seats' than marginal seats: although trade unions appeared to have sponsored some seats from time to time in Newcastle, the practice has been neither widespread nor systematic.

Among Independents, shopkeepers have also been less

successful than other non-manual groups. There were more candidates but less councillors from this group than from other categories of business proprietors. Businessmen and professional and managerial people clearly tend to be selected for the middle-class wards of the Borough while shopkeepers are more likely to stand for some of the more difficult working-class wards: on the Independent side, candidates are more likely to stand for the wards in which they live and the only business proprietors who commonly live in working-class wards are small shopkeepers.

As a result, the middle class is even more over-represented and the working class more under-represented among councillors than among candidates in general. While slightly over half the candidates come from the non-manual groups (54 per cent), slightly over three-fifths of the councillors (62 per cent) have a non-manual occupation. The manual workers are not un-represented on the Newcastle Council, but, even with the growth of the Labour Party, they remain in a minority. The Borough of Newcastle may be mainly inhabited by manual workers, but a large number of its local election candidates and a majority of its councillors come from non-manual workers' groups: the 'solid middle class' may not be preponderant, but middle- and lower-middle-class people are mainly in charge of local affairs.

(ii) CAREER OF COUNCILLORS

Many councillors have a short career: over two-fifths of the Borough councillors remained in office for one term only and the percentage was even higher among Labour councillors alone. Yet the end of these careers did not seem to come about usually by defeat. Only 27 of the candidates who remained in office for one term had contested a ward unsuccessfully before or after being elected; 40 candidates were successful at their first attempt, spent three years on the Council and left local politics without further contest. Some moved from the area; a few died. But the majority appeared to have only a limited interest in local politics or were disappointed by the relatively small power and the relatively large burdens of local government (see Table 6).

No Newcastle councillor has ever been elected alderman after serving only one term on the Council. But some have come to the aldermanic bench in their second term, and half those who have spent more than three terms as councillors have eventually been elected aldermen. As a result, the figures shown in Table 6 underestimate the length of tenure in office of many long-term councillors and they also underestimate the break between the group

TABLE 6. TENURE OF OFFICE OF NEWCASTLE COUNCILLORS

	Independents		Labour		Others*		Total	
	No.	Percentage	No.	Percentage	No.	Percentage	No.	Percentage
One term	34	39·5	29	44·5	4	40	67	41
Two terms	22	25·5	12	18	1	10	35	22·5
Three terms	22	25·5	10	15	4	40	36	22
Four terms or more	8	9·5	15	22·5	1	10	24	15
	86	100	66	100	10	100	162	100

* Including councillors who left the Labour Party to join the Independents.

of transient one- and two-term councillors and the group of long-term councillors who remained in office, as councillors or aldermen, for a decade or more.

TABLE 7. RECRUITMENT OF ALDERMEN

	Number of councillors	Aldermen	
		Number	Percentage among councillors
Two terms	35	9	25·5
Three terms	36	10	28
Four terms or more	24	12	50
	95	31	32·5

Elections to the aldermanic bench tend to occur largely on a seniority basis: indeed changes in party control account for eight of the nine cases of aldermen elected from among councillors who were in their second term. But as six further years in office—and sometimes twelve when the alderman is re-elected—are thus added to councillors who have already spent a fairly long time on the Council, the gap between 'junior councillors' who spent three or six years on the Council and 'senior councillors' who spent fifteen years or more tends to be increased. If the six years on the aldermanic bench are added to the number of terms spent as councillors, a group of 43 persons only seems to have ensured continuity on the Borough Council by remaining in office more than twelve years, while 26 councillors had participated in local affairs for only half that length and 67 councillors for a quarter of that time.

These 43 councillors who had twelve years of office and the 26 others who had nine years did not monopolize all the posts of influence. Thirty-eight of the 43 and 12 of the 26 were at some time chairmen of one or more committees, but 13 other councillors, including one-term councillors, were also appointed chairmen. Yet clearly the main burden of the organization of the Council was, over the whole of a generation, in the hands of a fairly small group. If the turnover is rapid at the bottom, and if many candidates, quickly disillusioned, cease to contest elections, the leadership at the top remains very stable. Changes in majority, particularly at the end of the war, increased the turnover. But the last thirty years have shown that Newcastle can recruit dedicated councillors willing to stay in office. It is perhaps deplorable that so many have served for short periods, but the blame cannot be placed on those who appear to be the 'ruling few'.

Trends are not very different in the Rural District. The length of tenure of councillors is longer than in the Borough, but as the Rural District Council has no aldermen, councillors are clearly likely to stand longer for re-election. Ten of the 47 councillors representing rural parishes and the fringe of the coalfield remained on the Council for twenty years or more in the period 1919–60, while 8 served for three years or less and 7 between three and six years. Eighteen of the 37 Audley councillors remained in office for only a term. Since, in the rural parishes at least, the length of tenure in office was rarely broken by defeat at the polls, it seems that many councillors preferred to remain on the Council for short periods only; this tendency even increased in the course of the 1940's and 1950's. While it became difficult to find candidates (one councillor had almost to be forced to stay on the Council in 1958, although he had previously resigned), long-term candidates were much less numerous in post-war years than they were in the inter-war years: by 1960, there was no longer any Rural District councillor who had been on the Council before the war ended.

It is therefore not because a small group of councillors want to perpetuate themselves in office that there are so few councillors in the 'influential' group. Some probably do want to remain on the Council for as long as they can; some of those who abandoned local politics after a few years may have done so because they felt that they would never enter the circle of influential leaders; but, on balance, it seems that the number of influential councillors tends to remain small because competition is probably not

OCCUPATIONAL STATUS OF ELECTORS, CANDIDATES, & COUNCILLORS

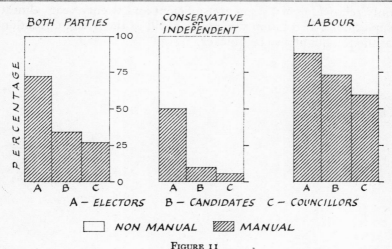

BOTH PARTIES   CONSERVATIVE or INDEPENDENT   LABOUR

A — ELECTORS   B — CANDIDATES   C — COUNCILLORS

NON MANUAL   MANUAL

FIGURE 11

great. Few long-term councillors did remain in office for periods of over twenty years, even in the Rural District, let alone in the Borough; and on the County Council, where the large majority of Newcastle councillors was drawn from members of the Borough or Rural District councils (19 out of 27), the average length of tenure of office was not longer than it was on the two other councils and only two Newcastle County councillors were elected for four consecutive terms.

COUNCILLORS AND CANDIDATES

Over a period of thirty years, local politics attracted only a tiny fraction of the Newcastle electors and party members. Among those who were attracted, few seemed to have enough interest, and some had too little luck, to be able to continue for long periods to contest elections or to sit on one of the councils. Those who contested were 'unrepresentative' of the social groups, and those who succeeded were even more 'unrepresentative' (Figure 11). But, despite this narrow recruitment and their relatively exclusive social background, influential long-term councillors do not constitute a 'group' in the strong sense of the word. Their seniority makes them more influential; the technical aspects of local administration tend to help professional and managerial people, as well as clerical workers. But the group is not closed; the seniority which the system seems to require is only relative, as ten years are sufficient and twenty years almost superfluous. If rotation was not so rapid at the bottom, rotation at the top might also be quicker.

CHAPTER SIXTEEN

THE POLITICS OF THE
RURAL DISTRICT

Local politics generally differs most from national politics in that it arouses slighter interest. In Newcastle constituency rather less than half the people who vote at General Elections vote at local elections. This puts a premium on good organization at municipal elections; because if only 40 per cent vote campaign organizers have to ensure only 21 per cent support for their candidate in order to get him elected. Well-organized minorities thus have some chance of winning local council seats. However, fewer party members, as we have seen,[1] are willing to help at local elections than at Parliamentary elections; and the party zealots' attempts to make the local elections rehearsals for the 'big day' are not always very successful. On the other hand one of the national parties, the Labour Party, is now responsible for the selection of about half the local government candidatures in the constituency and the Conservative and Liberal parties seem increasingly to be moving into local politics.

Yet the two local authorities in Newcastle constituency have very contrasting characteristics, and in only one respect have their post-war political histories been similar—the cycle of the growth of party organization and its collapse has coincided in Newcastle Borough and Newcastle Rural District. The peak of party effort and enthusiasm was reached about 1950: since then apathy has been a marked feature of both. Yet the feverish political activity of the immediate post-war years made quite different impacts on the two local authorities: in Newcastle Borough with its Borough Labour Party asserting 'Boroughwise'

---

[1] See above, Chap. 13, p. 266.

Labour Party precepts, Labour 'seized power' in 1947 and has held on to it, except for a few months in 1958, ever since. Consequently a familiar 'political system' has crystallized in the Borough—that of majority party government, involving whips, group decisions, and centralized policy-making. (This is described in Chapter 17.) In the Rural District, on the contrary, no such result followed the Labour victory of 1945. There has been no 'Rural District Labour Party' to impose its discipline on Rural District Labour councillors, and every attempt to construct a Rural District Labour Group has failed. Indeed so divided have the Labour ranks been that it is difficult to say whether Labour has ever been 'in power' or not. Thus majority party government and centralized decision-making have been absent from the deliberations of the Rural District Council.[1]

Two connected factors have been responsible for the inability of the Rural District to emulate the Borough. Even in Audley Parish, the most urbanized part of the Rural District, personality obviously counts for a good deal more in local politics than organizational contact. All the villages are 'face-to-face' communities in a way that most of the Borough wards are not. Moreover the parishes have developed separate political styles of their own and sectionalism has prevented the emergence of political issues dividing the whole Rural District on lines of principle. Councillors tend to promote parish rather than party interests.

In the post-war years the politics of Newcastle Rural District never achieved the equilibrium that distinguished political life in Newcastle Borough. Interest mainly lies in the failure of the Labour Party to take advantage of its apparent position of power and in the differences between parishes and local Labour parties that were the reason for this setback. Thus we shall divide the period since 1945 into the phase in which Labour looked likely to control the Council and the era since the 'rents row' of 1955 which put paid to Labour dominance for a long time. Furthermore we shall examine the parishes in the groupings we used in

[1] This account of Rural District politics is based on Minutes of the Newcastle Rural District Council, *Evening Sentinel*, *Newcastle Times*, Minutes of the Madeley Labour Party, Minutes of the Audley and Bignall End Labour Party, Minutes of the Newcastle Rural District Labour Group, and numerous interviews.

Chapter 7—the 'rural parishes', the 'fringe of the coalfield' and Audley.

1. The Post-war Years

(i) THE RURAL PARISHES

These are the parishes of Whitmore, Chorlton, Maer, Ashley, Mucklestone and Tyrley. Except for Ashley they might be described as 'semi-feudal' though, as we have seen, the local gentry in the past took little interest in local affairs, and tenant farmers and clergymen were usually councillors. In spite of the decline of the agricultural interest the only marked change in the post-war decade was the disappearance of the parsons, though Ashley, always something of an exception, began returning a pottery manufacturer during these years.

The rural parishes also shared the general post-war expansion of party organization. Though every village had a sprinkling of Labour supporters, usually known to everyone, the Conservative Party became the sole organized force, its advent coinciding with the incorporation of the rural parishes into the Newcastle constituency in 1949. Then at the same time local Conservatives found themselves within a constituency with a Labour majority and were blessed with a new Conservative candidate who, as we have seen, was untiring in his organizational efforts. In all these parishes he constructed efficient Conservative parties. For example, in Whitmore it is said that 90 per cent of the voters were recruited into the Conservative Party with the local squire deploying contingents of tellers and 'knockers-up'.

The Conservative Party, however, showed no sign of intruding into local politics, perhaps because though not all the Independent councillors were Conservative Party members none of them belonged to the Labour Party. In the first four post-war Rural District elections (the last one of these being in 1955), out of a total of twenty-four possible contests in these six parishes, three took place—all at Ashley. It was often difficult to find candidates and the practice grew up of councillors who wished to retire searching for and, in effect, choosing their successors.

Because there were so few contests organization had no place in local government politics save at Ashley, where a clash developed on the Parish Council in the early post-war years over the allocation of council houses. The conflict was resolved in a Rural District by-election contest in June 1948, between one of the 'commuters' and a farmer known as the 'uncrowned king of Ashley'. The former's machine, formed largely from fellow members of the Ashley British Legion, had been organized by a Labour supporter. This victory symbolized the rise of a new social force in the countryside.

(ii) THE FRINGE OF THE COALFIELD

There are four parishes on the western edge of the coalfield. Except for Balterley, which is very small in area and population, our survey showed that they were distinguished from the rural parishes by the presence of considerable Labour support. At Keele, Madeley and Betley about half the respondents said they had voted Labour in 1959. Yet only at Madeley, with its railway station and pit, had there been any Labour representation in the inter-war years, and it has been from Madeley that Labour influence has radiated to the surrounding parishes.

The first meeting of Madeley Labour Party in July 1943, part of a drive to promote the candidature of W. Simcock for the Stone division, was convened by the pre-war leadership of Madeley Labour—the 'railwayman', a shunter who was a Methodist lay preacher and an insurance agent. A temporary committee set up to organize lectures sponsored by the National Council of Labour Colleges and to recruit new members was superseded in April 1945 by an election committee on which all the adjoining districts, except Keele, were represented.

Thus it was preparation for the 1945 General Election which, for the first time in Madeley's history, provided an organized political party to contest Madeley's four seats at the 1946 R.D.C. elections. The Madeley Labour Party placed on its 'slate' the three leaders mentioned above and a farmer who had attended no party meetings, but who was well disposed to Labour. All four were elected, the farmer coming well ahead at the top of the poll. This victory was followed by two or three years of such intense interest in local government affairs—208 council houses were being built in Madeley—that it was eventually ruled that municipal business should not be discussed at party meetings.

Meanwhile the fortunes of the Madeley Labour Party had been fluctuating. The political revivalism of 1945, when average attendance at meetings was nearly thirty, was succeeded by the more workmanlike atmosphere of 1946 when 22 meetings averaged an attendance of twelve. Some interest was maintained by the council-house programme and two nights' canvassing in 1947 brought in 44 recruits; but the late 1940's saw a gradual diminution of keenness and a decrease in membership. In 1949 ten meetings averaged an attendance of seven and in the late 1950's only three or four meetings a year were held.

Yet on the credit side in these years must be set the successful sponsoring of another Labour Party at Betley where, in contradistinction to Keele, the Madeley Labour Party's emissaries were able to recruit a considerable number of members. At the R.D.C. election in Betley in May 1949 a local miller, a miner for most of his life, stood as a Labour candidate and ended the long rule of the Betley farmers. In the autumn of the same year the Betley Labour Party, with about thirty members, was set up under the miller's chairmanship. Standing again in 1952 he increased his share of the poll from 53 per cent to 64 per cent.

By the late 1940's the sort of Independent candidate of prewar days, a clergyman or tenant farmer, who was looked up to by the rest of the inhabitants, could no longer be encountered in Betley or Madeley. The one Independent councillor who survived was the Madeley farmer who had quickly quarrelled with the Madeley Party over a breach of party discipline on the Parish Council. His re-election to the R.D.C., time after time, usually at the head of the poll, depended on personal popularity rather than social deference.

Yet not only had the old type of Independent passed on by 1949, but also the older leaders of the Madeley Labour Party, who seemed unable to adapt themselves to new practices. For example, the 'railwayman' accepted the invitation of the Independent majority on the Rural District Council to be chairman of the Finance Committee, an act contrary to the Labour Party's Standing Orders. Yet he refused to resign his chairmanship, citing his thirty-three years as a Labour representative as proof of his loyalty to the Labour Party. Supported by the shunter he defied expulsion from the party; but in 1949 both men stood as

Independent Labour candidates and were defeated. Thus in three short years three out of the four pioneers of the Madeley Labour Party had left it.

The one who remained, the insurance agent, quickly became the recognized leader of the Madeley Labour Party. A former colliery clerk, who had been victimized after the 1926 General Strike, he belonged to a younger generation than the two railway workers. The older men had been associated with various denominations of the Christian church. Class feeling was alien to them and because they had developed their political habits while Labour was in a minority they saw no harm in co-operating with the Independents. Consequently the older leadership had not taken to party discipline and saw no harm in supporting Independent proposals if they so wished. Furthermore their view of local politics was that it was a matter for everyone to participate in: they scarcely envisaged it as an operational field for national parties.

The new leadership, formed of the insurance agent, a lorry driver and a Co-operative dairy worker, all elected in 1949, had different notions. They had little contact with organized religion, but in such places as the Co-operative Education Committee they had acquired many of the 'left-wing' ideas of the inter-war and war-time period. Towards the Independents they entertained some animosity and it was their intention to introduce party discipline to the Rural District Council through the medium of a Labour Group. By thus applying Labour Party rules they hoped to advance the Labour Government's programme.

(iii) AUDLEY

In the inter-war era Audley, as we have seen, was an industrial village which, because of the weakness of the unions and the strength of Wedgwood's influence, was controlled by a lower-middle-class oligarchy. Deep economic depression prolonged this situation. The coming of war, however, brought employment and with it Audley miners who had migrated to other coalfields returned to local pits, providing an element in Audley that had experienced external influences.

As at Madeley, the foundation of the Audley and Bignall End

Labour Party[1] dates from the adoption of a new Parliamentary Labour candidate in war-time. The initial meeting in October 1942 of the Audley Labour Party was called to support the candidature of Mr. J. Mack. It set off at a smart pace with 86 members at its inauguration and elected an executive of whom all but one were mineworkers. Several of the latter had worked for spells in other coalfields, the secretary having spent twenty years in South Yorkshire, the most militant of the English regions. At about the same time the Halmerend Labour Party was resurrected, largely at the instigation of a footrail owner who in his early days had been a fireman in the Minnie Pit. Thus at its inception the Labour organization in the whole of Audley Parish was dominated by the traditional industry.

It was this organization that helped in Mack's 1945 victory, but for the purpose of our story the decision to contest the local elections in 1946 was of far more importance. At the County Council election Audley Parish's one seat was won by the above-mentioned founder of the Halmerend Labour Party. He defeated one of the pre-war ruling clique, the Friendly Society secretary, who received only 37 per cent of the poll. Labour went on to win seven out of the nine Audley Parish seats on the Rural District Council and to sweep the Audley Parish Council. When the latter body met after the election for the first time there was no seconder when one of the prominent pre-war Independents was nominated for the chairmanship, but the hands shot up each time to carry all the Labour Party's list of nominees. One observer, perhaps aware that he was witnessing a social revolution on a parochial scale, resented the Labour Parish councillors as recent immigrants to the district, but there was only slight truth in this misjudgment which can be accounted for by the fact that a working-class leadership was emerging in Audley for the first time.

For the next three or four years enthusiasm was the keynote of the two Labour parties in Audley parish. Permanent party organization seemed to have arrived and, to a considerable extent in socials and whist drives, the life of the community was centred round the Labour Party. The approach of the next General Election led to a revival of activity in 1949 when a new Labour

[1] Henceforward described as the Audley Labour Party.

Party, 90 strong, was founded at the mining hamlet of Wood Lane. In 1950 there were about 300 members of the Labour Party in Audley Parish. No other party had any organization there at this date.

Already, however, the sort of internecine quarrel that was to become a feature of Audley politics had broken out. Differences of opinion about the merit of subcontracting and direct labour for building council houses found the leaders of the Halmerend and Audley Labour Parties on opposite sides. Halmerend was with Madeley and the majority in the Labour Group on the R.D.C. and in 1947 two councillors from Audley Parish, including the recognized leader of the Audley Labour Party, were expelled from the Labour Group for voting against a Group decision on this matter. As a result of this disagreement the Halmerend and Audley Labour Parties backed different men as Labour nominee for the whole parish at the 1949 County Council elections. The constituency agent and the Newcastle Constituency Labour Party then came down on the side of Halmerend and when the Audley Labour Party refused to comply by withdrawing its man it was disbanded in February 1949.

Although this was a disciplinary measure it was also in accordance with an attempt to re-form the Labour Party in Audley parish on the lines of the three wards into which it was divided (Audley ward, Bignall End and Halmerend) in 1949. This seems to have had no immediate consequence—the Audley Labour Party gained another seat at the 1949 Rural District elections—but the orderly official Labour Party philosophy on which this change was based was bound to create trouble, sooner or later, in an environment such as Audley. When the council-house scheme was completed it involved many people moving from Halmerend and Bignall End wards to Audley ward. Among these was the secretary of the Audley Labour Party (which, as we have noted, also included Bignall End). Since 1949 he had represented Bignall End as a Rural District councillor. Labour Party protocol stipulated that he should stand now for Audley ward and this was the verdict of his members. But the secretary refused to yield and put up for Bignall End as an Independent Labour candidate, receiving a good deal of help in his election campaign from Labour Party members and being not too easily defeated.

In the years before the Second World War Audley politics had been conducted by informal procedures and personal contacts, the style of politics associated with rule by a clique. Post-1945 politics had brought the manual workers to power. Their vehicle, the Labour Party, laid down various formal procedures for the conduct of internal party affairs. Thus post-war politics in Audley were directed in accordance with the relatively bureaucratic processes of a 'mass party'. When interest and membership began to decline, these became inappropriate if, indeed, they ever were appropriate to a milieu such as Audley.

(iv) THE 'RENTS ROW'

The decline in Labour fortunes in the Rural District in the early 1950's had its parallel in the decline of the national Labour Party. With the attainment of long-sought objectives there was a relaxation of effort and a slackening in enthusiasm. The building of the council houses and the completion of other long-awaited amenities, such as sewerage schemes, dissipated much of the basis for popular support. Those who had aspired to the fruits of social reform now became defenders of vested interests, and especially the council-house tenants emerged as the most obstreperous of lobbies. No doubt this was no more than happened elsewhere, but in Newcastle Rural District this process was dramatically accelerated by a spectacular controversy, locally known as 'the rents row', that left the local Labour parties in the Rural District in a parlous state.

By the autumn of 1954 it had become clear that the R.D.C. housing account was running a deficit and the Council decided that, wherever necessary, a 'lodger rent' of five shillings a week should be charged. But this was not enough to right matters and in December it was agreed that in the New Year a flat increase of three shillings a week should be imposed on all council tenants. As there had been two earlier increases since the war, it was not to be expected that the tenants would take it lightly.

Throughout the Rural District it appears that the reaction was spontaneous and hostile. Betley tenants may have taken the first step by writing to the National Tenants' and Residents'

Association; but leadership really emanated from Audley where many of the council tenants had formerly owned their own houses. The secretary of the Audley Tenants' and Residents' Association was the County councillor, a machine hand, who had been returned unopposed as a Labour candidate in 1954. Its chairman was the wife of a professional man, not a council tenant, who had fairly recently settled in the district. At one time this lady had been a Labour Parliamentary candidate in a southern constituency, and she was fated to play the role of a Thomas Hardy heroine, a rather exotic and disturbing influence.

Early in January 1955 representatives of tenants in all parishes, supported by a crowd of about two hundred people outside, presented their case to a special meeting of the Council, arguing that the tenants had not been properly informed about the increases which were unnecessary anyway. The deputation felt they received short shrift from the Council, and alleged that only the three Halmerend councillors, who had opposed the increases, and one of the Independents, a local squire, listened to them with sympathy. After this rejection of the tenants' case the Council refused to see another deputation in spite of the pressure of all the Audley councillors.

In the face of this steadfastness the Tenants' Association adopted two policies. One was not to pay the increases, though after council pressure this had little success. The other was to swamp the local Labour parties. The Association included supporters of all parties, but the majority of them were Labour voters who, if they could all be persuaded to become members of their local Labour parties, could influence the selection of local government candidates. At Madeley, however, this plan failed because the secretary of the Madeley Labour Party refused to take subscriptions proffered by members of the local Tenants' Association. At Betley where the tactics succeeded the Betley Labour Party disintegrated. In Audley Parish there was confusion because of the different fates of the two Labour parties. At Halmerend the local Labour Party was completely taken over by the tenants, but the Audley party was divided, some members supporting those Audley councillors who had voted for the rents increase.

Meanwhile in February 1955 the lady who was chairman of the Tenants' Association was adopted by the Newcastle Constituency Labour Party as candidate for Audley Parish in the April County Council elections. However, the constituency party later passed a resolution calling on its members not to support 'outside bodies' that brought pressure to bear on local councils. This had no effect on those Labour Party members who had joined the Tenants' Association so the Constituency Labour Party then ruled that all these delinquents should be expelled from the party; and that another candidate must be chosen as Labour's nominee for Audley in the County Council elections, an official repudiation that strengthened the resolve of the disowned candidate to stand.

In an attempt to prevent a final breach the constituency Executive decided that it would attend a special meeting of the Audley Labour Party to be held in March. The meeting opened peacefully—the Executive's decision that another candidate must be chosen seemed to cause no great stir—and everything was proceeding smoothly when a Borough member of the Executive, a young Trotskyist firebrand, who had publicly opposed the rents increase, jumped up and proclaimed that the Executive was dominated by the 'hatchet men' of the Newcastle Labour Party's two dominating figures, both of whom were present in the hall. One of them angrily stumped out, but the other, the Madeley leader who was then chairman of the R.D.C., retaliated by asserting that the Tenants' Association was controlled by Communists. One of the tenants threatened to throw him out of the window, whereat the meeting was declared closed and the police were called.

Compromise was now out of the question, and it became obvious that the County Council election would be contested. The Newcastle Labour Party selected a retired miner who, as a Rural District Councillor, had tacitly supported the rents increase; and called a special meeting of the Audley Labour Party to endorse his candidature. Those attending would be required to sign a declaration accepting the rules and policy of the Labour Party. At this nearly forty members of the Audley Labour Party—all of them adherents of the Tenants' Association—resigned, leaving only ten to turn up at the meeting and organize the official Labour candidate's campaign. The 'unofficial Labour' candidate issued an election address saying that she was standing 'at the request of the majority of the Audley Labour Party' who were protesting against 'the high-handed and undemocratic action' of the Newcastle Labour Party; and she expressed her conviction that it would be possible for her and her supporters to rejoin the Labour Party at some future date. With this appeal, using the Tenants' Association as the nucleus of a strong electoral machine, her campaign was successful, and she defeated the official Labour candidate by 1,446 votes to 1,313.

The Tenants' Association, cock-a-hoop at this triumph and claiming that none of them had disobeyed the Labour Party's constitution, asserted that they were the true voice of Audley Labour and asked to be readmitted to the Labour Party; and in furtherance of these claims put up nine Tenants' Association candidates in the three Audley wards for the Rural District elections in May. Faced with this situation the chairman of the Newcastle Constituency Labour Party and the Member of Parliament—an embarrassed arbiter between the two factions—together advanced a compromise plan suggesting the reinstatement of the newly elected County Councillor in the Labour Party, the withdrawal by the Tenants and the Labour Party of five Rural District candidates each and the acceptance by the Labour Party of any Tenants' Association nominee who was returned. The Newcastle Labour Party, however, would not countenance this appeasement, and disaster for the Audley Labour Party was only averted by eight Tenants' candidates withdrawing in response, they said, 'to the urgent appeal for unity' made by the M.P. with the approaching General Election especially in mind.

So ended the 'rents row' though its repercussions were to bedevil the Labour Party in the Rural District for many years. It revealed that there was a new pressure group in Rural District politics. Whether the disillusionment of the council-house tenants with the Labour Party was also expressed in their vote at Parliamentary elections it is impossible to say; but it is clear that the local representatives of the Labour Party suffered from this episode and in the late 1950's party membership was to decline even more. The failure of the Newcastle Labour Party to assert itself was a victory for local sectionalism and a blow to the prestige of its local leaders, who were to become even more divided in consequence of the 'rents row'. Above all, spontaneous popular feeling had found it impossible to make itself felt within the Labour Party which appeared in the hitherto unfamiliar guise of uncomprehending and unsympathetic authority.

2. Contemporary Politics in the Rural District

(i) PARTY ACTIVITY AND ALIGNMENTS

The later 1950's in the Rural District were characterized by a great ebbing of the tide of political activity experienced by both parties. With the exit of Major Friend, the Conservative organizational effort slackened until the only extant Conservative Party in the countryside was at Whitmore. The Labour Party, which had claimed 300 members in the Rural District in 1950, a decade later had about 50. Until 1961, when meetings became very infrequent, the Audley Labour Party managed to meet once a month and average an attendance of between seven and eight. Membership of the Madeley Labour Party which had been 83 in 1948 had fallen to 31 in 1959, and attendance at its three or four meetings a year during the 1950's averaged about seven.

Thus the 'rents row' did not set the tone of Rural District politics in the 1950's: it merely accentuated trends that were already operating. The revolt of the council tenants further depleted the rank-and-file in the local Labour parties and divided the militants. Moreover, though no particular Labour Party had been responsible for the decision of the R.D.C. to increase council rents, the fact that the Council's chairman and principal advocate of the policy at the time was the Madeley leader further exacerbated relations between the two largest parishes.

The impact of the 1955 contretemps was felt variously in different quarters. By August 1956 the Betley Labour Party had expired and its funds had been handed over to the Madeley Labour Party without, however, handicapping the Labour candidate at the 1958 Rural District elections, who received 74 per cent of the vote in a straight fight with an Independent. Meanwhile the Madeley Labour Party weathered the storm better than any other, its leader, the R.D.C. chairman, having successfully obtained a vote of confidence in his policy by eleven votes to five. The party continued to hold three out of the four Madeley seats, though the Independent farmer went to the head of the poll in 1955 and so consolidated his position that at the 1958 Rural District elections no fourth Labour candidate could be found for the Labour slate and the farmer and three Labour nominees were all returned unopposed. In 1961 these same four again retained their seats.

The unity of the Madeley Labour Party seems to be the consequence of two factors. In the first place, because of the necessity of producing a slate of eleven candidates for the Parish Council as well as the R.D.C. quota of four, there are a large number of elective offices which are potentially at the disposal of the party, a situation that tends to eradicate the normal Labour Party division between 'leadership' and 'rank-and-file'. The other factor has been the dominating personality of Madeley Labour leader, the insurance agent whom we saw oust the veteran 'railwayman' in 1949. By the mid-1950's he was widely regarded, especially at the Constituency Labour Party level, as 'Labour's strong man' in the Rural District. Allied with the 'strong man' in the Borough Labour Party, another firm adherent of the Silverdale Cooperative Party, he kept the Madeley Labour Party on the 'party line'. Thus though on national issues the Madeley Labour Party was often quite 'left wing', its reputation in local politics has been the opposite. Partly through their championship of official Labour Party policy in such matters as housing, partly through their anti-Audley coalition with the Independents, the Madeley Labour Party has won praise as being reasonable, moderate and pragmatic.

Thus the wheel has almost come full turn for Madeley Labour. The impatient younger generation who threw out the old pioneers in 1949 find themselves today in an undoctrinaire frame of mind, their revolutionary ardour blunted by the compromising necessities of representative government. But today's situation is different from fifteen years ago in one respect: at the moment the present leaders have to face no challenge from much younger men.

While Madeley Labour presented a picture of unity, Audley Labour was sadly in disarray. During the 'rents row' the Newcastle Constituency Labour Party wound up the Labour Party in Halmerend where the Tenants' Association had successfully gained control. In September 1955 a Newcastle-sponsored Labour Party was formed at Halmerend with a former Madeley councillor as its chairman. At first its membership was carefully screened by the constituency executive, but within a few months the County councillor was attending its meetings. Her subscription was also accepted by the secretary of the Newcastle Constituency Labour Party which in June 1956 chose her as the official Labour candidate for Audley parish at the 1958 County Council elections.

The reinstatement of the rebel leader was too much for that section of the Audley Labour Party that had, throughout the crisis, remained loyal to the policy as laid down by the Labour leaders on the R.D.C. and had incurred a good deal of local obloquy in the process. The Audley Labour Party had passed a resolution that subscriptions would be taken from no former members of the Tenants' Association and they threatened to resign if forced to go against this. As a result in January 1957 the National Executive of the Labour Party conducted an inquiry at Audley and ruled that as the parish's County Councillor had resigned from the Labour Party before opposing an official Labour candidate she had broken no Labour Party regulation. Accordingly she must be taken back into the fold.

This verdict seemed blatantly unfair to the Audley Labour Party, who showed no enthusiasm at all for the candidate who had been thrust upon them. When one of their members, who was already on the panel as an R.D.C. Labour candidate, announced suddenly in March 1958 that he was standing for the County Council no one appeared disposed to discourage him though the Constituency Labour Party threatened him with expulsion. Eventually pressure from the Regional Office at Birmingham forced the Audley Labour Party to expel the 'unofficial' candidate, but this did not prevent some of the bolder spirits in the Audley Labour Party from supporting him in his campaign. Halmerend Labour Party, on the contrary, naturally supported the sitting County Councillor, herself stigmatized as 'unofficial' in 1955 when she had represented the revolting council tenants. Perhaps she had then benefited from her rejection by the Newcastle Labour Party. Whatever the case, she was now defeated and the Independent Labour candidate returned with 51 per cent of the poll.

Independent Labour candidates thus became an accepted part of Audley's political life, both in County Council and R.D.C. elections. There seem to be three types: those who, as in the example above, have either quarrelled with or been expelled from the Labour Party; those who, as at Wood Lane, wish to be regarded as sympathetic to Labour though the local Labour Party has ceased to operate; and finally those who have no wish to associate with the Labour Party but who have generally working-class sympathies and realize that the word 'Labour' in their label is an electoral asset. In all cases the phenomenon of Independent Labour candidates has emphasized the failure of the 'official' local Labour parties.

We have seen how in the early post-war days social life revolved around the Audley Labour Party and its large membership. Its leaders, drawn from the dominant industry, were widely respected miners. With the great decline in membership, however, the leadership of the party tended to pass into the hands of less representative people who became discredited as a result of their support for the increase in council rents. By the mid-1950's membership of the local Labour Party could be something of a social handicap in Audley.

In fact by the mid-1950's the presence of a Labour Party in Audley parish was merely one more complicating factor amongst all the personal and village rivalries, which were intensified by the division of the parish into wards, making it a common practice for a local politician who was *persona non grata* in one ward to stand in another, thus spreading dissension further. Moreover the need to comply with the regulations of the Labour Party, further emphasized by another National Executive inquiry in 1960, postulated a bureaucratic urgency that was hardly appropriate to a small body of party workers scattered through several small villages.

The feuding local politicians were the consequence of the failure of any Audley leader to assert himself above the rest. It is said that in the nineteenth century Audley's chapel leaders quarrelled in the same way. Certainly it is noteworthy that one of the few people who ever commanded and held a large following, the chairman of the Tenants' Association, was a stranger with no local connections. Among the local inhabitants a contempt for punctilio, a memory for family disputes and a strong egalitarianism make it difficult for anyone to set himself above anyone else. Those who, like party leaders, assert national principles carry little weight because the Audley electorate seems to have accepted the concept of national parties in local politics only in the immediate post-war years. Since those days the Audley voters' persistence in discriminating between different candidates of the same political party proves that personality is still the most important factor in Audley's local politics. Nearly twenty years after a strong Labour Party entered the field there are many signs that Audley has in this respect reverted to the inter-war situation. On the other hand at the leadership level the united lower-middle-class oligarchy of the 1920's and 1930's has been supplanted, to some extent, by general factiousness.

Outside the two largest parishes politics has changed little since 1955. In the last decade there have been few contested elections and in most cases the same councillor has been returned without contest. Yet in 1961 there was one innovation that might be portentous. The advent of a Conservative agent in 1960 was the signal for the reconstruction of a network of ward organizations throughout all the Rural District save Betley. At Whitmore where the Conservatives had always been strongest the ward party decided to take the unprecedented step of running a Conservative candidate. This alarmed the Independent farmer councillors from Keele and Madeley who, dependent as they certainly were on some Labour votes, did not wish to see party politics brought into parishes where it had formerly been absent. They persuaded the local vicar to stand as an Independent, but he was narrowly defeated by three votes. Together with Conservative candidatures at Madeley and Audley this intervention implied a concerted attempt by the Conservative Party to end its non-participation in Rural District politics, a new departure that might herald the beginning of a new era.

After the immediate post-war years of great organizational activity party machinery in the Rural District lapsed or became moribund, and was only refurbished for the General Elections or the triennial County and Rural District elections—when these were contested. In many parishes neither the Conservative nor Labour Party ever ran a candidate, but at Madeley and Betley some tradition of Labour councillors was established, while at Audley a very complicated situation emerged. Whatever the party alignment in these parishes, however, personality remained of the greatest importance and the sort of impersonal party contests that were fought in the Borough were unknown in the Rural District.

(ii) ELECTORAL ORGANIZATION

Organization in the Rural District has become rather perfunctory. The Independents have scarcely used organization at all, confident as they are of unopposed returns in many parishes. As for the national parties, in between General Elections their organization has either lapsed altogether or it has become moribund except for its use in the triennial County and Rural District elections. These elections in 1961 were, in spite of Conservative intervention in the Rural District for the first time, typical enough to produce a fair picture for the observer of political organization.

For the County Council elections which take place in the second week in April the Rural District is divided into two wards —Audley Parish and the rest. The latter is known as 'Madeley ward' though, of course, it includes nine other parishes besides Madeley. Thus one ward is relatively concentrated and one is scattered.

Madeley had not been contested in the County Council elections since 1949, its Independent councillors having been returned unopposed since then. But in January 1960 the Constituency Labour Party had selected a candidate, one of Madeley's Rural District councillors. At Audley, however, the Labour Party was in a dilemma. Should they or should they not oppose the Independent Labour councillor who had defeated an official Labour nominee in 1958? Eventually, because of his record in supporting the Labour Group at Stafford, they decided not to oppose.

On the other side preparations were a good deal less advanced. At Madeley Conservative intervention was threatened, but finally the potential Conservative candidate was prevailed upon to withdraw and the Madeley Independent, the popular farmer, defended his seat against the Labour challenge. The contest was thus a straight fight between two Madeley personalities. At Audley, believing that the Labour vote might be split again, a 21-year-old Conservative candidate took the field. He was the grandson of one of Audley's inter-war rulers and a minor public schoolboy who two months before had founded a branch of the Young Conservatives at Audley. Because his nomination went forward secretly, for fear that Labour disunity might end, it was not endorsed by the Newcastle Conservative Party.

The most striking feature of the 1961 County Council elections in the Rural District was the similar behaviour of the two candidates who bore the labels of the national parties. Both the Labour candidate at Madeley and the Conservative candidate at Audley had canvassed before the election and distributed literature mentioning national as well as local issues, both had committee rooms, well-marked registers, a number of 'knockers-up' (though here the Conservative had the advantage in cars) and tellers at some of the polling booths. There was only one noticeable difference between the Audley Conservative and his Labour counterpart at Madeley—Newcastle Conservatives sent help to Audley. Madeley received no help from Newcastle Labour.

There were also parallels between the party candidates' two opponents—the Independent at Madeley and the Independent Labour man at Audley. Neither did any door-to-door canvassing though both issued election addresses in which they dealt solely with *local* affairs. At Madeley the Independent was anxious to stress that he was 'non-political'; but the Independent Labour man at Audley did not dissociate himself entirely from party politics, mentioning that his father had founded the Audley I.L.P. and recalling his own expulsion from the Labour Party. However, the personal electioneering of both men was the most striking characteristic of their campaigns. Neither had a committee room or plot, but both depended very much on local contacts and spent the entire day driving round their respective wards, from time to time taking people to the poll. Neither used 'knockers-up', but the Audley man did have some tellers. That both men won, the Independent at Madeley getting 69 per cent of the poll and the Independent Labour man at Audley 73 per cent, cannot necessarily be cited as proof of the superiority of their method of fighting elections. Even so it did seem that the electoral style of the national party candidates was inappropriate to the occasion.

The Rural District elections[1] which followed three weeks later showed many similar trends. In particular the Labour candidates at both Audley and Madeley had been selected some months before. The Audley Labour Party actually nominates six candidates, four for Audley ward and two for Bignall End, where the other two Labour candidates are supposed to be nominated by the defunct Wood Lane Labour Party. On this occasion, however, the six nominations were divided equally between Audley ward and Bignall End. Six Conservatives, put forward by branches at Audley, Madeley and Whitmore, were the first candidates of this party to stand at Newcastle Rural District elections. Among non-party candidates there were three Independents and four Independent Labour standing in contested seats. The three Independents, all nominated by friends, stood at Whitmore (in a straight fight against a Conservative), at Halmerend and at Madeley where the newly elected County councillor ran in harness with three Conservatives against four Labour men. One of the four Independent Labour men stood on his own in Audley ward: he was a retired trade-union secretary and a chapel leader who depended on his personal reputation. The other three Independent Labour candidates were at Bignall End: two of them were residents in Wood Lane and the third was the Independent Labour County councillor. It was characteristic of Audley politics that these last three Independent Labour men received more support from Labour Party members than the official Labour candidates in Audley ward. In Halmerend, though the official Labour Party nominating procedure could not be complied with because the Halmerend Labour Party had ceased to exist, there was a slate of four Labour candidates.

The campaigns tended to be in keeping with the politics of

[1] This account is based on reports by Miss J. Lavender and Messrs. C. Barnett, J. Borland, A. Grant, J. Pye and J. Stewart. We are grateful to all those councillors who co-operated by answering our questions.

the candidates. The official Labour candidates, both in Madeley and Audley ward, distributed leaflets identifying local with national issues and canvassed for about a fortnight before polling day, when they were provided with all the accoutrements of modern electioneering. Except at Whitmore, where there was embarrassment at having any contest at all, the Conservatives ran campaigns very similar to those of the Labour Party, except that they had more cars. The sole Madeley Independent candidate ran the same sort of campaign that had gained him the County Council seat three weeks earlier; while at Halmerend the Independent, a prominent councillor in pre-war years, was elected as he lay in a hospital bed. In the latter ward, as at Bignall End, personal groupings for the purposes of electoral organization seemed to have little to do with party affiliations. At Bignall End while two of the three official Labour candidates appeared to have no organization at all the third, and the only one of them elected, teamed up with the Independent Labour candidates, of whom the most important was the County councillor. The latter sent out an election address to all voters, had his posters on 100 walls and his bills in 100 windows, and on polling day relied on three cars as his sole organizational support.

Whatever one induces from the 1961 elections in the Newcastle Rural District it is clear that the type of electoral organization employed by the political parties for Parliamentary elections is not a necessary guarantee of success at local polls. A well-known Independent can still be a successful politician if he skilfully constructs his own machine based on personal contacts and if he remains in the public eye. Furthermore the Rural District electorate is also still capable of discriminating between candidates of the same party on personal grounds with fine disregard for party labels. It is too early yet to say whether Conservative intervention will finally put paid to this fluid situation.

(iii) THE RURAL DISTRICT COUNCIL AND ITS DECISION-MAKING PROCESS

(a) The Decision-makers

The Rural District Council increased its size from 24 to 27 in 1955 when Audley was given three more seats and Audley's representation rose in consequence from three-eighths to four-ninths of the whole. Three-ninths of the councillors now come from what we have designated as the 'rural parishes' and two-ninths from the 'fringe of the coalfield'.

Extent of representation, however, is no necessary measure of participation and here Audley was not to the fore. The thirty-four councillors who served Audley between 1946 and the present day averaged 5·6 years compared with 6·8 years for the twelve from the 'fringe of the coalfield'. There was a similar pattern in the attendance records for June 1960–May 1961. Out of a possible total attendance of forty-seven council and committee meetings the Audley contingent averaged 24, compared with a corresponding figure of 32 for the 'rural parishes' and 42 for the 'fringe of the coalfield'. Clearly both distance and availability of transport are partially responsible for these figures and though the Council changed its time of meeting from morning to evening in 1950 it is still difficult for poorer people from remoter parishes to serve. One Audley councillor, a former miner who had become an engineering worker, told the authors that on days when there was council business in the evening, his wife gave him two packets of sandwiches, the second to be eaten between finishing work and the meeting. After the meeting, having missed the last bus, he was often faced with walking six miles home to Audley.

Attendance and length of service are also of some consequence in a councillor's prestige. Of the councillors elected to committee chairmanships in the last ten years one-third have been from Audley, one-fifth from the 'fringe of the coalfield' and the other 47 per cent from the 'rural parishes'. But over the last five years the proportion has been very different: 7 per cent from Audley, 33 per cent from the 'fringe of the coalfield' and 60 per cent from the rural parishes. Thus at all times Audley has been under-represented in the seats of power (it has nearly half the population of the Rural District), but in recent years the alliance between the other two regions has deprived Audley of nearly all the important positions; and the rural parishes with about a quarter of the population have been very over-represented.

The division of the Rural District councillors into classes, as shown in Table 1, reveals that fairly consistently two-thirds of

NEWCASTLE RURAL DISTRICT

the R.D.C. has been composed of non-manual groups, but that in the period 1955–61 this fell to a little more than a half. At the 1961 Rural District election the balance of parties and occupational groups swung back to something approximating to 1946.

TABLE I. RURAL DISTRICT COUNCIL, 1946–61:
ANALYSIS OF OCCUPATIONAL GROUPS

Election year	1946			1949			1952		
	Lab.	Ind.	Total	Lab.	Ind.	Total	Lab.	Ind.	Total
Business proprietors	1	10	11	1	11	12	1	11	12
Professional and managerial	—	3	3	1	1	2	3	—	3
Clerical	4	—	4	2	—	2	2	—	2
Manual	6	—	6	8	—	8	7	—	7
Total	11	13	24	12	12	24	13	11	24

Election year	1955			1958			1961			
	Lab.*	Ind.	Total	Lab.*	Ind.	Total	Lab.	Ind.	Con.	Total
Business proprietors	—	11	11	1	11	12	2	9	3	14
Professional and managerial	2	—	2	1	—	1	2	1	—	3
Clerical	1	—	1	2	—	2	2	1	—	3
Manual	13	—	13	12	—	12	7	—	—	7
Total	16	11	27	16	11	27	13	11	3	27

* Includes Independent Labour.

The numbers involved are so small that one should hesitate before generalizing from them. It does seem, however, that in 1955 the Labour councillors became more proletarian as a group possibly owing to the increase in size of the Audley contingent in which there was in that year also a higher proportion of manual workers. It appears also that when Labour is strong it has a working-class preponderance which it loses when it is weak. But in all cases the Labour councillors are always more of a cross-section of the social composition of the Rural District than the non-Labour councillors.

(b) Groups on the Rural District Council

It would be wrong, however, to conceive of party and social class as factors that have played a large part in the deliberations of the Rural District Council. Before the war the Council was a gathering of Independent members among whom parish loyalties were the strongest sentiment. Decisions were reached after discussion between all councillors though ideas about future policy often originated in officials. This situation might end, it was thought, when the R.D.C. elections of 1946 returned eleven Labour councillors out of the total of twenty-four.

A predominant theme of the immediate post-war years was that Labour councils were helping to implement the policy of the Labour Government. In April 1946 the Audley Labour Party's local election address had read, 'unless the County . . . and Rural District Councils work in co-operation with this new Government their plans will be frustrated'; and two months later Madeley Labour's leader had said that the Labour councillors had been elected 'on a Labour mandate to carry out the Labour Party's vast programme of social reform'. To further these ends according to the 1930 Standing Orders of the national Labour Party, the R.D.C. Labour councillors should have constituted themselves a Labour Group, held meetings, elected a chairman and secretary and embodied projected council policy in resolutions which, as majority decisions of the Labour Group, would be binding upon all Labour councillors at subsequent council meetings. Thus the Group would stand in more or less the same relationship to the R.D.C. as the Parliamentary Labour Party to the House of Commons. This ideal was never realized for two main reasons—dislike of party discipline and disagreement between Labour councillors from different villages.

The oldest Labour member of the Council, Madeley's 'railwayman', never adjusted himself to the concept of a Labour Group with discipline and Standing Orders. With Independent support he was elected vice-chairman of the R.D.C. in 1947, defeating a Labour nominee. This roused tempers that were only calmed by the intervention of the Labour Party's West Midland Regional Office. Elected in 1948 as R.D.C. chairman, on this occasion by a Group decision, the 'railwayman' was soon objecting to the advisory sub-committee set up by the Newcastle Constituency Labour Party in order to 'help' the Labour Group. He stopped attending Group meetings, stood as an Independent Labour candidate at the 1949 elections and though defeated insisted on exercising his right to chair the first meeting of the new Council which was evenly balanced with twelve Independent and twelve Labour councillors. His intention to give his casting vote to the Independent nominee for the next year's chairman exemplifies the distaste with which the older generation of Labour councillors regarded party discipline. In later years many other Labour councillors were to follow his example.

Incipient parish sectionalism has been an even more serious factor militating against the establishment of a Labour Group. The two main disputants have been Audley and Madeley, the two parishes with large Labour contingents. As early as December 1946 the Madeley Parochial Committee (with its large Labour majority) recommended to the Council that the Audley Parochial Committee (also with a large Labour majority) when allocating Audley's new council houses should bear in mind the overcrowding in Madeley. The chairman of Audley Parochial Committee, who was also chairman of the Audley Labour Party, angrily pointed out that Audley had her own overcrowding problem. This episode exemplified the personal and parochial antipathies that still endure.

Throughout 1947 the Newcastle Constituency Labour Party attempted to arbitrate but, in spite of its efforts, by the end of the year five councillors had defected or been expelled and the Labour Group only numbered six. After the 1949 elections, when Labour for the first time had a majority on the R.D.C., a new attempt at reconciliation was made, assisted by the close working relationship between the Madeley and Halmerend Labour Parties' respective leaders, both of whom were co-operators. The Madeley leader, the insurance agent, was elected chairman in January 1950 and was re-elected chairman for the session in the following May as the result of Labour backing. Some *frondeurs*, however, must still have been active in Labour ranks, because the Labour nominee for the vice-chairmanship was defeated by an Independent candidate in spite of Labour's majority.

There were in fact little grounds for Labour optimism. From 1951 until 1954 at every Annual General Meeting of the R.D.C. there was a clash between Audley and Madeley nominees in elections to the chairmanship, when the Madeley leader was always elected with the help of Independent support. The conflict spread to the election of the chairmanships of council committees so that lines of division on the Council became established with Audley on one side and Madeley plus the Independents from the rural parishes on the other. In these circumstances no Labour Group could ever be a place for discussing and formulating future policy.

The 'rents row' in 1955 brought some measure of co-operation between all the Labour councillors because the decision to increase the council-house rents had not led to dissension between the parishes. But hopes that the quarrel might be patched up were soon dashed when some of the Audley Labour councillors, under pressure from their constituents, introduced a resolution at the Council in favour of the sale of council houses to tenants. In consequence a representative of the Newcastle Constituency Labour Party chaired the next meeting of the Labour Group. He enunciated the national Labour Party policy and secured the Group's condemnation of the offending resolution. The Group then decided to support an Audley councillor for the chairmanship of the R.D.C., and the meeting closed with a homily from the chair about the beginning of a new era 'in which party would take precedence over personalities'.

The general trend of events in the 1950's was to make Audley appear as the disaffected and culpable parish, both within the Rural District and the Newcastle Constituency Labour Party, and the dominance of the Madeley leader in forming the policy of both these bodies emphasized this impression. It was the leader of Madeley Labour who, as chairman of the R.D.C., was blamed most by Audley when in 1953 £350 compensation was awarded Audley—the value of the water mains under the Audley streets—for the pre-war sale of Audley waterworks, a transaction that had realized £17,000. In 1957 Audley demanded £5,000 and, meeting opposition on the Council, obtained it after taking the matter to the Courts. Meanwhile in 1955 the Madeley Labour councillors had obtained a ruling on the Council that in future council-house tenancies should be allocated by the whole Council instead of the Parish Councils, a decision that was hurtful to Audley; and a year later an unsuccessful resolution from the same quarter sought to abolish the Audley Parochial Committee, the last vestige of Audley's autonomy.

Audley also seemed to be at a disadvantage in its relations with the Newcastle Constituency Labour Party which sent two delegates to the R.D.C. Labour Group. Though, as its chairman said in 1958, the Constituency Labour Party had 'no authority over the Group except to consult and comment', it took these functions very seriously. When in 1955 five Audley councillors voted for the sale of council houses to tenants, against a Group decision, a special committee of the constituency party interviewed the offenders reporting one of them as 'contrite' and the others as 'aggressive'. As far as possible in the late 1950's the Constituency Labour Party kept the R.D.C. Labour Group under surveillance and from time to time intervened unsuccessfully to reconcile the Audley and Madeley factions.

By this time, however, the Audley councillors were determined to exert their power as three-quarters of the Labour Group. At a Group meeting they decided that a council minute relating to the dismissal of an Audley employee of the Council should be rescinded, a virtual motion of censure on the Madeley Labour leader who was also council chairman. Eventually only the casting vote of the Independent chairman of the Housing Committee prevented this being passed. A little later the eleven Audley councillors met in conclave and drew up a list, consisting entirely of Audley names, for the positions on the Council. When the Labour Group assembled, the Audley contingent had no difficulty in making every one of these nominations a Group decision. But this had no impact on the Annual General Meeting of the Council for the combination of Madeley Labour and the Independents again frustrated Audley's intentions, and most of the Audley nominees were defeated.

During the post-war years the Independents were not unaffected by the vicissitudes on the other side. In the late 1940's the threat that a Labour Group might change the nature of the Council, as it had done in the Borough, caused the Independent councillors, who formerly had consulted with each other over the telephone before council meetings, to begin to meet as a Group in order to counter Labour's plans. When in the 1950's the possibility of an effective Labour Group disappeared the Independents reverted to their former practice. They appeared quite content to support Madeley Labour against Audley until at the R.D.C.'s Annual General Meeting in 1960 they decided to support for Chairman of the Council an Independent councillor who was serving his last year. The Labour Group's nominees were this time sponsored by Madeley and the Audley councillors refused to vote for them. Consequently the first Independent chairman since 1950 was elected for a council that still nominally had a Labour majority. It was an almost inevitable outcome of Labour's internecine strife.

(c) Making Decisions

It is thus clear that party politics is a phenomenon that scarcely troubles the R.D.C. A rare issue, such as whether or not the sole shop on a council estate should belong to Silverdale Co-operative Society, might evoke a party response. Otherwise the Council gives the impression to the observer of discussing local issues with warmth, enjoyment and informality. The ceremony of the Borough is lacking though the Chairman with the Clerk at one elbow and the vice-chairman at the other sits on a raised dais. Facing them in a semicircle are the councillors who tend to sit grouped according to parish. The atmosphere is often one of camaraderie and good-natured chaff between the representatives of different parishes and political parties.

As in Newcastle Borough the work of the Newcastle R.D.C. is carried out within the administrative shadow of the Staffordshire County Council. Of the R.D.C.'s 8s. 8d. rate, 6s. 8d. goes in County Council precept and the functions over which the R.D.C. exercises control are delineated in the titles of its four Committees—Finance and General Purposes, Public Health, Housing and Planning (the last a recent addition). In these circumstances the powers of the Rural District are somewhat restricted.

Unlike the Borough there is no Labour Group in which policy can be hammered out. Decisions are made first in Committee—all Committees are of the full Council—and then ratified by Council ten to fourteen days later. By this system everything can be debated twice, and though most Committee recommendations are accepted by the Council without objection the R.D.C. shows more inclination to raise points than the Borough Council. Someone who may have missed the Committee meeting may raise objections to a minute and repeat arguments that have already been heard. It is unusual for the full Council to make important modifications, however, without first referring the issue back to the appropriate Committee.

In this situation the individual member may have considerable power. Without the shackle of party discipline he can be persuaded by argument or swayed by a speech, and the Council is a relatively free debating chamber in which members are seldom called to order by the chairman. More often the sentiments expressed are those of parish interests and this is especially the case with the strong Audley contingent whose representatives often clash with those of other parishes.

Circumstances, then, do not make the Committees or the Council a very suitable place for articulating policy and this feature is accentuated by the rather weak position of the Committee chairmen. The Chairman of the Council not infrequently attempts to draw up a list of possible chairmen of committees before each Annual General Meeting of the Council; but this list will usually be subject to the convention that the chairmanships should rotate annually. There have been occasional breaches of this custom, notably in the tenure of the chair of the Finance and General Purposes Committee by an Independent squire for six years, but the strength of parish feeling is the chief factor in maintaining the circulation of the major council positions. Therefore, unlike the Borough Council, the committee chairmen on the R.D.C. do not have time to 'dig themselves in' and forceful personalities are unable to gather power around themselves.

In the absence of party groups and strong, long-serving committee chairmen, much of the co-ordination of present policy and even thinking about future policy has passed into the hands of the Rural District officials. The Clerk of the Council often has a close relationship with the Chairman of the Council and the committee chairmen. They usually discuss items of policy with the Clerk and consult him shortly before Council or Committee meetings. It is not uncommon also for Rural District officials to act as the 'Brains Trust' to the Council, and the 1962 Rent Rebate Scheme, though originally mooted in the Finance and General Purposes Committee, was worked out in detail in the council offices. Thus without a party system, and in the face of the parishes' refusal to submit to guidance from one another, initiative has tended on occasion to stem from the Clerk of the Council.

It is difficult to assess the influence of the electorate in this scheme of things. Between the triennial elections, unless the voters know their local councillor—and, of course, many more voters do than in the Borough—their information can only come from the local press which gives very little coverage. Agendas of both committee and council meetings are sent to the local paper and to the libraries at Audley and Keele University. Yet distances are great in the Rural District; and the fact that the Council itself meets not within the District's boundaries, but in Newcastle Borough, makes immediate pressures by the voters most unlikely. However, the length of time between Committee meetings and Council meetings can allow discontent to organize, and outbursts such as that in 1955 are not completely impossible.

3. Conclusion

The most important year in the recent history of the Newcastle Rural District was not, it seems, in the late 1940's when the Labour Party was sweeping to power and transforming the political systems of so many local authorities; but 1932 when the incorporation of the former Audley Urban District Council brought an unassimilable element into the hitherto fairly peaceful deliberations of the Council. A pattern of politics was developed in the 1930's that not even the turbulent post-war years could eradicate. Party control was not imposed on the Rural District Council because no Labour Group, with a centralized decision-making process, was able to establish itself; and the division between Labour and the Independents quickly became a nominal one. The real line of conflict on the Council has thus remained, 'Audley versus the Rest', and as the years have progressed the likelihood of party conflict characterizing council debates has come to depend on the Conservative and Liberal Parties extending their activities to the Rural District. Certainly the Labour Party has signally failed to adapt its procedures to this particular environment.

The lack of political change is in sharp contrast with the social and economic transformation that has overtaken the Rural District since 1932. Especially in the post-war years the villages have benefited from the provision of much more sewerage, always the standing issue in Rural District politics, and the manual workers particularly have profited from the council housing programme, though this in its turn has provided causes for discontent. Moreover, changes in farming have brought about the decline in the size of the farming interest in the rural parishes, some of whose representatives have been replaced by 'commuters'. The social composition of the Council has thus become more heterogeneous.

In fact the post-war representation on the Council and the post-war leadership in the parishes have been rather different from that in the inter-war period. In Madeley and Betley the tenant farmers have largely disappeared and five Labour representatives led by an insurance agent have taken their place. In Audley the lower-middle-class oligarchy of the inter-war years has not, in spite of the post-war emergence of the Labour Party, been replaced by a group of working-class leaders. Indeed the experience of Audley may suggest that in industrial villages, where there is no strong trade-union branch or co-operative society to provide leadership, it may be difficult among manual workers for anyone—save an unusually firm personality—to impose his hegemony on quarrelsome working-class factions. In Audley there has been no working-class political 'leadership', in the true sense of the term.

Consequently the advent in post-war years of new social and economic forces in the Rural District, as in the Borough, has brought a new leadership to the fore. Unlike Newcastle Borough, however, the *bouleversement* has not coincided with any change in decision-making procedures, illustrating that on occasions political processes can be independent of their social and economic environment. The reasons for this lack of change lie in the gradual—if sometimes reluctant—acceptance by the Labour Party leaders in the Rural District of the strength of 'personality politics' and parish sectionalism.

Thus as far as local leaders can affect the Council's policy-making it will be through the influence they can exert on the Rural District officials who, in the absence of majority party government, are forced willy-nilly into the roles of policy-makers. This is a very different situation from that in Newcastle Borough which we must now examine.

CHAPTER SEVENTEEN

LOCAL POLITICS IN NEWCASTLE BOROUGH

T he municipal politics of the Borough are in striking contrast to those of the Rural District. In the Borough Labour's electoral triumph of 1945 was followed by its gaining control of the Borough Council, a position that has been virtually unchanged for fifteen years. Thus though the politics of the Rural District have undergone numerous vicissitudes, within Newcastle Borough the pattern has not altered very much in the last decade and a half. Consequently it is a less difficult (though not easy) task to locate power within the Borough and to deal with the process of decision-making as something that has remained more or less the same since 1947, the year in which the Labour Party for the first time secured a majority on the Council and the pre-war style of Borough politics was swept away.

The crux of the post-war change was the overthrow, almost overnight, of 'Independent politics', and its replacement by what is best called—though not, as we shall see, without important reservations—a two-party system. More recently the two-party system has moved a little towards a three-party system, so that the local development has reflected political evolution at the national level. Today it is still true that the law allows anyone who can get his nomination papers signed by eight voters to stand for the Council, and that such 'independent Independent' candidatures are still not unknown, especially in wards like Ward 4, with a highly concentrated population and some sense of community; but in the great majority of cases the Independent candidates will be nominees of an Independent organization while the other candidates will bear the label of one of our three national parties.

343

Thus the framework of politics in the Borough is fifteen years of Labour government, except for a brief interval in 1958, and in opposition an anti-Labour coalition of Independents, Conservatives and Liberals, from which the Liberals withdrew in 1960. But we must first trace briefly the fortunes of the parties in the years since the Second World War.

1. The Plight of the Independents

The Parliamentary victory in 1945 put the Newcastle Labour Party on its mettle and its next natural objective, declared quite openly at the 1945 local elections, was to win power in the Borough.[1] Because only a third of the Council is elected annually this aim was not achieved until November 1947 and even then, owing to the defection of one Labour councillor, the Labour majority rested on the support of a Communist alderman and the casting vote of the Labour mayor. It was not until the next election in May 1949 that Labour firmly secured control after substituting six Labour for six Independent aldermen. By this time, however, it had become clear that the Labour Party was intent on sweeping away the old order.

The main feature of the old political régime was the domination of the Newcastle Borough Council by Independents, a domination that had been based, as we have seen, on personal influence and ephemeral electoral organizations. The Independents of the inter-war years had had attachments to political parties. In the 1930's about half the Independent council members were Liberals, while the other half were Conservatives or were unattached—but in all cases national political allegiances were not carried into local politics for it was the firm Independent belief that 'party politics had no place in local politics'.

The political atmosphere of Britain after the Second World War, when organized national parties were highly in vogue, was hardly favourable to the survival of the Independents and the nationwide tendency for the latter to disappear from local politics has also been apparent in Newcastle. In 1945 there were

[1] This account is based on the *Evening Sentinel*, 1945–62, Minutes of the Newcastle Borough Council, Minutes of the Newcastle Liberal Association, Minutes of the Ward 2 I.C.A. Committee, and numerous interviews.

37 Independent members of Newcastle Council; by 1962 there were only 12, a decline brought about by the increasingly successful intrusion of the national parties into municipal affairs. First Labour, then the Conservatives and finally the Liberals all challenged Independent candidates and introduced new methods of political operation into Borough politics.

We have seen in Chapter 2 that the gradual advance of Labour in the 1930's had tended to lead to only one Independent candidate per ward. Labour's gains in 1945 and 1947 and the party's expressed intentions about the organization of the Borough Council alarmed all the non-Labour forces. In 1948 one of the prominent Independent councillors, an official of the Conservative Association, formed an Independent bloc which went into action against Labour at the 1949 Borough elections. This body, however, had largely grown out of the Independent Group which had been forced to organize itself on the Council; it was much more of an electoral combination than a highly organised political machine.

On the side opposed to Labour the first defection from 'Independence' was threatened in 1947 when the Newcastle Liberal Association was only with the greatest difficulty dissuaded, by some Liberal Executive members who were also Independent councillors, from running candidates with Liberal labels at the Borough elections. But inevitably a more serious threat came from the Newcastle Conservative Association which, as we have observed, had greatly expanded in membership and potential by 1950. In that year a leading Conservative in Ward 3, styling himself 'Anti-Socialist', beat the sitting councillor, the last of the 'independent Independents'; and yet more ominously for the Independents in Ward 5, where Labour stood no chance of winning, the Conservative ward party ran a Conservative candidate against the incumbent Independent. The Chairman of the Conservative Association, in spite of the embarrassment of being an Independent councillor, eventually announced his support for the Ward 5 Conservative candidate who, on polling day, gained an absolute majority with the Independent third, below Labour. Here the Conservatives, with little respect for the Independent tradition, had not hesitated to deploy their new organizational strength.

345

NEWCASTLE BOROUGH

Perhaps conscious of their new position of power the Conservative Association, in the autumn of 1950, invited both the Independents and Liberals to meet its representatives in order to plan a concerted electoral strategy for May 1951. This met with some opposition from the Liberals who at first rejected the proposed alliance by a narrow majority, but the pressure of the President of the Liberal Association, who was an Independent councillor, and the threat of resignation from the Liberal Party of another prominent Independent councillor forced the Liberals to reverse their decision. By the end of January 1951 an anti-Labour alliance, of Independents, Conservatives and Liberals, known as the United Civic Association, had been formed. It set up ward committees for local elections and began to collect individual subscriptions. As a result of the agreement there was in May 1951 a straight fight against Labour in all twelve wards by candidates who were all labelled 'U.C.A.' But it achieved little: indeed, it lost one seat to Labour. Some of its supporters claimed that its unfamiliar name had lost it support so it changed its name to Independent Civic Association for the election of 1952 without, however, arousing much enthusiasm. At the last minute it issued a leaflet, 'Wake Up, Newcastle', pointing out that because six aldermen were to be elected after the poll, the I.C.A. must win four seats for the Borough or be 'socialist dominated for ten years'. The electors remained deaf to these entreaties and no seats changed hands.

As an alliance against the Labour Party it has been difficult for the I.C.A. to adhere strictly to the 'non-party' position in local politics. Five members of the present (1962) I.C.A. Group of seventeen on the Council have been elected as official Conservative candidates. Of the other twelve who still bear the label 'Independent', three are possibly members of the Liberal Party, two are defectors from the Labour Party and some of the other seven are members of the Conservative Party. Thus only a small minority of the I.C.A. Group is completely 'independent' of party politics.

There has, not unnaturally, been some shifting of forces within the I.C.A. and friction between the partners in the alliance. Until 1954, when they fought five wards, the Conservatives demanded increasingly greater concessions, but in the mid-

346

1950's their impetus slackened and by the late 1950's it was the Liberals who were 'rocking the boat'. As early as November 1955 the Liberal Executive decided to run Liberal candidates in Wards 2 and 6, but the two candidates chosen finally succumbed to pressure from the I.C.A. and stood as Independents in May 1956. By 1957, however, the Liberal Executive was refusing to negotiate any longer with the I.C.A., and in May of that year the first Liberal candidate ever to stand in a Newcastle Borough election came second to the Labour candidate in Ward 2 and forced the Independent to the bottom of the poll. As a result in 1958 and 1959 the I.C.A. allowed the Liberals a free run against Labour in this ward, a sign that the new militancy of the Liberals, like that of the Conservatives in earlier years, had brought about a realignment of forces within the anti-Labour coalition.

With the growth of party organization it became more difficult for the Independents to compete in local politics. The I.C.A. initially set up ward parties which, as they were only for local elections, found it difficult to establish separate identities because they were often infiltrated by the members of the national parties. For example, the Ward 2 I.C.A. committee, formed in April 1951 and chaired by a well-known Conservative, recommended their Independent candidate after his defeat in May 1951 to make himself better known by joining the Ward 2 Conservative Association. The Ward 2 I.C.A. Committee also decided that though the I.C.A.'s candidate in the ward in May 1952 should be an Independent the election campaign should be in reality conducted by the Ward Conservative Association. Young Conservatives, in fact, provided many of the workers and the Ward 2 Conservative Association was approached for a grant towards expenditure. On the defeat of the candidate both in May and in the aldermanic by-election in July 1952 the Ward 2 I.C.A. committee decided that the next candidate should be 'straight Conservative or anti-Labour'. By 1956, however, when the Independent candidate in Ward 2 was a member of the Liberal Party, the *ad hoc* committee was formed of Liberals; and at the same time in Ward 6 another Independent, who was actually on the Liberal Executive, received official Liberal support.

By the late 1950's the I.C.A. ward committees had virtually

collapsed and individual membership of the I.C.A. had ceased. To fight their elections Independent candidates assembled their own extempore organization often with the help of those Independent councillors who did not have to seek re-election. Thus because the I.C.A.'s ward committees had failed to take root the organization had, for electoral purposes, become nothing more or less than a clearing house for anti-Labour candidatures; and today it exists as the opposition to Labour within the council chamber, a party caucus without a permanent organization.

Meanwhile the Labour Party had just about held its own. Though it lost four seats in the years 1953–7, all to the Independents, it had held all the aldermanic seats since 1952 and so maintained a small but steady majority based on always winning Wards 1, 2, 9, 10, 11 and 12, and more often than not Ward 7. In 1958, however, the defection of two Labour councillors to the other side resulted in the return of six anti-Labour aldermen. As five of these aldermen were from safe Independent wards the aldermanic by-elections in June 1958 were likely to give the anti-Labour forces a slight majority. Perhaps because of this they revealed some of the tensions within the I.C.A. The I.C.A., including by now some Conservative council members, had chosen an Independent candidate in Ward 3, but the Ward 3 Conservative Association, feeling that they had a better candidate, ignored the agreement and a three-cornered fight was only avoided by the Independent withdrawing. The leaders of the I.C.A., angry with the Conservative rank-and-file, retaliated by encouraging an Independent candidature in Ward 5 where a Conservative candidate was already in the field and where the Conservatives held all three seats. The Conservative again won with Labour second and the Independent at the bottom of the poll. Thus though an anti-Labour majority was assured (only lasting until the following November when Labour made a gain in a by-election) the victorious coalition was riven with dissension.

By 1960 two new factors were upsetting the stability of the I.C.A. The arrival of a full-time Conservative agent at the end of 1959 heralded more Conservative candidatures in local elections. In 1960 there were three, in 1961 five, and in 1962 six. Yet in spite of these efforts, to the Conservatives' chagrin, by 1962 they still had only five council members while the Independents had twelve. Of ten Independent candidates in the preceding three years eight had been elected, of fourteen Conservative nominees only three had reached the council chamber. This was easily explained by the fact that the Independents had become entrenched in the safe wards leaving the Conservatives to fight the Labour strongholds, a situation which the Conservative rank-and-file resented.

The rise of the 'new' Liberals, as described in Chapter 6, is the other factor hastening the end of the Independents in Newcastle politics. One of the staunchest of Independent council members among the Liberals—the man who had threatened to resign from the Liberal Executive in 1951 if negotiations were not opened with the I.C.A.—on losing his aldermanic seat in 1961 became converted to the idea of municipal Liberal candidates, stood as one in 1962 and was returned as a Liberal councillor. The younger Liberals were thus winning over some of the older members to the policy of the Liberal Party fighting local elections.

At all stages the challenges of the national parties with their much less makeshift organizations have affected the Independents. Enmity towards the Labour Party, regarded not unfairly by the Independents as the chief purveyor of national issues into local politics, led the Independents to make an agreement with the Liberal and Conservative Parties. This electoral alliance became subject to stress with the changing fortunes of its members. The Conservatives, inclined to throw their weight about in the early days of the alliance, became more attached to the Independent label for municipal candidates in the later 1950's when they feared that the description 'Conservative' might repel rather than attract voters. The Liberals made their exit from the I.C.A. when their party appeared to be on the ascendant.

In spite of their setbacks the Independent council members are still the largest of the three anti-Labour groups. None of the Independents seems likely to desert his Independent position to stand as a candidate of either the Liberal or Conservative Parties. On the other hand there is always the possibility that a Conservative Party that has recovered its buoyancy might want to take over more traditionally Independent seats; or that it might withdraw from the I.C.A. and leave the Independents to their own devices. Whatever the case, unless present trends are startlingly reversed it seems Independent councillors will become more and more of a rarity in Newcastle politics. This impression is reinforced by the finding in Chapter 12 that the Newcastle voters have little cognisance of the Independents in local politics and regard the elections, save for one or two exceptional wards, as a contest between Labour and the Conservatives.[1]

Consequently we must now turn to examining the national parties in Newcastle Borough politics, and especially to the position of the Labour Party from within whose ranks has come the leadership of the Borough since 1947.

2. The National Parties in Local Politics

There is considerable variation in the extent to which the national parties concern themselves with local politics.[2] The formal institutional position is not always a clear indication of who controls the parties. It must be remembered that even where there are no direct representational links between different committees a coincidence of membership may exist.[3]

(i) THE LABOUR PARTY

The Newcastle Constituency Labour Party has been described in an earlier chapter. Except for the selection of candidates for the County Council elections it rarely interferes in local politics which it leaves to the Borough (misnamed the Central) Labour Party. Institutionally the division of function is recognized by the fact that though the Borough Labour Party has its representatives at constituency party meetings there is no reverse relationship. The Constituency Labour Party is largely concerned with Parliamentary elections and the selection of a Parliamentary candidate.

[1] See p. 241 above.
[2] This account is based on Minutes of the Newcastle Constituency Labour Party, Minutes of the Newcastle Borough Labour Party, Minutes of the Ward 6 Labour Party, Minutes of the North Stafford Miners' Federation, Minutes of the Silverdale Co-operative Party and the Silverdale Co-operative Society, Minutes of the Newcastle Liberal Association, and interviews.
[3] See Figures 4, 5 and 7.

NEWCASTLE BOROUGH

The Borough Labour Party is involved with little else save local politics. Occasionally it may pass resolutions on national Labour Party policy as when in 1949 it supported Communist Party affiliation to the Labour Party or in 1961 blessed the Free Church campaign against Portuguese rule in Angola. But usually its time is taken up with organizational work of a seasonal nature. About the end of the year the nominating of candidates for the Borough elections begins. In January the list may be drawn up, by March election strategy will be under discussion, a month later the wards choose their nominees and in May the party workers will be on the streets. After the election there may be a post-mortem and then between June and September there is relative quiescence.

The Borough Labour Party is a federal body to which the ward Labour parties, trade unions and other bodies send their delegates. When it has a full meeting of all delegates it is known as the General Management Committee, about half of whose membership comes from the wards. At its Annual General Meeting the G.M.C. elects an Executive Committee composed of six officers chosen by the votes of the whole gathering and nine other delegates, of whom three are trade unionists, three are from the ward parties and one each from the Young Socialists, the Women's Section and the Silverdale Co-operative Society. Both committees meet monthly. Usually the E.C. precedes and reports to the G.M.C., but there are occasions, such as a sudden by-election, when the G.M.C. delegates authority to the E.C. The E.C. also interviews prospective nominees for the Council and, in conjunction with the Policy Committee of the Labour Group, writes the party's municipal election addresses. Thus though the G.M.C. has final power the E.C. has some say by virtue of its crisis function.

The wards are the only channel for the representation of the individual member though the fall in party membership in the late 1940's robbed them of much of their vitality. Ward 6 meetings, for example, averaged 30 members in 1946, but by 1950 the number had fallen to 9. This has been more like the average attendance in the years since and the shortage of active members has been one of the reasons why some of the ward Labour parties have combined. At other times the problem of finding a secretary, an official always in short supply, has had the same effect. Otherwise the accidents of ward boundaries have prevented any tidy pattern. Ward 11 as we have seen includes southern Chesterton and Knutton; but the Chesterton members prefer to foregather with their fellow villagers in the Ward 10 Labour Party. Thus the Ward 10 Labour Party is effectively the Chesterton Labour Party and the Ward 11 Labour Party is effectively the Knutton Labour Party. In spite of these idiosyncrasies Labour Party protocol is not usually infringed. For example, on occasions the votes of Chesterton members at candidate selection meetings in Ward 10 have been taken to Knutton and added to those of the Ward 11 Labour Party. An attempt is also made to insist on attendance registers at ward meetings to ensure that people do not participate in the activities of two wards at once.

The eight ward Labour parties try to meet monthly but rarely succeed. In 1962, 46 ward Labour Party meetings were reported to the Borough Labour Party—an average of about six for each ward party annually. The corresponding average for 1961 was four and it was three in 1955 and 1956; but the pattern of ward activity is uneven. Since 1958 Ward 3 Labour Party, for example, seems to have been the most lively (judging by reports of successful meetings) but this has not always been the case. Ward 11 was very flourishing in the early 1950's, with its cohorts of Co-operative women, but it has since become relatively inactive. Ward 10 has been fairly active for some years. Where membership is small, however, the loss—or gain—of a secretary may be the factor on which the collapse or survival of the ward Labour Party depends. Besides the decline in ward party activity since the late 1940's the most marked feature has been the tendency for ward Labour parties such as Ward 3 or Wards 5, 7 and 8, operating where Labour finds it difficult to win seats, to show the most energy.

Nomination of candidates for municipal elections is the prerogative of all bodies affiliated to the Borough Labour Party. The E.C. examines the nominations to make sure that all Labour Party regulations are being observed, requires from all nominees an undertaking to accept the Standing Orders of the Labour Group on the Council and in November sends the list to the G.M.C. The number of nominations varies: in 1950 it contained

25 names but the 13 in 1962 is probably nearer the mean. The G.M.C. may demur at one or two names but will usually endorse them and the list then becomes known as 'the Panel'.

Between November and March the G.M.C. must decide how many wards are to be fought. Finance enters into this decision for wards who are reluctant to fight may have to be subsidized. Six of the wards are regarded as safe for the Labour Party and selection as a candidate for them is tantamount to election. The marginal Wards 6 and 7 are always contested, but Wards 3, 4, 5 and 8 where Labour has little chance are sometimes the subject of dissension. On one occasion Ward 3 Labour Party was solidly against fighting but the rest of the Borough Labour Party, arguing that token candidates were necessary to divert enemy cars and workers from more favourable wards, insisted on a contest.

The ward Labour parties, in those wards it has been decided to fight, will next hold selection conferences at which the E.C. can attend with the full voting powers of its fifteen members and thus have a large say in the choice. The elaborate procedure of drawing up a short list in each ward is not commonly undertaken, however, because the candidates are so few that they average not much more than one per ward. The ward Labour party will normally select from the Panel the one name it has already submitted and sitting councillors especially are usually readopted without being even interviewed. Chances of disagreement are thus minimized.

Most disagreement about nominations has largely been the result of the intervention of the E.C. The E.C. ruling in 1947 that anyone on the Panel should be prepared to fight any ward was later rescinded by the G.M.C. as a result of protests from the wards; and a decision of the E.C. in 1951 that the Panel, once closed, could not be reopened was almost immediately annulled by a G.M.C. meeting at which the ward affected complained vigorously. On the whole candidates are so scarce that, as when Ward 9 adopted a candidate who was not on the Panel, minor transgressions are often overlooked. Thus the E.C. has not been able always to assert its authority over the wards and the strict letter of the law has sometimes gone unheeded.

Another source of pressure, much less frequent but more

embarrassing, has been the miners' union. Almost all the trade-union nominations for the Borough elections are people who are active workers within the Borough Labour Party and are also individual members of their wards. But the North Stafford Miners' Federation occasionally sends names unknown to the Borough Labour Party. As miners, even in the 'mining wards', are not very active in ward Labour parties it is always likely that the union's candidate will not be adopted. In Ward 12, for example, there have been refusals to adopt an N.S.M.F. nominee in spite of the financial reward in so doing. Sometimes as a result there has been opposition to the Labour candidate in Ward 12 by officials of the Silverdale branch of the miners' union or their nominees. At the same time the N.S.M.F. has only contributed to local election expenses when one of its own candidates has been adopted in one of the wards.

Until recent times the Silverdale Co-operative Society was more to the fore than the miners' union in the affairs of the Borough Labour Party. After the tentative relations of the inter-war years, in 1942 the Society affiliated to the constituency party and from 1944 until 1957 expressed itself politically through the Silverdale Co-operative Party. The latter was soon a considerable force, paying for half the cost of political propaganda in the Borough; but there was trouble in 1947 when the Borough Labour Party forgot to ask the Co-operative Party for its nominees to the Panel. Consequently an agreement between the two bodies in 1948 laid down that the Silverdale Co-operative Party could send to the Borough Labour Party its list of nominees who, if selected by the wards, would be known as 'Co-op and Labour' candidates. Two-thirds of their expenses would be paid by the Co-operative Party. In 1949 not only were four out of the seven Co-op nominees adopted and two of them returned to the Council, but also all the official positions in the Borough Labour Party were held by members of the Co-operative Party. However, the failure of the Silverdale Co-operative Party to obtain the selection of its nominee as Parliamentary candidate in 1950 led to disenchantment and by the early 1950's its meetings were sometimes inquorate. Between 1950 and its demise in 1957 the Silverdale Co-operative Party only secured the acceptance of four of its sixteen nominees as Labour candidates at the Borough elections.

NEWCASTLE BOROUGH

The wards have thus been generally reluctant to accept the candidatures of other bodies and the Borough Labour Party has been unable or unwilling to counteract this tendency. One result has been that political processes, of which nomination procedure is probably the most important, have not been completely centralized in the Borough Labour Party. The post-war attempt at centralization, epitomized in the policy of the agent between 1947 and 1951, often aroused resentment and since the agent resigned correct party procedures have not always been observed. The wards have complained because, unlike the local Labour parties in the Rural District, they have no direct representation on the Constituency Labour Party and at other times they have objected to the Executive Committee of the Borough Labour Party intervening to install a municipal candidate without reference to the G.M.C. There has also been considerable reluctance to answer appeals for work in other wards, and only a few enthusiasts are willing to journey long distances and canvass in wards, like Ward 4, where there is very little hope of winning. Local sectionalism is thus a force to be reckoned with.

In spite of the partial failure of centralization through its institutions, the Borough Labour Party is centralized in effect because only a small number of people are concerned with its affairs. Table 1 shows the average attendance at both the

TABLE I. AVERAGE ATTENDANCE AT MEETINGS OF THE NEWCASTLE BOROUGH LABOUR PARTY COMMITTEES

Year	1946	47	48	49	50	51	55	56	57*	59	60	61	62	1949–1951	1959–1962
Borough Labour Party E.C.	11	11	10	9	9	8	6	6	6	4	5	6	7	9	6
Borough Labour Party G.M.C.	30	21	31	28	35	34	20	24	12	16	15	15	19	31	17

* Attendance in this year is exaggerated because inquorate meetings are not included in the average.

Borough Labour Party G.M.C. and E.C. for many of the years since 1946. Apart from the very obvious recent decline in party activity these figures show that the E.C. has maintained a higher proportionate attendance than the G.M.C. In fact about half

355

the E.C. turns out as against a quarter of the G.M.C. The overall picture, however, is one of a handful of people running the Borough Labour Party.

(ii) THE NON-LABOUR FORCES

It is more difficult to examine the forces opposed to Labour because in some cases the absence of documentation, and in the case of the Independents the lack of formal organization, limits analysis. But the earlier account of post-war Borough politics fills some of the gap. Moreover it must be remembered that the Labour Party has virtually been the ruler of Newcastle since the late 1940's. With this in mind let us investigate the role of the Liberal and Conservative Parties in Borough politics.

(a) *The Conservative Party*

The structure of the Conservative Party is less complex and less highly integrated than that of the Labour Party, chiefly because the Conservatives have no separate Borough party. The Newcastle Conservative Association controls all party matters in the constituency including Borough and Rural District affairs. The Executive Council endorses all local government candidatures, but this is a mere formality and the effective control in municipal matters within the Conservative Association is the Local Elections Committee, set up in March 1958, comprising the officers of the Association, Conservative councillors and any other interested members who wish to attend its meetings.

At first the purposes of the Local Elections Committee were not strictly adhered to; for example, in October 1958 it defined its aims and objects as 'to get our candidate returned to Parliament'. But since the advent of the agent in 1960 the Committee has confined itself to local government matters, discussing electoral policy and tactics. It has shown a tendency to select and even to arrange the nomination of candidates especially where the Conservative ward parties have been moribund or non-existent. Otherwise it receives nominations from ward parties and helps them in their electoral efforts.

The Conservative ward parties have rather more autonomy than ward Labour parties. Where they exist, as in Wards 3, 5, 6, 7 and 8, they select their own candidates without interference from the central Association. They should meet monthly, and one or two do so, but an annual average of the Conservative ward party meetings would be about six or seven. At these meetings national Conservative policy is rarely discussed and municipal affairs seldom raised, though where Conservative candidatures have become a regular feature, as in Wards 5 and 7, a cycle of activities co-ordinated with the local elections in May motivates political life. Ward meetings also, to some extent, have a social function, though within the ambit of the constituency the most important duty of the wards is the raising of funds. Each ward has a quota, allocated by the constituency association, a quota which it is supposed to attain every year.

As the Local Elections Committee largely consists of the Association's officers the people who run the Constituency Conservative Party are, at least nominally, in charge of its local government activities. In fact of the ten Conservatives who are on all three of the Association's important committees—the Executive Council, Finance Committee and General Purposes Committee—eight sit on the Local Elections Committee. Only three of these eight, however, are Borough residents, a reflection of the greater relative strength of the party in the countryside. This may partly explain the disagreement that has arisen over strategy at Borough elections in 1959 resulting in one important Conservative, who was an Independent council member, resigning from the Executive Council because he disapproved of the Conservatives fighting more seats.

In general today the 'top ten' are in favour of more Conservative candidates at Borough elections, a policy supported by the Conservative ward parties, but made difficult by a shortage of candidates and recent Liberal incursions. The fact that the Conservatives are far from power in the Borough and, indeed, are outnumbered by the Independents on the Council can be little encouragement to the five Conservative council members. Only two of the latter are also members of the Conservative Executive and neither of them is in the 'top ten'. One may perhaps conclude that though those chiefly responsible for directing the effort of the Conservative Association would like to see more Conservative local government candidatures they are not always encouraged in this policy by prominent Conservatives within the Borough.

(b) The Liberal Party

Like the Conservatives, though unlike the Labour Party, the Liberal Party has no separate organization for Newcastle Borough. Yet the Liberals, alone of the three parties, have built up their strength in the process of fighting local elections and as a result of successes in this field they have today (1962) a remarkable enthusiasm. It is significant that when in 1962 this keenness materialized in the selection of a Parliamentary candidate they chose one of their Borough councillors to fight the next General Election.

Institutionally the Liberal Party is decentralized. The existing Liberal ward parties are responsible for adopting their own candidates without endorsement from the centre and thus they have a high degree of autonomy which may at some date prove embarrassing. At the moment, however, the position has hardly been tested, for the ward parties in Wards 4, 5 and 7 have grown out of organization set up at the first contests in these wards where the Liberal candidate or councillors have been prominent in constructing these machines. As in the other two parties there is a system of ward representation at the centre by four delegates— the ward chairman and secretary and two other elected nominees.

From those wards without organization the Liberal Council at its annual meeting deputes people to attend the executive meetings. If the political prospect seems promising in these wards nomination of a candidate will be made by the policy subcommittee consisting of the Liberal councillors, prospective candidates for other wards and the chairmen of the ward parties. As yet there seems to have been little friction over the choice of a Liberal candidate in any ward. The Liberals have the unity of a party that has recently arrived on the scene and, like the other two parties, they suffer from a dearth of people willing to stand for the Council.

Though the Liberal Party is decentralized in structure it tends to be centralized in fact. Table 2 shows that though, unlike the Labour Party, the number of active Liberal workers has increased since the mid-1950's, only a few people nevertheless run the party. In fact the attendance at the Liberal Executive's monthly meetings is about the same as at the monthly meetings of the Borough Labour Party. Thus the Liberal and Labour parties are not very different in this respect.

TABLE 2. AVERAGE ATTENDANCE PER MEETING OF THE NEWCASTLE LIBERAL EXECUTIVE PER YEAR

	1950	1954	1955	1956	1957	1958	1959	1960	1961	1962
Average attendance	12	9	9	12	11	13	10	11	15	15

The Liberals hope to continue the policy, so far quite successful, of expanding outwards from an organizational and geographic centre. This may modify their present extraordinary compactness. Three out of the four Liberal Borough councillors represent Ward 4, the smallest and one of the most central of the wards. The Liberal councillors and the part-time agent also dominate the Policy Sub-committee where all the most important policy decisions of the party are first taken. Consequently though power is formally less centralized in the Liberal Party than in the case of the other two parties in actual fact it is a good deal more centralized.

3. The Municipal Decision-makers

There are 48 council members—12 aldermen and 36 councillors. The former are not elected for a three-year term by the voters but for six years by the councillors. Six aldermanic vacancies fall triennially and are filled by a slate of nominees from the majority party though the procedure has not always been a foregone conclusion.[1] Because of Labour's slight majority, Borough politics are tense and balloting for the aldermanic bench can result in shocks. In 1956 the defection of one Labour councillor plus the fact that another voted for himself secured the election of an Independent alderman, and in 1958 there was a more serious sequel when the defection of two Labour councillors returned another five Independent aldermen and paved the

[1] This account is based on the *Evening Sentinel*, 1945–62, Minutes of the Newcastle Borough Council, and interviews. We should like to thank the many officials of Newcastle clubs and societies who co-operated by sending us lists of their committee membership.

way for the anti-Labour forces to seize power. Thus the political balance of the Council is not entirely in the hands of the voters.

The electors return annually a third of the councillors who are more likely to be in touch with the feeling in the wards than the aldermen. Table 3, associating the representation and residence of all council members, shows that half the aldermen live

TABLE 3. RESIDENCE OF COUNCIL MEMBERS BY WARDS

	1	2	3	4	5	6	7	8	9	10	11	12	Outside Borough	Total
Aldermen	—	—	6	—	—	1	—	1	—	1	2	1	—	12
Councillors	3	5	6	—	3	2	2	2	5	2	—	4	2	36
Total Council members	3	5	12	—	3	3	2	3	5	3	2	5	2	48

in Ward 3 and that six wards have no resident aldermen. Councillors are more evenly distributed, but the total effect is that more than half the council members live in four wards, a quarter of them residing in Ward 3.

Table 3 takes no account of whether the councillors living in particular wards actually represent those wards. This is examined in Table 4 which shows that just over half the councillors

TABLE 4. REPRESENTATION AND RESIDENCE OF COUNCILLORS

	Labour	Independent	Conservative	Liberal	Total non-Labour	Total
Live in ward they represent	15	2	2	1	5	20
Live elsewhere	6	5	2	3	10	16

live in the wards they represent. The table also shows a significant tendency for Labour councillors to live in the wards they represent and for non-Labour councillors not to. Thus Labour councillors may be more in touch with feeling in the wards.

In the Council the Independents are probably least in touch. Besides showing a creditably high attendance for the Council as a whole, Table 5 reveals that it is the councillors who stand as political party nominees who are most conscientious; and the Labour members, perhaps as the ruling party, have the best record of all.

TABLE 5. POSSIBLE AND ACTUAL ATTENDANCES OF COUNCIL MEMBERS
AT COUNCIL MEETINGS IN 1962

	Lab.	Percent-age	Ind.	Percent-age	Con.	Percent-age	Lib.	Percent-age	All Council	Percent-age
Possible	274	100	151	100	59	100	44	100	528	100
Actual	236	90	88	58	45	76	36	82	405	77

Table 6 examines the social composition of the Council and shows that the business proprietors are the most over-represented group on the Council; with 8 per cent of the Borough's population they hold 31 per cent of the council seats. The clerical

TABLE 6. OCCUPATIONAL GROUPINGS OF COUNCIL MEMBERS

	Labour	Inde-pendent	Con-servative	Liberal	Total non-Labour	All
Business proprietors	3	9	3	—	12	15
Managerial and professional	3	1	1	3	5	8
Clerical workers	6	1	1	1	3	9
Skilled workers	8	1	—	—	1	9
Less-skilled workers	7	—	—	—	—	7

workers with 9 per cent of the population and 19 per cent of the seats are also well favoured, though the professional group, 17 per cent of council representation and 11 per cent of Newcastle inhabitants, are not grossly over-represented. Finally the manual workers, with a third of the council seats and 70 per cent of the population, have about half of the seats to which their numbers might entitle them. Not surprisingly women without occupation and husband have no seats.

The comparison between the social composition of Labour and non-Labour council members is not unlike an analysis of the House of Commons where there are scarcely any manual workers outside the Parliamentary Labour Party, while the latter is much more a social cross-section of the nation than its opponents. If we examine the Newcastle Labour Group we see a similar state of affairs with the manual workers having 56 per cent of the Group's membership. Clearly the Labour Group is much more 'representative' of Newcastle's citizens than are its opponents.

The Labour Group, moreover, shows little connection with the social and cultural leadership of the Borough. Figures 12–15 depict the 'cobweb' of leadership in Newcastle by associating the

NEWCASTLE LABOUR GROUP: CONNECTIONS OF MEMBERS

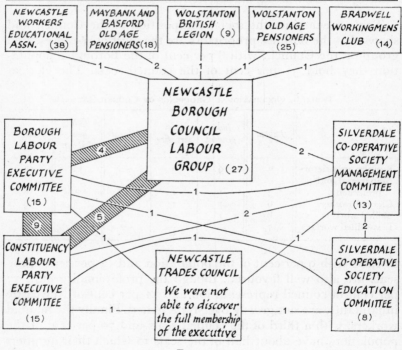

FIGURE 12

membership of the four groups on the Council with the committee membership of Newcastle organizations in all cases but two. The two exceptions are the Rotary Club and the Round

Table (a sort of junior Rotary) which restrict entry so narrowly that it was thought more appropriate to consider their whole membership.

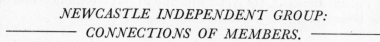

NEWCASTLE INDEPENDENT GROUP:
——— CONNECTIONS OF MEMBERS. ———

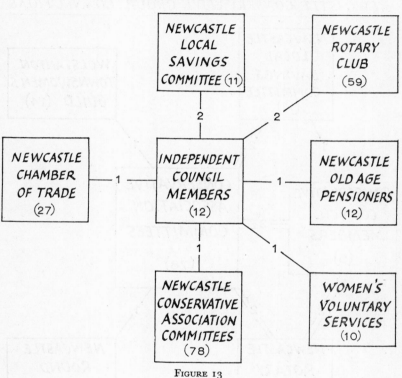

FIGURE 13

The Labour Group is isolated from the leadership of social and cultural activity in Newcastle—a situation that Margaret Stacey[1] also found in Banbury—and the corporate life of the Labour movement is obviously the most important field in which the Labour council members exercise their organizing abilities. Otherwise they are to be found on the committees of Old Age

[1] Margaret Stacey, *Tradition and Change* (1960), p. 50.

NEWCASTLE BOROUGH

Pensioners' Associations (old age pensioners have been used for collecting Labour Party subscriptions) and workingmen's clubs. It is noticeable that the organizations they help to direct tend to be outside the centre of Newcastle and at the Wolstanton end of the Borough.

NEWCASTLE CONSERVATIVE GROUP: CONNECTIONS

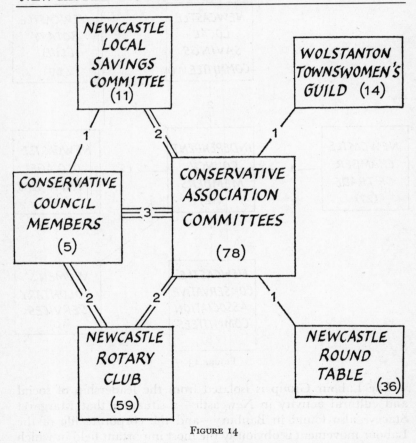

FIGURE 14

Of the four council groups the Independents are nearest to identification with the social and cultural leadership of Newcastle. A quarter of them are members of the Rotary Club, but even the Independents are not overloaded with connections. The Liberals and Conservatives are too small to generalize much about; but it is not surprising, in view of their recent arrival, that the Liberals have few extra-council committee activities, while the Conservatives are only a little more involved.

NEWCASTLE LIBERAL GROUP: CONNECTIONS

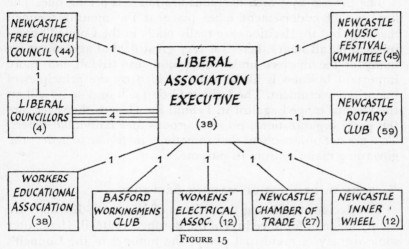

FIGURE 15

In conclusion the Borough's decision-makers may be divided according to their characteristics in two ways. In the first place there is the difference between the Labour Group and the others. The Labour council members are much more a cross-section socially of the electorate and more likely to live among the people they represent. But secondly there is the contrast between the council members who are nominees of parties and the Independents. The former with a better council attendance record have fewer connections with the leadership of Newcastle's social and cultural organizations. It seems as though the Independents combine politics with other activities, while the party men specialize in taking part in political life.

4. The Process of Making Decisions

The decisions of Newcastle Borough Council, like those of any local authority, are very much circumscribed by the powers of

the Government in Whitehall. The post-war Labour Government was centralizing services when Newcastle Labour Party
came to office; but since 1951, except for a few months in 1958,
Labour has ruled in Newcastle but not at Westminster. Yet in
both periods there are examples of both sides of the Council
protesting against Government interference.[1]

The process by which decisions are made is a long one. The
final act of endorsement takes place at the monthly council
meeting; but the decisions are really made in the Council's committees. At all stages there is a very great deal of agreement for
many of the matters under discussion are trivial; but more
important business is likely to be decided by the principles of
majority government. The Labour Group will impose its will on
the Groups ranged against it. Behind the Groups, however, are
the party organizations, pressure groups and individual voters.
To a greater or less extent they sometimes intervene to deflect the
governing majority from its purpose.

(i) FORMAL PROCESS OF MAKING DECISIONS

The decisions affecting the citizens of Newcastle Borough are
finally made at full meetings of the Borough Council. Here, after
some display of municipal pomp, the minutes of the Council's
committees are introduced by the appropriate committee
chairmen. The Mayor, who presides, from the aldermanic
bench above the councillors reads merely the numbers of
the minutes '1, 2, 3, etc.', only stopping when some council
member indicates that he or she wishes to query one of them.
An intervention may occasionally be important and one of
the Groups may wish to rescind the minute concerned, in
which case it is more usual to refer it back to the appropriate
committee. More often, however, the subject raised will be
some small item that will be settled after a short debate, often
by a cross-bench vote. But the great majority of the minutes
will not be challenged and the council meeting will end in about
an hour and a half.

---

[1] This account is based on the *Evening Sentinel*, 1945–62, Minutes of the
Newcastle Borough Council, Minutes of the Newcastle Borough Labour
Party, and interviews.

(ii) DECISION-MAKING IN COMMITTEE

There are twenty committees of the Newcastle Borough Council, each relating to some aspect of the Borough's functions. Some of them, such as Baths, or Road Safety, deal with day-to-day problems of municipal life. Others such as the Watch Committee are largely reminders of past glory. The Education Committee, because of its quota of co-opted members and other distinctive features, tends to lead a somewhat separate life of its own. Finance and General Purposes are distinguished by being full Committees of the Council. Housing is such an important function that it is divided between two Committees, Housing Management which is concerned with the allocation of tenancies and the repair of the council houses, and Housing which decides terms of tenancy and plans future housing development.

Though the most important work of the Council is done in committees there is not a great deal of delegation to committees. In fact no committee has delegated powers in respect of all its functions, though the Town Planning Committee has delegation in the matter of applications both for planning permission and under the building by-laws—about half its functions. Otherwise odd functions are delegated on an *ad hoc* basis and in the case of what might be called trivial emergencies, the Town Clerk and the chairman and vice-chairman of a committee, after consulting one another, may act subject to later ratification by the Council. Special powers are also delegated to the committees by the Council during the May and August recesses. No deliberate attempt is made to co-ordinate the work of committees, though the General Purposes and Finance Committees sometimes fulfil this function because matters which are not clearly the province of a particular committee may be referred to them. The control of the purse strings also is bound to give the Finance Committee some co-ordinating powers.

The informal nature of committee procedure is symbolized by the chairman sitting in the well of the council chamber with a Borough official at his elbow. Debate in Committee has, therefore, more spontaneity than in a full council meeting, there are more interruptions and interjections. This mood is further encouraged by the fact that at this stage the party Groups will not have selected speakers or adopted a position on the subject under discussion. There are no inhibitions about disagreeing with one's party colleagues and the discussion proceeds with cut and thrust. It is chiefly in Committee that councillors' reputations are made and ruined. Silence wins no rewards, but the ability to give and take in decision-making may mark one out for promotion.

Although future policy must come through a committee, it is not always shaped in the course of committee discussion. In fact the sources of policy seem to be varied. It is often asserted that much policy in local government today emanates from the officials so that the councillors only ratify its implementation, holding watching briefs for the voters.[1] This picture certainly does not apply to Newcastle though it is difficult to assess how much influence the officials have on the making of the Borough's policy. Generally speaking the more expertise needed for policy decisions the more likely are the officials to affect the outcome. Town planning and finance, for example, are two fields where technical knowledge is bound to carry much weight. Furthermore the Town Clerk gives legal advice to the Council and its Committees whenever it is necessary.

The impact that the officials make on policy varies with the field of activity and with the personalities involved. The Town Clerk attends in person the Finance, General Purposes and Staffing and Salaries Committees and by conferring with the other officials, who attend other committees, or by occasionally attending the latter himself, he exercises some co-ordinating control over policy; but he does not hold an 'administrators' cabinet' which in some local authorities is the sign of a good deal of policy being centralized in officials. Nor are there, in Newcastle, any regular and formalized meetings between the Town Clerk and the chairmen of committees though naturally consultation is common.

Many ideas about future policy, however, stem from the chairmen of the committees. Council Standing Orders give them no special powers; but the chairmanships do not rotate annually in Newcastle, as they do in some municipalities, and there have

[1] For a discussion on this point see H. Maddick and E. Pritchard, 'Conventions of Local Authorities', *Public Administration*, Part I, Summer 1958, p. 146, and Part II, Summer 1959, p. 137.

only been two Labour chairmen of the Housing Committee and three of the Finance Committee since 1947. At the present moment (excepting the brief Independent interregnum in 1958) the Housing and Finance chairmen have had five years in office and the Education chairman has had six, as against an average length of tenure of chairmanships of 2·6 years. Thus the more important committees less often change their chairmen.

These circumstances allow the chairmen the opportunities of framing continuous policies for some years ahead. If any chairman is desirous of giving a lead he is assured that his ideas will be put forward either in committee or in the Labour Group. In either case it is more important to persuade the other Labour council members than the opposition. A strong-willed and capable chairman, who is well advised on the technical and legal aspects, is likely to get his way. Thus the Newcastle Council's land-buying policy is said to be on the initiative of the energetic Housing chairman. Where chairmen have definite policies of their own there is much less chance of the officials providing the stimulus for the Council's policy deliberations.

In conclusion it should be said that a good deal of power in Newcastle Borough is in the hands of the elected representatives. Indeed in the pre-war days when the Independents were in a majority the Borough officials almost certainly had more say in policy formation; for the difficulties of framing a programme were inevitably greater when there was no majority party to co-ordinate the policies of the different committees. Conversely the situation has changed since Labour introduced party politics to the Council: today policy decisions are largely beaten out on the anvil of the Labour Group by the hammer blows of the Labour committee chairmen.

(iii) DECISION-MAKING IN THE GROUPS

Since 1947 council decisions have been made within the framework of majority government—one party in power and ranged against it a coalition. The Labour Group in November 1945 announced that it would take no committee chairmanships or vice-chairmanships until it was in a majority: then it would take them all and all the aldermanic vacancies in addition. In 1947 the Labour Group also proposed a resolution, passed by the

Council, declaring that all committee membership should be allocated according to the proportionate strength of the 'Labour and Independent Groups'. By this Standing Order, which is still in force, the Independents are forced to caucus at least once a year in order to organize their representation on the Council's committees. Thus it was the deliberate policy of the Labour Party that brought the formal Group system into being.

This system was contrary to all the assumptions underlying the old ways of carrying on council business. Three Labour veterans who had been elected to committee positions by the Independent majority refused to resign immediately and they were expelled from the party. Like their counterparts in the Rural District the 'Old Guard' in the Borough had been unable to adapt itself to the new scheme of things. A similar fate befell two Independents who refused to caucus with the Independent Group and took 'Independence' so seriously that they sometimes voted for Labour motions. One of them, a very prominent alderman, was left off the Independent slate for the six aldermanic vacancies in 1949; the other was defeated in 1950, as we described above, by an 'Anti-Socialist' who was a well-known member of the Conservative Party. Thereafter until 1961 the arrangements of the Council were subject to this dual Group system; but in that year the two Liberal councillors, in order to obtain committee representation, were unwilling attenders at the Independent Group. In consequence in 1962 the Liberals, by this time four in number, were accorded representation as a Group on every council committee.

Today the Group system is firmly established and it is from the Groups, and especially, as we have seen, the Labour Group, that policy initially stems. The present (1962) Labour Group consists of six aldermen and twenty-one councillors, though not all members usually attend and there have been a few cases of the Group meetings being inquorate. Two delegates from the Borough Labour Party also have the right to attend. The Group meets on every Monday before the monthly council meeting. Until 1962 they systematically considered all the committee minutes that were to be submitted to the Council, but this procedure has recently been streamlined. The first half-hour of the meeting is now devoted to the discussion of future policy and only if notice of motion has been raised before this time elapses will the Group debate a specific minute. Thus unpremeditated argument is less likely to arise as a result of this innovation.

The policy of the Labour Group is *not* usually decided in its Policy Committee, which consists of the Group's chairman, vice-chairman, secretary and two whips. This Committee's most important task is to make the recommendations for membership of the council committees and even these suggestions are often rejected subsequently at the Group meeting. In fact, the Policy Committee seldom meets and rarely discusses important items of policy.

While the Labour Group remains in the majority all important matters must, sooner or later, pass through it. Policy that projects a year or more into the future will often be introduced as a topic of discussion by a senior member of the Group, probably the chairman of the appropriate council committee. But other council members who may be the spokesmen of a particular point of view may raise issues that are controversial and debate may range freely over the topic. It may happen that no 'party line' will be laid down until absolutely necessary. In all such arguments an assertion that a policy is the national policy of the Labour Party is regarded as the trump card. For example, the Labour Group was not disposed to support comprehensive schools until the educational innovators in the Group reminded their colleagues that the Labour Party was nationally committed to this policy.

On matters that arise from the committee minutes read at the Group meeting, the Group may decide sometimes to reverse a decision made in free committee discussion perhaps with the backing of a majority of the Labour men at that council committee. This may occasionally be the result of the full Group meeting differing from the views of its representatives on the particular committee; but it is more likely to occur as the consequence of second thoughts. Someone may point out that the minute in question, perhaps formulated in the heat of debate, is inconsistent with past policy, or is against the interests of the Labour Party or the people of the Borough.

Thus many decisions of the Labour Group are necessarily of a trivial nature and infringement of them hardly brings retribution unless the transgression is constantly repeated. It is only a 'Group decision', a resolution on some important issue of policy, that is expected to be obeyed and even then the normal right of conscientious abstention can be invoked. In recent years 'three-line whips' have only been issued for the balloting for the triennial list of Labour Party candidates for the aldermanic elections. Labour council members are not always conscious of the whip as are M.P.s in the House of Commons. Indeed party loyalty much more than party discipline is likely to be the force restraining a Labour man from attacking a colleague in the council chamber or voting for an Independent motion. It is therefore quite misleading to envisage the Labour Group as a dragooned and pliant body.

The impression that party discipline within the Labour Group is severe, hardly confirmed by the fact that the authors could not find any members (except the whips) who knew the names of the whips, has probably gained ground because since 1945 a series of defections has taken place at first sight provoked by strong resentment against Group control. Closer examination reveals, however, that it was not the severity of the discipline, but the principle of obeying majority decisions that was resented. In the early post-war years it was the 'Old Guard' of Labour who, as we have seen, were expelled for their refusal to conform to this principle. Some of the later expulsions, however, seemed to be of people who were genuinely unaware of the Labour Party's declared policy. Doubtless the dearth of candidates accounts for such people being selected.

Though our final conclusion is that the strictness of discipline within the Newcastle Labour Group has been exaggerated there can be no doubt that the procedure of taking Group decisions has altered the nature of council politics. On many issues that are trivial there can be multilateral discussion in council Committees and on the full Council; but when in a field such as Housing or Education the party lines are approached then the debate may become bilateral or, today perhaps, trilateral. It is also true that on occasions a Labour Group decision, later passed by the Council, may not really represent the wishes of a majority of the Council. Thus a determined minority of the Council may be making council policy.

On the other side discipline is scarcely exerted at all, though if the I.C.A. came to power they would have to maintain some sort of system to keep a majority. Since 1947, according to Council Standing Orders, the non-Labour council members have of necessity met to apportion Committee assignments and for the triennial aldermanic elections they have voted as a bloc. Furthermore since the late 1940's they have met once a month before the council meeting in order to achieve some measure of understanding. Frequently at these meetings they reach agreement about important issues, though no whip is wielded and no form of coercion on the twelve Independents in the I.C.A. is possible. As for the five Conservative members of the Group, party practice as suggested by Conservative Central Office should be for them to meet as a Conservative Group with the agent as secretary. But they feel that five is too small for this and consequently they attend the I.C.A. Group meetings with the Independents from whom they are not always very indistinguishable. For instance, there do not appear to be any marked divisions of opinion within the I.C.A. Group between Independents and Conservatives as such, perhaps because of the similarity of social background between them. In fact the whole Group tends to be in general agreement on controversial matters such as housing and municipal finance, though because they have little chance of policy-making they do not often discuss important issues. On small matters such as street lighting or parking they may disagree and vote against one another in Committee and on full Council, but they will never make a point of deriding the arguments of members of their own Group in the way they would those of Labour spokesmen; and it would certainly be an exaggeration to say that they discuss and vote on each issue on its merits. Their solidarity, almost as great as that of the Labour Group, is based on opposition to the latter and no discipline is needed to persuade the Independent and Conservative council members not to vote with the Labour Party on important motions.

The Liberals by 1962 were four in number on the Council. As their appeal to the electorate had stressed independence from the I.C.A., Liberal councillors from the beginning made a point of not attending I.C.A. Group meetings, though under the

Council's Standing Orders they were obliged to go to its meeting in May 1961 in order to place their nominations for Mayor and the aldermanic vacancies. Since that time they have rejected all overtures from the I.C.A. Group and have upheld Liberal independence. Though they have no Group meeting the four Liberal councillors, with a Liberal County councillor who sits for Wards 5 and 7, meet together once a month in what is called the Liberal Forum. This body is primarily intended as a 'clinic'— a place for citizens to bring their complaints to Liberal councillors—but it also serves the purpose of providing an opportunity for an exchange of views from which may emerge a common policy. Such agreement, however, will be general rather than specific, will not be embodied in anything like a resolution and cannot be used to coerce any Liberal councillor to undertake any action he or she dislikes.

5. Pressures from Outside the Council

It is clear that making municipal decisions is a lengthy process. At the three main stages—Committee, Group and full Council— as well as at other times, there is some opportunity for pressure to be applied by interests and interested individuals. In fact pressures stemming from the party organizations, the voters and organized groups all play a part in the formation of municipal policy.[1]

(i) PRESSURE FROM THE PARTY ORGANIZATIONS

The members of the political parties, and especially that small proportion of them who take part in political activity, are naturally more likely to be interested in the actions of the Borough Council. Moreover three-quarters of the council members owe their initial nomination to being a member of a party: only the Independents, who make up the other quarter, are free from party ties. Thus the relationship between the parties and the Council is bound to hold some significance.

The five Conservative council members are perhaps least affected by the connection with their party organization. There

---

[1] From here to the end of the chapter the account is based on all the sources mentioned above and interviews.

is no Conservative Group, as we have noted, and the Conservative Association brings no pressure to bear on them. Conservative council members are *ex officio* members of the ward associations in the wards they represent and they are therefore accessible to rank-and-file Conservatives. Though there is no formal method of exerting pressure the threat of refusing renomination always exists. In general, however, the Conservative ward parties show little interest in council matters and only in Ward 5, where Conservative representation by now is an established fact, is it the common practice for the ward's Conservative councillors to report back to ward meetings. There is no evidence of individual Conservatives, either here or elsewhere, attempting to influence the opinions or actions of Conservative council members.

The Liberal councillors, as we have seen, stand at the centre of their constituency organization. They make monthly reports on the council committees they attend to the monthly meetings of the Liberal Executive; but as they are among the dominant figures in their constituency party—unlike their Conservative counterparts—they are in a strong position to withstand pressure. When the 1962 rents and rates controversy was raised at the Liberal Executive it was decided that the Liberals as a party should not become involved in the issue—a decision that relieved the Liberal councillors of possible embarrassment. But there is no evidence of the Liberal councillors coming under fire from their ward parties, presumably because these organizations have only recently been constructed, largely by the councillors themselves. Whether the present harmony of the Liberal Party will be shattered because of its decentralized structure is something that only time can tell.

Labour council members face the most pressure from their organization—and from elsewhere—for two reasons. In the first place the Labour Party is alone amongst the three in having an almost Borough-wide coverage and its highly integrated organization would seem to be well suited for making representations to the Labour Group. The fact that the latter has both a relationship with the Borough Labour Party in the centre and the wards at the perimeter leaves plenty of scope for friction. Secondly, the Labour Party's almost permanent and yet narrow majority makes the Group a natural target for criticism and suggestions for future policy. A spell in opposition, one Labour councillor confessed to the authors, would be welcome in order to relieve many of these pressures.

The Labour councillors, we have observed, are more likely to live in the wards they represent than those of the other parties. Those who do not reside in their wards may face especial difficulties though much will depend on the wards. Where the ward Labour Party is not very active and the ward has little geographic or social cohesion, as in some of the 'central' wards, the councillors may have a relatively easy time; but in other wards absences at ward meetings will be noticed and a few lapses may bring a complaint to the G.M.C. In 1961, for example, Ward 9 Labour Party complained that none of its councillors were attending ward meetings. Since the early 1950's such protests have been common and there is a general feeling at the ward level that Labour council members are remote from the work of the ward parties.

Besides reporting on council business to ward meetings the Labour council members also receive complaints about failings in the municipal services from ward members, a few of whom seem to specialize in acting as a funnel for criticism of the Borough's administration. Most Labour councillors agree that they receive a good deal more comment on the details of local government from the ward Labour parties than they do from the public. Matters of more general policy are likely to be referred from the ward Labour party to the Borough Labour Party.

While individual Labour representatives may feel most pressure from their wards the Labour Group as a whole is more likely to be called to account by the General Management Committee of the Borough Labour Party. All Labour council members have the right to attend the G.M.C. meetings, though without votes unless they are delegates from their ward or other organization. In addition, since 1958 the Labour Group itself has appointed three delegates to the G.M.C. But in spite of these close formal connections in 1962 only about a dozen Labour council members attended G.M.C. meetings and only about three people in the Labour Group are at all active in the Borough party's work. Of course council business often deters many council members, especially the most senior, from under-taking a great deal of extra-council activity.

Relations between the Labour Group and the Borough Labour Party have not always been smooth. Only three years after Labour came to power, in 1950, the Borough party was complaining of 'absenteeism' in the Labour Group and three years later a suspicious request that all Labour council members should show their party cards met with some opposition. In 1956 the Borough party ordered the aldermen from Ward 6 to reconstruct the party there and two years later issued a general appeal for more help in party work from all members of the Group. There is thus a disposition on the part of the Borough Labour Party to censure the Labour Group for being out of touch with the 'doorstep work' of the party.

On occasions the Borough Labour Party has asserted some authority over individual councillors. For example, in 1955, by six votes to four, the Borough party expelled one of the Labour councillors, then the Deputy Mayor, who, contrary to standing orders, had insisted on compiling her own municipal election address. The Labour Group, who had not withdrawn the whip, were anxious to reverse this decision and only the unwillingness of the victim to appeal prevented a clash between the two bodies. But direct conflict is not the inevitable relationship and sometimes the division of opinion has been within both the Borough party and the Labour Group. In 1956 when the Labour Group asked the Borough Labour Party to expel two Labour councillors who had voted against the whip at an aldermanic election the Borough party divided nine to nine and only the casting vote of the party chairman swung the verdict in favour of the Group's request. Again in the autumn of 1959 it was only by six votes to five that the Borough party condemned the intention of the Council, and of its Labour majority, to build 'luxury' flats. However, in the following spring the Borough Labour Party made a claim to take over the control of Newcastle's housing policy from the Labour Group. The Group refused to consider this bid for power seriously.

The disagreements within the Labour Party in Newcastle Borough are partly a result of institutional relationships and partly ideological. On the institutional plane the disputes between the Labour Group and the Borough Labour Party are similar to those between the Parliamentary Labour Party and the national party organization. The Labour council members are nearer the sources of power and the responsibilities of decision-making and consequently they realize the limitations imposed upon them by representative government. The active Labour Party workers who are not on the Council feel frustrated by their inability to influence municipal policy and they resent the apparently uninfluenceable council members whom they regard as 'compromisers' and 'slackers'. Thus whereas the majority of the Labour Group is inclined to the 'right' the majority of the Borough Labour Party is inclined to the 'left'.

In Chapter 15 we saw that there is no consistent pattern among Newcastle Labour Party members of 'rightness' and 'leftness' in national political issues and these terms probably have less meaning when applied to local affairs. Even so it does seem that many Labour Party members do see an ideological spectrum with more of the Labour Group on the 'right' and more of the Borough party on the 'left', a situation in which 'left-wing' councillors, after finding their suggestions falling on stony ground in the Group, take their ideas to the more fertile field of the Borough Labour Party.

Local tradition has it that the 'right' in the Newcastle Borough Labour Party has formed around the nucleus of the Roman Catholic councillors, often of Irish descent, an analysis that, as we have observed, has some basis in earlier history. But today there appear to be only three or four Catholic Labour council members and their influence is almost certainly exaggerated by the 'left'. The strength of the 'left' was originally based on those councillors who had been active in the Silverdale Co-operative Society and especially the Silverdale Co-operative Party; but since the demise of the latter in 1957, and since the political co-operators became established in the seats of power, the 'running' on the 'left' has been taken up by younger men who in 1960 formed the Newcastle Young Socialists.

Whatever the exact position it does seem as though the 'right' and the Labour Group have been able to wield power without much difficulty. In sheer size alone the 27 members of the Group are no match for the average of 17 members who have attended the meetings of the Borough party over the last three years. Only in the renominating process can a sitting councillor be seriously threatened and even then the shortage of candidates will inevitably strengthen his hand.

The Conservative, Liberal and Labour organizations all sponsor candidates for the Newcastle Borough Council and they are all bodies that have existed in some form for more than forty years. Consequently they are a permanent force in Borough politics and the possibility that they will bring pressure to bear on their councillors must always be present. In actual fact, however, it does not seem as though the Liberal and Conservative Associations exert much influence in this way while the Borough Labour Party, which at times does make an effort to intervene, has little success. As only about 3 per cent of the Borough's electors are members of a political party and only about one-tenth of these are active in party work it is hardly surprising that the party organizations provide little guidance and have little power; but they are a restraint of a sort that the Independent councillors do not experience, and perhaps as a result they fulfil some democratic function.

(ii) PRESSURES FROM INDIVIDUALS AND GROUPS

The attitude of the electorate to local politics has been discussed in Chapter 12. Only 40 per cent of the electorate vote at Borough elections and only 25 per cent are able to name even one of their councillors who, as one might expect, do not feel under constant pressure from the voters. Even chairmen of important council committees are not approached by individual members of the public very often; councillors might expect four or five such representations a year and aldermen (unless they are also committee chairmen) even less, for aldermen are not chosen by the voters. Of course the practice of buttonholing councillors varies from ward to ward and pressure of this sort is most likely in those wards with some social cohesion, and more often than not is concerned with the problem of housing.

Some council members encourage individual voters to approach them, but on the whole there is a feeling among the council members that one is more likely to lose than win votes by soliciting the public in this way. The voter brings his grievance to his councillor, expecting redress. Usually the latter can only behave as a sort of postbox between his constituent and the Council: the council member either passes on the complaint, if it is relevant, to the appropriate Borough official, and then conveys the reply back, or he raises the matter in his Group or on Council. As the individual councillor may make little impact, the expectant voter is often disappointed. Thus the councillor may offend rather than please, losing votes rather than gaining them, by being too zealous in the services of his constituents.

Some pressure on councillors is also exerted by organized groups of two kinds, the permanent and the ephemeral, the latter causing the Council more trouble. Some committees of Council co-opt members from established organizations. Thus Parks, Cemeteries and Gardens must by law co-opt members from the various smallholders' associations and the Education Committee also has to co-opt representatives of religious bodies. On the other hand the Chamber of Trade is sometimes consulted by the Council on such minor matters as parking and street lighting though its wishes may not be granted. On important matters, for example rates, the organized shopkeepers are more likely to make representations through the Independent Group than directly to the Council. The Newcastle Trades Council is in a rather similar position, sometimes writing letters to the Borough Council expressing its opinions on local matters, though in the case of Borough employees' salaries it writes to the Council Establishments Committee. But on issues of more moment the Trades Council is likely to express its views through its delegates to the Borough Labour Party or more directly through its councillor members in the Labour Group. A very similar procedure has usually been followed by the Silverdale Co-operative Society. The Old Age Pensioners' Associations are another pressure group that finds help from councillor members sufficient. At one time the secretary of the Newcastle Old Age Pensioners was an Independent councillor, but she found that old people's interests could be quite as well safeguarded from a position outside the council chambers.

The established organizations with social and economic interests need to apply little pressure because they are naturally represented on the Borough Council. Their activities are unspectacular in comparison with those of groups that suddenly emerge as the result of some single issue, such as a rise in rates or council-house rents. The most recent of these outbursts was in the late summer of 1962 when the ratepayers, already faced with the prospect of a revaluation of their property, strongly reacted to their shouldering an additional burden of £33,000, the equivalent of a 10d. rate, instead of the council tenants as was originally intended. A protest meeting convened by some of the Conservative and Independent councillors and by the Stoke Property Owners' and Ratepayers' Association was attended by over 2,000 people and an almost unanimous vote of no confidence in the Council was passed. The Labour chairman of the Housing Committee, who courageously defended the Council, was fiercely attacked from all sides, but little came of the meeting, because instead of using it in order to initiate a ratepayers' party, the organizers chose to exhort those present to join the Property Owners' Association. Thus the chance was lost and a piece of financial wizardry which reduced the £33,000 to £7,500 to some extent mollified the ratepayers.

Protest at the Council's monetary demands has also been voiced by the council-house tenants. A Council Tenants' Association, with branches on every council-house estate, was formed in 1944, in order to complain about the second war-time increase in rents. The organizers of this association, up in arms against an Independent Council, were naturally associated with the Labour Party, and in the immediate post-war years several of them became Labour councillors. Until Labour came to power on the Council they vigorously pleaded the tenants' case in the Housing Committee and secured the abolition of lodger rent in January 1946. When Labour gained a majority, however, the tenants' leaders faced an embarrassing situation and in 1949 the Tenants' Association became defunct.

The present Tenants' Association dates from the middle of August 1962 when a notice of rent increases varying between 6s. and 8s. a week was sent to all tenants of council houses together with a four weeks' notice to quit and a form which the tenant had to sign to maintain tenancy. Resentment was great—there had been a rent increase in 1961—and people on several estates began quite spontaneously, without reference to or knowledge of one another, to collect the unsigned forms. Protest became organized with the calling of a meeting in the Municipal Hall at which 3,000 tenants voted in favour of paying no increase until their representatives had met the Council. The meeting also set up the Newcastle Council Tenants' Association, uniting all the organizations on all the council-house estates.

·At the end of September 1962 a formal constitution was drawn up which stipulated that there should be a branch and committee of the Newcastle Tenants' Association on each estate, sending two delegates each to a central Management Committee. When the latter was elected it consisted entirely of 'white-collar' workers or their wives. By this time, however, some of the initial impetus of the Association had been lost and many of its members were satisfied with its success in obtaining some reduction in the proposed increases.

Both the outbursts of the ratepayers and of the council tenants illustrate how large sections of the municipal electorate, long apathetic and politically dormant, will suddenly become aroused by an action of the Council. It may be significant that in both episodes financial loss was involved though in the case of the tenants the sums were larger and at least the majority of those called on to pay were poorer. But with both bodies of citizens the feeling of outrage was obviously great and the Council heeded and mollified the indignation. It is as though the voters most effectively make the weight of their opinions felt, not by voting, but by a 'spontaneous overflow of powerful feelings'.

6. The Framework of Public Opinion

Freedom of speech and of the press are of less account in a representative democracy when the electors are unaware of what decisions are being made in their name. In Newcastle Borough, as we have seen, most important decisions are framed in the Committees of the Council and only two of these—Finance and General Purposes—are open to the press and public. The agendas of these two Committees, though not available to spectators at their meetings, are released to the press on the day before they assemble. But in the case of all the other Committees, of which the most important is Housing, the sessions are held in private. The decisions of the closed Committees will first be known when their minutes become available at the reference desk of the Newcastle Public Library two days before the Council meets, or the gist of them is published in the local press a day before-hand. Numerous copies of these minutes are also provided for the public at the council meeting.

Thus at most forty-eight and more probably twenty-four hours is the time in which the public has the opportunity to discuss most of the items which will arise for formal endorsement at the Council, hardly long enough for responsible and informed discussion or for interested groups and individuals to air their opinions. It is true that on occasions word of committee decisions can travel quickly. For example, the council chamber was packed when the full Council met towards the end of July 1962 in order to confirm the rise in council rents recommended by the Housing Committee a week earlier. On the other hand, it is clear that there were many council tenants who were surprised and shocked when the announcement of the increases and the notices to quit dropped through their letter-boxes in the middle of August 1962.

One can be too indignant about the state of 'local democracy' for the situation in the country as a whole is hardly one of vigorous political discussion at all levels and at all stages of decision-making. However Parliamentary sessions are public and *Hansard* provides us with an account of the debates. If all the Newcastle Council Committees were open to the citizens then there could be a period between the committee and council meetings when pressure might have an effect and decisions modified or annulled. Moreover, it would be likely that the Group of the majority party, though assembling in private, would be discussing the committee minutes and would there-fore be open to the persuasion of the voters and party organiza-tions. This would be especially welcome where a party had held power as long as Labour has in Newcastle. The sang-froid with which some Labour council members seemed to face the outcry of the angry council tenants, one of Labour's most loyal sources of electoral support, may have been induced by a conviction that this anger would be turned against the Government for increas-ing municipal loan charges; but it may also have been a reflec-tion of long years of power without serious challenge. This type of situation can perhaps only be ultimately resolved at the polls by the voters.

The fact is, however, that the mode of electing the Newcastle Corporation, as of all Borough councils, does not encourage great responsibility on the part of the electorate. One-quarter of the Council—the aldermen—are not responsible directly to the voters, and only another quarter of the Council has to face annual election. Thus the political colouring of the Council can only change slowly and the relationship between those who make and those who suffer the decisions cannot be properly expressed in a vote for or against a past record or a future programme.

7. Conclusion

In Newcastle Borough party government is the norm and the Labour Party has been firmly if narrowly in power for a decade and a half. The Independent Civic Association, an anti-Labour electoral alliance of Conservatives and Independents who act as a Group on the Council, has recently faced the challenge of the resurgent Liberals. Meanwhile the number of Independent council members has gradually declined and in a few years' time they may be a rarity. The party organizations will then be almost everywhere in control of the selection and promotion of municipal candidatures; and local 'professional' politicians will have taken over from 'amateurs' who tended to regard politics as an expression of social pre-eminence and who thought in local terms of issues to be decided on their 'merits'.

The Labour Party is probably best equipped for Borough politics because it alone of the three parties is organized on a Borough, as well as a constituency, basis. The Liberals, however, are at the moment well deployed for these purposes, while the Conservatives with much of their leadership in the Rural District are least well organized for Borough politics. Yet all these parties, operating on a ward basis, are able to provide more candidates than would otherwise present themselves; and the domination of the Council by the Labour Group has given it a co-ordinated policy that did not exist in the pre-war days of the non-party majority.

Labour's virtually unbroken spell of power has tended to separate the Labour council members from their rank-and-file and especially from their voters. Many of the Labour councillors have seldom had to make an effort to defend their seats and consequently they have become somewhat unheedful of public opinion. The wrath of the council tenants might have been mitigated by a little more sympathy and tact; and it might have been avoided altogether if discontent could have been properly expressed within the ward Labour parties by Labour Party supporters.

As so few take part in the activities of the parties the electoral process remains as the main institutional method by which voters can make their weight felt; but unfortunately the electoral system makes no provision for the public to pass judgment on the record of the Council. Even if the voters did not regard local elections as an opportunity to register their verdict on the national parties they would still be prevented from ousting a council of whom they disapproved, because it takes three years to change all the councillors. Thus the voters have only slight influence on council policy at election time and when occasionally dramatic pressure is applied it stems from the spontaneous outbursts of angry citizens.

CHAPTER EIGHTEEN

LEADERSHIP IN NEWCASTLE-UNDER-LYME

B y implication the question, 'Who runs Newcastle?' has been partially answered at various stages in this work. Here we are concerned with collating all our findings and, as far as possible, tracing the pattern of leadership in the constituency.

The concept of leadership implies the acquiescence of the many in the designs of the few. Social leadership, for example, is a generally accepted position at the highest level of the status hierarchy. It will involve setting (perhaps not consciously) standards of taste and behaviour that will usually be looked up to by the rest of the community; and it may carry with it leadership of associational life in such organizations as churches, clubs and trade unions. Economic leadership consists of taking the most important decisions in the trade and industry of a community. Large bankers, employers and landlords will thus be economic leaders. By the political leaders we mean those who hold the most important positions in the formal institutional system: they are the 'top people' in the constituency organizations and on the councils. Depending on circumstances, they may or may not be able to make decisions which affect social and economic leadership.

It is not uncommon for different forms of leadership to coincide in the same people. Sidney and Beatrice Webb's description of the rural English parish on the threshold of the Industrial Revolution is a classic example of this situation.

'[Parish government] . . . was . . . subject to a very real, if somewhat spasmodic control at the hands of the squire, the parson, or other neighbouring Justices of the Peace. Moreover, the official relationships between the parties were inextricably woven into the economic relationships that existed between the same individuals in their private capacities. The J.P. was probably the landlord of the whole of the parish officers; the officers were the employers of the paupers; and even the clergyman . . . often owed his position to the squire. . . . Hence though there might be grumbling, there could be no effective resistance to the action of the governing group. . . .'[1]

Here we have a position in which the economic and political leadership of the landlord and the J.P. were combined in the person of the squire who, the Webbs imply (though they do not say), was also at the peak of the status pyramid, the ultimate object of deference in a community in which everyone knew 'their proper place'.

This exceedingly simple form of rural society was disappearing in the nineteenth century under the impact of industrial change. Our account of the constituency of Newcastle-under-Lyme has contained no example of such a society. Even in the countryside as early as the 1830's political arrangements were, as we have seen, passing into the hands of tenant farmers and clergymen and the landlords were largely withdrawing from their administrative chores. In Audley and the industrial area, on the other hand, there was a disposition on the part of the mine-owning and manufacturing employers, in the later nineteenth and early twentieth centuries, to fulfil some of the functions of a squirearchy and to take the lead in political life. This tendency did not survive the First World War. In the inter-war years the political leadership of the Wolstanton U.D.C. passed out of the hands of large employers into those of shopkeepers and clerical workers; but the heterogeneity of the area and the struggle between the Labour Party and the Independents precluded any tidy coincidence of political, social and economic hierarchies. In Audley, on the other hand, a small oligarchy, described by one inhabitant (without prompting) as 'the little squires', continued the tradition of the combination of different forms of leadership. Similarly in Newcastle Borough, especially before 1932, the Council was dominated by shopkeepers and small businessmen whose economic leadership was given corporate embodiment in the

[1] S. and B. Webb, *The Parish and the County* (1906), p. 48.

Chamber of Trade and whose social pre-eminence was expressed in membership of the Rotary Club.[1]

The picture that thus emerges is one of great complexity. The area which now comprises the constituency was in no sense a community. Constituency organization consequently imposed a unity of control that was alien to the social structure. Anyway, as far as we can ascertain, until the 1940's there was little correspondence between those who ran the constituency associations and those who ran the councils.

Our historical examination of the three forms of leadership is in part handicapped by the difficulty of estimating the extent of social leadership in the past. In the absence of a good deal of evidence one can only assume that the degree of deference declined as social groups of lower status became the political leaders. Furthermore the rise of a labour movement, especially in the industrial area, is an indication that the working classes were becoming less inclined to look up to their 'betters'. Even so, the acceptance of Wedgwood by the Labour voters, if not by the Labour Party militants, is an indication that to be a member of the most respected of all the dynasties of potters was, in the inter-war years, no handicap politically at the constituency level.

But we must now turn to our own times. What are the social, economic and political leaderships in contemporary Newcastle and to what extent do these leaderships coincide?

1. Social Leadership

In the absence of an examination of the status hierarchy, such as that undertaken by Lloyd Warner,[2] we must consider what are the social attributes that are likely to confer the highest prestige and compel the most respect. In a medium-sized Borough such as Newcastle it seems likely that being a Justice of the Peace or a member of the Rotary Club or Round Table might provide the cachet that is needed to be recognized as a social leader. Figure 16 indicates the associational connections of J.P.s and members of the Rotary Club. (The Round Table's single link was with the Conservative Executive Council.) The 37 Borough and

[1] See above, Chap. 2, pp. 52 ff.
[2] Lloyd Warner, *Social Class in America* (Chicago, 1949).

LEADERSHIP

12 Rural J.P.s clearly have many more links with the political parties than do the Rotary Club members. This situation is doubtless the result of the way in which the selection procedure for magistrates takes account of the need to represent all political parties in the district. Otherwise the J.P.s have fewer connections than the Rotary Club members. The latter, however,

Links between Newcastle J.P.s, members of the Newcastle Rotary Club ———— and committee membership of other organizations ————

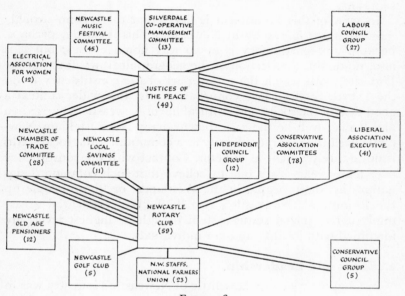

FIGURE 16

beyond their links with the Chamber of Trade have few connections with the leadership of other organizations. There are only four Rotarians on the Borough Council and only three others with political connections. Consequently one would not be warranted in describing either the J.P.s or the Rotarians as being in a position of 'leadership' *vis-à-vis* the rest of the constituency.

An examination of the other organizations in the constituency revealed that there were none that had many links at committee level with other associations or with the committees of the political parties; and it is thus difficult to escape the conclusion that in Newcastle there is no small group that runs social and cultural life. There is a wealth of associational activity in the constituency, but its management is in many hands. This wide diffusion of what we might call 'associational leadership' is no new thing for, as we have observed, over most of the constituency, since the nineteenth century, ordinary people have been used to organizing collective action without the help of social superiors.

In view of this situation it is likely that there is no strongly marked status hierarchy in Newcastle. This is partly, perhaps, because the constituency is in no way homogeneous; but it is also, no doubt, a reflection of the geographical proximity of the Potteries, with which the urban part of the constituency forms the 'North Staffordshire conurbation'. In this wider context a good deal of the social and cultural life of Newcastle is carried on and it may well be the case that to many Newcastellians Newcastle has little separate identity as a community. But local status is not entirely absent as a factor. Contact with the constituency over many years leads one to believe that such common designations as 'those people in the Westlands' or 'those people up the Brampton' (Newcastle's two 'high-class' residential areas) imply a recognized status system though its highest levels are identified with locality and not individuals.

2. Economic Leadership

In Chapter 7 we saw how little of Newcastle's industry was in the hands of Newcastle people. Consequently it is not surprising that an examination (Figure 17) of the twenty-five proprietors or managers of the largest firms shows that they play little part in social or political life.

Political Leadership

(i) LEADERSHIP IN THE PARTY ORGANIZATIONS

Decisions made by the active party workers do not make a regular or heavy impact on the man in the street. Only at election times do the militants come much into contact with the voters. Moreover, the sort of choice in which the most powerful of the party workers are likely to exert an influence on the eventual decision is seldom more important than 'Shall we fight this ward or that?' or 'Shall we canvass tonight or tomorrow night?' Occasionally, it is true, Parliamentary candidates have to be selected, but the Conservative and Liberal militants have not, since 1918, chosen one who has subsequently been returned to Westminster. Nor are the Labour Party's militants always in command of their own household, as the events of 1951—described in Chapter 4—demonstrated. Then the most active party workers were unable to get their favourite chosen as Labour candidate because the trade-union delegates, usually absent from party meetings, turned up in order to obtain the nomination of a different aspirant.

Links between proprietors or managers of enterprises employing more than 100 people and committee membership of organisations

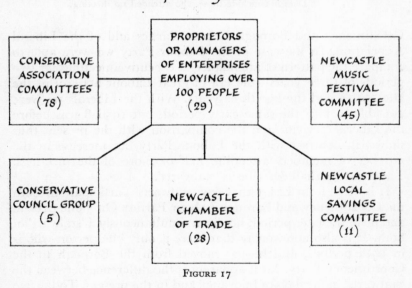

FIGURE 17

Thus there are few rewards for party workers and control passes into the hands of those members who have the enthusiasm to bear the brunt of the work. These few are the nucleus of the

391

party leadership: they hold the power (such as it is) for it is difficult for the members who attend irregularly or not at all to have much say in the direction of the party organizations. As in all voluntary bodies the dedicated few call the tune.

How small the minority can be that runs the parties is shown in Table 1 which analyses the attendance at the Executives of the

TABLE 1. ATTENDANCE AT EXECUTIVES OF THE CONSTITUENCY AND BOROUGH LABOUR PARTIES AND AT THE LIBERAL PARTY EXECUTIVE

Percentage of attendance	Constituency Labour Party		Borough Labour Party		Liberal Party	
	1949–1951	1960–1962	1948–1950	1960–1962	1956–1958	1960–1962
'Stalwarts' {80–100%	1	3	—	1	3	4
{50– 79%	6	2	6	3	4	6
25– 49%	14	7	9	6	9	8
Less than 25%*	26	12	11	15	36	41

* Does not include those who attended no meetings.

Constituency and Borough Labour Parties and of the Liberal Association. In the case of the Labour Party we were able to compare the pattern of attendance at executive meetings for two periods of three years—the era of great Labour activity in the late 1940's and the last three years. With the Liberals we were not able to take the same early period, but 1956–8 was before the Liberal 'revival' and the comparison with the present thus shows, in contrast with the Labour Party, an increase in the number of members attending half or more of the meetings. These last we shall describe as 'stalwarts'.

It is clear from List 1 that few 'stalwarts' participate in both the Constituency and Borough Labour Parties. Only one person, and he in the later period, has been simultaneously a 'stalwart' in both. It is also noteworthy that there is only one person who is in both periods, and he has moved from the Borough to the Constituency Party. Most apparent is the difference between the 'stalwarts' in the days of buoyancy and in the present. Today five out of the eight Labour 'stalwarts' are non-manual workers or their wives as against only three out of thirteen in the late 1940's. But the overall impression is of a Labour Party leadership

LEADERSHIP

springing from a variety of backgrounds with a sprinkling of railwaymen and rather more than a sprinkling of Co-operators, the result of the strength of 'the Co-op' in the area and its willingness to allow its employees time to serve.

LIST 1. 'STALWARTS' IN THE NEWCASTLE CONSTITUENCY AND BOROUGH LABOUR PARTIES

Constituency Labour Party E.C. 1949–51

A.1. Manager of Co-operative store. Councillor 1946–52. Alderman 1952–5. Chairman Constituency Labour Party 1949–51.
  2. Engineering worker. Councillor 1946–52. Alderman 1952–8. Secretary of Constituency Labour Party 1951.
  3. Warehouse manager. Councillor 1947–52. Alderman 1952–8.
  4. Heating engineer. Councillor 1952–61.
  5. Wife of retired miner.
  6. Co-operative dairy worker. Rural District councillor 1955– . Delegate from Rural District.
  7. Miner. Delegate from Rural District. Son of County and Rural District councillor.

Constituency Labour Party E.C. 1960–2

B.1. Wife of schoolteacher. Secretary of Constituency Labour Party 1957–61.
  2. Wife of Co-operative employee. Rural District councillor 1955–1958. Delegate of Rural District.
  3. Railway clerk. Chairman of Constituency Labour Party 1960–2. Chairman Borough Labour Party 1959–62.
  4. C.5.
  5. Clerk.

Borough Labour Party E.C. 1948–50

C.1. Manager of Co-operative store. Councillor 1936–51, 1952–5. Alderman 1955– . Chairman Constituency Labour Party 1951–2. Chairman Borough Labour Party 1948–9.
  2. Woman social worker. Councillor 1952–5. Treasurer Borough Labour Party 1946–52.
  3. Brickyard worker. Secretary Borough Labour Party 1948–50.
  4. Railway signalman. Councillor 1945–53. Alderman 1953– . Secretary Borough Labour Party 1950–2.
  5. Retired miner. One of two 'strong men' mentioned in Chap. 16, p. 321.
  6. Wife of storeman at steelworks.

Borough Labour Party E.C. 1960–2

D.1. B.3.
  2. Railway worker. Councillor 1962– .
  3. Schoolteacher. Councillor 1956–1958, 1960– . Chairman of Constituency Labour Party 1955. Secretary Constituency Labour Party 1962. Secretary Borough Labour Party 1955–8.
  4. Retired Co-operative Insurance agent. Councillor 1932–4, 1935–1938, 1945–9, Alderman 1949– .

LEADERSHIP

List 2 shows a not very dissimilar picture in the case of the Liberal 'stalwarts'. Unlike the Labour Party there are a few more active members in the later period than the earlier, a feature to be expected in view of the recent Liberal 'revival'; on the other hand, in spite of the nearness in time of the two periods, here

LIST 2. 'STALWARTS' IN THE NEWCASTLE LIBERAL PARTY

1956–8

A.1. Grocer. Former chairman of Executive. Justice of the peace.
2. Insurance agent. Secretary of party 1954–8.
3. Builder's clerk. Treasurer of party 1956–9.
4. Company director. President of party 1958–61.
5. Clerk. Former Labour and Independent councillor.
6. Heating engineer.
7. Labourer.

1960–2

B.1. A.1.
2. University student, former Army officer, businessman and colliery recruit. Unpaid agent.
3. Railway executive. Secretary of party 1960– . Councillor 1961– . Chosen Parliamentary candidate 1962.
4. Woman schoolteacher. *Liberal News* officer 1958–61.
5. A.4.
6. Journalist. Editor of *North Staffs Liberal*.
7. Daughter of A.4.
8. Woman mental health worker. Treasurer of party 1960– . Councillor 1962– .
9. Schoolteacher. President of party 1962– .
10. Woman nurse, wife of university lecturer. County councillor 1961– .

also there has been with two exceptions a complete turnover among the 'stalwarts'. More than that, the active members of the later era are drawn from rather different strata of society. They include no manual workers at all—compared with two in 1956–8 —and the non-manual workers in the later period are, on the whole, people with more education and professional qualification. In terms of our survey classes, of the seven 'stalwarts' in the earlier period, two were A, three were C, one was D, and one was E: in the later period two are A and eight are B. Thus the change the Liberal leadership has undergone in recent years represents an upward movement through what are popularly known as the 'middle classes'.

Besides this the recent leadership is twenty to thirty years younger than that of the earlier period, doubtless corresponding to the division between the generations in the Liberal membership that we noted in Chapter 13. Four out of the ten Liberal 'stalwarts' are women, an example of feminine influence not paralleled in the other two parties, and especially odd in view of the preponderance of men amongst Liberal members. Three of the five Liberal councillors are numbered amongst the Liberal 'stalwarts', reflecting the connection between the Liberal resurgence and its manifestation in the new tactics of fighting municipal elections. Finally it is noticeable in both periods that many of the active members are officials of some sort. This is in common with the Labour and Conservative Parties.

The type of analysis we are able to make with the Labour and Liberal Parties is not possible with the Conservative Party. In the absence of data about attendance of Executive Council meetings for the purpose of comparison we were forced to make the assumption that the direction of the Conservative Association was vested in the ten people already mentioned as being on all the three important committees. We are only able to present this group of interlocking committee men for the present day. Such information as we have, however, suggests that though people of similar social background ran the Conservative Party ten or twelve years ago, very few of them have survived and the bulk of these ten cited below have come comparatively recently to constituency politics.

LIST 3. TEN CONSERVATIVES ON ALL THREE ASSOCIATION COMMITTEES

1. Accountant. Chairman of party 1946–51. President of party 1952– . Independent Borough Councillor 1945–54. Justice of the Peace.
2. Jeweller. Deputy chairman of party 1958–60. Chairman of party 1961– . Rural District Councillor 1952–61.
3. Wife of 2. Vice-chairman of party 1961– . Justice of the Peace.
4. Pottery colour manufacturer. Chairman of party 1958–60. Vice-president of party 1961. Justice of the Peace.
5. Pottery manufacturer. Son of former Conservative candidate. Vice-chairman of party 1961– .
6. Wife of estate agent. Vice-chairman of party 1962. Husband Rural District Councillor 1955– .
7. Solicitor. Candidate for Borough Council 1960. Vice-chairman of party 1962.
8. Director of pottery works. Treasurer of party 1962.
9. Engineering manufacturer. Vice-chairman of party 1962. Candidate for Borough Council 1962.
10. Bank manager.

LEADERSHIP

Some features of this list are not dissimilar from those discovered in the cases of the other two parties. For example, there is a preponderance—eight out of ten—of officers of the party. There is also some connection with Borough and Rural District politics, though any direct participation is in the past. At the present moment none of the ten are council members in spite of the fact that eight of them are members of the Local Elections Committee. Finally, in one way this hierarchy is reminiscent of the Labour Party's. Only two of the ten are women, in spite of the fact that the latter provide twenty-seven of the fifty-nine members of the Executive Council.

The social standing of the Conservative Association's leadership is from 'higher' social groups than that of the other parties. Though there is perhaps not quite the wealth of professional training there is in the Liberal Party, there is a good deal more commercial and industrial substance, and among the six from the countryside three are J.P.s. There is a notable and expected absence of manual workers while possibly the nearest thing to a clerical worker among them is a bank manager!

The four men among these ten who are residents of the Borough are younger than the others and of less social standing. Though they may play their part in the affairs of the constituency Association they have no influence in the decision-making processes of Newcastle Borough. In fact, because the Conservative council members are so little involved with the Association's affairs, the Association has little or no impact as a corporate body in Borough politics. For the very opposite reason, as we have seen, the Liberal Party has behaved much more vigorously in the municipal field. It remains to be seen whether a large contingent of Conservatives on the Borough Council would provide any leaders for the Conservative Association.

(ii) LEADERSHIP ON THE COUNCILS

Many of the important decisions affecting Newcastle's citizens that are not made in Stafford or Whitehall are not made in the party Executives either: they are reached by the two local government authorities. It is their decisions that, as we have seen, can make thousands of people angry.

In Chapter 15 we saw that 43 Borough council members had

had 12 years or more of office since 1932 and 10 Rural District councillors had had 20 years or more of office. Seniority, however, was not the only qualification for committee chairmanships which sometimes went to more junior councillors. Furthermore, in the Rural District there is the problem, as we observed in Chapter 16, of apportioning the chairmanships among the parishes. In the Borough where the effective choice is made in the Labour Group, a gift for tenacious argument and informed criticism in Committee and the ability to make a good speech on the full Council are likely to compensate for lack of seniority.

On the Rural District Council, as we have seen, the system of rotating chairmanships prevents the emergence of powerful political leaders if not of forceful personalities; and consequently the leadership has tended to stem from the permanent officials. Conversely, in the Borough the lengthy tenure of committee chairmanships and the fact that Labour has held almost unbroken control since 1947 have produced firm and consistent political leadership. It is the strong men of the Labour Group who are the political leaders in Newcastle Borough.

Observation and discussion with many council members of all parties make it clear that there are four members of the Labour majority who hold most sway over the activities of the Borough Council. Three of these are Committee chairmen. One of them is the 'Co-op' manager mentioned as C.1 in List 1. Another is a schoolteacher who has been on the Council since 1945. He was chairman of the Education Committee for eight years and has been chairman of the Finance Committee for six out of the last seven years. The third, a bank official, who has been on the Council since 1951, was treasurer of the Borough Labour Party for four years and, except for the few months of Independent control in 1958, has been chairman of the Housing Committee since 1957. His predecessor in this position had held it for ten years and during that time had become the acknowledged leader of the Labour Party in the Borough. In a Borough rightly proud of its extensive housing programme, the chairman of the Housing Committee has become the Council's main 'troubleshooter'. We have already seen how the present chairman has dealt with the anger of both council tenants and ratepayers and made himself pre-eminently conspicuous in the process. The fourth of these 'men of power', D.3 in List 1, is the only one who is not a chairman of a committee; but as secretary of both the Constituency and Borough Labour Parties he naturally has considerable influence in the Labour Group, especially over the more recently elected councillors with whom he will have become acquainted in the nominating process.

Except for the last-named, the four most important members of the Labour Group are not among the 'stalwarts' in the Borough or Constituency Parties. In fact the demands that council chairmanships make on a man's time are such that tenure of them is hardly compatible with organizational work in the wards. Thus three out of the four most important figures in the Labour Group are not closely in touch with the 'doorstep' workers and two of these, being aldermen, do not have to present themselves triennially to the voters. Furthermore, none of the four are manual workers, the class that makes up the majority of Labour councillors, Labour Party members and Labour voters. They are all, in fact, men who through their occupations have acquired skills such as commercial management, financial expertise, public speaking and dialectical disputation that stand one in good stead in local council work.

Finally it should be noted that political leadership does not often coincide with the leadership of other associations. None of the Conservative 'stalwarts' serve on the committees of other Newcastle organizations, though one of the Liberal 'stalwarts' is a member of the Workers' Educational Association Committee. Two of the Labour 'stalwarts' are members of both the Silverdale Co-operative committees and one of these two is also treasurer of the Newcastle Trades Council. One of the Labour Group's quadrumvirate is the president of this latter body while another of these four is both a committee member of a workingmen's club and president of an old age pensioners' association. The Labour leadership has thus rather more contact with Newcastle's associational life. Even so, eight of the Labour 'stalwarts' and two of the Labour Group's four 'men of power' have no such connections.

4. Conclusion

It thus becomes apparent that leadership in Newcastle is widely diffused. Figure 18 shows that there is most connection between social and economic leadership, that is, between the highest social status and business ownership or management. Even in this case, however, there were only eight out of 143 social leaders who were also economic leaders. On the other hand there is no connection between economic and political leadership. The withdrawal from local politics of the large-scale employers began, as we have seen, before the First World War and those Conservative 'stalwarts' who are employers are resident in Newcastle constituency but in business elsewhere. Doubtless there is embarrassment in carrying on a business in a Labour-dominated constituency while being a Conservative leader there.

Relationship between social, economic and political leadership

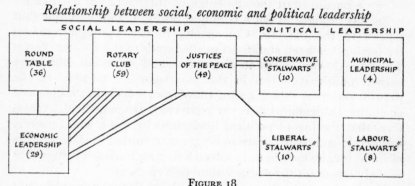

FIGURE 18

Between social and political leadership the connection is slight and entirely on the side of the Conservatives and Liberals. The three Conservatives and the one Liberal who are social leaders are not so by virtue of being Rotarians or members of the Round Table but by virtue of being J.P.'s; and, as we have noted, there is a sense in which the appointment of magistrates is a 'political' act. Moreover, all four of the magisterial 'stalwarts' live in the countryside: none of them are resident in the Borough. Consequently there is no coincidence of social and political leadership in the Borough. None of the Labour 'stalwarts' and none of the Labour quadrumvirate on the Labour Group are social and economic leaders; but neither are any of the Conservative or Liberal 'stalwarts' who live in Newcastle Borough. Political control in Newcastle Borough is independent of high status and economic hegemony.

LEADERSHIP

Historically this situation, as we have seen, has been developing for quite a long time. The rise of the Labour Party was slow during the inter-war years in both the Rural District and the Borough though after 1932 the absorption of the Audley Urban District into the former and the Wolstanton Urban District into the latter was likely, in the long run, to provide bases from which the rule of the tenant farmers, shopkeepers and small businessmen could be threatened. In the post-war years the emergence of a strong Labour Party threw the Rural District into such a state of flux that, as we observed in Chapter 16, it is difficult to discern any stable political leadership. Tenant farmers still lead in some parishes but the challenge of other types of local councillor has brought about a confused position. Initiative has thus passed to the officials. Conversely, in the Borough political leadership has been stabilized in the hands of the Labour Party. Thus the lowest levels in the social and economic hierarchy gained political control in the late 1940's, a reversal of the natural order of things and a blow from which the social and economic leadership has never recovered. It seems likely, therefore, that the loss of political leadership by those who formerly wielded it and their failure to regain it, resulting in sixteen years of Labour rule, may have involved a decline in their prestige that already has upset the status system of Newcastle.

Leadership by the leaders of the Labour Party has not brought about, however, rule by manual workers. Only two out of the eight Labour 'stalwarts' and none of Labour's municipal leaders work with their hands. Thus after the early post-war years of Labour domination, leadership of the Borough Council again became vested in the middle classes. But with a difference; shopkeepers and small businessmen are no longer supreme, and in command one finds members of the professional, managerial and clerical classes.

CHAPTER NINETEEN

CONCLUSION

Newcastle-under-Lyme has had a Labour Member of Parliament for forty-three years (1962) and at the last General Election Labour had a majority of over 6,000 votes. The constituency is poorer than the average, more working class and with a higher proportion of coal-miners, salient features which all connote a 'safe' Labour seat. Yet this does not completely prevent us from drawing conclusions from Newcastle that may have some general validity. Party organization, voting behaviour and the politics of local government are all topics that concern every constituency in the country. Furthermore, the analytical method we have adopted reveals that the constituency is a heterogeneous union of rural with mining villages and working-class with middle-class residential areas. Though the overall impression is of an 'old-fashioned' setting, the constituency has not escaped from the influence of contemporary trends. Its industry is becoming more modernized and compact, while Newcastle Borough's record of post-war housing is one of the best in the country.[1] Thus many different aspects of Britain's social and political pattern are observable in the constituency even if the relative proportions are not commensurate with those of the nation.

The preponderance of manual workers and the fact that the largest occupational group among them are coal-miners account for some of the voting characteristics of the constituency, such as the 'swing' away from Labour in 1959 being smaller than the national average. This is doubtless a case of the influence of dominant social groups, noted by Trenaman and McQuail in West Leeds and Pudsey,[2] and confirmed by the authors at ward

[1] C. A. Moser and Wolf Scott, *British Towns* (1961), p. 140.
[2] J. Trenaman and D. McQuail, op. cit., p. 136.

level in Newcastle by two types of analysis. There is more difficulty in explaining why the skilled workers are so much more Conservative in Newcastle. This may be merely a classificatory problem (that is, in other studies the skilled manual group may be defined differently); but it is possible that it is the result of the presence of craft industries, such as pottery and iron and steel, in which Conservatism among the workers is strong.

Possibly the feature of the constituency most characteristic of British politics in general is the small amount of political interest and activity on the part of the vast majority of voters. Figure 19, assembling material from several chapters, shows that while

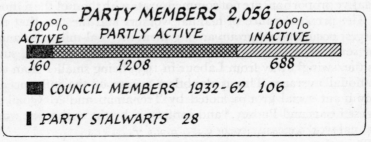

INTEREST AND ACTIVITY

ELECTORATE 63,504

	VOTERS	NON VOTERS
1959	84%	16%

	VOTERS LOCAL ELECTN	NON VOTERS LOCAL ELECTIONS
1960	38%	62%

POLITICALLY AWARE	PASSIVE	POLITICALLY UNAWARE
40%	33%	27%

POLITICALLY "KNOWLEDGEABLE"	POLITICALLY "UNKNOWLEDGEABLE"
25%	75%

MEMBERS (3·2%)	NON PARTY MEMBERS
	96·8%

PARTY MEMBERS 2,056

100% ACTIVE	PARTLY ACTIVE	100% INACTIVE
160	1208	688

■ COUNCIL MEMBERS 1932-62 106

▍ PARTY STALWARTS 28

FIGURE 19

402

CONCLUSION

more than four out of five voted at the General Election, only about two-fifths voted at local elections. One in four voters can name one of their ward's councillors, one in thirty-six is a party member, one in approximately four hundred a '100 per cent party activist', and one in over two thousand a party 'stalwart'. Among party members about a third are '100 per cent inactive' and about one in thirty-seven is serving on a local council. Thus the only political act committed by more than half the electorate is voting at General Elections. In fact, here the constituency with an 84 per cent turn-out was in 1959 5 per cent above the national average. On the other hand membership of parties in Newcastle is only 3·2 per cent of the electorate, over 6 per cent below the national average. Judging by these criteria it is possible that there is more political interest but less political activity than in the nation as a whole. Whatever the case, a small minority of people actively concern themselves with politics and the great majority only participate by marking their Parliamentary ballot papers.

Another feature of politics in Newcastle that has been noted elsewhere is the variation of activity and interest as between different groups. Younger people are on almost every count less politically active and interested than their elders; and women who, at the level of party membership, are almost proportionately represented, are noticeably under-represented at the higher levels of party organization and on the councils. But it is the differences between social groups that are the most important and interesting. Here Figure 20 shows that the 'higher' the social class the greater will be its political activity and conversely the 'lower' the social class the smaller part it will play in political life. Just about half the Conservative voters but only 18 per cent of the Conservative members are manual workers, and there are no manual workers at any higher level in the Conservative Party. More than nine-tenths of the Labour voters are manual workers and 77 per cent of the party members. But 44 per cent of the Labour council members are non-manual workers though only 9 per cent of Labour's General Election vote comes from the non-manual classes; and among the party 'stalwarts' non-manual workers easily predominate.

Thus the manual workers are clearly less active in politics.

403

CONCLUSION

On the other hand we have cited evidence to show that in both Parliamentary and local politics the manual workers are as well informed as the other voters, so that political knowledge and interest do not seem to vary much as between the manual and non-manual classes. Consequently we must conclude that though political activity in Newcastle is more of a characteristic of non-manual workers, political interest does not significantly vary with class. The manual workers have, perhaps, less time and inclination to participate in politics, but this is not an indication of less political awareness on their part.

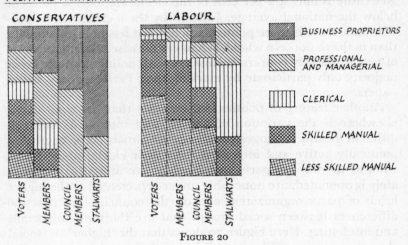

FIGURE 20

The early story of the constituency's political development reveals some features that are common elsewhere and others that are unusual. The growth of party organization, for example, seems to have closely followed the national pattern. Until the last quarter of the nineteenth century party differences between Parliamentary candidates were not clearly defined and electoral machines tended to be set up purely for the purposes of the contest, disappearing when it was over. Party life was centred around clubs which had more a social than a political function. It was in the 1880's that the modern form of party organization —with individual membership based on permanent ward and constituency parties—first emerged. Before the First World War especially, the Liberal organization attained an efficiency that was not surpassed by any party for over thirty years.

As nearly everywhere else, modern party organization in Newcastle predated the Labour Party. The rise of the latter, however, was accompanied by rather uncommon circumstances. As the largest trade union in the constituency was the miners' and as they were the last large union to affiliate to the Labour Party (in 1909) at the national level, a Constituency Labour Party came rather late to Newcastle; and when it did, it chose the sitting M.P., a former Liberal, as its candidate, largely at the miners' behest. Consequently a representative of the most aristocratic potters' dynasty became the first Labour Member of Parliament. The constituency had moved from radical Liberalism through 'Lib-Lab' sponsorship to Labour almost painlessly and without many of the ructions that enlivened this process in other places.

Wedgwood's defection from the Liberal Party seems to have brought about its virtual collapse. It hovered between independence and alliance with the Conservatives. The latter, having won no victory since 1886, except at the 'khaki' election of 1900, were obviously confused by an opponent who was a Socialist employer and, lacking leaders, fell into disarray. In the 1930's Wedgwood came to personify the constituency to such a degree that it became a sort of twentieth-century feudal fief. Keeping the Labour Party militants in check, Wedgwood after 1930 enjoyed years of political truce at a time when, in the rest of the country, party conflict became more embittered. Consequently by 1939 party organization was weaker than in 1914. Only in the Second World War, with the selection of a successor to Wedgwood, did the Newcastle Labour Party for the first time begin to find its organizational feet.

Indeed if there is any evidence for the belief that Newcastle politics has been conducted by 'mass parties' it must spring from the period between 1943 and 1951 though in retrospect these years may seem an episode brought about by exceptional causes rather than as a stage in party development. During that time, however, a phenomenal interest in politics characterized the politics of Newcastle as elsewhere in Britain. The peak of

CONCLUSION

Labour achievement, around 1949, was reached with a membership of about two thousand (nearly five times as many as when we carried out our membership survey in 1960). With the Conservatives the summit of over five thousand members (nearly three times as many as in 1960) was attained about a year later. Thus when the constituency, as at present territorially constituted by the redistribution of 1949, faced the General Election of 1950 there was a clash between well-organized parties with large memberships.

These circumstances in which one in every eight voters was a member of a political party soon gave way in the early 1950's to the more normal position as described above. The Liberal 'revival' displayed some of the characteristics of the other two parties in the immediate post-war years; but though Liberal enthusiasm was great and Liberal organization technically superb this resurgence, both geographically and numerically, was restricted. The fact that Newcastle was acknowledged as a 'safe Labour seat' was doubtless partly responsible for the running down of the party organizations, but general political apathy was also widespread. In spite of some increase of interest in more recent times there is little indication that a return to the 1943–51 style of politics is likely; and here there may be more deep-seated and permanent causes. As one commentator has remarked:

'Perhaps in retrospect it will be evident that the mass party saw its hey-day during the period when the extension of the franchise had created a mass electorate, but when there was as yet no effective means of reaching the voters in their own homes.'[1]

Our findings on the impact of television in the 1959 General Election go some way towards substantiating this prophecy. It is clear that a large number of people saw the television election programmes and that those who saw them had a greater knowledge of General Election issues than those who did not. Further, it seems that television made its greatest impact on those with the least interest in politics. Thus the party organizations may indeed be deprived eventually of their 'educating' and 'agitating'

[1] R. T. Mackenzie, *British Political Parties* (1955), p. 591.

functions and be left with the humdrum task of 'getting out the vote'.

However, for a few years in the 1940's the two main parties in the constituency came close to being 'ideological parties'. This was especially the case with the Labour Party in the mining villages where social life, in the form of dances, socials and whist drives, revolved around the local organizations. But historical perspective enables us now to see that this period was exceptional and that its end was a return to a normality in which party activity is not widely regarded as a suitable spare-time activity. Even at their centres, in fact, the parties in Newcastle have had to struggle to maintain a permanent organization, while in the wards numerous parties have been inaugurated and then collapsed, to be re-formed only to collapse again. In the Borough the annual local elections and the need to provide candidates for them has helped to keep party organizations in trim; but in the Rural District, where local elections are triennial, party organization has often completely disappeared between General Elections. There has thus been, especially in the countryside, almost a cycle of political organization dependent on General Elections, reminiscent of those American electoral machines whose lives only last for the short period of the campaign. The history of Newcastle's three constituency parties certainly gives one cause to regard them in this light.

It seems probable, indeed, that the events of the late 1940's left their most lasting mark on local politics. The appearance of a Labour Party determined to fight for control of both Newcastle Borough and Newcastle Rural District Councils was a complete departure from past practices. So ebullient was the Labour Party of these years that when after the local elections of 1945 the vastly expanded Labour Group attended the Council for the first time the Chief of Police was in attendance, presumably to deal with any outbreak of disorder. The real revolution, however, after Labour seized control was in the changed relationship between political power and the social structure and in the way the Council made its decisions. Before the Second World War the political leadership of the Borough had largely reflected the social hierarchy and the Borough's decisions had been made by shopkeepers and small businessmen inspired to a considerable extent by the Borough officials. With Labour in the majority almost 'unknown men' with slight status in the Borough came into the seats of power and policy was hammered out in the Labour Group with less dependence on the Borough officials.

In the Newcastle Rural District highly organized parties were even more of a novelty. The Labour Party had the same declared intention of gaining control and the post-war years witnessed many of the same developments as in the Borough, with the party's leaders ousting the old rulers. But for various reasons the record of Labour in the Rural District is not a 'success story' as it is in the Borough. The clash between Madeley and Audley, and the existence in the latter parish of feuding leaders and a sort of Socialist 'peasant proprietorism' made it difficult to impose Labour Party procedures and policies. Furthermore, the 'face-to-face' nature of the villages put personality at a premium while robbing organization of much of its *raison d'être*. Consequently though the post-war years saw many changes in the Rural District, it proved impossible for the Labour Party to apply the same sort of decision-making process that it had conferred on the Borough, and the R.D.C. continued in its pre-war routine. Interference by the Newcastle Constituency Labour Party and later the West Midlands Regional Office of the Labour Party only strengthened local sectionalism and in this rural context the Labour Party appeared as the party of uncomprehending urbanism.

Thus there is evidence in Newcastle constituency that might be used both for and against the operation of national parties in local politics. In the Rural District the abortive attempt to organize the politics of the Council on party lines appeared to complicate the situation without adding any compensatory features. In the Borough, on the other hand, the Labour Group had given the Council a policy to support or oppose and provided some committee chairmen of considerable ability. Also the Borough Labour Party has ensured a steady stream of nominees to fight elections though in recent years candidates have not been so forthcoming. It is difficult to adjudge whether the standard of candidates and councillors has deteriorated: what is clear is that neither the loss of local government powers nor the rise of the Labour Party can be fairly cited as reasons for the gentry and professional people not participating more fully in Borough politics. As we have seen, this tendency dates from the mid-nineteenth century.

The introduction of party discipline into local politics was the innovation that was greeted with most disfavour by local opinion. It was an experiment doomed to failure in the Rural District, while in the Borough after considerable trouble discipline has had to be relaxed. It is interesting to note that on both local councils the leadership of the Labour Party, as a result of experience of office, has gradually come round to the opinion that on many local issues the assertion of party protocol is a superfluous gesture. In this way the Labour leaders have made some concessions to the practice of judging issues on their merits, though this departure from party Standing Orders has not endeared them to all the rank-and-file.

One of the most important conclusions of this book is that the character and style of leadership in any sort of society have a great influence on the flavour of its politics; and an attempt to interpret the local politics of the wards and parishes in terms of the background and opinions of the voters failed for this reason. The political personality of the leaders contributes much to the folklore of politics. Thus the beliefs that Wards 1 and 2 are Roman Catholic wards or that Audley Parish is dominated by the Nonconformists, widely accepted by Newcastellian political practitioners, were proved by our survey to be somewhat exaggerated. Yet it is true that Catholic councillors are still returned from these Borough wards and that many Audley councillors still originate in the chapels. The groups—and often the families—with a tradition of political leadership continue to provide it long after the social basis of their pre-eminence has ceased to be in a preponderance amongst the electorate in their areas.

Our study has also implied that an examination of the ordering of political power must be largely concerned with the important decision-makers in local government and not with the leadership of the constituency associations. The latter from the nineteenth century have appeared as the emissaries of national and extra-Newcastellian forces. Even in the case of the Labour Party with its policy of introducing national issues into local

CONCLUSION

politics, a division of labour quickly arose between those who ran the Borough Labour Party or were on the Borough Council and those 'stalwarts' who ran the Newcastle Constituency Party. Only with the Liberal Party which is small and new to Borough politics are the local and Parliamentary functions in the hands of more or less the same people.

The changing patterns of local leadership have been summarized in the last chapter, and here we are content to describe the differing values that successive leaderships have implied. The age for positive leadership, untrammelled by central control, was in the nineteenth century before much power passed to Stafford and Whitehall. The 'Improvers' with their visions of civic splendour were then defeated by 'Economizers' whose dominance was symptomatic of a community largely untouched by industrial expansion and economic buoyancy. Where, as in the industrial area, these conditions were present the lack of leadership militated against municipal progress. Thus the Independents who ruled until the Second World War were social leaders first and local politicians afterwards, envisaging local politics in terms of the exercise of local functions. Occasionally, as in their support for the Westlands project, they gave forward-looking leadership (though the then chairman of the Housing Committee was a Labour councillor). More often their concern for the 'merits of each individual issue' led them into short-sighted cheese-paring and opposition to a co-ordinated policy.

This type of localism was eradicated by the arrival in power of Labour, the party of nationalization and centralization, whose traditions of working-class action based on collective solidarity were inimical to the lower-middle-class political individualism of the Independents. The policy of the Labour leaders was not a collection of *ad hoc* decisions but stemmed from the declarations of a national programmatic party. In the days of the Third Labour Government, in both the Borough and Rural District, leaders of the Labour Party considered they were helping to implement that government's legislative programme. Later the acceptance of the idea of comprehensive schools, once it was recognized as Labour Party policy, exemplifies the position. The Labour leaders in the Borough have also tended to be local politicians *par excellence* with few other attachments. In the Rural

District, however, leaders with personal followings are still common as illustrated by the Labour councillor at Betley who received many Conservative votes. Thus social prominence often characterizes the Labour Party leaders in the countryside, while in the Borough as likely as not they will be socially obscure. Of the two councillors among the Labour Group's four 'men of power' one was named by two respondents in his ward and the other by no one at all.

As leadership in the Borough has become more impersonal it has also become less concentrated. The present relatively slight coincidence between social, economic and political leadership, contrasting with the situation of thirty or forty years ago, is a consequence of the growing complexity of the society. Moreover, the operation of representative institutions and the rise of the Labour Party have contributed to this division of functions and sharing of power which, interestingly, Professor Dahl has also observed in the development of the local politics of New Haven, Connecticut.[1] But these changes have not brought manual workers into the stratum of political leadership. Only in the immediate post-war years were many manual workers prominent among Labour Party 'stalwarts' and in the Labour Group. Most unusually at this time miners were, as we have seen, active in the local Labour parties in the mining villages. But the skills needed for political leadership are not easily acquired by manual workers and when the period of enthusiasm was over they were ready to relinquish their control to non-manual workers whose occupations often fitted them for political work. It may well be that only on rare and urgent occasions will the working class be roused enough to participate in large numbers at the leadership level. At other times they will be willing to give voting support to those white-collar and professional Labour Party leaders who have sympathetically identified themselves with working-class aspirations.

These changes in political precepts and political leadership have been paralleled by a transformation in the position of Newcastle. In the nineteenth century, besides having more political control over its destiny, Newcastle was more economically and socially independent. Today it is much more part of

[1] Robert Dahl, *Who Governs?* (New Haven, 1961), pp. 223 ff.

CONCLUSION

the North Staffordshire conurbation and of a 'national society' and it is not only *political* decisions about its future that are made elsewhere. The growth of population, the construction of new housing estates and the concentration and nationalization of industry have all completed the process of destroying the former 'face-to-face' society whose early death-knell was sounded by the amalgamation of 1932. A larger, more scattered, more impersonal Newcastle is now the one in which the voters form their opinions.

For a study of local politics it is not unimportant to estimate the electorate's conception of the place of its own community in the scheme of things. Unfortunately our evidence here is conflicting and even puzzling. In the nineteenth century the voters seem to have had little desire for the municipal franchise in the Borough, or elsewhere for local autonomy; and there seems to have been little protest at the County's and Government's accretion of powers. Yet in 1930 local patriotism was outraged by Stoke's attempted annexation of Newcastle; and the voters almost unanimously condemned it. Again as recently as 1960 when the same thing was mooted there was another outcry. On the other hand there is much to demonstrate that the electors are ignorant of the functions of local government,[1] unaware of local political personalities and generally apathetic about local politics. Only half as many of them vote in local elections as in General Elections and when they use their municipal franchise, in spite of numerous Independent candidates and a long Independent tradition, they see their choice as one between the two large national parties. Here again there is a residual feeling, especially strong in the Rural District and among the professional classes, that the personality of candidates should count for more at local elections. We cannot reconcile these apparent contradictions which indicate scope for investigation of the electorate's image of the processes of government.

Perhaps the growth of a more impersonal society in which the national parties dominate the voters' minds is counterbalanced by some fundamental and ineradicable assumptions about personal relationships. Whatever the truth may be it is apparent that ideological concepts have not made any great inroads into the

[1] F. Bealey and D. J. Bartholomew, loc. cit.

412

CONCLUSION

mentality of the electorate. As we have observed, among Labour Party militants there is no left-wing syndrome such as one might find among Labour M.P.'s;[1] the Liberals' central position obviates against ideological development; and the Newcastle Conservatives, far from betraying a tendency to a right-wing syndrome, are shown as remarkable for their moderation. Thus the whole constituency is characterized by a lack of extremism.

The evidence about the voters' attitudes to the parties tends to confirm the findings about the party members' lack of ideological consistency. Both the Conservative and the Labour voters were prepared to give credit to the party they opposed. The Conservative voters, though more attached to the party of their choice than the Labour voters, were ready to acknowledge that the Labour Party had some merits in the realm of ideas about policy: where they vastly preferred the Conservative Party was in the field of competence to execute policy. In this latter sphere the Labour voters were prepared to give the Conservative Party as much credit as the Labour Party; though the Labour voters were more inclined to view the party struggle as a conflict over general principles. This picture, besides depicting an electorate that, in spite of its lack of political interest, is a good deal more sophisticated than politicians and political scientists often assume, also reveals a considerable amount of consensus between the two sets of electors about the policies and performances of the parties. In this situation it is difficult for an ideological division to develop.

These findings do not conflict with what we have said about 'working-class consciousness' in the constituency. We noted that there was no significant disposition for the skilled manual workers to consider themselves any less 'working class' than the less-skilled workers; and that a third of the business proprietors also placed themselves in the 'working class'. In addition many of the Labour Party leaders are professional men or clerical workers; while half the Conservative voters are manual workers. Thus there are elements in common on both sides of the political fence, a circumstance which hardly predicates a 'class struggle'. 'Class consciousness' there certainly may be in Newcastle, but class hatred is very uncommon.

[1] S. E. Finer, H. B. Berrington and D. J. Bartholomew, *Backbench Opinion in the House of Commons* (1961), pp. 48 ff.

CONCLUSION

This is borne out by the constituency's recent social history. Strikes have been infrequent and the outstanding expression of the life of the local Labour movement has been, not the trade union, but the co-operative society symbolizing working-class thrift and collective self-help. Furthermore, a high rate of working-class owner-occupation of houses, by no means a very recent feature, has given the workers a proprietorial sense in spite of their poverty. On the other side the employers have usually been self-made men without social frills. Those few who have been involved with the leadership of the Conservative Party have seldom adopted the accents and standards of dress and behaviour commonly associated with the nation's 'ruling class': they do not generally give the impression of expecting deference and they do not often seem to receive it. Though a confrontation of class with class was nearest to reality in the years immediately after 1945 the passage of time and the workings of representative democracy appear to have eased the situation. One persistent impression gained from interviewing councillors and ex-councillors today is their readiness to admit to qualities in their political opponents.

What are the reasons for this lack of social bitterness that supports the consensus underlying the party struggle? Doubtless many of the answers to this question lie in the way national experience has fashioned national values: the answers are thus applicable to many other constituencies. But in Newcastle there are local factors, as we have seen, that have blunted the edge of social and political conflict. The ghost of Wedgwood still seems to haunt the constituency, manifesting itself in the liberalism of the Conservatives and the unwillingness of many Labour Party members to submit to party discipline. Beyond this perhaps there is a certain local unity exemplified by the lack of superficial social differences and the absence of self-consciousness between the different parties on the two councils. In traits of character such as independence, kindness, outspokenness and 'awkwardness' many of the councillors reveal the legacy of their Staffordshire origins. After all, the bond of experiences shared together may prove to be the most effective cause of consensus in the end.

APPENDIX 1

PARLIAMENTARY REPRESENTATION IN NEWCASTLE-UNDER-LYME, 1868–1959

Two Members of Parliament

1868	*Sir Edmund Buckley, Bt.	Cons.	1,423
	*William Shepherd Allen	Lib.	1,081
	H. T. Salmon	Lib.	744
1874	*Sir Edmund Buckley, Bt.	Cons.	1,173
	*William Shepherd Allen	Lib.	1,116
	H. T. Davenport	Cons.	1,037
1878	(By-election)		
	*Samuel Rathbone Edge	Lib.	1,330
	Charles Donaldson Hudson	Cons.	990
1880	*Charles Donaldson Hudson	Cons.	1,484
	*William Shepherd Allen	Lib.	1,252
	Samuel Rathbone Edge	Lib.	1,175

One Member of Parliament

				%age of votes cast
1885	*William Shepherd Allen	Lib.	4,031	58.5
	A. R. Scoble	Cons.	2,848	41·5
		Maj.	1,183	
1886	*D. H. Coghill	Lib. Unionist	2,896	51·2
	H. R. Brindley	Lib.	2,752	48·8
		Maj.	144	
1892	*William Allen	Lib.	4,204	59·4
	D. H. Coghill	Lib. Unionist	2,936	40·6
		Maj.	1,268	

* Elected.

				%age of votes cast
1895	*William Allen	Lib.	3,510	50·9
	A. M. Lee	Cons.	3,399	49·1
		Maj.	111	
1900	*A. S. Haslam	Lib. Unionist	3,751	51·3
	William Allen	Lib.	3,568	48·7
		Maj.	183	
1906	*J. C. Wedgwood	Lib.	5,155	63·6
	A. S. Haslam	Cons.	2,948	36·4
		Maj.	2,207	
1910 (Jan.)	*J. C. Wedgwood	Lib.	5,613	56·9
	E. S. Grogan	Cons.	4,245	43·1
		Maj.	1,368	
1910 (Dec.)	*J. C. Wedgwood	Lib.	5,281	56·4
	E. S. Grogan	Cons.	4,087	43·6
		Maj.	1,194	
1918	*J. C. Wedgwood	Lib.	Unopposed	
1922	*J .C. Wedgwood	Lab.	14,503	60·5
	A. Shaw	Cons.	9,573	39·5
		Maj.	4,930	
1923	*J. C. Wedgwood	Lab.	12,881	65·6
	L. Ravenshaw	Cons.	6,746	34·4
		Maj.	6,135	
1924	*J. C. Wedgwood	Lab.	14,226	57·7
	A. Hassam	Cons.	10,425	42·3
		Maj.	3,801	
1929	*J. C. Wedgwood	Lab.	20,931	69·9
	C. K. Tatham	Cons.	9,021	30·1
		Maj.	11,910	

* Elected.

PARLIAMENTARY REPRESENTATION

				%age of votes cast
1931	*J. C. Wedgwood	Lab.	Unopposed	
1935	*J. C. Wedgwood	Lab.	Unopposed	
1945	*J. D. Mack	Lab.	25,903	66·1
	G. A. Wade	Cons.	8,380	21·4
	N. W. Elliott	Lib.	4,838	12·5
		Maj.	17,523	
1950	*J. D. Mack	Lab.	30,249	57·7
	J. A. Friend	Cons.	22,132	42·3
		Maj.	8,117	
1951	*S. T. Swingler	Lab.	30,814	58·0
	J. A. Friend	Cons.	22,278	42·0
		Maj.	8,536	
1955	*S. T. Swingler	Lab.	28,314	56·8
	F. H. Taylor	Cons.	21,569	43·2
		Maj.	6,745	
1959	*S. T. Swingler	Lab.	29,840	55·6
	T. Prendergast	Cons.	23,838	44·4
		Maj.	6,002	

* Elected.

APPENDIX 2

THE SURVEY

The survey, begun in November 1959 and completed in March 1960, was largely carried out by undergraduate students though some professional interviewers were used in the closing stages. A sample of 100 respondents was selected by random sampling in each of the twenty-one wards designated in Chapter 7. In reality, therefore, we were conducting twenty-one separate sample surveys with 2,100 people to be contacted. Unfortunately there were the usual refusals, while deaths and removals made the 1959 electoral register somewhat out of date. The final result is contained in Table 1.

TABLE 1. FINAL SURVEY FIGURES

Ward	Answered	Refused	Not contacted	Moved	Dead or ill	Total
1	81	4	7	8	—	100
2	76	3	4	12	5	100
3	66	8	4	16	6	100
4	81	3	6	8	2	100
5	81	5	—	9	5	100
6	74	3	5	14	4	100
7	80	2	7	11	—	100
8	66	18	1	8	7	100
9	70	17	8	4	1	100
10	66	19	4	10	1	100
11	72	14	2	8	4	100
12	70	17	3	1	9	100
Ashley	75	8	7	6	4	100
Audley—Audley	68	15	5	7	5	100
Audley—Bignall End	73	2	14	3	8	100
Audley—Halmerend	72	1	18	7	2	100
Balterley and Betley	69	18	5	4	4	100
Chorlton and Maer	70	16	5	6	3	100
Keele and Whitmore	69	13	5	7	6	100
Madeley	70	15	3	10	2	100
Mucklestone and Tyrley	67	11	1	14	7	100
Total	1,516	212	114	173	85	2,100

The refusal rate at rather more than 12 per cent was high, but it is not possible to make comparisons between the different wards because the fluctuations are sometimes the result of differences between amateur and professional interviewers. All the 5·4 per cent of respondents who were not contacted were called on at least three times. Lorry drivers, commercial travellers and shift workers were the most difficult to find at home. The fact that 258 people or 12 per cent of all the sample were dead, seriously ill, or not at the address given, demonstrates how quickly the electoral register becomes out of date.

When the data were tabulated we made 179 associations in each of the 21 wards and carried out χ^2 tests on the distributions. In Figure 21 we record every factor which provided significant results in four or more wards in at least one of its associations. This is, of course, only a rough indicator of the importance of the various factors. The following reservations must be borne in mind:

1. The table does not distinguish between different degrees of significance—10 per cent, 5 per cent, 1 per cent and 0·1 per cent.

2. We were faced with many tables in which the constituent groups were too small. Where there were ordered sequences much grouping together was carried out in order to apply the χ^2 test, but we were not always able to group the same categories as between ward and ward.

3. The groups could not always be realistically combined. For example, the 16-and-over school-leavers' group needed to be isolated and yet it was often too small to be tested statistically. Where no test was possible the association is regarded as 'not significant' for the purposes of our figure. Thus some important factors are only recognizable as such in the weighted tables where they cannot be tested.

4. We should point out that the fact of significance in itself is not necessarily very revealing, and only relates to numerical distribution. For example, the association of 'political knowledgeability' and readership of the *Evening Sentinel* showed that in one significant case it was readers, and in the other non-readers, who were most knowledgeable. However, there were few cases of this sort and usually the significant tables confirmed known and expected tendencies.

The following factors were significantly associated with others in fewer than four wards:

Religion	Ability to name one's councillor
Being a juror or not	Ability to say who held the
Club membership or not	majority on the Staffordshire
Occupation	County Council

FIGURE 21. ALL FACTORS SIGNIFICANTLY ASSOCIATED IN FOUR

	1959 G.E. vote	1959 G.E. vote	Class	Self-assigned class	Form of house tenancy	Had phone	Had standard lamp
Class	11	—					
Self-assigned class	8	12	—				
Form of house tenancy	9	9	10	—			
Had phone	x	8	x	x	—		
Had standard lamp	x	4	x	x	x	x	
Age	1	6	3	4	x	x	
Sex	3	5	3	x	x	x	
Devoutness	2	2	2	0	x	x	
Length of residence	2	5	1	0	x	x	
Would vote for 'man' or 'party' at local elections	2	5	1	x	x	x	
Local election vote	1	6	1	5	x	x	
School-leaving age	4	4	6	x	x	x	
Knowledge of friends' addresses	0	5	0	2	x	x	

x—No association examined.

Vote at the 1955 General Election

Possession of a vacuum cleaner, refrigerator, or television

Number of children in family

Whether place of work in the Borough (in the Rural District in the parish) or not

All the questions about broadcasting and television programmes and reading newspapers

Ability to name an issue at the 1959 General Election

Attendance at 1959 General Election meetings

Discussions with people outside the family before the 1959 General Election

Knowledge of friends' politics

Satisfaction with one's neighbours

Satisfaction with council services

Age							
—	Sex						
6	—	Devoutness					
4	1	—	Length of residence				
x	x	x	—	Would vote for 'man' or 'party at local elections			
2	3	x	x	—	Local election vote		
1	1	x	4	0	—	School-leaving age	
x	x	3	x	x	1	—	Knowledge of friends' addresses
0	0	x	x	x	x	x	—

All the questions about the party image

Preference for the 'man' or 'party' at General Elections

APPENDIX 3

PERCENTAGE DISTRIBUTION OF FACTORS BY WARDS

Borough wards	Class						Self-assigned class				Form of house tenancy		
	A	B	C	D	E	X	'Upper and upper-middle'	'Lower-middle'	'Working'	'No class'	Council-house tenants	Owner-occupier	Other tenants
1	9	1	7	27	53	2	4	6	85	5	26	38	36
2	9	1	8	29	49	3	13	8	68	11	60	21	19
3	17	21	12	32	15	3	45	8	45	2	38	48	14
4	10	5	9	32	42	3	10	15	73	2	—	51	49
5	6	22	12	33	23	3	45	10	41	4	—	64	36
6	3	9	14	36	35	3	20	10	57	12	33	33	34
7	3	11	5	44	25	13	12	27	60	1	8	61	31
8	11	15	15	32	18	3	38	14	39	9	12	69	19
9	4	12	7	50	26	—	24	19	49	8	22	47	31
10	4	4	4	52	35	—	15	12	68	5	50	13	37
11	3	4	7	44	38	4	13	9	71	7	47	31	22
12	6	3	6	44	41	—	13	7	71	9	36	30	33
Rural District 'wards'													
Ashley	31	14	4	26	20	5	31	16	46	7	20	58	22
Audley—Audley	10	6	9	35	38	1	16	5	75	5	19	43	38
Audley—Bignall End	10	5	3	36	37	10	1	3	94	1	4	69	27
Audley—Halmerend	9	4	9	29	47	3	3	9	87	1	14	72	14
Balterley and Betley	18	16	6	31	28	1	26	13	51	9	10	37	53
Chorlton and Maer	37	6	3	26	27	1	40	9	45	6	10	44	46
Keele and Whitmore	20	15	13	25	24	3	33	15	42	9	10	53	37
Madeley	14	9	10	22	42	3	19	16	59	6	21	45	34
Mucklestone and Tyrley	16	18	7	18	37	3	28	7	42	22	18	24	58

Borough wards	Religion				Last attended church or chapel			School-leaving age		
	Church of England	Roman Catholic	Nonconformist	None	Last month	Last year	More than year ago	13 or less	14 or 15	16 or over
1	58	10	32	—	24	41	35	18	74	7
2	58	12	30	—	36	35	30	42	53	5
3	65	13	23	—	26	41	33	19	53	28
4	72	10	19	—	42	41	17	20	73	7
5	63	9	28	—	51	25	25	25	40	35
6	80	11	9	—	36	38	25	27	63	9
7	66	5	29	—	32	51	18	31	57	12
8	52	15	32	—	35	32	33	33	52	16
9	68	4	26	2	34	36	31	21	73	6
10	62	8	29	2	39	28	33	24	74	2
11	63	6	31	—	36	32	32	35	64	1
12	61	9	30	—	36	30	34	29	65	5
Rural District 'wards'										
Ashley	74	1	23	1	51	35	14	33	44	23
Audley—Audley	58	2	41	—	40	33	27	16	81	3
Audley—Bignall End	55	—	45	—	27	36	37	11	87	1
Audley—Halmerend	49	—	52	—	39	31	30	23	74	4
Balterley and Betley	84	3	12	2	58	20	22	30	53	17
Chorlton and Maer	90	—	10	—	50	33	17	18	64	18
Keele and Whitmore	85	2	14	—	60	25	16	29	44	27
Madeley	74	3	19	4	40	32	28	31	61	8
Mucklestone and Tyrley	76	11	11	3	56	26	18	16	63	20

DISCREPANCY BETWEEN THE SAMPLE RESULTS AND THE GENERAL ELECTION RESULTS

As was said in Chapter 8, there were discrepancies between the results of the survey and those of the 1959 General Election. The largest affected the turn-out: 7 per cent of the electors who were interviewed claimed to have abstained, while the official abstention was 16 per cent. A discrepancy was to be expected, however. Electors who were in the sample but refused to answer are not included: yet the proportion of abstainers is probably larger than average in that category. Moreover, electors who could not be contacted because they had moved, had died, were too ill, or simply could not be found at home despite repeated 'call-backs' were obviously not included among respondents: but, in General Election returns, electors who died and many electors who have moved simply become abstainers. Overall, it is not unreasonable to believe that, on a register as old as the one which was used for the 1959 General Election (and which was also used for this survey), 7, 8 or perhaps 9 per cent of the electors were no longer in a position to exercise their vote in Newcastle. Detailed results of refusals, removals, etc., are given in Appendix 2.

The discrepancy between the abstention rate in the sample and the abstention rate at the General Election is thus probably very small. The other two discrepancies concern the swing and the distribution of the voters among the two main parties; they are also very small and are of the same magnitude as those which have been found in other surveys; they fall within the margin of usual sampling errors. Admittedly, there may be other reasons accounting for the difference. As in other surveys, the Conservative share of the poll may be exaggerated in the Newcastle survey (47 instead of 44 per cent) because Conservative voters are often more easily contacted than Labour voters; more Labour electors are to be found among social groups with long and irregular hours. Moreover, Labour electors are perhaps more reluctant to disclose their allegiance than Conservative electors, particularly when they live in areas of strong Conservative support, of which there are some in the Newcastle constituency, both in the Borough and in the Rural District.

The swing is also too large in the sample (2·8 per cent instead of 1·2 per cent), but this swing is somewhat different from the swing which is calculated from election results, as these take into account voters who died or moved from the constituency while this survey's swing is based only on electors appearing on the register at the time of the study. Although it is, of course, impossible to know whether the discrepancy was due to real changes in the composition of the electorate, such changes are not to be discarded. If, for instance, electors of 1955 who died or moved contained a greater proportion of Conservatives than average, the apparent swing in the sample would tend to exaggerate the extent of the Conservative gains.

INDEX

INDEX

INDEX

INDEX

Hanley, I. L. P., 74, 75
Haslam, A. S., 66
Hassam, A., 109, 121, 125
Hat manufacturers and the hat trade, 37, 38
Hewitt, E. P., 71
Heathcotes, 26 f.
Hoteliers, 38, 39 (see also inn-keepers)
House tenancy, forms of, 174 f., 230, 236, 237
and class, 151, 152, 170
Housewives without either husband or employment (class X), 147 f., 229, 230, 361
Housing, 26, 35, 49, 54, 141 f., 165, 278, 291, 324, 367, 373, 377, 397, 401, 412
Hustings, 41, 58

Improvement Commissioners, 37
'Improvers', 43 f., 410
Independent Civic Association (I.C.A.), 132, 346 f., 373, 384 (see also Independents in local politics and United Civic Association)
Independent Civic Association Borough Council Group, 346
Independents in local politics, 33, 35, 36, 45, 47, 50 f., 87, 93, 101, 119, 126 f., 130, 133, 138, 161 f., 220 f., 240 f., 245, 247, 265, 271, 298, 300, 302 f., 315 f., 320, 323, 324, 327 f., 337 f., 343 f., 387, 397, 410, 412 (see also Independent Civic Association)
Independent Labour, 46, 222, 316, 318, 322, 326, 328 f.
Independent Labour Party (I.L.P.), 27, 73, 78, 79, 82, 84, 86, 329, 335
Industrial groups, 159, 160, 237, 252
Industrialists, 22, 144, 145

Industrial Revolution, 21, 52, 139, 386
Inglis, J. M., 99
Innkeepers, 27, 44 (see also hoteliers)
Insurance agents, 78, 90, 314, 316, 335, 341
Irish, 45, 57, 378
Irish Home Rule, 61, 63
Ironmarket, 17
Iron ore mining and iron industry, 17, 21, 22, 34, 37, 54, 402
'Island site', 50, 51
Issue most important at 1959 General Election, 188 f., 203 f.

Junior Imperial League, 111
Justices of the Peace, 22, 25, 27, 29, 386 f., 396, 399

Keele, 21, 24, 25, 29, 118, 127, 154, 155, 221, 254, 314, 315, 327
Keele, University of, 144, 155, 340 (see also University College of North Staffordshire)
Keele and Whitmore, 155, 157 f., 181, 184, 238, 244
Kelly's Directory, 25
Kennedy, L., 288
Kidsgrove Urban District Council, 47
Knocking-up, 50, 67, 313, 329, 331
Knutton, 21, 22, 29, 31, 59, 95, 162, 253, 352
Korea, 101

Labour Church, 78
Labour Government, 1945–1951, 96, 316, 334, 366, 410
Labour Groups on councils
on Borough Council, 51, 351, 352, 362, 363, 365, 366, 369 f., 397 f., 407, 408, 411, 413
on Rural District Council, 312, 318, 334 f.

432

INDEX

Madeley Parish Council, 315, 324
Madeley Parochial Committee, 335
Madeley Tenants' and Residents' Association, 320
Maer, 22, 24, 118, 154, 228, 254, 304, 313 (see also Chorlton and Maer)
Maer Hall, 24
Mainwarings, 24
Managerial, professional and technical classes (class B), 147 f., 168, 169, 229, 236, 243, 247, 250, 272, 302 f., 333, 361, 394, 400, 412, 413 (see also professional people)
Manufacturers, 31, 32, 38 f., 45, 54, 387
Marginal Seat, 203
Market Drayton, 22, 143
Market Drayton Poor Law Union, 22
Marsh Trustees, 37
Mass media, 187 f., 192, 197, 203, 215, 217
Mass parties, 56, 95, 104, 114 f., 130, 319, 405 f.
Matthias, J., 82
Mayer, J., 45, 46
Mayors, 36, 46, 85, 109, 112, 113, 125, 270, 344, 366, 374
Means Test, 49, 87
Member of Parliament (see Swingler, Stephen)
Membership of clubs, 199 f., 230, 239
Methodism, 126, 314 (see also Primitive Methodism)
Midland Coal, Coke and Iron Co., 29
Migration, 19, 139, 140
Miners, 27, 31 f., 39, 40, 45, 47, 59, 60, 62, 68, 78, 79, 83, 86, 88, 89, 103, 125, 126, 162, 163, 166, 178, 179, 181, 182, 302, 305, 315, 317,

318, 321, 326, 332, 354, 401, 405, 411 (see also North Stafford Miners' Federation)
Miners' Eight Hours Bill, 63, 64
Mines Regulation Bill, 63
Mining villages, 18, 33, 48, 86, 99, 114, 125, 126, 138, 253, 271, 401, 407, 411
'Mining wards' (Wards 10, 11 and 12), 162, 182, 183, 253, 354 (see also Chesterton, Knutton and Silverdale)
Minnie Pit, 162, 317
Moran, Alderman 'Tony', 49, 51
Moreton House, 33, 35
Mucklestone, 22, 24, 25, 98, 118, 154, 304, 313
Mucklestone and Tyrley, 155, 157 f., 181, 190, 238, 244, 245
Munich, 87
Municipal Corporations Act, 1835, 22, 37, 38, 40
Municipal Corporations Act, 1882, 38
Municipal Reform Association, 44

Nairobi incident, 69
National Assistance, 49
National Coal Board, 144, 145
National Council of Labour Colleges, 314
National Government, 88, 112
National Labour Electoral Association, 62
National Labour Party, 113
National Liberals, 108, 124
National Tenants' and Residents' Association, 319 f.
National Unemployed Workers' Movement, 87
National Union of Distributive and Allied Workers, 90

434

INDEX

Party finance
    Conservative Party, 113, 114, 117, 118, 357
    Labour Party, 80, 81, 88, 90, 92, 94, 97 f., 103, 353, 354
    Liberal Party, 65, 127 f., 132, 135, 136
Party images, 202 f.
Party members, 187, 194, 249 f., 310, 402, 405 f.
    Conservative Party, 106, 111, 113, 115, 117 f., 249 f., 274 f., 323, 403, 406
    Labour Party, 91, 92, 94, 95, 97, 98, 100, 102, 104, 249 f., 281 f., 298, 319, 322, 323, 351, 403, 406, 407
    Liberal Party, 126 f., 249 f., 287 f., 358, 406
Party membership surveys, 249, 250, 274
Party militants, 390 f., 402
    Conservative Party, 106, 120, 267 f.
    Labour Party, 89, 99, 267 f., 323, 378, 388, 405
    Liberal Party, 126 f., 267 f., 358, 359
Party organization, 56 f., 85, 88, 93 f., 111, 114 f., 137, 203, 247, 312, 314 f., 350 f., 405 (see also electoral organization)
Pease, Mrs. Helen, 77 n. (see also Wedgwood, Helen)
Plural voting, 22
Political activity, 191, 201, 227, 261 f., 280, 294 f., 355, 402 f., 407, 411
Political interest, 187, 188, 191, 193, 194, 196, 198 f., 209, 219, 227, 233, 238, 261 f., 294 f., 304, 319, 402 f.

Political knowledge, 197, 198, 219, 230, 235 f., 246, 270, 271, 284, 285, 294 f., 402, 403
Political opinions, 202 f., 219, 268 f., 294 f., 411, 412
Poor Law Amendment Act, 1834, 22
Poor Law Guardians, 22, 24, 26, 29
Population, 22, 23, 139 f., 154, 155, 412
Porthill, 118
Potteries, the, 17 f., 31, 38, 42, 66, 79, 84, 89, 118, 131, 139, 142, 145, 154, 161, 164, 216, 254, 390
Pottery industry, 17, 19, 37, 142, 147, 252, 271, 402
Pottery manufacturers, 29, 32, 33, 114, 405
Pottery workers, 32, 39, 40, 161, 179
Poujadism, 204, 209
Prendergast, T., 116, 121, 236
Primitive Methodism, 48 (see also Methodism)
Professional people, 25, 32, 38 f., 43, 130, 133, 137, 146, 177, 296 (see also managerial, professional and technical classes)
Protection, 108, 124, 125 (see also Free Trade)
Public Health Act, 1848, 30
Pudsey, 401

Questions in surveys, 188, 203, 204, 208 f., 212, 213, 228, 233, 235, 242, 245, 246, 268 f., 274 f.

Radicals and radicalism, 57 f., 70 f., 83, 89, 107, 123, 295, 405
'Railwayman', the, 26, 48, 314, 315, 324, 334, 335
Railwaymen, 78, 99, 163, 178, 179, 181, 302, 305, 314 f., 393
Ratepayers' Association, 45

436

INDEX

INDEX

Twemlows, 24, 53

Tyrley, 22, 24, 98, 118, 154, 304, 313
(see also Mucklestone and Tyrley)

Uncontested seats at local elections,
24 f., 42, 50, 163, 219 f., 240, 246,
299, 301, 303, 327

Unemployment, 22, 28, 48, 49, 69,
77, 84, 86, 87, 90, 105, 206

Unilateralism, 274, 281 f., 287, 291,
292, 295, 296

United Civic Association, 346 (see
also Independent Civic Association)

United Front, 87

United Nations, 101, 131

United States of America, 101, 282,
284, 407

University College of North
Staffordshire, 129 (see also Keele,
University of)

Unpolitical, the, 192, 194

Unskilled manual workers, 146 f.

Victory for Socialism, 100, 102, 295

Voting

and age, 166, 169, 170, 172, 229,
231, 234

and class, 148, 166, 168, 169, 195,
229, 234, 235

and club membership, 184, 230

and discussions outside family, 196

and geographical distribution,
155 f., 229 f.

and house tenancy, forms of, 169,
170, 173 f., 230, 234, 235

and industrial group, 177 f., 182 f.

and length of residence in area,
184, 230

and political allegiance of friends,
185

and political interest, 197

and political knowledge, 230, 237

and religion, 166, 169, 170, 173 f.,
230

and school-leaving age, 166, 169,
170, 172 f., 230, 234, 235

and self-assigned class, 175 f., 183,
184, 229, 234, 235

and sex, 166, 169 f., 229, 230, 234,
235

Voting for either the 'man' or the
'party'

at General Elections, 242 f.

at local elections, 234, 236, 237,
242 f.

Wade, Colonel George, 114, 115,
121, 126

Waller, Sam, 75

Ward, Colonel, John, 82

Wards, character of, 154 f., 422 f.

Ward 1, 155 f., 181, 237, 238, 240,
244, 348, 360, 409

Ward 2, 155 f., 181, 236 f., 244, 347,
348, 360, 409

Ward 3, 154 f., 181 f., 192, 195, 223,
224, 238, 240, 244, 254, 270, 272,
345, 348, 353, 360

Ward 4, 132, 136, 138, 155 f., 181,
182, 238, 240, 244, 254, 262, 270,
353, 355, 360

Ward 5, 132, 136, 138, 155 f., 181 f.,
196, 224, 238, 240, 244, 345, 348,
353, 360

Ward 6, 155, 156, 181, 182, 192,
196, 224, 238, 240, 241, 244, 347,
353, 360, 377

Ward 7, 132, 136, 138, 155 f., 181,
192, 224, 225, 232 f., 238, 240,
244, 245, 254, 262, 348, 353, 360

Ward 8, 155 f., 181, 196, 224, 238,
240, 244, 353, 360

Ward 9, 101, 154 f., 181, 224, 238,
240, 244, 348, 360

INDEX